# SWIMMING
# AGAINST THE

## THE DIARY OF AN ESSEX COPPER 1953-1983

## GEORGE P RAVEN

FORMER SUPERINTENDENT, ESSEX POLICE

# SWIMMING AGAINST THE

## THE DIARY OF AN ESSEX COPPER 1953-1983

**MEREO**
Cirencester

## Mereo Books

1A The Wool Market Dyer Street Cirencester Gloucestershire GL7 2PR
An imprint of Memoirs Publishing www.mereobooks.com

### Swimming against the tide: 978-1-86151-178-2

First published in Great Britain in 2014
by Mereo Books, an imprint of Memoirs Publishing

The address for Memoirs Publishing Group Limited can be found at
www.memoirspublishing.com

Cover design - Ray Lipscombe

The Memoirs Publishing Group Ltd Reg. No. 7834348

The Memoirs Publishing Group supports both The Forest Stewardship Council® (FSC®) and
the PEFC® leading international forest-certification organisations. Our books carrying both the
FSC label and the PEFC® and are printed on FSC®-certified paper. FSC® is the only
forest-certification scheme supported by the leading environmental organisations including
Greenpeace. Our paper procurement policy can be found at
www.memoirspublishing.com/environment

Typeset in 10.5/16pt Plantin
by Wiltshire Associates Publisher Services Ltd. Printed and bound in Great Britain by
Printondemand-Worldwide, Peterborough PE2 6XD

To my wife Joan

"Every man who is high up loves to think that he has done it all himself; and the wife smiles, and lets it go at that. It's our only joke. Every woman knows that."

(Sir J. M. Barrie - What Every Woman Knows)

# Contents

# Introduction

*"A constable is a citizen, locally appointed, with authority under the Crown for the maintenance of order, the protection of life and property, the prevention and detection of crime and the prosecution of offenders against the peace."*

Many who contemplate writing, or who are persuaded to write, their memoirs, are people of great renown; those who are 'born great, have achieved greatness, or have had greatness thrust upon them' (Shakespeare). Perhaps they have become renowned through their own efforts, or through the labour of others. I was once told by a fellow cynic, also an ex-police officer, that the difference between an MBE and an OBE, which awards some are lucky enough to receive, is that the former stands for 'My Bloody Effort' and the latter for 'Other people's Bloody Effort'.

This distinction might well be the difference between an interesting autobiography, written by a genuine achiever, and one full of tales for whom the writer claims the credit, but did little or none of the work. Famous, even infamous, politicians, successful actors, bestselling authors, even some policemen whose careers have been unusually meritorious, have penned their memoirs with varying degrees of success. Most of those I have read seemed as though they had been written by Jack Horner, who also said, "Oh what a good boy am I!"

There is a great deal of difference between those persons of fame and fortune whose identities have already become household words and one such as myself, whose name is, and will undoubtedly remain, uncelebrated. In the case of well-known authors of memoirs, whatever their field of endeavour, there are already many thousands of people 'out there' waiting to read avidly every detail of their past achievements, their professional and particularly their personal lives, no matter how dull and uninteresting they might have been.

Apart from my own immediate family, of which very few remain, personal friends and acquaintances, a few former colleagues and perhaps even a few old 'customers', no one knows or cares that I even exist. How many eager eyes therefore will ever have the desire, or the opportunity, to read these memoirs of an ordinary, unexceptional police officer I know not.

I have written four crime novels and a book about Spanish food since my retirement, and while I am encouraged to know that Jeffrey Archer had his first novel *Not a Penny More, Not a Penny Less* turned down seventeen times, perhaps it should be gratifying to know that I have already beaten his record. One morning after reading yet another rejection slip from yet another publisher, I said to my wife Joan, "I think I should write my memoirs, perhaps I'll have more luck with those".

"What a good idea!" she cried with great enthusiasm. "I'd love to know what you got up to in the police force."

I have been retired for thirty years now, and married to Joan for twenty-four. She has not therefore had to suffer the trials and tribulations of a policeman's life. It is said that a policeman's lot is not a happy one, but I believe it is a policeman's wife who has to suffer most in a marriage to a policeman and to a service such as the one I chose. Joan of course knows of my police background, but except when we are in the company of other ex-police officers, talking of the past and reminiscing about cases and personalities, I have seldom discussed with her details of my police service. However, in the light of her encouraging response to my somewhat jesting comment about writing my memoirs, I began to think more seriously about the prospect of doing just that.

I would add here that I was married throughout my thirty years' police service and I have, since my second marriage, always regarded that part of my life as a closed book. In my private life I was an ordinary man, and so far as I am aware did little that was extraordinary or that might interest any other average person. I am not a reformed drug addict, a cured alcoholic nor a sexual athlete, nor have I committed murder, robbed a bullion train, or done any of the other things that sometimes make the private life of another so interesting to read about.

My memoirs will, I concluded, if they are to be of any interest at all to others, be about my professional life as a police officer. My private life will therefore remain, to all but me, a closed book.

Perhaps some good will come from such an enterprise,

apart from the diversion it will provide for me. If my wife is the only person who ever reads the manuscript, perhaps she will better understand why I became the person I am today. She did as a matter of interest know me as a youth, and the account of how we met and married, so many years later, is an entirely different and quite romantic story. The years between however have made me, so some have said, a somewhat hard and misanthropic individual. I admit to having a critical eye and a cynical way of looking at life, and at my fellow men, but I don't believe I am a misanthrope. I do not hate my fellow men, I don't believe I hate anyone, but I do despair for many of them and trust very few.

I am reminded of a story I once heard of a successful businessman who took his six-year-old son aside one day and said to him, "Son, you are now old enough to learn your first and most important lesson in life". He lifted him, stood him on top of a tall cupboard and told him to jump off.

"No! No!" cried the boy. "I'll hurt myself."

"No you won't," said his father. "I'll catch you, just trust me."

The boy jumped. To his horror his father moved away and he crashed to the floor, bruised and disillusioned.

"There," said his father. "That's your first and most important lesson in life. Never trust anyone." Perhaps being a police officer for so long, while not such a drastic lesson, nevertheless leaves a similar mark upon one.

At first the task of writing my memoirs seemed too daunting to proceed further and the idea remained dormant for several years. The rich and famous, to whom I have already referred, are usually blessed with cash, ghost-writers and researchers and have access to documents, records and information to help them in their task. I have none of these things, only my memory, the internet and a word processor. Many of the documents and records that might assist me with times, dates and places are now no longer available to me, and many will in any event have been destroyed. I cannot vouch for the complete accuracy of my recall, so I apologise in advance to anyone who might read this chronicle at some future time, and who finds therein errors of fact. I can only attempt to recall the events within the limits of my somewhat tired memory. Opinions expressed are of course my own, and as often in the past I would expect them to be out of step with those expressed by our leaders and politicians.

The more I think about the prospect of writing about the past, the more little snippets of information jump into my mind. I feel rather as an archaeologist must feel who digs for old relics and fossils, seeking clues of bygone days and events. Sometimes something of great value and interest is unearthed, but often only scraps of old bone, or pottery that are a dime a dozen are brought to the surface. I have wondered too whether perhaps the past should stay buried: many of my experiences, after all, were not pleasant ones, nor were many of the sights pretty.

Now, sitting here on the terrace of our very modest house in Spain, with the Mediterranean sun warming me on the outside and the red wine of Jumilla doing a similar good job on the inside, I have become enthusiastic and optimistic. The decision made, I find that I am looking forward to the trip down memory lane, albeit with some trepidation, and am already planning the task ahead. Naturally the names of any persons with whom I had dealings as prisoners, suspects or about whom 'police enquiries' were made, have been changed or omitted. I have no wish to embarrass them, their friends or relatives, nor with my advancing years have I any wish to appear in court as the defendant in an action for libel, or defamation of character. However the names of my fellow officers, where I am able to remember them, are real enough.

These police officers actually exist or existed - sadly many have now preceded me to another place. I may have been at odds with one or more of them, senior or junior, from time to time, but I have nothing but the greatest admiration for them all as fellow police officers. With few exceptions I cannot contemplate saying anything herein to their detriment, or that might be either embarrassing or actionable. I would be proud to think that they held me in the same esteem.

My career in the police service was neither distinguished nor notorious. I won no medals, except for 'Long Service and Good Conduct', nor was I prosecuted for any crime, except careless driving (see Chapter Two). I am satisfied to have reached the rank of Superintendent and to have come through it all without serious injury to mind or body. At the same time I would have like to have achieved more. Perhaps if I had managed to learn humility, and to have been able to learn sooner that to be a senior police officer you need also to be a politician, I would have done so.

While I would not describe myself as a maverick, I am

aware that I did from time to time, when I had become a senior officer myself and perhaps even before that, irritate my superiors with attitudes and actions which, while they may have reflected my ability as a police officer, were at the same time considered to be imprudent. I did eventually learn, too late to do me any good, that tact, diplomacy and perhaps a little deviousness are often far better weapons against a boss who is wrong than simply telling him so.

I well remember having dinner with the Chief Constable of Essex, then Robert Bunyard, just prior to my retirement. It was the custom at that time for senior officers who left the force without ignomiy to be given this treat, together with several other fellow officers who might be available at headquarters on that particular day. I do have some doubts that their main motivation was to say goodbye to me. However it is not every day you are invited to a free meal with the Chief, and it would perhaps be imprudent to refuse!

After the meal the Chief would present the retiring officer with a certificate of service, and take the opportunity to say a few words about him to those assembled. In my case he said he was aware that I had a small boat and planned to do some sailing in my retirement.

"He should be quite good at that," he continued. "After all he is well used to sailing against the wind and swimming against the tide."

I genuinely believe that when I joined the police force, most recruits sincerely wanted to serve the public and were dedicated to the pursuit of justice and upholding law and order. Most of us were ex-servicemen who had worn a uniform before, and had 'served' and understood the meaning of the word.

I would therefore have liked my thirty years' service to the community in general and to the Essex Police in particular to mean more than a few sarcastic remarks by a pretentious man like Mr Bunyard, whose first act when he took office was to issue to every senior officer in the force a copy of his book on Police Administration. He obviously thought that until that moment no one knew anything about the subject. His book contained, by way of acknowledgements, a long list of the other books from which he had compiled his own.

I would also have liked to look back upon my career with pride, and with the knowledge that I had achieved what I had set out to do. Someone who had been a doctor for thirty years might reflect that, with or without his help, there was now a cure for this or that disease, that new technology had made such and such an operation quicker and less painful. A teacher might count her success in 'A' Level passes achieved by her pupils. A soldier could ponder that the war he fought was won with his help.

There is certainly a good deal of satisfaction for a police officer who makes a good arrest and 'puts away' a criminal who would otherwise plague society with more crimes, but it is short lived. Sadly, upon retirement, a police officer sees only that crime is worse than ever it was, getting an accused to court is more difficult, and the likelihood of a conviction smaller. Riots and civil disobedience abound, and the efforts of those young officers who now strive to put all this to rights are frustrated at every turn.

The British police were once proud to be independent of government, answerable only to the Monarch, but successive administrations have done their best to erode this independence and to shackle the police force until it becomes, as it is in many other countries, an instrument of the state.

However it is said that 'The public gets the police force it deserves'. And they, 'the great unwashed', as they are known in police parlance, now demand 'squeaky clean' policemen 'at all costs.' They elect politicians who pass more and more laws, dream up more and more regulations and issue more and more directives to the police, to tie their hands and make enforcing both the good and the ridiculous laws they pass an almost impossible task.

The cost of all this is that today they have a police force that is disillusioned and unhappy, one that is motivated by fear of criticism and one which has little or no effect on rising crime. No politician is going to admit this but you need only ask any officer, who does not think he might be overheard or quoted to find the truth of this statement, or even to read the daily press.

I will be giving many actual examples in this book of how and why the police force today does not have the support and backing of the public as it did in my day, and why the results in terms of 'clearing up' crime, and preventing it, are so poor. It is not going to get any better, however much money successive governments are prepared to throw at the problem, until the pendulum begins to swing back the other way and the public starts to demand that criminals are caught and locked up, 'at all costs!'

I have no doubt that every police officer, in this or any other country, has many tales to tell after thirty years of service to his community. Some of the most popular series on television purport to chronicle the everyday lives of policemen and women. I have read many books by ex-policemen who had a particular message to impart, or careers to boast of. I have rarely seen one which describes what life is really like in the police service. Do policemen really beat up prisoners? Do they really plant evidence on suspects? Do they really fabricate false confessions? These are the sorts of questions people often used to ask me. Perhaps the answer is not a simple "Yes" or "No". Probably people do not really want to know the answer, and the question is posed to put the policeman on the defensive. It's a bit like the question, "Have you stopped beating your wife yet?" A simple, "Yes" or "No," will not do from a man who has never beaten his wife and the only answer the questioner will believe is the one he wants to hear. Witnesses in court who have been asked a question by defence counsel often start by saying, "Yes, but…" They are cut off with a perfunctory wave of the hand and told, "Just answer the question, 'Yes' or 'No.'"

The question might have been, "Did you hit my client?" The answer, "Yes" is condemnation of oneself, and an admission of guilt. The answer, "Yes, but he was coming at me like a madman with a carving knife" is justification of one's action and a denial of guilt.

The question I myself often ask is, "Why?" Why do people sometimes believe that the police are all thugs and dishonest fabricators of evidence against innocent people? Why do the media, defence solicitors, minority groups and some individuals in high places continually propagate this image of our forces of law and order? Why has the word 'Bobby' now become 'Pig' or 'The Filth?' The answers to these questions are not clear-cut, but I believe that the opinion of an ex-police officer is as valid as that of a politician, psychologist or criminologist, perhaps more so.

There have been many changes within the police force since I joined it in 1953, with successive Home Secretaries trying to stem the tide of crime. None has succeeded. A series of 'incidents' of one sort or another has brought changes in the law that politicians thought would plug the gap. Most of these changes have made life more difficult for the police officer. It is one thing to make a law, quite another to enforce it. Of course laws are often made to appease a certain minority section of the public and it is not really expected that they could or should ever be enforced. The Litter Act, for example. God forbid that there should be a prosecution every time someone threw a cigarette packet, a drinks can or sweet wrapper on the pavement!

My life and service in the police cannot, except in a few minor ways, be compared with the life of the present-day warrior. Clad in his riot gear with reinforced helmet, clutching his American style riot stick, wearing his bullet proof vest, brandishing an armoured plastic shield, and his can of nerve gas, he presents an image more like 'Robocop' than the constables I knew. Perhaps it is as well to remember those days when the copper on the beat had the love and respect of the entire community, and did his job 'without fear or favour, malice or ill will' as he had sworn to do.

I have decided that this will not be a book solely about me. I am not that important in the scheme of things. Rather it will be about the police service, including some cases in which I was personally involved, with informed comment on the law, law enforcement and the development of the police service during the years 1953 to 1983. I say my comments are 'informed' because I believe thirty years in the police service qualifies me as an expert to make such comment. So many pronouncements on the police, the law and law enforcement are made these days by politicians, newspaper reporters and other commentators whose knowledge of these subjects is often scant and coloured by pressures upon them, by prejudice and by self interest. What I have to say is, "The truth, the whole truth and nothing but the truth".

Shall we now lift the lid and peep inside at the police force as I saw it?

CHAPTER ONE

# First steps (1953)

*Down here it was still the England I had known in my childhood: the railway cuttings smothered in wild flowers…the red buses, the blue policemen - all sleeping the deep, deep sleep of England, from which I sometimes fear that we shall never wake till we are jerked out of it by the roar of bombs.*
*(George Orwell - Homage to Catalonia (1938) ch. 1)*

In 1948 National Service for young men of eighteen years was still something for them to look forward to, although not necessarily with great pleasure. At that time I was myself anticipating being 'called up' to do my duty for King and country: King George VI was on the throne at that time. Faced with the prospect of a humdrum life of going to work at eight o'clock each morning and returning at six in the evening, and the probability of doing this for the rest of my life, I became somewhat disillusioned with 'Civvy Street'. I felt restless and impatient for something more exciting.

I was then working in the Engineer's Department of the West Ham Borough Council as a very junior 'something or other', and one morning I just couldn't face it any more. Instead of going to work on the bus full of the same old men smoking, reading their newspapers and coughing their hearts up, I walked thoughtfully the five or so miles from Seven Kings in Essex, where I lived, to the Army Recruiting Office at Romford. That same day I signed on for five years with the colours in the Kings Royal Rifle Corps.

By the age of twenty-three I had come to a crossroads in my life, one of those we all find ourselves at from time to time. It was necessary to make an important decision. In which direction shall I travel? Once embarked upon a particular road and in a specific direction there is usually no turning back, so it is well to ponder. Maybe one will wonder in the years to come what would have happened if another road, a different direction, had been taken. Perhaps there will be regrets. Maybe, on reflection, the other road would have been better. Most of us don't get the chance to go back and start again. When it is time for reflection, it is too late.

After I had completed my five years' military service, I had to decide whether to sign up for another period of army life or to leave the services and return to 'Civvy Street.' It had been a wise decision to enlist rather than wait for 'call up.' Regular soldiers were given certain privileges, and I had soon won my first stripe and a period at a Junior NCO training establishment in Northern Ireland - It was quite a safe place for British soldiers to be posted at this time.

Circumstances had led me to be transferred from the

Kings Royal Rifles, and the last five years of my service had been in the Intelligence Corps. I was now a Staff Sergeant, having seen some of the world. I had served in Singapore and Germany, as well as spending a year at the RAF Russian Language school at Kidbrooke in Sussex. I had enjoyed my service in the forces immensely, and I was naturally reluctant to leave. Being employed on peacetime field security duties was a bit like being a military policeman, but I was mostly working in plain clothes and 'snooping' rather than parading up and down in a big red-topped hat and being objectionable.

Leaving the service was a big step into the unknown. I had already decided I would like to join the civil police and become a detective, but one couldn't very well do so while still a serving soldier. I was then still single and had no one to worry about but myself, so I made my mind up, hastily as usual, and came out. I have never had cause to regret it.

The first step was to decide which police force to join, as there were so many, but my local force, the Essex Constabulary, seemed the most logical. There were more than a hundred police forces in England and Wales in 1953. Most cities had their own force and there were many Borough Constabularies as well as County Constabularies.

The words 'constabulary' and 'constable' actually relate to the early days of policing, when a single constable was appointed by local communities and was aided when necessary by local people. Hence the expression "Hue and Cry" the old English common-law practice of pursuing criminal with "horn and voice" ("hue" from the old French verb huer, to cry or shout). The word 'police' came into use after the formation of the Metropolitan Police in 1829 and gradually the use of 'constabulary' and 'constable' has been dropped.

The words 'police' and 'politics' are related. Both are derived from the Greek term for city-state and have to do with the administration and oversight of communities of people. Police operations vary from nation to nation. In some states police forces are highly militarised and almost indistinguishable from the armed forces. This subtle but distinguishable difference between a constabulary and a police 'force' may have gone unnoticed by many of our citizens.

My local force was then The Essex Constabulary (now Essex Police) and there was also the Southend Borough Constabulary within the county. Before 1953 there had also been a Colchester Borough Constabulary, but this had been absorbed by the county prior to my joining.

During my early years of police service, first the City and Borough forces slowly disappeared until there were only eighty or so police forces remaining, then began further 'amalgamations' as they were called. At the time I left the police service there were only forty-three forces left (excluding the Metropolitan Police). The 'taking over' of the smaller city and borough forces by the larger county ones had caused much ill feeling and discontent amongst the ranks. Time has healed most of these wounds, and the young men joining today will know nothing of them. Their concerns are far more important than the petty squabbles occasioned by political desire for more control of the service as a whole. The official reason for the amalgamations ('take-over' was a dirty word) was "to improve efficiency".

On the contrary the millions of pounds of public money that it cost to implement these amalgamations - new uniforms and badges, printing of forms and signs and training of officers - did little if anything to improve efficiency. It was however one small step nearer to every government's dream; a 'National Police Force.' (Part I of the Police Reform Act 2002, gives the Home Secretary sweeping new powers and has been described by some MPs as the first step towards a National Police Force).

My letter of application was duly written, and sent off to the Police Headquarters at Chelmsford. I was to learn later, as you can see from the definition of a constable at the beginning of this introduction, that officers are 'locally appointed.' While it is now possible to join a force in another district, away from where you live, in those days it was usual for Essex officers to be recruited from Essex men. There is a historical reason for this which is pretty obvious, but that has now all changed and forces can even recruit from abroad. Likewise politicians are supposed to represent constituents of places in which they live, but now it suffices if they own a recently purchased (or rented) flat there.

The application form wanted to know such things as the names of my grandparents and where they were born. I assume that the reason for these questions was important in assessing my eligibility to become a police officer in England. I can only wonder what such forms contain today when for politically correct reasons forces are desperate to recruit from other ethnic groups, now represented within our society, regardless of whether or not they are in every other way suitable.

Some years ago a Labour Home Secretary, David Blunkett, suggested that we should recruit foreigners into the British police! You can imagine how ex-police officers like me feel about that, but it is a sad reflection of the state of the service that it cannot appoint sufficient officers 'locally' as the definition of constable requires. What it will do to our already depressed, unhappy and demoralised police only common sense can tell, but then what does common sense have to do with politics?

One of the spaces on the application form was a request for two references, and I remember that I gave the name and address of my father's best friend Charles Tapping, who had known me since I was born. My other reference was my own best friend's father, a respectable architect. At the time it didn't occur to me that I should, as a matter of courtesy, have asked their permission to give them as references. I had naturally no doubts that they would speak well of me if asked.

Subsequently an appointment was made for me to visit my nearest police station at Chadwell Heath to take the entrance examination. Chadwell Heath was within the Metropolitan Police District, while still within the Administrative County of Essex. Had I known this at the time of my original application, I would undoubtedly have joined the Metropolitan Police. As it turned out I think I made the right choice. I had many dealings with officers of the Metropolitan Police in the years to come, particularly as our territorial borders adjoined. I was never impressed with either their efficiency or the lack of professional courtesy with which I was often treated. Until the Regional Crime Squad was born in 1964, about which I will say more later, a police officer from a county force who strayed into the Metropolitan Police district, for whatever reason, was viewed with great suspicion and regarded as a country bumpkin.

The entrance examination was in three parts, Geography, English and General Knowledge. For Geography I was given a large outline map of England, and asked to mark on it various large towns and rivers etc. Fortunately there were a few places I did know, but many that were sheer guess work. The English wasn't so bad, and one had a choice of subjects about which to write a short essay. I realised that an essay says a good deal about the person who is writing it and so made sure I kept off subjects like politics and religion. General knowledge too was pretty 'general', although I still remember one question which catches most people out. It went like this: "A little boy is digging in the garden and finds a coin. It appears to be a very old and the little boy runs in and shows it to his father who examined it closely noting that there was a date that said 200 BC. He looked at his son and said, "Son this is a fake". How did the father know this?" Later when discussing the exam with others who had taken it, several of us were still scratching our heads. While the examination was not so difficult for someone with a good general education and some intelligence, I have absolutely no doubt that it has now been made easier to enable the requisite number of recruits from all sections of society to get through. It would be little use any government saying that there is more money for more police if the recruits couldn't get past the entrance exam! You may think I am suggesting that the calibre of recruits has fallen. In my opinion, it has.

One evening shortly after taking the exam a somewhat irate Charlie Tapping came to our house. It seems a local police Inspector had called upon him, in full uniform and in a marked police car. The officer only wanted to ask whether George Raven was in his view reliable, honest, sober and trustworthy. However the idea of a policeman calling upon him unannounced was quite scandalous to a gentleman of his standing. Whatever would the neighbours think etc, apart from the shock to his system? After all policemen calling unexpectedly are usually the bearers of bad news.

Suitable apologies were made and well received, and a few weeks passed before I was called up to police headquarters for an interview with the Chief Constable, whose decision would of course be final.

The Chief Constable of the Essex Constabulary at the time was Captain Jonathan Peel, later to be Sir Jonathan Peel, who boasted some relationship to the former Prime Minister who introduced the Bill that was to establish the Metropolitan Police in 1829. Perhaps it was fitting, if this was so, that he should have been a Chief Constable. Interestingly enough the name Peel is still very much associated with the police in Essex as Sir Jonathan's son Anthony Peel was at one time chairman of the Police Committee.

For some years up until the time I joined the police force, Chief Constables had been recruited from retiring army officers, who it was thought were ideally suited, and still young enough, to lead a disciplined force of men, and later men and women. Most of the eighty or so forces had former captains, majors and even a brigadier or two as their Chief

Constable. The fact that they were not themselves policemen was not important, and to a large extent this policy was successful. Later this practice was to be changed, so Captain Peel was the last of his breed in Essex County. With him and those like him, sadly in my view, went the military discipline he stood for which I so much admired.

There was also at that time still a distinctly defined 'upper class' in most societies, particularly in the more rural areas, and an ex-army officer fitted in nicely with the social structure of a Borough or County. One of the landed gentry who had reason, heaven forbid, to have dealings with the police could ring up the Chief Constable and feel comfortable. Many a young officer of those times who dared to stop or even talk to someone who considered his social status above average would be told, "I am a friend of the Chief Constable". That would often effectively terminate the interview. I was instructed quite early in my service to which of the local dignitaries I should touch the peak of my helmet and address as "Sir".

Soon after I joined however, the climate began to change somewhat and Chief Constables were chosen through a scheme known as the Trenchard Scheme. Suitably-educated candidates would be trained at Hendon and eventually turned out as inspectors and rapidly rise to fully-fledged Chief Constables. Many of these men had been to university and were more liberal in their views and far more amenable to political interference.

I arrived, wearing my demob suit and trilby hat, at the impressive old red brick building that was Police Headquarters at Chelmsford. Today this lovely old building still houses the Chief's office, but it is now dwarfed by the great and ugly concrete edifice standing behind it, which can be seen for miles around. I was carrying with me a large suitcase, as instructed, which was to contain my uniform when I returned home, if I was fortunate enough to be accepted.

Two other applicants were parading for interview that day. One was Peter Wright, an ex-naval man a little older than me, from then on known to all as 'Sailor' Wright, and the other was Peter Taylor, a pleasant young man about my own age; I don't recall his background. We three sat in a small waiting room getting to know one another and waiting for our turn to be marched in to see Captain Jonathan Peel, the Chief Constable.

True to military tradition we were called in alphabetical order, so I was first. Captain Peel, who was not a large man, was nevertheless impressive in his Chief Constable's uniform, the wreath and crossed battens, signifying his rank on his epaulettes. He sat majestically behind his huge desk, studying me as I was led in by the recruiting Sergeant, and directed to sit down in a chair directly facing him. We chatted about my army service naturally and the obvious question was asked: "Why do you want to join the Essex Constabulary?"

I was expecting the question, and had practised a dozen or more different ways to answer it prior to the interview. Today I honestly can't remember which one I advanced; perhaps it was none of them. So many, I recall, had seemed trite and probably none would have been novel to Captain Peel, who was an old hand at interviewing candidates. In these circumstances I suppose the truth is probably the simplest, but so often it is not the answer that is expected of you. Some might be joining because it was considered a secure job with free housing, uniform and medical treatment. Others because they couldn't get a job doing anything else. I may have mumbled something about having the desire to become a public servant, to serve my fellow citizens and rid the streets of crime, but I doubt it. The truth is I wanted to be a detective, not a 'bobby' on the beat, although I knew that that was a necessary step towards my goal.

Finally I was dismissed and told to wait outside. I grinned sheepishly at Peter Taylor as I passed him on his way in, and sat down again with Sailor Wright. We naturally discussed how I had got on and soon Peter Taylor re-appeared and Sailor Wright went in. When he came out we sat waiting for some time before the recruiting Sergeant came back into the room and announced that we had all been accepted. However we were not yet 'in.' First there was the medical, but that would be after lunch.

We were taken to the canteen, fed, watered, and later driven into Chelmsford Town to visit the Police Surgeon, Doctor Catlin. I was not too concerned about my physical fitness, because having been in the army, I considered myself to be in good shape. I was a little apprehensive however, because there is in my family a tendency to colour blindness, and I was aware that this was an important aspect of the police medical examination. Sailor Wright on the other hand was a little overweight and was concerned that this might cause him to be rejected.

We were subjected to the most rigorous examination I

had had since joining the army. On that occasion I had been shown some cards with masses of different coloured dots on them. I had been asked to say what number I could see among the dots. I had got it wrong, and was told that I was slightly colour blind and that I could not, under certain conditions, distinguish between red and brown. It was not a problem for getting into the army, since in those days, as I was told by the Medical Officer's Orderly, "They don't test your eyes, they just count them!" It later years it did prove a slight problem, but only when playing snooker!

I had a similar test on this occasion, and once again stared at the coloured dots with a complete lack of awareness. Perhaps the lighting conditions were different, or perhaps I guessed right this time. In any event all three of us passed, and were carted off back to headquarters to visit the Uniform Store.

At this time policemen were still wearing the tunics which buttoned up to the neck, with their number on it. Even today, when officers are wearing shirts and ties with open necked tunics, and numbers are worn on epaulettes, it is still referred to as your 'collar number.' There were then no summer-weight or winter-weight tunics, just tunics, made of heavy and rather coarse material, which had to be worn in both cold and warm weather. Two sets of everything except boots were provided, including capes. The cape is a thing of the past now, but it was a most useful item of the police officer's equipment, and was often used to conceal the odd hot dog, cup of tea or even a smoke. Likewise the white gloves, the only item of ceremonial dress we had in Essex, are not often seen today. Policemen always carried, and often wore, black leather gloves. It is reputed that some officers put a marble in each finger in order to make a handy weapon for striking wayward youths and other 'ne'er do wells' but I cannot confirm this; I certainly never did.

The last items to be issued were the tools of the trade, to be known from then on as one's 'appointments', the truncheon or baton, as it is more properly called, handcuffs and whistle. The handcuffs were heavy and solid, not the lightweight ones with a ratchet that are issued today, and which, if the film representations are to be believed, can be opened with a hairpin. There were two other 'appointments,' in many ways the most important, that were not issued yet, the Pocket Book and Warrant Card. All of these appointments a constable was expected to carry with him at all times when on duty in uniform. The Warrant Card had to be with you whether in uniform or not, both on and off duty.

Most of this vast quantity of uniform and equipment was just about squeezed into the large suitcase, which I proudly carried home, with the two helmets separately in a large paper bag. At home I tried on the uniform once again and looked at myself in the mirror, watched by my mother, who immediately burst into tears. Why do mothers do that? I asked her what there was to cry about, and she said that when I had been born in a nursing home in Croydon, one of the nurses wrapped me in a blanket after being fed on one occasion. It seems I managed to wriggle my arms out of the covering and wave them about. "Look at him," said the nurse. "He's going to be a policeman!"

It seemed to my mother that the nurse's prophecy had come true. She burst into tears again.

When her tears had dried, she began to exhort me with words of advice, as mother's do. I was too busy fixing the numbers on the tunics and overcoats and picturing myself patrolling down Romford High Street to listen to them, but have no doubt it was good advice. I was to be Constable Number 937 and like my army number it was one I was never likely to forget.

Boots had to be provided by you, although there were guidelines as to type, and plenty of advice as to where to buy them. A 'Boot Allowance' of sixpence was included in the weekly wage of some £10. There would also be a bicycle allowance, for those who were required to use a bicycle in their duties, and a typewriter allowance. All reports had to be typed personally; typing pools, typists and recording devices were something for the future.

There were now several weeks of waiting before I was due to go on the next 'intake' of recruits to the police training school at Hartley Wintney in Hampshire, during which time I bought my first motor car. I recall it was quite an old Singer Le Mans sports model in British racing green, with an exhaust that produced a throaty roar even at a modest thirty miles an hour. Under the bonnet, which was as long as the rest of the car put together, was a once-powerful engine. There were also a lot of polished brass pipes and gadgets, which the previous owner had fastidiously kept shining bright. The huge chrome headlamps were covered with a chromium-plated grille to prevent stones from breaking the glass, and there was a thick leather strap over the bonnet, I suppose to prevent it from flying open at speed. In its day it must have been an awesome machine. Now, still a 'clean car,' as I heard many a car dealer say in later years, it did rattle a bit and drank petrol and oil like a thirsty giant. None the less I was very proud of it. When the day arrived, I drove to the training school in the car, one of the few who were fortunate enough to own his own transport.

Eynsham Hall, as the establishment was known, like many a government institution of the time, was an old manor house of a past era which the noble owner had been forced to sell when no longer able to maintain it. It was a fine old mansion, now somewhat tarnished by the hordes of heavy-booted young men constantly assailing the oak floors and staircases once trodden by fine gentlefolk. The otherwise beautiful grounds were now spoiled by various buildings of many shapes and sizes, which had grown up like mushrooms within them. There was also, I noticed with some disquiet as I approached the main house, a large parade ground. It looked very much like those I had seen at many an army camp in the past, and brought back unpleasant memories of sore feet and aching limbs.

There was no sign of a Sergeant Major bawling across the square, I noticed with some comfort, although I was to meet the formidable Sergeant Horton very soon. I never knew whether this menacing gentleman had ever been a Regimental Sergeant Major in this or perhaps another life, but he surely would have made a good one. His title here was Drill Sergeant, and drill was one of the disciplines we learned, and experienced, daily.

For ex-servicemen, which many of us were - although the Intelligence Corps in those days could hardly be called a regimental sort of unit - drill was no real problem. The august Sergeant Horton did, however have considerable trouble with some of the complete greenhorns, who had to spend many an extra hour tramping up and down to his thunderous, "Left, right, left, right, left!" late into the evening. Still, all this was to come a little later; first we had to be addressed by the Commandant and then 'processed.'

Eynsham Hall was then the police training school for what was known as Number Five District. Each of the hundred or so police forces which then existed in England and Wales was part of a district or group. So far as Scotland was concerned from a policing point of view, and with respect to many other aspects of the law, it was, and remains, a foreign land. No one force, apart from the Metropolitan Police, could afford its own training school, driving schools, forensic science laboratories etc, and these 'central services' were provided on a 'district' basis, financed partly by central government and partly by the forces that used them.

Each intake consisted of thirty officers - more correctly trainees, since none of us had yet been sworn in as constables - from forces which included Essex, Surrey, Suffolk, Buckinghamshire, Bedfordshire, Oxford and the City of London. There were others within the district, but the entire list is of no importance, and many of the smaller forces then within the district no longer exist. The ravages of time and government efforts to improve efficiency were soon to destroy many of them.

There was one intake each month and the course lasted for three months. This meant that there were some ninety officers undergoing training at any one time. It also meant that there was a passing-out parade once a month, when those who were then 'fully trained' officers would parade before their various Chief Constables, and be given their final address and details of their postings. 'Fully trained' is perhaps not the right description of the woefully inexperienced young men who were soon to be let loose on the streets of our cities. There were years of 'on the job' training yet to come.

There were no female officers in training at Eynsham Hall, for which the staff there were truly thankful. There was another establishment, the name of which escapes me, where both men and women recruits were trained at the same time. While at Eynsham Hall, we heard many a tale of the 'goings on' there, Of the instant dismissals of recruits caught in the women's quarters, and worse, of drunken orgies, one of which was said to have culminated in a woman recruit being 'shaved' by some of the men, after being stripped and covered in shaving foam. I will leave the rest to the imagination of the reader. I am by no means a woman hater; on the contrary I am a red-blooded heterosexual and proud of it. However I do have strong views about the desirability of treating men and women as equals in a service such as the police, and I will be expounding them in due course.

Arriving at Eynsham Hall on that morning, the recruits of the new intake were all in plain clothes. After being identified and duly ticked off on the list, we were assigned to our various quarters and 'fell out' to find them, change into our uniforms and 'get fell in' again. I was assigned to a room in the 'big' house, with five other officers. Some were less fortunate and had to manage in less salubrious accommodation within the grounds. I can recall that in my room there was a chap called Dave Pronger from the City of London. Sailor Wright was also with us and Ron Staggs from the Southend-on-Sea Borough Constabulary. Sadly I read of his death several years ago in *The Law*, a newspaper that used to be published by the Essex Police and distributed to all retired officers. The names of the other two trainees who were to share this accommodation with us for the next three months escape me now, but we all soon got to know each other.

From a fairly well-mixed cross-section of citizenry, in an assortment of suits and sportswear, one would have thought that changing into uniform would have levelled the playing field somewhat and make us all look alike; not so. It is of interest at this point to say that for each of the forces represented at Eynsham Hall there was a different uniform, some black, some blue, a different badge, different buttons, and different physical requirements. In the City of London, for example, the minimum height was six feet. Most other forces required their officers to be at least five feet ten inches tall. Many forces have reduced this today to five feet eight inches. In the politically-correct world we live in there must be no discrimination against the 'shorties.' The City also had a differently-shaped helmet.

On our first parade we were reminded that we were a 'shower' and not fit to be let loose on the unsuspecting public, most of whom had done nothing to deserve us. Those who have seen the film called *Carry On Constable* will have an idea how we must have looked.

During the next three months however, a remarkable transformation took place and there began to emerge a smarter, more confident and knowledgeable bunch of men. The day always began with a parade. Uniform, appointments and white gloves were the order of the day, and while standing around waiting for the call to 'get fell in' we each took turns brushing the backs of each other's uniforms. The slightest speck of dust or dandruff was likely to cause comment. Whether the material was black or dark blue, barathea or gabardine, it showed the slightest speckle of dirt. Helmets too had to be spotless, and chinstraps had to be down at all times. Today those officers who do wear helmets never have the chinstrap down across the chin as was intended, and I often flinch when I see the state of dress, or undress, of some of the police officers I see on duty.

A police officer has to enforce the law. It follows that he should know what the law is, and fully understand his powers and authority. A solicitor has to study for years to become qualified, albeit in more than just Criminal Law, however a police officer has just three months to learn the entire range of offences that may be committed by both the criminal and the ignorant. We all learned at an early stage that ignorance of the law is no excuse for committing an offence.

Ask any solicitor, experienced or fresh from law school, what is the maximum permitted width of a caravan, and he will be unable to tell you. He will of course know where to look it up, and immediately reach for the appropriate book on his shelf. The police officer on the beat has no library to consult, and is expected to know the answer to this and hundreds of other similar questions that used to be contained in the Motor Vehicles (Construction and Use) Regulations. This thick volume, together with a copy of the Offences Against The Person Act of 1861 and the Larceny Act of 1916, were issued to all recruits on his first day at training school, and they were some of the first legal authorities I ever saw. With them we all received a copy of *Moriarty's Police Law*, a thick bound tome which was to become our 'bible.'

There are three basic areas of the law that a constable needs to know about. They are 'Offences Against Property,' including burglary, housebreaking, robbery and all crimes relating to what is known today as stealing, but were in my early days called 'Larceny.' Then there is a large group of crimes relating to 'Offences Against the Person,' ranging from Murder, as the most serious, through Grievous Bodily Harm, down to Indecent and Common Assault. Traffic Law is the third and perhaps the most difficult, since it contains many more offences than practically all the other laws put together, and each of them has to be learned in order that the constable may deal with any transgression that he sees committed. In addition to these three main classes of offence there are simply too many more than I could possibly mention, but they include Public Order offences, Diseases of Animals, Firearms, Dogs, Itinerant Traders, and many more.

I learned at Eynsham Hall that the law, which had to be learned, was also in three parts. There is the Common Law of the land, Statute Law, made by governments, and Case

Law (Stated Cases) which law is made by judges in the High Courts, by way of their decisions in deciding what a particular statute really means. In such cases these decisions, usually applicable to only one case, are used as a precedent in later cases whose facts are exactly the same, or as nearly the same as would justify the same interpretation.

To prosecute a person for committing any offence, whether a serious one, the penalty for which is imprisonment, or a lesser or 'summary offence,' as it is known in the trade, certain facts have to be proved to the court. These facts are known to the police recruit as the 'points to prove'. To learn the points to prove for each particular offence the recruit is given a 'definition' to learn, parrot fashion. The first definition I learned was that of 'constable'. It is one I have never forgotten and one of the most significant, in the light of the changes I have seen in the police service.

The word 'constable' had been in use from at least the 5th Century. A constable was then the "count of the stable" and in charge of the King's horses. After the Norman Conquest in 1066, the new rulers added the office of constable to the justice system. By the 11th century the constable had become one of the chief officials of state, with power over the King's cavalry. He also acquired judicial authority. The constable had command of the army, since the main fighting force was composed of knights on horseback. Local constables were also given law-enforcement powers as assistants to sheriffs. Constables were responsible for putting down riots or armed uprisings, a far cry from today's humble policeman, but an indication of the honour it once was to be a constable.

Let me give you another example of a definition, perhaps one of the most important I ever learned, 'larceny': "A person steals who, without the consent of the owner, takes and carries away anything capable of being stolen, with the intent, at the time of such taking, permanently to deprive the owner thereof".

It was essential both for the forthcoming examinations at the end of the course and for one's future on the street to learn these 'points to prove', since without one or more of them a case would not hold water in court. I shall be discussing the law in general in another chapter and giving some illustrations of how important this is. In addition to his 'definitions' there were also many 'Powers of Arrest' to learn, which I shall also refer to in a later chapter.

Incidentally there is no such thing in English law now as 'larceny'. The law was changed by the introduction of the Theft Act 1968. Now there are only various forms of 'Theft' and quite a new definition. Theft is now defined as the "dishonest appropriation of the property of another".

Many of the complexities of the law of larceny were simplified by the introduction of the Theft Act, although in every case when governments make laws they make new problems. Already there are almost as many 'cases stated' about theft as there were about larceny. To illustrate just one example of how difficult it was to prove larceny, a person had to actually 'take and carry away' the item stolen. Those four words were the cause of a great deal of difficulty in proving a case. Today that proof is not necessary, so if I put my hand through an open window and merely touch a purse I can now be said to have stolen it. Further, the intent to steal must have been at the 'time of such taking', so that if I borrowed your pen fully intending to give it back but later decided to sell it, I couldn't be convicted of larceny. These and many more difficulties that had been in existence for many years were eliminated by the introduction of the Theft Act, which brought with it its own difficulties.

There were of course many more 'definitions' to learn and all of them had several 'points to prove'. Each morning after breakfast at Eynsham Hall there was, if one got up early for breakfast, an hour or so before the first 'parade.' During this time most of the students used to walk round the grounds, learning their definitions. A stranger would have been puzzled to see dozens of individuals walking slowly round the huge lawn in front of the main building, mumbling aloud to themselves, occasionally stopping to glance at a little book, tuck it away again and carry on walking and mumbling.

Having learned the law, the next important subject for the police recruit to learn about are the laws of evidence and how to give his evidence in court. Another of the definitions I remember well is the definition of evidence:

> "Evidence is the name given to the means by which any point, or points, are proved, or disproved, according to the rules governing the subject."

Yes, you guessed it: there are different rules for different subjects. Fortunately for the police officer, there are solicitors, who can help him through the minefield of evidence, after the smoke has cleared from the scene of the crime and he is sitting quietly in the office preparing his case papers. Giving evidence in court is all important, and one of the class rooms at Eynsham Hall was rigged out to look much like many of the old Police Courts or Magistrates' Courts did in those days.

As I have already said, the recruit was not issued with an official pocket book upon joining; this was given to him later when he returned to his force fully trained. At the training school however, all recruits were given a pocket book for the purposes of training only. Learning to make entries in this precious, and accountable, document was a whole subject in itself and no constable should ever underestimate its importance. One learned to dread that moment when the defence solicitor held out his hand and said, "Let me see your pocket book, officer". If this happened and you were found to have said something that was not in your notes, or failed to say something that was, you were in big trouble.

We were taught early that one of the rules of evidence was that if you learned your evidence and gave it without reference to your pocket book, the defence solicitor could not ask to see it. It was always wise therefore to learn your words the night before going to court. In today's courts things have changed considerably and I have no doubt that if a defence solicitor gave some plausible reason for wanting to see a police officer's pocket book, or any other document, he would be allowed to do so.

One was to learn also that a constable could only refer to

his notebook when giving evidence of an incident if those notes were made at the time, or immediately afterwards. It was believed also that magistrates were far more impressed by an officer who gave his evidence without reference to his notebook. We were taught that after reciting our evidence we should always look directly towards the Chairman of the Bench and say, "That, your Worship, is my evidence".

Criticism of police officers and casting doubts upon their credibility had not yet begun in earnest, particularly in magistrates' courts, where the officers were usually all known by the local magistrates – after all they used to touch their forelocks to them and call them "sir" in the street. Solicitors who did attack officers in this way without very good cause were rebuked sharply by the Chairman of the Bench, who would promptly add another month to the sentence he proposed passing on his client or another few pounds to the fine.

Following a practical exercise, when one or more of the class would 'report' a motorist for an offence, or a 'pedlar' for peddling without a licence, we would all adjourn to the 'court' for the 'case' to be tried. Training school staff acted as prisoner, magistrate and solicitors. This resulted in some educational but hilarious episodes. On one occasion the officer gave his evidence and concluded by saying, "That, your evidence, is my worship". On another the 'defence solicitor' shouted at the officer, "Who makes these allegations against my client?" The officer, somewhat shaken, thought for a moment, looked at the 'magistrate' and said proudly, "I sir, am the alligator".

In this way many of the pitfalls of giving evidence in court were learned, but not all of them. I was later to hear many more howlers such as this in real courts, when to have fallen about laughing, as we did at the training school, would have been severely dealt with. Magistrates in those days were a highly respected and dignified breed, and constables and citizens alike regarded them with necessary reverence.

The physical side of being an officer of the law is also important, and the more academic lessons were punctuated with periods of physical training. These consisted mainly of long cross-country runs, obstacle courses and self-defence. The physical training instructor was, as one might expect, an expert in self-defence, but at the same time I believe he must also have been a sadist. One saving grace was that for the lesson on how to defend oneself against a man coming at you with a knife, the knife was made of wood. I am quite sure that had this not been the case, the local hospital would have run out of sutures very quickly. Fortunately throughout my service I was never required to find out if I had actually learned that lesson well. There have been occasions when I have had to face an aggressor, but so far as I recall, self-defence learned in the gymnasium some time before was forgotten, and it was a case of survival of the fittest, no holds barred and hit first and hardest. Time was when the sight of a police uniform was enough to quell most 'trouble' or to make a villain think twice about assaulting an officer. Sadly those days are now gone.

One afternoon when we should have been out on a cross-country run the weather was as they say inclement, so the instructor decided that we should spend the time boxing. He paired us up according to approximate size and I found myself 'gloved up' and facing a another recruit. Having done a bit of boxing in the army I decided I could hold my own with the ginger-haired, somewhat gormless looking individual from Buckinghamshire with whom I was paired. When my turn came I touched my gloves together a couple of times, flexed my shoulders and danced up and down on my toes, hoping I looked confident enough to induce fear into my opponent. I had learned in the army that to gain a psychological advantage over your opponent, the 'body language' had to be positive. My opponent just stood there, his arms by his sides and his head hung low looking at the ground.

The instructor blew a whistle and we squared up to each other. I threw a couple of left jabs, neither of which landed, much to my surprise, and then all hell broke loose. It was as if I had stepped into a bar-room brawl with a couple of dozen rowdies. Punches landed on my head and body from all directions. Then I took a direct hit on my nose, stars flashed and I was on the floor. I did hear a whistle blow in the distance, and in my dazed state realised that my nose was streaming blood, and that I was being helped up. The ginger-haired chap led me to a wash basin, apologising profusely all the way, and I was quickly cleaned up. Still a bit shaken and with my pride severely dented, I sat and watched the rest of the afternoon's boxing without a great deal of interest.

It was not until some time later that I learned that before joining the police force, my opponent had worked in a fairground boxing booth. He had challenged all comers to last a minute with him for £5, and had not often had to 'pay up.' If I learned nothing else that day, it was that you could never tell by appearances. I thought of this many times during my early service when I was tempted to raise my hands to defend myself or even to respond to a vile insult or two. "Lose your temper, lose the advantage" I always found to be a sound maxim, although one I was not always able to follow.

The day eventually came for our passing-out parade, and I learned that I had been posted to Romford, which was so far as Essex was concerned about the busiest and roughest area of the county. Peter Wright was going to Colchester, formerly Colchester Borough force and now considered a good posting, and Peter Taylor went to Brentwood. I was to serve at Colchester many years later as Divisional Superintendent, while Peter Wright was still a Constable at Copford. He was well respected and dearly loved by the people of that village and sorely missed when he retired. He has since died. Like many other detached beat officers, he was never replaced.

Peter Taylor left the force after only a few months. One night in Brentwood high street, he was badly beaten up by a gang of three drunken louts. Someone dialled 999 and help arrived quite quickly. Peter was taken to hospital for treatment, and the three thugs were arrested and taken to Brentwood police station. Sometime later Peter returned from hospital bandaged and sore. He was absolutely disgusted to find that the three prisoners were together in the charge room, drinking cups of tea and laughing about what had happened along with the duty Sergeant. He resigned the very next day, and I can't say that I blame him.

As for me, well that is what this book as about isn't it?

It was to be another two weeks before Sailor, Peter and I were to part company. First we had to report to headquarters at Chelmsford for a Local Procedure Course, our pocket books and final briefing, before the big day when we would be sworn in.

We were to discover that there was yet another group of laws to learn. We had had Common Law, Statute Law and Case Law, and now there were bylaws. These are laws made by local authorities, under various statutes, for the control of dogs fouling footpaths, street vendors, children playing games in the street, and a host of other minor crimes against Good Order and Local Government. Copies of the various laws made by the Essex County Council were added to the growing pile of 'bumph' that each of us had to carry with us to all lectures.

Every police force in the country was a proud and independent body of men doing a similar job. However each had different procedures, different coloured forms, different policing policies and priorities and vastly different terrain and problems. It was impossible for all these differences to be incorporated into the general training at Eynsham Hall, so every officer had to undergo a Local Procedure course before he finally set foot on the streets of his particular 'manor'. This word manor has been used by police officers to describe the area of his or her authority since the time when the Manor House was the focal point of most villages or beats.

Another valuable document we were issued with was a copy of the Essex Constabulary Standing Orders. At the time

I joined this was a loose-leafed volume about an inch or so thick. Each month amendments would be issued which had to be meticulously made by each individual officer to his own personal copy, and his work checked and certified by a Sergeant. The book contained all the information concerning local procedures, which differed from national standards. Later this book grew and grew, until at the time of my own retirement it was contained in three volumes, each more than two inches thick. I can remember that one of the deputy Chief Constables I served under, John Duke - sadly now deceased - used to say that Standing Orders were a catalogue of other people's mistakes. To a large extent that is true, since a new order appeared each time someone did something worthy of criticism to remind others not to do the same.

If an officer was ever in doubt as to the action he should take in a particular case, or which form to complete, he could find it in Standing Orders; at least that was the theory. In practice of course, this laudable document was not available to refer to on the street, when it was all happening, and mistakes were often made. There was always a member of the 'hindsight brigade' to tell you later, "But it is in Standing Orders!"

We were now issued with our pocket books, and given further instructions on their completion. At the beginning of every tour of duty, the day and date had to be written in and underlined. The time, date and place of every incident which occurred during your tour of duty was to be methodically entered, together with your evidence if such incident was likely to result in a court case. The name, age, occupation and address of persons interviewed had to be entered. Ladies for some reason don't like to be asked their age, and if this was refused, the trainee was advised to look her up and down and say, "Ok, I'll put approximately forty," or an age that was obviously an over estimate. The response was invariably, "Don't be rude young man, I'm only thirty". Why this insistence on the age of everyone being meticulously entered I don't know. Today I believe the approximate age is all that is required in most cases. Giving offence to a member of the public cannot be tolerated in today's police force.

The pages of the book were numbered and it was a mortal sin to tear out a page. Every error had to be clearly marked as such, and a thin line drawn through it so that what had been written previously was still visible.

I mentioned earlier that if notes of an incident were made at the time, then an officer could make use of his notebook to refresh his memory in the witness box.

An officer who was a little unsure of how he should word his evidence might be tempted to wait until he was back at the station and could consult a more experienced man. This would of course result in notes that were not made at the time, so an officer might put an earlier time his book, indicating that they were in fact made at the time of the incident. This habit of 'making up' your notebook after an event, when you'd had time to reflect on the right things to write down, was a great temptation for all officers. It was also a further good reason for learning your evidence by heart.

One way of preventing this improper practice was the making of 'points'. On every tour of duty you could expect a

Sergeant or Inspector to pop up at any moment to make a point with you. When he did so he would write the time, date and place in your pocketbook and sign it. Any entry you made after that would have to be at a time later than the time of the 'point.' If you still had some evidence to go in of an earlier incident and at an earlier time, you were in trouble.

You may have noticed that a constable has two breast pockets, and wondered what he kept in them. The pocket book, naturally, was in one, and in the other an 'Information book.' This contained details of recently stolen bicycles and motor cars, descriptions of missing and wanted persons and some forms knows as HORT1. (Home Office Road Traffic Form 1). When a person was stopped driving a motor vehicle and the driver did not have his driving licence and insurance with him, this form was issued to him requiring him to produce them at a police station of his choice within five clear days. This practice is still I believe carried out today, in contrast to most European countries where it is an offence not to carry all documents, particularly Insurance, in the car with you; a much more sensible idea! Hours and hours of police time are wasted chasing up people who have for various reasons failed to produce their documents within the five days allowed.

Finally there was the Road Accident booklet. Since the list of items of information required to be noted down at the scene of a road accident was too long for any human brain to remember, a booklet was completed rather than the pocket book. Naturally a pocket book entry had to be made as well, to the effect that an accident had been attended at whatever time date and place, but all the relevant details were recorded in the Accident Report Book, under the various headings. This completed booklet was later handed in to the Sergeant and was an 'accountable document,' that is to say it had a serial number. A new one was issued only after a completed one had been handed in. There was not, or should not have been, an opportunity for any alterations to be made later.

I recall that there were also some further physical training sessions on this local procedure course. The instructor was a man named Tom Pinch. He was an old - in service - police constable who was, we all thought, somewhat punch drunk. Nevertheless he taught us all a good deal about unofficial methods of self-preservation. We also had instruction on when and where to use our batons - in short, never - and how to handcuff a person. In practice, with the old style handcuffs, it was very difficult to do this without removing a big chunk of skin from the victim's wrist.

Now we were ready, or as ready as we would ever be, to be sworn in as constables of the County of Essex. On the great day we were paraded in our best uniforms (we had been issued with two) and taken to County Hall in Chelmsford. In the Magistrates' Court the business of the day was temporarily suspended while we were wheeled in front of the 'Bench' and each in turn took the oath and swore to do his duty "without fear of favour, malice or ill will". What a long time ago that seems now. I often have a little smile to myself since the oath taken by police constables is much the same today, and the words "without fear" are still used. Today, whatever anyone else may tell you, all police officers from the very highest rank to the very lowest are motivated by fear; fear of criticism, fear of complaints, and worst of all fear of violence so frequently used against them and which frequently goes unpunished.

The Chairman of the Bench said a lot of encouraging words to us and applauded our public-spiritedness in wanting to serve our fellow citizens of Essex. When I left the court that day I was ten feet tall and ready for the task ahead, for ridding the streets of Essex, of crime and criminals. We were now given our Warrant Cards, a mark of the authority that had now been bestowed upon us, and instructions to report for duty at our appointed stations.

In contrast, after thirty years of serving the said citizens of Essex, there was no visit to the Magistrates' Court for a few words of thanks. Just lunch with the Chief Constable and his sarcastic jibe about sailing close to the wind.

# The Probationer (1953–955)

*No man, not even a doctor, ever gives any other definition of what a nurse should be than this - "devoted and obedient". This definition would do just as well for a porter. It might even do for a horse. It would not do for a policeman - Florence Nightingale - Notes on Nursing (1860) p. 200*

My arrival at Romford police station one October morning in 1953 was something of a culture shock. I don't really know what I had expected, but having been to training school, followed by police headquarters for local procedure training, I was used to fairly modern buildings with modern equipment and a general air of efficiency. Romford was none of these things, although, as I was to find out, efficiency is not always apparent at first glance.

Romford Police Station in those days was quite an old

building in South Street close to the railway station. Like many police stations in Essex it had originally been built for a different purpose: many were old schools or other public buildings which had been taken into use by the police many years earlier. Also like many other stations, it housed the Magistrates' Court. These courts were also called Police Courts, perhaps by reason of their close association with and often proximity to the local police station, more probably because justice used to be dispensed there by police and magistrates without the aid of lawyers!

There was a narrow side way leading to the Magistrates' Court and on past it to the two garages used by the Chief Superintendent and his deputy and then the 'backyard'. The backyard was where the police cars (area cars) were able to park when they were not on patrol and it housed a cycle shed, dog kennels and at the very bottom a long air-raid shelter. The air-raid shelter was a store for all kinds of unwanted items - including unexploded bombs.

In 1953, only eight years after the end of the Second World War, sundry items of ordnance such as incendiary and other devices dropped by the enemy were still being found, especially along the railway embankments. It was usual for an area car to be despatched to investigate any such reported find and bring it back to the police station, if it was not thought dangerous, in the boot of the police vehicle. It was then deposited in the air raid shelter until such time as some greater authority, who bore the title 'Civil Defence Officer,' at police headquarters, made arrangements for its collection by the army.

Some time later when I had graduated to become an area car driver, I had occasion to answer such a call. A couple of small boys had discovered an 'object' near the railway embankment. It looked like other small incendiary bombs I had seen, but to be sure I radioed for confirmation. There was a considerable wait while the Civil Defence Officer, a Sergeant, was contacted and eventually he called me on the radio.

"Does it have three studs on the base?"

"Yes," I replied.

"What colour is it?"

"Black."

"Ok that's fine, it's incendiary and is OK to transport to the station."

I carefully placed the bomb in the back of the car and drove through Romford market, which was crowded with people, arriving at the station some ten minutes or so later. I took the object to the air-raid shelter and left it there.

Back in the car the radio was calling me; the Civil Defence Sergeant.

"Whatever you do don't touch it. I just checked and three studs black is H.E". (high explosive). I think that was probably the first time I was abusive to a senior officer. But I digress.

I entered the small foyer of the police station and told the officer on duty there that I was a new arrival reporting for duty. He lifted the flap in the counter and ushered me in. Today undoubtedly I would have had to be searched, vetted and passed through two or three security doors before being allowed inside, an unfortunate necessity in these times of fear and uncertainty.

The duty Sergeant, named Bennett, was a man in his early fifties who always wore an amiable smile that disguised a less agreeable nature when dealing with the 'ungodly', as he called all wrong doers. Sergeant Bennett was affectionately known as Wag Bennett, I learned later, although constables always addressed him as 'Sergeant,' 'Sarge' or 'Skip'. I was used to discipline in the Army; I think it does a lot for a uniformed service, and abhor the current fashion of calling almost everyone, as well as your peers, by their first name.

A 'wag' is a facetious person or a 'joker' and I soon realised why Sergeant Bennett had earned this nickname. I was standing with him at Golden Lion Corner, then a focal point in Romford, when a Bentley came round the corner too fast and almost collided with another vehicle on its offside. Sergeant Bennett stepped out into the road and stopped the car, and the driver sheepishly wound down the window. Sergeant Bennett threw back his cape, took out his pocket book, stepped up to the window and peered in. "For such a nice-looking car," he said, "I expected to see a far more intelligent-looking driver". He proceeded to 'advise' him about the manner of his driving, put his pocket book away and signalled the driver to drive on.

I was led through the parade room to the Sergeant's office. The parade room was a long narrow place that had no doubt once been a corridor of some kind. There were several high old-fashioned desks along one wall reminiscent of the one used by Bob Cratchit in Dickens's *Christmas Carol* and a long row of numbered coat pegs along the other. Beneath the coat pegs was an equally long low wooden seat, the top of which was divided and also served as the tops of some twenty or more lockers that coincided in number and position with the coat pegs. Like the other officers, I was later to be allocated a peg and a locker, none of which were lockable!

At the far end of this long room was the only window, in front of which was a table and beside it two fifteen-drawer metal filing cabinets. These, I was to find later, contained the dozens of different forms that were required to be filled in for every conceivable occurrence, from stolen bicycles to missing persons and from descriptive forms for suspects and prisoners to crime complaints. Getting to know all these forms and their purport was a major task for the probationer.

For the thirty years of my service, no doubt for the thirty years before that, and probably for the next thirty years, people will be complaining about the amount of paperwork generated by police work and trying to decrease it. No one has succeeded so far. The computer era has improved some aspects of the job, but the information still has to be written down on paper before someone can enter it into a computer. Every piece of paper is also a potential court exhibit and so must be correct, and if at all possible unambiguous.

Above the table were the 'pigeonholes.' Each officer had a pigeonhole bearing his collar number, and this was his own particular communications centre. Messages from his Sergeant, from other officers and anyone else who wanted to contact him when he was not on duty went in here. It was the first place an officer looked when he came on duty and the last before he signed off. Failure to see a message in your pigeonhole was a serious matter. When coming on duty, work that had been allocated to you would be waiting there - such things as summonses for personal service, warrants for non-payment of fines and enquiries from other divisions or forces.

The Sergeant's greeting was formal but friendly. He shook hands and had there been a chair for visitors in his office he would probably have asked me to sit. There was little for him to tell me at that stage, except that I would be reporting for night duty the following day on 'C' Shift. New recruits always started with night duty, for reasons that were never very clear to me. I was shown to my locker and told that this was where I would keep my Standing Orders, any files and papers that I might be working on and my typewriter. It was also where I would keep my sandwiches and thermos flask when I came on duty until my refreshment break. Sergeant Bennett did, to be fair to him, suggest that I should keep my sandwiches in a tin box. I didn't realise the importance of this advice at the time and my mother (I was not married then) prepared my supper sandwiches on my first spell of night duty and wrapped them in a plastic bag. At 1.15am when I went to my locker to retrieve them there was the plastic bag in shreds, and nought but a few crumbs for me to eat. The station rats had made another score! I bought myself a metal lunch box next day. It was one of the many lessons I learned the hard way.

I suppose now would be a good time to familiarise and perhaps bore the reader with the general organisation of the Essex constabulary in 1953. Like the other hundred or so provincial, city and borough forces, Essex had a Chief Constable and a Deputy. The Metropolitan Police is different in many respects from other police forces, one distinction being that it is led by the Commissioner. Already in 1953 this had become much more a political appointment, the occupier of that office being personally chosen by the Home Secretary. The Police Committee on the other hand selected Chief Constables in counties and watch committees in cities and boroughs. Oddly enough, anyone could apply for the job of Chief Constable, although by the time I joined the police it was usual for the short list to be made up of senior police officers from other counties or 'Trenchard' chaps.

It is important to note that Chief Constables were, and so far as I know still are, solely responsible for the day-to-day policing of their territory and for all operational matters. Today of course there are politically-appointed police and crime commissioners, who replaced police committees. At the time of writing these memoirs I am not sure what the relationship is between the Commissioner and the Chief Constable, but I am sure that in most cases it is not a comfortable one. In so far as finance is concerned however, the police and watch committees (in the days of borough forces) were in charge, since it was they who had to raise the money through local taxation. This division of jurisdiction or control was naturally the cause of much conflict between the chief and his committee. He would tell them how much money he needed to carry out his operations efficiently and they would tell him how much he could have. I suppose, although police committees and watch committees no longer exist, that the same annual bargaining still goes on.

Political influence from the Government of the day could

not be avoided, since only half of all police expenditure comes from local taxation, the other half being provided by the Government. However this half will only be provided if the Government is satisfied that the force is being run efficiently. Each year Her Majesty's Inspector of Constabularies visits each force for about three days and examines every aspect of its day-to-day business. His report to the Home Office determines whether half the next year's police revenue will be provided. I have never known the money to be held back, although occasionally the Inspector's report will contain adverse comments about certain matters which the Government will expect to be put right by the following year.

It will be seen therefore that the independence of Chief Constables could not be total. Many Chief Constables hope to be rewarded at the end of their service with a knighthood. There was also promotion to one of the ranks considered higher than that of Chief Constable to think about, that is to say HM Inspector of Constabulary or Commissioner of Police of the Metropolis. It behove them therefore to 'toe the line' in respect of Government policy. There have been some examples during my service of Chief Constables who from time to time insisted upon their independence, but none of these were ever knighted, or rewarded by promotion.

The Essex Constabulary was divided into divisions, which generally corresponded with the administrative divisions of the county. Each division had a Chief Superintendent in charge and he always had a deputy, who would usually be a Superintendent.

Divisions were again divided into sub-divisions under a

Chief Inspector. The urban sub-division was usually housed at Divisional Headquarters, and the other sub-divisions, which had their own headquarters within the division, were known as rural sub-divisions. In each sub-division there might be one or more section stations with a Sergeant and two or three constables; I was reminded of these whenever I saw *Heartbeat* on television. Perhaps the most sadly missed officers of all were the 'detached beat' men who lived and worked alone in small villages.

Romford, being a mainly urban area, had no detached beats. There were sub-divisional stations at Hornchurch and Harold Hill and sections at Emerson Park, Plough Corner, Upminster and Rainham.

The ranks in the police service are there for organisational and administrative purposes only. Every constable from the Chief Constable downward has the same legal powers bestowed upon him when he is sworn in. In theory, therefore if a constable decides to arrest someone he does so on his own authority and no one could or should stop him from doing so. That's the theory!

At every divisional and sub-divisional station there are members of the Criminal Investigation Department. These are known as divisional CID officers, although they are actually part of the force Criminal Investigation Department. The senior detective at divisional level was a Detective Chief Inspector, who usually had a deputy who was a Detective Inspector.

When I was at Romford the DCI was a man named Vic Cook, an experienced detective of the old school. I didn't see much of him during my stay at Romford. His deputy was

Billy Girt, a small but formidable man who was somewhat of a legend in his time. Not only was the CID staff terrified of him, so were the local villains!

I was leaving the station one day as he was coming in. He looked at me rather quizzically; I was a new boy and he didn't know me.

"Do you know Ginger S......g?" he growled.

Ginger, I leave his surname out, was a local 'CRO' with a bad record of violence and dishonesty. PC Russell had pointed him out to me during my two weeks with a tutor constable. I therefore had a vague idea what he looked like, but could hardly say I knew him. I was however out to impress.

"Yes sir" I said.

"Go and tell him I want to see him."

"Do I tell him what for sir?"

"No, just tell him to get his arse down here sharp like."

Ginger was standing at Golden Lion Corner with some of his associates as I walked up.

"What do you fucking want?" he said aggressively.

"Mr Girt wants to see you" I said.

His attitude changed immediately. "What for?" Now there was a touch of nervousness in his voice.

"I don't know, but I'd hurry if I was you, he was breathing fire when I saw him a few moments ago".

Ginger scooted off as if his tail was on fire. I never did know what Mr Girt wanted Ginger for, but it was an indication to me of what a formidable man he was.

At sub-divisional level there would be a Detective

Inspector and a Sergeant in addition to one or more Detective Constables in the larger sub-divisions and usually only a Sergeant and one Detective Constable at the smaller ones. Sections did not usually have CID officers.

The officer in charge of the divisional CID was rather unfortunate in that he had two immediate bosses, the Divisional Chief Superintendent, who was his administrative head, and the Detective Chief Superintendent at police headquarters, Chelmsford, who was his operational boss and responsible for making sure that reported crimes were properly investigated. This could occasionally lead to conflict, as there were often divisional Chief Superintendents who 'interfered', as that was how their interest in crime detection was seen by detectives, in the daily running of the CID. Of course the Divisional Commander, as the Chief Superintendent was known, had a duty to see that the CID was running efficiently, and was expected, if the Chief Constable rang him early in the morning, to know chapter and verse of what was going on in his division. For this purpose there was a daily early morning 'conference' when the departmental heads were expected to update him on everything that was happening. This was irreverently referred to as 'morning prayers' by all who had to attend, and it was here that those more 'interfering' divisional commanders would occasionally try to tell the CID Chief how to run his department or deal with a particular investigation. These meetings could be and often were uncomfortable for this reason. Of course it would be a long time before I was a party to one of them.

Finally there were the divisional women police officers. Like the CID the Women Police Department, as it was known in those days, was a specialist department of Headquarters. There were other specialist departments at headquarters such as Fingerprints, Scenes of Crime, Police Dogs and the Training School and the officers attached to these departments had all applied to specialise after completion of their probation and receiving the necessary specialist training.

Each division had a WPS (Woman Police Sergeant) and two or three constables. At headquarters the head of the department was a Woman Superintendent and a deputy who was a Woman Chief Inspector.

As I have said they were a specialist department and had their own office, duties and administration. They were always referred to as the Women Police Department and rarely, if ever, did normal uniform patrol duties. Their function was to assist in dealing with women prisoners, to keep records of and make enquiries relating to missing persons and to generally assist the male officers of the uniform branch whenever the assistance of a woman was required. This might be to search women prisoners, or to console a distraught female who had just been told some tragic news such as a loved one being killed in a road accident. Occasionally they were required by the CID to act as 'decoys' for handbag snatchers in the market.

The usefulness of women in some aspects of police work cannot be overlooked and I for one would be the last to say otherwise. Equality and women's rights however eventually caught up with the police service, and you might be surprised to hear that the women of the Women Police Department were the first to protest that their department was to be disbanded. Women's rights activists, not women in general, believe that women are equal in all aspects of life. Of course women should have the same rights as men, but only the foolish or the blind cannot or do not want to see that they are also different.

Women are now fully integrated into the police service. There is no 'Women Police Department' and even their collar numbers, which used to show WPC, are now indistinguishable from a male officer. The word 'woman' has been dropped from all the ranks held by female officers. They are members of shifts, do night work and officially carry out all the duties that their male counterparts do. This pleases the politically correct, women activists, and some politicians. It is of course nonsense; everyone has limitations, whether due to physical size, intelligence and most of all sex.

The insistence that women must, and therefore can, do all the jobs once required to be performed only by men, has caused a great deal of trouble in the police service. What Sergeant for example would send four-foot-two inch Constable Wendy Bloggs to deal with a six-foot-two drunk causing havoc at the local pub? The reality is that while a shift might have had eight male officers it now has six men and two women (four of each if there were enough women). This means effectively that the duty Sergeant now has only six officers instead of eight for the majority of the requirements of the shift. In practice women police still do the things they are good at, like dealing with women prisoners and witnesses, where the sympathetic female does a far better job than a man could.

The police force after all is here to serve the public, not the interests of minority groups who would have us all eating out of their hands if they could. One of the less obvious, but none the less real manifestations of having women in the police service and considering them as equal to their male counterparts is attitude. Because of the historical reasons why women are now considered equal in the police service, as in other fields of endeavour usually regarded as 'men's' work, it is usually only a certain type of woman who wants to join.

Many of them are setting out to prove something; not only that they are equal to, but sometimes that they are better than men. I have been appalled at the sight of women in police canteens drinking pints of beer from a 'jug' and using the 'f' word to punctuate their sentences. A good many have sued their forces when they have been treated as equal to men and screamed 'sexual abuse!' Who is being discriminated against? Women receive months off duty when they become pregnant, and many of them do whether married or not, so now it seems their duties have to be adjusted to allow for them to be at home to look after their children!

Perhaps the very thing that distinguishes men from women, sex, causes the most serious source of difficulty now that men and women share a parade room. Wherever men and women work together, such as in offices, hospitals and more recently the Armed Services, there is always a great deal of inconvenience caused to the organisation by 'love affairs' that spring up between various members of the team. Internal discipline is involved and people have to be moved from their stations to split them up. A senior officer has to be mindful that he can't send PC Wendy Bloggs out on a job with a particular male officer, and a thousand and one other minor and more serious administrative problems occur. In terms of policing, does the job get done better or worse? I rest my case!

At the time of my arrival at Romford there were always three shifts of constables designated 'A', 'B' and 'C' with an equal number of constables, each with a Sergeant and an Inspector. At Divisional Headquarters there would also be an Administration Department headed by an Inspector or Chief Inspector responsible for the day-to-day administration of the Division. There was also a court office where all the 'process' or summonses were dealt with.

There were only three tours of duty for beat constables and these were nights, 10pm to 6am, earlies, 6am to 2pm and lates, 2pm to 10pm. Each officer was allowed three quarters of an hour for a refreshment break which had to be taken at his station. Officers would be required to work seven consecutive days and then have one day off, his rest day. With this system you got a different day off each week and one weekend off in six. Each of the three shifts would be worked for two weeks before the 'quick change over.' On 'quick change over' officers on nights would sign off at 6am and report back for duty and 2pm for late turn. Those on early turn who finished at 2pm were back on at 10pm for nights and the late turn off at 10pm would be on again at 6am for earlies and so on.

From time to time during the past thirty years the Police Federation (which is the policeman's equivalent of a union, although it doesn't deserve to be called one), through individual officers or groups of officers, have sought to get the shift system altered. Many experiments have been tried to see whether a better system could be devised. At the time of writing I don't believe it has. This experimentation is an example of how an organisation becomes unstable if it is not run from the top, and allows the 'men' to dictate such things as how and when they should perform duty. How would it be if the Army allowed groups of junior officers and men to hold meetings to decide when and how they should fight the enemy?

It was occasionally necessary for an officer to work what was called a 'day shift' from 9am to 5pm. This might be because of a court appearance or other administrative duty or even to play sport. Those willing and able to get into the various force teams for cricket, football, bowls etc could expect to be given time off to play at the discretion of the duty Inspector. I wonder if the public realises how many police man-hours are spent, they may say 'wasted', playing games! There were many instances of a team member refusing to play because he was on rest-day!

There is one other department of the police force that I have yet to mention and that is the Traffic Division. Officers of this division, also administered from headquarters at Chelmsford, received special training to deal with traffic matters only, especially on the main roads and motorways that run through the county. Such things as policing the motorways, serious road accidents, abnormal and indivisible loads etc, were left to them. It was considered somewhat of a 'cushy number' and a transfer to Traffic Division was considered to be promotion and was highly sought after.

It was an unwritten law that an officer had to parade for duty fifteen minutes before the start of his shift; this time was unpaid and nobody complained. The quarter of an hour was used by the shift Sergeant to allocate duties and to brief his shift as to current crime and matters of importance such as stolen cars, stolen cycles, missing and wanted persons and current crime. Each officer had to write down these details and carry them with him when he went out onto the street. Each man was also required to read the *Police Gazette*, *Metropolitan Police Informations* (published and distributed nationally and containing details of serious crimes and wanted criminals, missing persons and bodies found) and all the incoming telephone and teleprinter messages since he was last on duty.

After all this was done there would be a parade, when officers going out on the street would be inspected for smartness – chin straps down – and his appointments would be examined. In many of the small City and Borough forces this parade extended to the street and the file of officers was marched along to relieve those going off duty, who tagged along behind as someone else took their place.

Carrying out all these tasks before the appointed time for duty to commence ensured that officers went out on the street on patrol at the same time as the shift going off duty came into the station to sign off. In this way there was no gap in 'coverage' and woe betide any officer not out of the station on the dot of his appointed time to start patrol, or any officer who put a foot inside it before he was due to sign off.

No working man today would be expected to give his organisation fifteen minutes of his time unpaid every day, and it was only to be expected that this custom was soon to erode. Anyone, especially the 'ungodly,' knows that today there is little or no police coverage in any town for at least a half an hour between shifts.

Some of the things with which constables were not issued included a bicycle, a typewriter and boots. These three items were an absolute necessity, and one was given an allowance for them. In the case of boots it was sixpence a week and the typewriter two and sixpence per month. A cycle allowance was only payable if you were actually required to use your own machine on duty. I was not, since Romford Division proudly owned four county bicycles. I did however need a bicycle to get to and from work, so I bought the latest Raleigh model suitable for the task. It was a very large bicycle with 28" diameter wheels and a three-speed and dynamo which had a battery operated backup pack that allowed you stop at traffic lights without your lights going out. I was very proud of my new machine, and rode it gingerly for a while as I hadn't ridden a bicycle since I was at school.

Police officers were required to live where directed by the Chief Constable, which was supposed to be within your particular division. Housing was free, as were medical and dental treatment. Married men were housed in police houses and single men were found suitable digs; there were no 'section houses' as there were in the Metropolitan Police District. After

I was married I had to wait for six months before a house was available for me and then it was in an adjoining division, one of the many deviations from the usual rules that I was to experience when expediency was preferable.

The idea of police houses was to enable the Chief Constable to move officers around as he wished for the good of the force. This practice meant that when an officer left a station he took with him all his local knowledge, which was bad from a practical policing point of view but was designed to prevent an officer from becoming too cosy at one station. Later in the mid-sixties as rules were relaxed the Chief began to allow some officers to buy their own properties, which meant that they were less likely to be moved around.

No matter where you lived, you had to travel to work in uniform. It was a disciplinary offence to wear a civilian coat over your uniform. You were a locally-appointed citizen with special powers and expected to be available to answer any of the 'great unwashed' at any time as soon as you left your house. I lived at Seven Kings and five miles from my station, so my cycle journey to work was partly through the Metropolitan Police district. For a while I was terrified that I would be stopped and asked to deal with an accident or some other incident, the procedure for which in the MPD I hadn't a clue.

Worse was the prospect of having to travel to work on the bus, in uniform, not being sure whether I should pay or not. It was customary for Metropolitan Police officers to travel on all public transport without paying, but I was not officially allowed to do this.

I was cycling home along the same route soon after six

o'clock in the morning only a few nights after I became a constable. I was so tired that I fell asleep on my bicycle and fell off. I was awake soon enough, picked up my fallen and scratched new bicycle, straightened my helmet and quickly glanced around to see how many people were laughing. Thankfully there were none.

I hadn't been a police officer very long when one day I visited the library at Seven Kings, fortunately off duty and in plain clothes. I secured my bicycle to the railings outside the library with a padlock and chain, but when I returned it had gone. I looked up and down the street in disbelief, but was forced to conclude that it had been stolen.

Some way away I saw a Metropolitan policeman standing beside one of those blue police boxes they had in the Met and made my way towards him, feeling rather stupid and rehearsing what I would say. He was a portly, and to me elderly officer, who listened to my story without interest. Then he got out of his pocket, not a pocket book, but a pad of HORT1s, and began to make some notes on the back of one of them. When he got to the question, "Your occupation?" and I answered, he threw back his head and did the best impression of the laughing policeman I have ever seen. I walked home extremely crestfallen and with little confidence that I would ever see my cycle again.

There was a happy sequel to this story. A few days later an officer at East Ham arrested a man who was distributing obscene pictures by putting them in women's shopping baskets. One wonders what pleasure he might have derived from this, but it takes all sorts, so they say. He was in possession of a fairly new bicycle, which when the serial number of it had been checked, turned out to be mine. I revised my opinion of the constable who took the details of my bicycle, although I expect when he told his mates about this green Essex Copper who had his bike nicked, they all had a great laugh at my expense.

Later I was duly warned to attend East Ham Magistrates' Court at Stratford in East London to give evidence, and dreaded the part when I would have to say I was a serving police constable. The press would have had a field day! Luck was with me however, as the man decided to plead guilty; the prosecuting solicitor was able to give the facts of the case to the court without revealing that the cycle's owner was a policeman. Some years later when I was on the Regional Crime Squad I had the hub caps stolen from my Ford Zephyr. Somehow the local press got hold of that and I did get a roasting. The story didn't quite end there, as I had to go to the local station to sign for and collect my machine. The tool kit was missing from the saddlebag and when I got outside I found the saddle had been raised to its highest level and I couldn't reach the pedals. I didn't have the nerve to go back in the station and ask for a spanner, so I wheeled the bike until I found a cycle shop at Manor Park, where I borrowed a spanner before riding the rest of the way home on my trusty steed. Apart from the missing tool kit it was happily none the worse for its experience in the hands of a real criminal, who incidentally went to prison for six months.

Within a few months I was offered police accommodation at Coxtie Green in Brentwood, as there were no police houses available at Romford. It was a fine new house and I accepted readily, although it meant an even longer cycle ride to work each day.

For the first two weeks, a probationary constable, for that is what I now was, is accompanied around the beat by a senior constable who was called your 'tutor constable' for obvious reasons. It was his job to supervise and instruct the new man on all aspects of actually patrolling a beat. Most of what a policeman learns is through on the job training. He will, during his service attend many courses, but where he actually learns his trade is on the beat, and he never stops learning it. In this respect he is as much a trainee the day he retires as he was on joining.

My tutor constable was a man named Bob Russell, who at the time had about eight years' service, having served all this time at Romford. He was knowledgeable and unlike many police officers I met subsequently, ready and willing to pass on his knowledge. Many a crime has gone undetected because one officer will not share his bit of information with another for fear that he will lose the chance of an arrest himself. This tendency for officers to jealously guard their own little data banks of information is still a problem today, despite training and Standing Orders!

You will not be surprised to hear that I was issued with a set of Divisional Standing Orders when I arrived at Romford. Not only did each police force vary in procedures etc, but so did each division. In each police division there were different problems, and each had to have specific instructions about them. For example the coastal area of Clacton has seasonal problems associated with holidaymakers; Colchester has problems connected with the Essex University, and so on. It was therefore necessary for officers in each division to be aware of their own special problems and how it had been decreed that they should be dealt with, hence Divisional Standing Orders.

Romford was conveniently divided into four main beats, which radiated in a cross from Golden Lion Corner, in the centre of the town. They were known as beats 'A', 'B', 'C', and 'D', that is, High Street, London Road, North Street and the Marketplace. There were also a number of 'cycle beats' which were a little further afield, and as their name suggests were patrolled on the county bicycles. Due to other priorities these outlying beats were not always covered during the daytime, but at night they were, and depending on the number of officers on duty one might have to work more than one beat in order that they all received coverage. Whenever a beat had no constable on duty covering it the area car would pay special attention to it.

Like divisions, each beat had its own particular features and problems. No, there were no more standing orders, but it was necessary for the new recruit to learn the problems associated with each beat, for example, the railway station on the High Street beat, the brewery on the London Road beat, and particularly the Market Place. Things happened at certain times of the day and night on each beat which the officer on duty was expected to monitor. 'Being about' is the police jargon for this aspect of police work. The last train from London for example, pub closing time, even the Chief

Superintendent coming to work in the morning. He would expect to see the man on 'A' beat, and if not he would want to know where he was.

Romford had two area cars which each patrolled half the division. The northern half included Harold Hill, Emerson Park and Collier Row, the southern half Upminster and Hornchurch. It was a very large area and the cars covered a lot of miles each day.

Area car drivers were a breed apart. They were of course more senior men who had received the necessary training to drive the patrol vehicles, and who were identifiable by their shiny trousers due to constantly sitting in a car. They had names like 'Fangio' Reed and 'Stirling' Jones, which I suppose was to distinguish them from us ordinary officers. On each shift, manpower permitting, the area cars had to have an 'observer', which was one of the more interesting duties, a variation from normal beat work and a pleasant change, especially when the weather was bad. 'Observer' is a misleading name, for it was the observer that did all the work during his period in the car. The driver drove, and rarely did anything else, except when two heads, or bodies, were better than one. It was always a busy tour of duty.

For the next two weeks I patrolled with PC Russell, who showed me the ropes. There was a great deal to learn and my tutor constable pointed out to me daily far more than I could ever remember in two short weeks. Unlike detached beat officers we did not work the same beat every day, and it took some time to be familiar with every postman, milkman and shopkeeper on the various beats, although that was your aim.

After a few months a constable, even in a busy town like Romford, could spot a stranger walking along the street late at night or early in the morning.

One example of how this 'local knowledge' worked occurred about 5.15 am one morning in North Street. The Sergeant, a man named Grey, affectionately known as 'Wonky-eye Grey' because he had a bit of a squint, was making a final point with me at the telephone box there.

It was always, and I believe still is, customary to greet your Sergeant or Inspector - he too made points occasionally - with the words, "All right Sarge?" or "All right Sir?" In the case of the Inspector a salute was required (it was in Standing Orders). I don't know the origin of this greeting in the Police Service, they never wore helmets with visors to raise (the origin of the salute) but it is no doubt part of an old tradition and one that no one has yet sought to change. Although the "All Right," was no doubt intended to inform your senior officer that all was well on your beat, it was always said with an inflection in the voice that made it a question.

We were chatting in a shop doorway and had said, "Good morning" to a train driver and one or two other people who were on their way to work as usual, when we saw a young man approaching.

"Who's he?" said Sergeant Grey.

"I don't know, never seen him before" I replied.

"Well you'd better find out hadn't you?"

I stepped out of the shadows and stopped the youth, who seemed at once nervous and suspicious.

"Good morning" I said, "Do you mind telling me where you're off to?"

"I'm going to work, officer" was the reply.

"Where do you work?" I asked.

"At the Co-Op bakery" he said.

During our short conversation the youth had been holding the left land pocket of his jacket as you might do if there was something heavy in it. I knew the Co-Op bakery was not in the direction in which he was walking.

"What have you got in there?" I asked tapping his pocket. There was a 'chink chink' of coins rattling, whereupon the youth made a dash for it with the Sergeant and myself in hot pursuit, after a brief pause to get over the shock.

If he hadn't been weighed down with a good many pounds of coins that he had spent the night stealing from cigarette and chewing-gum machines, we might not have caught him, but of course we did, and very pleased with ourselves we were too.

I sometimes think it is a pity that there are no longer any officers with this kind of local knowledge, or the opportunity to catch petty thieves in this way. It was good police work, I was told later by the Inspector, and I still believe the public was far better off when this was the way it was done.

Another memorable incident comes to mind in relation to this same telephone box. It was about three o'clock one morning when a man in his late twenties came running along the centre of the road in an obviously distressed condition. He ran up to me in a state of panic.

"Can you help me? My wife's having a baby," he said.

"Have you phoned for an ambulance?" I replied.

"No! No! There's no time, it's coming it's coming!"

"What's your address?"

He lived in a flat above the shops not fifty yards away. I phoned the station and asked them to get someone, a doctor, anyone, up there as soon as possible, and went with him to his flat.

The poor chap was still in a blind panic; his wife, much calmer, was in the bedroom in the throes of giving birth. I tried to visualise the relevant page in the First Aid book, now reposing in my locker at the station. I sent the husband to the kitchen to make tea, and took off my cape and helmet.

For the next few minutes I sat by the woman's bed doing what I supposed her husband should have been doing. She gripped my hand as she pushed and panted until out popped a baby boy, who commenced to scream his head off almost immediately.

Fortunately the woman had given birth previously and so knew a little more about it than I did. However she was rather weak after all her efforts and I was able to make mother and baby comfortable, by placing it in the crook of her leg, as the book said. I was not supposed to do anything else until help came.

The tea came first; both husband and I drank nervously before I instructed him to go and put the kettle on again. Everyone knows you need lots of boiling water when a baby is born - maybe someone will enlighten me one day why this is. Soon afterwards the midwife arrived, having been summoned by the station, and I was off.

When I returned to the station later and informed the duty Sergeant that I had just had a baby and which form should I fill in, he was not at all fazed and barely looked up from his work as he said, "Just put in a 57b".

There was a sequel to this little story. A few months later I was on patrol in North Street again, this time during the day, when I saw a woman wheeling a pram. I didn't recognise her, but she stopped me and said, "Hello Constable!"

Then I realised who she was. I asked how she and the baby were.

"We're both fine, thanks to you" she said.

"What's the baby's name?" I said.

"George," was the reply. "My husband enquired at the police station and we named him after you". I was as proud as if I had just been awarded an OBE.

As we patrolled together PC Russell pointed out to me many of the local 'CROs' as well as magistrates and other important folk who were qualified to receive a salute.

CRO is used by police officers all over the country and is spoken as three words, "see are oh". The letters stand for Criminal Record Office, and indicate that a person has a criminal record. The Criminal Record Office is housed in London and naturally all the records are now contained on the Police National Computer. In those days they were all in files that had to be referred to in any case when you might be investigating an individual. A phone call to Criminal Record Office giving a person's full name, date and place of birth and height would tell you whether the person was wanted or if he or she had a criminal record. With a name like John Smith you were likely to get several names to choose from.

It was useful to know your local thieves, since experience showed that these were the most likely persons to become suspects in future crimes, especially if the crime fitted their particular MO. "Em Oh" is another expression used a lot by policemen. The letters stand for modus operandi, or in English, "Method of Operation". Criminals are prone to leave their calling card by reason of their MO, and the study of this subject is quite an advanced one in the realms of criminal psychology. In addition to the National Criminal Record Office, Essex Police had its own records at headquarters. There used to be a PC Patmore in charge of it, who had a remarkable memory and a huge collection of card index records, and who was instrumental in bringing many a criminal to justice.

Naturally in these days of computer records much more can be accomplished in theory than one man's brain could hope to achieve. However there are legal limits on what can be kept on a computer and since the introduction of the Data Protection Act a person about whom you have records has the right to see the record, so it must be accurate. Information about suspicions, rather than convictions and matters of fact, cannot therefore be stored on computer, but can quite safely be held on a card index. Rather silly really, but there it is.

I had pointed out to me many convicted local criminals and was told their MO. For example one local burglar always used to put a sixpence in the light socket when he entered a house and replace the bulb. That way if anyone in the house was disturbed and switched on a light the fuse would blow, and hopefully the burglar could escape without being identified.

Some thieves only stole particular items, some only cash. Bicycle thieves were quite common then and there were several on the Romford 'Manor' for me to keep an eye on.

If you hadn't had an arrest for a while you could very often get one when on market duty by keeping an eye on the second-hand bicycle stall and waiting for 'matey' to arrive offering to sell a bicycle. Even if you didn't recognise the seller as a local villain it was always worth a check as there were not many genuine cycles offered for sale there. The stall holder purported to be co-operative and helpful to the police in this task of preventing and detecting the theft of bicycles, but when there was no police officer in sight there was a great deal of doubt about his honesty. Who was it said, "If there were no receivers there would be no thieves"?

There were also a number of 'barrow boys' and other unlawful street traders, with suitcases full of dodgy watches or fluffy toys, whose names I still well remember, but for reasons I have said earlier I will not now identify them. There were a few places where they could legitimately sell their fruit or other wares from their barrows or suitcases, such as public house yards and little private alleyways. However, if they did it in the street, where they preferred, they committed an offence against the bylaws. Usually they saw the helmeted figure approaching above the passers-by and were off before you got there, however by a little cunning you could hide in a doorway and wait till one of them came along and stopped at a favourite spot and then pounce. It was great fun, and the barrow boys for the most part took it in good spirit, paid their small fine and were back next day. One of them I remember did occasionally lose his temper and shout and wave his arms a lot. He drew the line at physical assault on a police officer however, for he was well aware, as were most of the 'ungodly' in Romford at that time, that to assault a police officer was considered a heinous crime by the local magistrates and carried a certain six-month prison sentence.

Another activity that was considered good sport concerned the Crown & Anchor boys at the Romford Dog Stadium. On the evenings when there were race meetings, two or three officers would volunteer for extra duty, for which they would be paid by the dog track authorities. Outside, amongst the crowds of people entering for the evening's event would be one or more Crown & Anchor operators. The Crown & Anchor 'board' would be on a printed cloth that could be thrown down on the ground quickly. At each corner would be a jam jar with a candle in it and the operator would throw the dice and take bets which would be placed on the 'board'. Of course all this was illegal.

The idea was to sneak up as near as possible to the Crown & Anchor operator unseen. If you were seen he would grab up his board and money and disappear into the crowd. If you were lucky you would be there before he could grab the money and the board and he would disappear without it. You were able to confiscate the board and the public was served in preventing this serious crime, at least for this evening, and you didn't really want the trouble of a prisoner. What happened to the cash? You may well ask, but there were several charity boxes on the police station counter, the favourite being for the Police Sports Fund.

The Chairman of the Magistrates at Romford during my period of duty there was a Mr Hole, who ran an ironmonger's shop next door to the police station. He was a gentleman in every sense of the word and took his civic duty very seriously.

An assault on a police officer was a relatively unusual event, and although scuffles with drunks and other ne'er-do-wells were common enough, policemen were robust enough to withstand the odd bruise or torn tunic without complaint. However, should the assault result in a visible injury such as a black eye, sprained finger or even bruised knuckles, the offender would be arrested.

One of the early rules of the game a probationer learned was that if it were ever necessary to subdue a member of the public by actually laying hands on him in more than a gentle way, then it would be wise to arrest him for assault. This avoided any possibility that when he sobered up, or came to his senses, in the morning he would look at his own bruises and rush off to make a complaint. More about complaints later, but suffice it to say that in those days the only place for a defendant to make a complaint against a police officer that was likely to be taken seriously was to the magistrate before whom he or she was appearing.

Having been arrested for 'assault on police', the prisoner would be kept in a cell overnight and paraded before the magistrate next morning. Mr Hole in every case would listen with great care to everything the prisoner might say in his defence, including any complaint he may have about the conduct of the officer. He would pause and look very stern.

"I have listened very carefully to what you have said. You and the public in general must know that an assault on one of my constables will not be tolerated. You will go to prison for six months."

I never knew an exception to this. The police had the confidence and the support of the entire bench and if Mr Hole wasn't sitting the words might be different, but the sentence was the same.

I was assaulted only once at Romford and never knew an officer who was assaulted badly enough to require time off duty to recover. Nor can I recall, in the last few years of my service, anyone in my Division being sent to prison for assaulting a constable in the execution of his duty. During my last few months of service in 1983 it was not unusual for at least two officers per shift to be off sick with injuries incurred on duty and awaiting claims for compensation! Assaulting a police officer is now treated far less seriously and therefore occurs regularly.

So my education had begun, and I learned a great deal during those first two memorable weeks. As well as the geography of the beats, the people, events and places of interest to the police, I learned where I could get a good cup of tea and the occasional sandwich.

Although strictly speaking it was frowned upon for policemen to scrounge a cup of tea, however provided you didn't stray off your beat to do it and weren't actually caught doing it, it was seen as part of 'keeping your finger on the pulse' of your territory.

The local taxi office at Golden Lion Corner in Romford

was a good example. It was open all night and often occupied by only one person. He or she would be pleased for a policeman to pop in for a chat and a cup of tea. During the few minutes that dialogue took place all sorts of useful snippets of information were exchanged. The information exchange between taxi drivers, postmen, milkmen and many others was vital to a policeman's general knowledge. Whenever a serious event or crime had to be investigated, the investigating officer always called in the 'local' man, who was often able to provide him with a great deal of essential local knowledge and information.

The bakery in London Road was another port of call I was introduced to. They started early and there was always a warm bun to go with the tea. There was a cinema I recall in South Street and by arrangement the boiler room door was always left unlocked. It was only a few yards from the police station and it was a good place to have a quick warm up on a cold night and even a few 'drags' of a cigarette for those who smoked. To be seen smoking in public or in a police car was practically a hanging offence!

No doubt PC Russell had other little places he kept to himself, and I soon found that after a few months on the beat one found one's own little 'bolt holes' where a bit of useful chit chat might be exchanged along with a cuppa.

Probation in the police lasted for two years. During that time you were learning your trade out on the street and being quietly assessed and reported upon by your senior officers. No one could move on in the force either to become a CID Officer, Area Car Driver, Traffic Patrol, or to take the first steps on the ladder of promotion until after those two years were complete, your probation had been confirmed and you were judged to be a satisfactory if not a good, or even an excellent, all round police officer.

Two of the most daunting of all the tasks that beset the probationer are his first arrest and his first process report. Reporting a member of the public for an offence generates a 'process report' and was called an "A22" since that is the number of the form used for the purpose. The second of these tasks invariably precedes the first and although quite harrowing is by far the less stressful experience.

It was PC Russell's job to see that I did several 'process reports,' and in Romford it was not difficult. My first was a gentleman who had parked illegally on the double yellow lines in Romford market place. Perhaps he was a little unfortunate that a probationary constable was having his first real experience of 'nicking' a motorist. In other circumstances he might have got off with a warning.

As the gentleman in question approached the car I threw my cape back to allow me to get out my pocket book and pen.

"Is this your car sir?" I said, my voice all of a tremble.

"Yes officer, I'm sorry, I've just been a minute."

"Did you leave the car here?" I was bearing in mind all the points I had to prove to secure a conviction.

"Yes, but like I said I have only been a few minutes."

Then I pointed out to him the 'No Waiting' sign just a few feet from his car.

"It is an offence to leave your car parked here between 8am and 6pm." Out came my book.

"Yes I know, but for Christ's sake I wanted a piss!" He pointed towards the back yard entrance of a nearby public house where I knew there was a toilet open to the public day and night.

"You will be reported for the offence" I said. "You are not obliged to say anything unless you wish to do so but anything you say will be taken down and may be used in evidence."

I opened my book and waited while the gentleman went first red in the face and then white.

"I really don't know what I pay my fucking taxes for" he said, and I carefully noted every word.

He was about to get in the car to drive off when PC Russell nudged me.

"Don't forget to get his particulars."

During the next few minutes I checked the driving licence and certificate of insurance handed to me and noted down the chap's name and address, age and occupation as I had learned to do at training school. I almost forgot to note down the registration number, make and colour of the car, but was prompted by PC Russell.

A few weeks later when the accused appeared in Court in answer to his summons, there was no pleading guilty by letter or on the spot fines in those days, I recited my evidence to their worships. Satisfaction and some amusement replaced any nervousness I had felt when I reported the offender as I repeated his reply after caution. These words were known as 'verbals,' often denied by the accused, and a word that was to take on a far more sinister meaning as I became more experienced.

The Chairman of the Bench looked coldly at him and said, "I can tell you what you pay your taxes for. It's so that we can have constables like PC Raven here to keep our streets free of obstructions by inconsiderate and selfish motorists like you. You will be fined twenty-five pounds."

After two weeks of schooling along with PC Russell I was ready, or so the system believed, to be let loose on the general public on my own.

CHAPTER THREE

# On the beat at Romford (1955-1957)

*My object all sublime,*
*I shall achieve in time.*
*To let the punishment fit the crime,*
*The punishment fit the crime.*
*W S Gilbert, The Mikado (1885) Act 2*

I'm sure that one of the most memorable moments of my life was when I first walked along South Street, Romford, in my uniform, alone and with the slow realisation of the huge task that was before me. I had worn uniform before, but that had been quite different. Then I had been one of a Regiment, a Corps, never alone in the face of the enemy. Yet now here was I in the front line, on my own, with nothing but a whistle and a stick to help me enforce the law.

Fear, excitement, anticipation, pride, satisfaction were

just a few of the feelings that assailed my consciousness that afternoon, for I was now on 'late turn'. It was 2pm and I was on 'A' Beat. Later as confidence grew I also began to feel a sense of power. I could walk out into the road, hold up my hand and the traffic would stop. I could beckon to an unruly youth and he would stop being unruly and come towards me, meek and fearful. The ungodly feared me and the public at large respected me and called me "Officer", "Constable" or even "Sir".

I was also aware that I was a new boy and that while I might have looked the same as the rest of the policemen on my shift, to the locals I was 'new' and green as grass. I was all too mindful of the fact that there were those who would want to test me out in the days ahead. I knew too that for the next two years I would be under the microscope of my senior officers.

I didn't really expect to enjoy my experience on the beat. I wanted to be a detective, but it would be quite a time before I achieved that distinction. It is fair to say that from the first day you walked the street alone you were treated by fellow officers and senior officers alike, exactly the same as any other constable. The only people who even knew you were a probationer were your immediate superiors, members of your shift and yourself.

I use the word 'superior' in this context for the first and only time in this book, and only to illustrate the point that police officers regard their peers as colleagues and often friends, and those in authority above them as senior officers. The idea that they are superior in any way is unpalatable to them. Although they are given the respect due to their position in the organisation, superior they are not. I had come from the Army, where other ranks were accustomed to referring to their officers as 'superior'. I was soon to learn that police officers were very sensitive about the distinction between 'superior' and 'senior', and were all well aware that in the eyes of the law all officers were equal, and constables, whatever their rank.

At the time of the formation of the Metropolitan Police, policemen were indeed considered inferior. They were recruited from the uneducated and the 'lower classes', which were thought to be ideal for dealing with criminals. What was wanted was brawn rather than brain, and policemen tended to be large, thuggish men with little more than muscle to qualify them for the job. They were not expected deal with, or even address, the upper classes, and there are stories of lords in their fine carriages running down a constable and laughing and boasting about it in their club later without the slightest fear of apprehension or prosecution.

From that time the status of the constable grew until he was well thought of by all classes of society. Sadly that situation peaked in the 1960s, and has declined since. Some blame for this has to be borne by the service itself and by the few individual officers who have let the side down. However, instead of punishing just those officers for their misconduct, the whole service has been blackened and discredited by a series of Government measures and press campaigns.

There were however in 1953 still a few remnants of the old class differences. One of them was in the manner of reporting. In addition to the form A22 already mentioned there were two others in daily use, the A57 and the A56. Any request, from a minor matter such as to change a rest day to a more important one concerning a domestic matter or request for a move, specialist appointment etc, had to be submitted on an A57 (or A57b, the smaller version if it was only a small request). Any such report containing a request had to commence with the words, "I beg to report". No one thought that this was in any way obsequious at that time, but it wasn't long before the more forward thinking had it changed to, "I have to report".

The A56 was used whenever a request was sent to another department or force asking for some action to be taken, perhaps requesting a statement in the case of a road accident or to ask that a person resident in another area be reported for failing to produce his driving documents with the permitted five days.

One of the ways an officer was assessed, not just probationers, was by keeping a record of how many process reports and arrests he had each month and also by the quality of his reports. The shift Sergeant, who wrote the first paragraph on all officers' assessment reports, knew first hand whether PC 937 was doing his share of keeping the ungodly at bay. However the Chief Superintendent, who only saw the reports as they passed across his desk, didn't have this advantage. Some Superintendents used to keep what were referred to in the ranks as a 'league table'. Each man would have an appropriate tick against his name every time an "A22" or other report came through him. This 'league table' system was highly frowned upon at headquarters, I learned much later, since some thought it encouraged officers to make unnecessary arrests and process reports - as if one would!

The Chief Superintendent at Romford was a man named Arthur Ruggles. I know very little about him, and fortunately there were very few occasions when I had to see him. Of course I saluted him in the street, and tried to make sure I was visible whenever he walked from the police station either to his home in Western Road just opposite, or along South Street to the market, as was his custom.

If he failed to see an officer during this walk of a hundred yards or so he would enquire immediately on his return, "Who's on 'A' Beat?" Then, when you came in for refreshment break, or for any other reason, you would be called in to his office to explain where you were, and why you were not on your beat. It had better be good!

It was rather odd however, because my tutor constable instructed me that if I saw Mr Ruggles in the market place as opposed to South Street I was to ignore him, as he would me. I did indeed see the Chief Superintendent in the market on occasions, always in plain clothes and usually standing at the back of the crowd listening to a particular stall holder, who I was told was favourably disposed toward police officers, offering his 'bargain of the day'. Occasionally over the top of the crowd a package would be passed over to the Chief Superintendent. I didn't see any money change hands, although I'm sure it was.

Just before Christmas one year I asked this chap, whose name escapes me, if he had any large turkey dishes - It was that kind of stall. He handed me a very large china dish for which I believe I paid half a crown. Hiding it under my cape just before I was due to go in for refreshment break, I began to walk away from the stall when the plate slipped and crashed to the ground in a thousand pieces. There was quite a fuss with people wondering what was happening, and my face was as red as could be. Later I called at the stall again, just as he was packing up and got a replacement at no charge.

Regular reports were submitted on probationers, and as they went along from Sergeant to Inspector and on upwards to presumably the Chief Constable, each senior officer completed a paragraph. The Inspector would usually endorse what the Sergeant had said in a few different words, while others would add such expressions as, "Making good progress" or "I am hopeful that PC 999 will become an efficient constable".

I never knew of a probationer who was not finally accepted, although I believe there were one or two who fell by the wayside by committing some serious disciplinary or criminal offence before their two years was up. To have rejected a constable as unsuitable would be a serious reflection on the three months' training, where any weeding out should have been done - and which had already cost the taxpayer a great deal of money - or on the Sergeant under whose wing you had been for two years. I myself have, when I was of senior rank, been overruled when trying to get an absolutely useless individual dismissed during his first two years, after which time it would be impossible. However the probationer does not know these things and is consequently on his toes and eager to impress during those early years.

The number of officers on each shift at Romford was about twelve on paper, but there were always one or more on 'rest-day', one on annual leave, perhaps one having some time 'off his card', another on a course, another sick, playing sport and so on. The Sergeant had to do his best to man all the beats, provide an area car observer and a man for the front office. In these heady days no member of the public would be expected to come into the police station, even to ask directions, and not be able to speak to a police officer. Today you will be lucky if anyone comes to the bulletproof screen in answer to your insistent ringing of the bell, for at least ten minutes, and then it will be a civilian clerk!

It will be obvious that by the nature of the job of policing there were times when overtime was accrued. This was recorded on a card in units of a quarter of an hour and for every three-quarters of an hour worked, authorised and signed by the Sergeant, an hour could be taken off at the discretion of the Sergeant.

Manning the front office was usually a task given to the more senior, perhaps older and less fit members of the shift. During the day there was a civilian telephone operator in a little cubicle in the front office, but at night the 'front office man' had to man the switchboard as well as his other duties, which included looking after prisoners in the cells. There was a counter where members of the public would present themselves, under which were a number of registers and books which had to be kept up to date. These included the Crime Complaint Book, Lost and Found Property Register, Unoccupied Premises Register, Key Holders, Dog Book and so on. Every shop and business premises was requested to provide a name, address and telephone number so that someone could be contacted in the case of an incident occurring at their premises during the night or at some other time when they were unoccupied.

The Charge Book was also under his control and all visits made to prisoners had to be duly recorded and occurrences entered, meals supplied and so on. During the daytime there was usually a station Sergeant on duty in addition to the shift Sergeant, although they shared the same office, who dealt with the reception of prisoners. It was his decision alone to decide whether to accept or refuse a charge in respect of any prisoners brought in.

All the various tasks associated with the front office man, together with his own report writing, were enough to keep him busy, but it was still considered to be a cushy number, especially on a cold wet night. If an officer had asked to do some reports he might be lucky enough to get 'front office duty' for four hours in order to write them.

Communications within the police service generally were very limited, and when an officer went out onto the street, he was virtually lost to his supervising officers. Of course he had his whistle, which might have been very useful in the streets of London a hundred years ago, but in a modern town the size of Romford it would hardly have been heard above the traffic. However as part of the uniform it looked quite smart, the chromium chain linking one breast pocket to the other.

In order for others to keep in touch with officers on the street, it was the custom for them to make 'points'. That is to say they had to be at a certain place at a certain time where there was a telephone box so that the station could get in touch to give instructions or just to enquire if all was well. It was also at these points that sergeants and inspectors, and once in my service a Superintendent, came out to visit you.

There were various lists of points available for each beat, probably a dozen or so, which avoided officers habitually being at the same place at the same time every day. Villains keeping watch on a bank or other premises and planning a future crime might well spot this. When you were sent out on your beat you would be given a list of points to make, a different one each day. During the fifteen minutes you were parading, the duty Sergeant would have written into the duty book what beat and list you were working and what time you could come into the station for your refreshment break. For example, "PC 937 - 'A' Beat list 'D' - Refs 5.15pm".

Each officer had to sign on in this book, and at any time a senior officer could look at it to see who was on duty and where he was. There was also a space in the margin by each name, and each officer when signing off would have to write in any matters he had dealt with that would require a report later on. The Sergeant would note this and ask you for the report if it wasn't on his desk in a few days.

When did you get time to do your reports? You may well ask, and the answer is not straightforward. You would say to the Sergeant when you came on duty, "I've got reports, Sarge". If you were lucky he might say, "Ask me again when you are on Refreshment break". If you were unlucky he would say, "They'll have to wait". Naturally he was considering all the other calls upon his manpower on that shift, but realised that reports, like everything else, had to be done eventually. It was surprising how many officers had reports to do when it was raining hard or during the night shift! All these things the Sergeant duly noted.

It might seem logical that night time was the best time for officers to be in the station doing reports, when all was quiet outside. Not so - night duty was the most important time for officers to be about their business, trying door handles and making the public feel secure in their beds.

'Trying doorknobs' is an expression that was often used by officers and others, and might seem to many a somewhat meaningless task. Not so, it was considered a very serious neglect of duty if premises which were insecure were not discovered by the officer on that beat during the first part of night duty. It was considered even more serious if some business premises had been broken into during any time of the night and the beat officer did not discover that 'break'. If this happened the Detective Inspector or Chief Inspector, who would be made aware of it as soon as it was reported next day, would want to know why it was not found. I myself have been summoned and dragged from a warm bed at nine in the morning after night duty because I did not discover a break at a golf club one night.

"What time did you last examine the premises?" said the Detective Inspector, hoping to discover by my answer when the break had occurred. This is the point where you either tell a lie and say the premises were all secure at a certain hour, or admit that you didn't examine the premises at all and suffer the consequences. I told a lie!

When you did get a turn to do reports, you sat at the table in the parade room, which was close to the Sergeant's office door. He was usually available for advice and assistance in completing the reports, but more especially keeping a sharp eye out that you were not taking longer than you should to avoid going back out on the street.

Probably the most frequent call for a report was when you had reported someone for an offence. Riding a bicycle without a light, leaving a vehicle on a road at night without the necessary lights, unlawful parking and many other minor offences called for a Form A22. The form contained sections on the front for the accused's name and details and then the charge. This was a strictly legal matter and had to show the time date, place and details of the alleged offence. The wording of most of the charges you were likely to need was in a dog-eared folder on a string and hanging on the wall beside the table. It was necessary to type out the appropriate charge and adjust the time, date and place to suit. After the charge was the Act and Section that it was alleged had been contravened. If you managed to report someone for a more unusual offence that was not in the dog-eared file, then you had to find it in the well-worn copy of *Oke's Magisterial Formulist*, which sat on the window ledge together with *Archbold's Criminal Pleading* and *Stone's Justices Manual*. These last two volumes contained all the current law likely to be referred to by a police officer, together with current case law on the various subjects. These books were published every year in view of the changes in and additions to the law, which were not inconsiderable. Because of the expense the station was allowed only one new copy of each new issue of these tomes. Naturally this went to the Chief Superintendent, who probably never ever used it. His old copy went to his deputy, his deputy's to the CID and so on down the line. The parade room copies were therefore always at least five or six years out of date.

On the reverse of form A22 was the place for your evidence, which corresponded pretty well word for word with what you had written in your pocket book, and which you would later recite to the magistrates.

When completed, the form would be handed to the duty Sergeant or placed in his tray. He, in due course, would go through it and recommend proceedings, or otherwise if for some reason the evidence did not cover all the points to prove. Some sergeants were more pedantic than others and would mark with red pencil any errors of spelling or typing. In the early days I had reports returned in this way several times before they were accepted and passed on to the Inspector. who would be the 'Informant'.

In order for a Summons to be issued by the Court an Information had to be 'laid'. It was always the Inspector who did this and the Summons later received by the accused would read, "Information has this day been laid by Reginald Ellis (if that was the Inspector's name) that you John Citizen did...." followed by the particulars of the offence and the date and time he or she was summoned to appear at Court. Summonses were regularly served by Registered Post, or by a police officer if there was some reason to believe the accused was unlikely to acknowledge the summons, and there were many of those.

Back out on the street there were many things to consider when dealing with a particular matter. Reports of crime, requests for assistance and allegations against individuals were all commonplace and required instant decisions without reference to the Sergeant or a textbook.

One of the more important areas of discretion a beat officer had was concerning his power of arrest. It was a very considerable power, and a decision to deprive another citizen of his liberty was never taken lightly. The main considerations were, "Have I the power?" and "Is the arrest necessary?"

One of the main distinctions between the powers of a constable and those of an ordinary citizen is that in many cases a constable has the power to arrest a person whom he 'reasonably suspects' of committing an offence, whereas a citizen may only arrest another if he actually finds him or her committing certain offences.

Almost every Act of Parliament which creates offences has a section concerning the power of arrest of a constable. The section usually started, "A constable may arrest any person…". Then came the differences. Sometimes the power was, "If found committing," on other occasions there was added, "or whom he reasonably suspects of having committed". Sometimes the power of arrest was only granted if a person failed to give his name and address, sometimes as in the case of a 'poacher' he had to be seen leaving the land where he was suspected of taking the game etc.

Crimes were also divided into three main categories so far as arrest was concerned. Until legislation classified certain crimes, British common law classified offences as treason, felonies and misdemeanours. Among the felonies recognised under common law were homicide, arson, rape, robbery, burglary, and larceny. The number of felonies has been significantly enlarged by legislation to include such offences as kidnapping, tax evasion and drug dealing.

Misdemeanour was a term applied in law to offences that were neither treasons nor felonies. Often a misdemeanour was referred to as a Summary Offence, because usually, but not always, misdemeanours could be tried at a Magistrates' Court. Among the more common misdemeanours or summary offences were disorderly conduct, public drunkenness and ordinary motor vehicle and driving offences. Some sex offences were misdemeanours, while others were classified as felonies.

Some misdemeanours were, like felonies, indictable offences, or those subject to a trial by a jury. Some types of assault, perjury, minor sex offences, selling liquor to minors, and operating an illegal gambling establishment were among the more common misdemeanours of this type. These differed from felonies largely in the punishments for them. There is a further distinction between crimes that may be tried by a Magistrates' Court if the accused agrees and those that can only be tried there. In the first case the accused has a right to trial by jury, if he so desires, and in the second he has no such right. This distinction is usually where the maximum penalty is six months' imprisonment or less.

In due course the distinction between felonies and misdemeanours was abolished and criminal offences classified as indictable and non-indictable (arrestable and non-arrestable offences). This has somewhat simplified the constable's plight when considering whether he has the power to arrest someone. However, now he has to remember also the maximum penalty for an offence, since an arrestable offence is one where the maximum penalty is five years' imprisonment or more. The Police and Criminal Law Act of 1984 (PACE) says a great deal more about a Police Officer's powers, but happily by then I was beginning a new life as a private investigator in retirement.

Generally speaking a constable would have no doubt that he had a power of arrest for a felony, but for the hundreds of other misdemeanours or summary offences there was a minefield of problems for him. At training school, as well as his 'definitions' he had learned to recite his powers of arrest for most offences he was likely to come across, but how many of them could he remember in the heat of battle?

One of the first arrests I recall making occurred at the same time as I first realised that there were a lot of inadequacies in the law, that in some cases the 'law was an ass' and that it was therefore occasionally necessary for it to be 'straightened out' rather than 'bent'.

It was a very cold night in November and once more I was patrolling 'A' Beat. Close to the police station there was a small arcade of shops and it was quite usual for the officer on 'A' Beat to lurk in the arcade prior to going back into the station for his refreshment break. It was just before 1.15 am and I was looking forward to a warm cup of tea and a sandwich after what had so far been an uneventful night.

I became aware of voices and saw three youths pass across

the entrance of the arcade some three or four yards from the shadows where I was standing. They were clearly in high spirits and making more noise than was appropriate at time of night. I began to walk towards them to tell them to be quiet and saw that one of them, I could not positively say which one later, was carrying a heavy object about the size of a house brick. For a few seconds only they were all out of my sight, and I then heard the crash of breaking glass.

I turned the corner almost at the same instant and there were the three, a foot or so from the broken shop window, all laughing and about to run off. There was no one else in sight, and a house brick, I was certain it was the one I had seen being carried, lay inside the window close to the jagged hole. There was no doubt whatever that they were responsible for smashing the window, whether for the purpose of stealing - it was a stationer's shop with various items of office equipment on display - or just for sheer wantonness I neither knew nor cared. I arrested all three of them and wheeled them into the police station, where they became less boisterous and exercised their right after being cautioned to remain silent.

It was the usual practice after an arrest for the arresting officer to relate the facts to the duty or station Sergeant in the presence of the accused.

"Which of the three threw the brick that smashed the window?" he asked me.

"I don't know" I truthfully answered. "They were out of my view for a second, and I didn't actually see the brick being thrown, and I can't be one hundred percent sure who it was that I saw carrying it".

The Sergeant paused and suggested we go to talk in his office.

"Look," he said. "Unless you can identify which one threw the brick I will have to refuse the charge."

"But why?" My surprise and disappointment were clear for all to see.

"Because that's the law. Three people can't commit the offence of wilful damage. They can conspire to commit the offence but not after the offence has been committed. So you will have to say which one it was."

"But I truthfully can't do that".

"Well that's up to you. If you point the finger at one of them I'll charge the other two with aiding and abetting. The result will be that they are all punished".

"I'm sorry Sergeant, I can't do that."

"OK, it's a matter for you. As it is we'll have to kick them out on a pink sheet."

"Can't we charge them with conspiring to steal from the shop window?" I asked.

"Well we could if it was a jeweller's shop, but that's a bit heavy for a stationers" the Sergeant said, quite sensibly you might think.

There are two different forms relating to arrested persons, a white sheet and a pink sheet. If the charge is accepted then a white sheet is used to record the arrest and all subsequent events relating to that prisoner. If it is refused then a pink sheet is used to record details of the original arrest and detention, together with the reasons for refusal of the charge.

I was completely shattered when the three grinning faces left the station, but I realised that to have achieved justice for the shopkeeper and satisfaction for myself I should have had to tell a lie and identify one of the three as the person who had thrown the brick.

I believe that if this had happened during the daytime and the three suspects had been interrogated by CID officers a different result might have been achieved, but I was green and still completely honest. I was later taken aside by the Sergeant, who told me not to be upset by what had occurred. He assumed I had learned an important lesson and applauded me for being honest on this occasion.

"To have told a lie or to have 'stitched up' one of the youths, as the jargon has it, would not have been right," he said. "Do you know why?"

"Of course, it's always wrong to lie".

"No, not always, but if you do have occasion to lie in similar circumstances make sure that only you and the prisoner know it. In this case I would have known also!"

I am not making any admissions here that I have ever 'stitched up' a prisoner, but I do know that occasionally it was necessary, and that probably a good many police officers who were made aware of this and similar loopholes in the law have at times done their best to block them up with their own remedies.

'Stitching up' or 'verballing' prisoners are expressions that were used quite often by police officers and villains alike. The former involved the alleged planting or inventing evidence and the latter attributing words to a defendant that he did not utter. I shall have more to say about both of these matters later, but suffice it to say that these expressions existed for a reason and such allegations were not infrequent.

A more successful arrest occurred some time later when I apprehended a young man for attempting to obtain money by false pretences. Between 1953 and 1956 there was quite a bit of news abroad about the suffering of the people of Hungary under the communists. One of 'the great unwashed' of Romford thought to take advantage of this and hung a placard round his neck which said, "Help Hungry". Having studied the law on the subject of fraud I felt sure that I could make it stick and took him along. He pleaded 'Not Guilty' and his lack of education and inability to spell Hungary correctly came to his defence when he pleaded, through his solicitor, that he was merely 'begging,' which was also an offence, but a lesser one. He was indeed hungry, he said on oath in his defence, and was trying to get some money to buy food.

"Have you ever heard of a country called Hungary?" The prosecuting solicitor said in cross-examination.

"Yes". Replied the defendant.

"How do you spell it?"

"H, U, N, G, R, Y" said the youth.

"No further questions, your worships".

"You are a dishonest rascal," said Mr Hole, the Chairman of the Bench, "and you will go to prison for three months". In his view obviously this was a far less serious matter than assaulting one of his constables.

I suppose I have been asked many times by friends and others whether policemen actually beat up prisoners as sometimes depicted on television in drama programmes. All too often when there is some sort of skirmish between rowdy youths and police it's the police on whom the cameras concentrate. If a policeman's fist, boot or truncheon is seen connecting with any part of another person's body there is the usual outcry of 'police brutality'. The fact that he is getting a pasting himself seems quite acceptable.

I believe that there are a few occasions when it is justified for a policeman to lay hands on his fellow citizen. The first of these is of course when he makes an arrest. The law often permits an officer to use 'as much force as is necessary' to accomplish this. Believe me, when a man doesn't want to be arrested it is difficult to see how he could be overcome without force, sometimes quite considerable force.

Secondly in self-defence. It is sometimes forgotten that policemen are human and if one is punched on the nose by a drunk he is likely instinctively to hit back. Temper is a thing that has to be controlled if you are a police officer, but occasionally in the heat of the moment this is impossible. John McEnroe, the US tennis player was known as much for his temper on the court as he was for his brilliant play; he was often fined and suspended because of it. I don't think there can be any doubt that he was unable to control his temper.

I have known some officers whose temper was less controllable than others, but while some tolerance was allowed by their senior officers, they were seriously in jeopardy of losing their jobs. The magistrates knew their local police officers, and if an accused complained that an officer had assaulted him once, they might take the view that the accused was making it up or exaggerating. However if different defendants consistently accused the same officer of assault, it would soon become apparent that the officer would have to be dealt with.

It was not unknown for a certain amount of controlled violence to be used against a certain type of suspect when being interrogated. I don't mean by that that rubber hoses were used, but when all else failed a sharp open-handed smack across the face often worked wonders. An ex-colleague of mine often recalls his early days in the force when he had brought in a young hooligan for allegedly stealing a woman's handbag. He didn't witness the offence and the circumstances were such that without a confession a conviction was unlikely. The officer interviewed him at length using all the techniques he knew and then gave up. He went to see the Detective Sergeant and explained all the circumstances.

"Have you hit him?" Said the DS.

"No" said my colleague.

"Well go and fucking hit him" was the reply.

I have been guilty on a couple of occasions of losing my temper when I should have held it. The first was when I saw a heavy goods vehicle travelling along a narrow one-way street the wrong way. I stopped the vehicle intending only to point out to the driver his error. The driver opened his window, looked down at me    and started to use the most abusive language and to threaten me with a good deal of unpleasantness. I wasn't long out of the army and as yet I'd not learned that this was what one had to expect and tolerate from 'the great unwashed'. Without any conscious thought I jumped up and wrenched open the cab door, dragged the driver onto the road and began to pummel him with my fists. The co-driver, a younger man, came quickly to his assistance, but didn't turn on me. Rather he tried to calm down his driver, who was by then a bit less irate and suffering a bloody nose. In due course he apologised to me and drove off.

Convinced that I would lose my job, I went sheepishly back to the station when it was time for my refreshment break and expected a warm reception. No one said a word, so neither did I. I never heard any more about the matter.

Then soon after starting patrol at 10pm one night I was called to a pub in Romford marketplace, where there was a fight in progress. On my arrival the fight had spilled out into the pub yard. It was between several men who were trying to restrain a soldier in uniform. I pushed my way to the fore and saw that the soldier, a corporal, was fairly drunk and very disorderly. While it was an offence to be drunk and disorderly in a public place, we were at that moment on private property. However at my approach Corporal Green MM, as I later discovered was his title, went for me like a madman and delivered a forceful blow to my midriff. Happily my thick uniform and cape saved me from any serious loss of wind or mobility and I punched him squarely in the face. He sat down and began to vomit.

I ushered all the onlookers back into the public bar and went out again to the yard to make my arrest for assault on police. Corporal Green MM was nowhere to be seen. I presumed he had decided to call it a night and gone home.

That night my refreshment break was at 1.15am and when I got back to the station there was a little activity. Corporal Green MM was there, sporting a beautiful black and swollen eye and complaining that an officer had assaulted him. I managed to speak to the Sergeant and tell him what had happened before he had to make his decision as to what he should do about it.

"Stay out of the way for a bit" he said.

Corporal Green MM was calmed down and invited to make a formal complaint.

"Who was the officer who assaulted you?" he was asked.

"I don't know, do I. He was in uniform, that's all I know".

"Did you take his collar number?"

"No".

"Well could you identify him?"

"Yes."

All the officers that were available, including the front office man, one 'Jock' Semple, and those having refreshments, were called to the front office, and the man on 'A' Beat was brought in.

"OK," said the Sergeant. "Who was it that assaulted you?"

Without hesitation Corporal Green MM picked out 'Jock' Semple.

"That's him, that's the bastard" he said.

"Are you quite sure?" said the Sergeant.

"Yes, positive" said Corporal Green.

The Sergeant dismissed the troops and took Corporal Green into his office. I don't know what was discussed, but some fifteen minutes later they came out and Corporal Green shook hands with the Sergeant and went on his way, apparently content with the manner in which he had been dealt with.

I shall have a lot more to say about complaints against police, but that is more or less how they were dealt with in 1953.

Another thing we dealt with differently was strikes. One early turn I was detailed to go down to Roneo Corner at 7.30am. Roneo corner, so called because the Roneo factory making duplicating machines was there, was just out of town to the south. There was to be a strike, so I was told, and I should take a County bicycle and go down there to keep order and "see there's no trouble".

I arrived and met the Union chap in charge of the strikers, who probably knew more about the law relating to strikes than I did. We agreed on the number of pickets that were permitted and that there should be no intimidation and so on. I remained at the gates with the six pickets, who fairly quietly tried to persuade their fellow workers to join them as they arrived for work. Few did, and by lunchtime it was all over.

Strikes in those days were usually concerning some minor demarcation dispute when an electrician wanted to do a bit of carpentry to save time and get his wires through a plank, and other such nonsense. Unhappily industrial disputes were gradually to become of more concern to the police force, culminating in the miners' strike of 1984 just after I left the force, which perhaps helped to exacerbate the already fast-declining public confidence in the police. This was not the fault of the police but of politicians who sought to use the police as strike breakers.

The police service concerns itself a great deal with other people's troubles, problems and often misery, and officers were usually themselves cheerful. A sense of humour when everything around you was, for others, something to weep about, was a way of keeping aloof and detached from it. My acquaintance with death until I joined the police was limited to seeing the body of my paternal grandmother, who had died while eating breakfast when I was only eight years old. Soon death was to become an almost daily routine part of my life.

I was standing beside the row of telephone boxes in Romford market one night just outside a wall of the churchyard. A young couple who had just walked through the churchyard ran up to me and said they had seen an old lady collapsed in there. They took me to the spot, pointed her out and then left. The lady concerned was unknown to me, but not I suspect to some of my more experienced colleagues. She was in her sixties, I judged, unconscious and smelled strongly of drink. She was breathing so far as I could tell and had urinated and defecated, if the stench was anything to go by.

I telephoned the station and in view of her condition they sent a van rather than a car for her. She was loaded rather unceremoniously into the back of the van and taken to the station, where the Sergeant decided that she was pretty ill and should be taken to the hospital rather than dealt with as a simple drunk; Oldchurch Hospital was not far away. I accompanied the driver to the hospital. A doctor came out to the van to examine her after hearing of her condition, and pronounced that she was dead.

Later it was to be determined that she had died of

alcoholic poisoning, and that nothing the police did or did not do had hastened her death or could have prevented it. The immediate task for me was to find out who she was and to inform her nearest and dearest. The identification was not difficult; her handbag revealed that. More difficult was the duty ahead of me, as it would be the first time I had been called upon to inform close relatives of a sudden death.

I knocked on the door of a terraced house on a fairly run-down part of town and a man of about thirty-five answered. Behind him stood a woman of similar age, who was carrying a glass of beer.

"What do you fucking want?" The man demanded.

"Are you related to Mrs M......?" I asked.

"Yes, she's my mother. What's the stupid cow done now, drunk herself to fucking death?" He began to laugh; well leer would be a better word.

"I'm sorry to have to tell you that your mother was found dead about an hour ago and is at Oldchurch Hospital. The Coroner's Officer will be in touch with you." I was going to add that he could go to the hospital to see his mother and recover her belongings if he wished, but further words were cut off.

"Serve her fucking right," he said, and slammed the door in my face.

Back at the station there was great amusement at my apparent distress at this harrowing experience. Most of them knew Mrs M. and her family, who were all 'CRO', and they had no doubt that her life of misery with them all had driven her to drink and to her eventual death.

This was by no means my only experience of the strange behaviour of the families of elderly relatives who have died suddenly in what might well be regarded by most as 'tragic circumstances'. One in particular that comes to mind was when neighbours who could smell gas called me to a terraced cottage in an old part of Romford. There had been no response to their knocking and the old lady who lived there was known to be a little eccentric and unsteady on her feet.

I too received no answer to my knocking on the front door, but found the back door to be unlocked. I went in to find the old lady lying apparently dead on the kitchen floor. A gas tap on the cooker was turned on but was not alight. There was an upturned plate over the ring and the gas was still escaping.

Sudden death, as this sort of incident was called, was often quite straightforward and the deceased's doctor would attend and sign a Death Certificate. In a case like this however it was usual for the Beat Officer, who was almost always the first police officer on the scene, to call the CID, who would attend and see if there were any suspicious or other circumstances that required investigation.

In this case the CID attended and the body was eventually removed to the local mortuary. I was instructed to wait at the house until relatives could be contacted and attend. A daughter and son-in-law eventually turned up and began to tear the place apart looking for valuables and money. When they had finished it looked worse than many housebreaking scenes I have attended, with drawers and their contents strewn about. Not one question was asked about their dear departed mother and mother in law. I later described them as being like scavengers.

"Where's her money?" I was asked.

"So far as I am aware there was no money found except the few shillings in her purse" I said.

"She always kept a large amount of money in the house. What have you done with it?" the daughter demanded in an accusing manner.

I could see where this was leading and didn't like it one bit.

"Now that you are here," I said, "my duty here is finished. I don't much care for your insinuations, but if you have any complaint to make you had better do so at the station." I left and immediately reported what had happened to the Coroner's Officer. The relatives did indeed make a complaint that money and valuables had been stolen from the house, but fortunately they were not taken seriously and were dealt with tactfully and efficiently by the duty Inspector.

This case was also the first post mortem examination I attended. It was customary for the officer who first found the body to identify it to the pathologist before he commenced his autopsy. I knew from training school that I would have to attend post mortems and had been told also of the various reactions experienced by officers carrying out this duty for the first time, to the great amusement of morticians who seemed to delight in other people's discomfort at such events. It was incidentally discovered that the old lady had died of natural causes. There was no evidence that she had breathed in any of the escaping gas, so she must have been dead when the gas began to escape. It was concluded that she had had a heart attack and fallen down, dropping the plate on the stove and extinguishing the gas at the same time. 'Accidental death' was the Coroner's verdict.

No police officer I ever knew really enjoyed going to a post mortem, although later in my career I found them most interesting, especially when the death was not from natural causes, and one was looking for evidence which might assist in tracing the person responsible for the death. But if one had to attend an autopsy for the first time there were many more salubrious mortuaries in the county than the one at Oldchurch Hospital, and many more sensitive morticians.

The mortician is the chap who usually prepares the body for the pathologist and in the case of Romford at that time, cut open the body for the doctor to examine. After the examination it was he too who sewed it up again with those big ugly stitches and thick thread. The mortician used to smoke continually during the examination and afterwards when he was 'sewing up' I once saw him take a last drag on his cigarette with bloody fingers and toss the butt into the chest cavity before finishing the stitches.

Romford was full of colourful people, and during my two years' probation I met a new one every day. Characters such as Ginger (not the Ginger I referred to earlier in this narrative), who sold papers at the railway station. He wore a ragged old khaki-coloured coat and woollen hat and in summer and winter a pair of tatty mittens of the same colour. Tied under his nose there was always a piece of rag, presumably to absorb the drips. He appeared at the railway station every morning dragging an old orange box with his newspapers in it. Later in the afternoon he could be seen dragging it back down South Street and up the market place.

A year or so after I arrived at Romford Ginger died one cold winter morning. There was nothing suspicious about his death, which was due to a combination of his age, the cold and malnourishment. Subsequently I learned that he lived alone in a house in Gidea Park and had died intestate, leaving the house and more than three-quarters of a million pounds in the bank.

Another character, a little old lady who was known to all the police officers in Romford, was a frequent visitor to the police station. On a daily basis for many years she came into the station with an envelope marked "For the CID". The envelope contained her daily information letter concerning a man named Ian. No one knew who Ian was and the letters always said that he was planning another robbery or burglary and gave details of where and when the crime was to be committed. She was quite mad of course, but this sad little woman was quite harmless. The office man used to call out, "Thank you Mary" and wave as she left her missive in the little green post-tray on the counter.

I also one day made the acquaintance of an old man who lived alone in Mawney Road. He would regularly dial 999 to say that he had been assaulted and robbed and although a car would be sent on each occasion, just in case, the majority of the Division knew of him and his calls.

I did not. I was the Area Car Observer on the particular day when he called again and the driver did not let me in on the situation. Instead he let me get out of the car at the old man's gate to 'deal'. He was sitting on a chair in the front garden, apparently tied with rope and with what at first glance appeared to be blood all over the front of his jacket. The handle of a kitchen knife protruded from the jacket and he was groaning and rocking from side to side as I approached in some trepidation. The Area Car Driver was coming up behind me as I got closer and I was startled by what he said.

"Now now Fred! What is it this time?"

Fred looked up and saw the driver's familiar face and smiled weakly. "They've done it again" he said. "Want to come in for a cuppa tea?"

The rope around Fred was quite loose, the knife was stuck into his clothing but not into him, and the blood was tomato ketchup. We helped him into the house and sat and had a cup of tea with him. He talked and talked and wanted to show us his family album, his war medals and his Masonic regalia. Fred was quite senile, but harmless. He was sad and lonely, wanting nothing but a bit of company. Nowadays I suppose the Social Services would drag him off to an old folk's home, where I doubt if he would be any happier. At home at least he still had a bit of dignity, even if he was a bloody nuisance to the local police. I used to pop in and see him occasionally for a few minutes when I was on that beat.

Policemen also used to be encouraged to call in and visit any retired officers who lived on their beat, just to say hello and let them know they were not forgotten. I used to have many an interesting chat with some of them. I have been retired now for over thirty years, but have never had such a visit. This tradition, like many of the old timers I used to visit, has sadly passed away.

Area car duty was usually rather more exciting than walking a beat, although there were many officers who liked nothing better than to pound the pavements. Area cars invariably brought the first officers to the scene of an incident that had been reported by 999 call, often a burglary or other crime scene, sometimes a road accident, or occasionally something more gruesome.

I attended many scenes of death and destruction on the roads of Essex. The call over the radio would be to an RTA (Road Traffic Accident). Often, if it was a very serious accident or a fatal one, it would be dealt with later by the Traffic Department Officers, but the local 'area car' was frequently the first on the scene. The sight of human beings suffering from torn limbs and flesh, broken bones, terrible shock and distress is something no one can ever really get used to and when a call came to a 'serious RTA' one always had to steel oneself before arriving at the scene.

I have often wondered why they call these disasters 'accidents'. An accident as defined in the Oxford Dictionary is "an event that is without apparent cause, or is unexpected". It also describes an accident as "an unfortunate event, especially one causing physical harm or damage, brought about unintentionally". To police officers road accidents are not unexpected. There is almost always a cause for a road 'accident', and as in law a person is responsible for the natural consequences of his actions, the fact that it was unintentional in my view does not make it an accident.

The majority of 'accidents' are caused by drivers who are breaking the law, either by speeding, failing to give way when they should, driving under the influence of drink or drugs or driving an unroadworthy vehicle. When the consequences of such action are damage or injury to a person or property it should in my view be regarded as a crime and not an accident.

There are also, as a police officer, enough occasions when one has to deal with real accidents. I reported for duty one morning at 5.45am and found that I was Area Car Observer for the first half of my shift. This was a very good shift to work because about 9.15am when you came in for breakfast Mrs Lilly was on duty. Mrs Lilly, the canteen cook, was the wife of PC Lilly, the Coroner's Officer; she used to cook wonderful breakfasts of eggs, bacon, sausages, fried bread and all the trimmings.

We were on the road by a couple of minutes past six and almost immediately were called up by Headquarters from where all area cars were controlled. We were to make our way to an accident at Hornchurch Railway Station; further details would follow.

Approaching the station some five minutes later the radio informed us that a woman had fallen onto the railway line and been injured. An ambulance was on its way. So far so good, it didn't sound too bad. However as we approached closer to the station we could hear a woman screaming. On the platform was quite a crowd of people, no doubt waiting to get on a train for work. The train was stationary just outside the station and the injured woman, a lady probably in her early forties, was still on the line. The screaming was not coming from her but from a younger woman, later identified as the injured woman's daughter who was standing looking at her mother, her hands clenched and pressed to her face.

It appeared from the station porter, who was at the scene, that as the train had started to move out the woman had opened a door and attempted to get in. She had slipped and fallen through the gap between the platform and the train. The guard had seen the incident and signalled the train to stop. It was thought best not to move the woman.

About now the ambulance arrived and the attendants began to get onto the line with a stretcher to remove the lady, who appeared to be conscious but crying with shock and pain. It was then that they noticed her right arm was missing at the elbow. Looking along the track I could see what was obviously the severed arm some twenty yards further along it. My driver grabbed a fire bucket from a nearby hook on the wall, emptied the sand out of it and handed it to me.

"Go get it" he said.

The next few minutes were some I will always remember. Although I have carried out rather more gruesome tasks since, this was the first. However, as I recovered the arm I noticed that it had two jewelled rings on the fingers. As I climbed back onto the platform the daughter, who had stopped screaming, approached me and insisted on removing the rings. The arm, the bucket and the daughter went off in the ambulance.

I never did know the outcome of this accident as the subsequent investigation and reporting was left to the British Rail Police, within whose jurisdiction it occurred. I do know that when it was time to go in for breakfast I wasn't at all hungry and even Mrs Lilly's 'scrummy' breakfast couldn't tempt me that morning.

During another period as Area Car Observer we were called to a house at Harold Hill, where a neighbour reported that her elderly neighbour, a gentleman in his seventies, had not been seen for a couple of days and milk remained on his doorstep. She feared that he might not be well and perhaps needed assistance. Such calls were not unusual and it was considered right and proper that we should attend, although not strictly speaking police work. At the time the police would answer any call within reason to help or advise a member of the public.

I knocked loudly several times and then went round the house, looking into the windows. Through the kitchen window I could see a plate with a partly-eaten meal and a cup and saucer. Then I got a ladder from the garage, which was open, and climbed up to look into the bedroom windows. In one of them I saw a man lying in a double bed. He was as white as the sheets that covered him and one arm hung limply out of the bed, almost touching the floor.

I banged on the window, but there was no response, and I concluded that this was a job for the Coroner. I went down the ladder, discussed the matter with my driver and decided to break a window and gain entry to the house and deal with the matter as a 'sudden death.' I took out my truncheon, the first and one of the few times I ever used it, broke a kitchen window, opened it and climbed in. As I walked into the hall I saw what appeared like a ghost, walking down the stairs towards me a look of shock and horror on its face. "What the bloody hell do you think you're doing?" he shouted.

It transpired that he had felt ill while eating his supper a couple of nights earlier and had gone to bed and taken sleeping tablets. He had stayed there taking more pills each time he woke up, hoping that eventually he would recover - which he did, the moment he heard his window being broken.

Explanations were made and accepted and the neighbour's husband, who fortunately was a builder, offered to repair the window. The gentleman assured me that he required no further 'assistance' from the police and I left him with a suggestion that he should keep his garage door locked. The matter was later reported on an A57b and no further action was required.

Domestic violence was unfortunately as prevalent then as it is today, and a good deal of police time was spent dealing with such incidents, especially on paydays, usually Friday, when they most frequently occurred. One had to learn to deal with these events sympathetically, although the police could do little more than give advice, as an assault upon a wife by a husband, unless broken bones or serious wounds were involved, was not a crime for which the police could prosecute. The wife - it was almost always the wife who had been assaulted - was advised to see the Magistrates' Clerk the following day and take out a summons for assault. They rarely did.

Even when the assault was serious enough to be actual bodily harm and therefore a criminal offence, and the husband was arrested, he would usually be bailed when he was sober. Experience had shown that rarely, if ever, would the wife make a statement the following day, or if she did would later wish to withdraw the complaint. A wife is not a compellable witness against her husband, and unless she is willing to give evidence there is no case for the man to answer. Police have in more recent years been criticised for not taking matters of this kind seriously and directives have been issued and legislation passed to try and improve matters. Husbands still beat their wives, and wives still refuse to give evidence against them. Wife beaters are potential killers, and I have known a good many cases where murder or manslaughter charges have eventually been brought against husbands who have habitually beaten their wives.

You have to be careful what advice you give to a woman in these domestic circumstances. I once attended a call to such a dispute and found the wife in the front garden wearing only a flimsy nightie. She was bruised and crying; the entire contents of her wardrobe were on the front lawn. After listening to her story, a familiar one of a husband coming home drunk and an argument ensuing, I managed to get the husband to dress and open the door, and after a good deal of persuasion I managed to get him to let the woman into the house. As they had both calmed down I left, having given her the usual advice. I might well have asked her why the hell she stayed with a man who would treat her like this, although there was no such note in my pocket book.

Some months later I was told that a local solicitor was coming to the station to see me, and an appointment was made for the next time I was on duty. The solicitor was representing the husband, who had told him that I had advised his wife to leave him. There is apparently some sort of civil tort that I knew nothing about concerning enticing a woman away from her husband, a law that I am sure was intended for quite a different situation. I referred to my pocket book and assured the solicitor that I had done no such thing. He took a statement from me about the incident and I heard no more about it.

There were some lighter moments of course, and occasionally one came into contact with the rich and famous. I once went to a road accident involving Frankie Vaughan, then a well-known singer and entertainer. He had knocked a young man off his motor cycle. Mr Vaughan was in no way to blame, but was insistent on making sure that the chap's injuries were not serious. While sitting in his luxurious American car, which smelled like a harlot's bedroom, I took a statement from him and he signed my pocket book.

On another occasion I was personally thanked by Anne Shelton, who was performing at a local Odeon Cinema with the Ambrose Orchestra, because I had managed to rescue her from being besieged at the stage door by autograph hunters.

During my probationary period I did a month attached to the CID to learn the different procedures and forms they used. This gave me a taste of the work, and I knew more than ever that this was what I wanted to do. During this attachment I was referred to as a CID Aide; all probationers had this one-month attachment and worked alongside hardened detectives. Some of them I remember well including Sid Maxted, Chalky (Len) White, 'Sniffer' Bert Sherwin and others whose names escape me.

One of the detective sergeants I won't name was well known for the blakeys he wore in his shoes (who remembers them?) His shoes tapping on the Battleship Linoleum floors used to signal his arrival in the station when still a long way from the CID office. He was a living example of the benefits of seeing dear little ladies across the road, one of the little services policemen used to provide. Many years before he had helped a lady across the street and subsequently when he saw her in the street he used to help her if necessary and pass the time of day. She somehow found out who he was, although until she died he didn't know her name. She was, it seemed, part owner, a large part, of the Romford Dog Stadium. Years later she died with no other living relatives and it was said that the Sergeant was favourably mentioned in her will.

The DI, Billy Girt, was around most evenings and CID officers who had been on duty all day, although they had been home for a break or two, dare not go home until he had dismissed them. It might be anything between 10 o'clock and 11 o'clock, usually after the pubs had closed, when he would come back into the station, demand to know what was going on, and if 'all quiet' would go home. It was then safe for the rest of us to go.

One evening when Billy Girt came back into the CID Office having had his usual quota of whisky, Chalky White was busy taking a statement from a suspect in an indecency case, a man in his fifties. Chalky was something of a touch typist and preferred to type a statement when he could, rather than write it in longhand. The suspect had not actually admitted the offence, but had said enough for the statement to be worthy of being taken 'under caution'. It was not uncommon for a suspect such as this to admit being in the vicinity and to having seen the victim, but not to having actually touched her. His statement would usually be long and verbose. Today society graces such sick individuals with the name 'paedophile'. What we used to call them is still not in the dictionary!

Chalky was onto the third typed page when Billy Girt came in. Everyone stood up, as his entrance demanded.

"All right sir?" we chorused.

Billy noticed the seated civilian. "What's 'e doin' 'ere?" He growled.

"He's in for that indecent assault earlier tonight, sir".

"Oh is 'e?" Billy walked over and glared down at him overbearingly. "Dirty bastard, are you?" he said.

There was no reply. Billy pulled the sheet of paper, currently being typed, from the typewriter and Chalky handed him the other two. He skimmed through the pages quickly, tore them in half and threw them on the floor.

"All a load of fuckin' lies" he said, "Tell this officer the truth or I'll be back and sort you out myself." Billy Girt stalked off into his office, whereupon the suspect confessed.

I enjoyed my month's CID attachment and resolved to leave the police force and seek other employment if I didn't make it within four years or so. My two years' probation passed quite quickly and I was one day called in to the Inspector's office to be told that I had been accepted as a fully-fledged constable. The same day I completed an A57 asking to be considered for transfer to the CID.

My first application for CID finished in the waste-paper basket of the Inspector's office. He called me in and advised me to apply again in a year or so. Normally no one went onto the CID with less than four years' service and there was "plenty of time", he said. I was aware that many officers who had served all their time in uniform did not like the CID and did their best to discourage young officers from specialising in this department. However the same advice came from other quarters, including the CID officers I had met during my attachment.

So my next application was for a driving course. No one could drive a police vehicle of any description until they had been on a Standard or Advanced Police Driving Course, no matter how much driving experience they had. Some months later I was sent to headquarters for a test to assess my driving ability and to see whether I should have a 'standard' or 'advanced' course. I was pleased to find that I was recommended for the advanced course. Several more weeks went by before I received my instructions to attend the course at Chelmsford Police Headquarters for five weeks.

Chelmsford Driving School was where all driving instruction for N° 5 District took place, so there were officers there from many other forces as well as Essex. It was a very valuable part of my police training, and one which has stood me in good stead ever since.

Later, when I once again applied for the CID, the Inspector asked me, "Why did you want an Advanced Driving Course if you want to go on the CID?"

"I want to be both a good driver and a CID Officer" I replied.

"Ugh!" he grunted. "You'll be the first then!"

This time however my application was processed and sent to the Detective Chief Superintendent at Headquarters, one Jack Barkway, who no doubt would look at it some time, and when there was a vacancy, make some enquiries about me at my Divisional Headquarters. Meantime I became an Area Car Driver at Romford and continued to attend to the many tasks allotted, but this time from the driver's seat.

During the daytime there are a number of routine things to do such as serve summonses, execute warrants for arrest, often for non-payment of fines, and even take the car to headquarters for service. At night-time however you were able to 'police' your area, and this could be done in a number of ways. Of course there were always accidents, 'suspects on premises' and other calls for assistance from the public to attend to. One of the more interesting tasks was to stop and check vehicles.

The Area Car was frequently called to deal with a 'Drunk and Incapable' who had been discovered in the gutter, on a park bench or elsewhere where his presence was considered to be inconvenient. It was common practice in order to avoid unnecessary paperwork, upsetting the duty Sergeant and dirtying a police cell, to pick him up and dump him in the Metropolitan Police district, which adjoined Essex. Occasionally, later in the night or early morning, we would often get another report of a drunk only to find that the Metropolitan Police had dumped him back on our 'Manor'. Quite often such an individual would wake up cold and miserable and many miles from where he thought he was. Let the punishment fit the crime, eh?

During the quiet periods between answering calls, particularly between 3am and 5am, it was your choice whether you did some police work or found some quiet secluded spot for a bit of shuteye until it got light and people and traffic began to move about. No doubt many of the 'old sweats' did a bit of skiving, but there were those among us who preferred to keep on the go.

At times, when one was available, there would be a CID Officer on night duty who would often come for a ride in the area car and add his weight and expertise to the tasks performed. On these occasions 'forty winks' was in any case out of the question.

Some of the more outlying places, country clubs, golf clubs, houses of the local gentry and so on, required a visit. Vehicles moving about late at night were always viewed with suspicion and were worth a check. Occasionally a dodgy-looking vehicle might go by and the CID Officer would say, "Give him a pull". One night when Sid Maxted was on the car he drew my attention to a big old car which appeared to be weighed down heavily at the rear. We stopped it and found a small safe in the boot which the occupants, two likely lads, had just stolen.

This expression "giving someone a pull" may have derived from the method used to stop a vehicle. In the police vehicle was a roller blind in the rear window that had the words 'POLICE STOP' in large black letters on a white background. The idea was to pass the vehicle you wanted to stop, pull the blind up and, at night-time, shine a torch on it from inside. This, one hoped, would induce the driver of the car behind to stop. It was a bit primitive, but it usually worked. One of the problems was that during the period the blind was up you couldn't see what was happening behind the car, and this could be a major handicap.

On one occasion I had seen three scruffy-looking youths in a rather nice car; the two didn't go together, so I decided to give them a 'pull'. Having passed the vehicle, the observer pulled up the 'stop' blind and shone his torch on it. I slowed the car, anticipating that the car behind had seen the stop sign and begun to slow also. But when the observer dropped the blind I could see the car behind much closer than it had been, almost touching the police car it seemed, and travelling faster. I accelerated and drove out of the car's path into a convenient layby, braked and watched the car go past; there was now no one in it!

The three youths, it seemed, had abandoned the car as soon as the police car passed them. When we got out we could see the three of them making off across a field. One of the advantages of being the driver was that you could instruct the observer to give chase while you did the important bit of radioing for assistance, not that there was much chance of getting any. Fortunately the abandoned car had come to rest in the centre greensward and was not a danger to traffic. I drove to a lane at the far side of the fields and intercepted three exhausted youths and an equally exhausted observer as they came through a gap in the hedge. On this occasion the car owner was pleased to get his car back in one piece, as often they were severely dented or even burnt out.

The 'theft of a motor vehicle' was then, as it is now, a

crime of great frequency. It is a very serious crime from the point of view of the victim, since his car is probably his second most valuable asset. There are three main reasons why cars are stolen; the first has been dubbed 'joy riding', wrongly, in my view, giving the impression that it is not such a serious crime. I mentioned in Chapter One the definition of theft, and you will remember that it was necessary to prove the offender intended "permanently to deprive the owner" of the item taken. If the 'joy riders' had already abandoned the car, or when caught said that they intended to do so, then this point could not be proved. It was for this reason that the offence of "taking a motor vehicle without the consent of the owner" was created, but it bore a lesser penalty and did nothing to curb this criminal act.

The second class of car theft was when criminals stole a car - there was usually a gang of them - intending to sell vehicle or otherwise dispose of it for gain, perhaps to dismantle it and sell the parts or, in the case of the more expensive cars, to take them to Europe and sell them there. It was not uncommon for a man to leave his car at the railway station car park in the morning and find it missing when he returned home in the evening. By this time his car, perhaps a BMW or Jaguar, was already in France or on its way even further afield. These vehicles were less likely to be recovered.

The stolen cars the police are most interested in are the third category, those that are stolen solely for the purpose of committing crime. These cars are often stolen several days before they are required for the 'job' and the police will have had the particulars reported to them soon after the theft. It was important therefore that patrolling officers had these details of recently stolen cars, which might then be identified either before, during or after they were used for committing a crime.

Details of all cars stolen within the Essex Police District and many from the Metropolitan Area that adjoined were passed to patrol cars every half hour or so, so that one was in possession of the very latest information. Stolen cars were then, as they are today, a big headache for the police and it is important that they are dealt with correctly for many reasons.

Whenever a stolen car was found abandoned it was regarded as an important find. This was not only because the total value of recovered stolen property was an important statistic, but because of the chance that it had been, or might be, used in the commission of another perhaps more serious crime.

Much could be ascertained from the circumstances of the car being found. Often thieves would set fire to a car after they had finished with it in the hope that this would destroy any physical evidence or fingerprints that might connect them with the vehicle. There was not, so the thieves believed, a lot of advantage in having such vehicles closely examined for fingerprints and other physical evidence.

On other occasions the vehicle would be abandoned after an accident or deliberately crashed or dumped in a river or quarry. Whatever the circumstances, the first priority was to search the vehicle and have it examined for fingerprints and other clues. In many instances the vehicle was in such a location that it indicated the thief or thieves might intend to return to the vehicle. In all such cases a certain amount of time was well spent keeping observation on it.

How times have changed! In the *Daily Mail* of Saturday 8th December 2001 there was a report of a woman who had her car stolen in Greater Manchester; of course she reported it. Some time later she saw her car parked on a road near where she lived. The number plates had been changed, but it still had the original number on the tax disc and there were several items of the loser's personal property in the car that she could identify. The car was locked and secured with a steering wheel clamp!

When she notified the police to whom she had reported the theft, they told her they had no manpower available to attend and advised her to 'steal the car back again' by using a hacksaw on the steering wheel clamp. As an alternative they offered her the use of the police recovery vehicle at a cost of £100. The advice given to this woman was wrong both in law and in practice. I only hope she took the matter further with the Chief Constable.

In my own personal experience this type of response to reports of abandoned vehicles is not uncommon these days and is another of the many reasons why public confidence in the police service has sunk to such depths. It is true that with modern technology not available in my day, the owner of a vehicle can be obtained in seconds together with any intelligence about its history or that of the owner.

I had my share of excitement and car chases during the relatively short time I was an Area Car Driver. I also did my share of damage to police vehicles! On one occasion my observer opened his car door as I was reversing in a country lane and the edge of the door caught in a culvert in the embankment and was practically ripped off. On another the car I was chasing stopped rather quicker than I did and I smashed the front of the police car. A bigger sin still, the thief got away while I was sorting out the mess. Fortunately I did recognise him, so he didn't escape justice.

Usually, as far as police drivers are concerned, there is only one set of circumstances when you can be adjudged 'not to blame' for an accident to a police car. That is if the car is stationary and parked on the correct side of the road with the handbrake applied. In any other circumstances there is always consideration given to the question of prosecuting you. In any case there are a great many forms to fill in and questions to answer before you are allowed back in the driver's seat. On these two occasions, all the circumstances being considered, I was just given a warning.

My last accident was one where I was not so lucky. I was answering a 999 call to 'suspects on premises' and was travelling in excess of the permitted speed. I passed close by a woman on a pedal cycle, who had both sides of her handlebars loaded with shopping; she wobbled and came off. Of course I was obliged to stop and deal with this incident and abandon the call I was answering. The woman was uninjured and so was her bicycle. However her husband later that day came to the station to complain and I was duly reported for driving without due care and attention. I later appeared in front of the Magistrates and was fined £3 with £2 18s costs. Later the rest of the officers on my shift had a 'whip round' for me and handed me the sum of £6, which meant I could pay my fine and costs and still have enough for a drink afterwards.

I was reminded at Court that police cars were not permitted to exceed the speed limit, even when answering emergency calls. Of course I knew that, as do all the drivers of ambulances and fire engines who regularly break the law in this way with the tacit approval of their senior officers and the public. It is just one more of the ways that such public servants have often to bend the rules to get the job done. For some weeks after my 'case' the Area Car Drivers at Romford refused to exceed the speed limits. They were soon advised that this was not the way to behave and things got back to normal.

Naturally I was taken off Area Cars, but the following week I was called into the Inspector's office to say I was to be posted to Harlow CID as soon as arrangements could be made for my house removal. I had been at Romford just four years.

The officers on my shift at Romford were all great characters and I remember them with feelings of warmth, comradeship and pride. They were the men from whom I learned my trade, the like of whom will probably never be seen again. They were a team of dedicated policemen; many of them have now passed on. Officers such as Fred Baddeley, a large round officer of great humour and patience. My fondest memory of Fred was the night he befriended a stray Alsatian dog on his beat. The animal followed him round until time for refreshment break when he brought it to the station to share his sandwiches. Afterwards he took it out with him again, hoping to lose it by six o'clock. This he was unable to do, the animal by now having become quite attached to this genial giant of a man. The dog was duly 'booked in' as a stray and attempts were made to put it in the kennels behind the station, without success. The dog became quite aggressive at the prospect of custody and was eventually tied to the kennel door with a piece of rope and a spare collar kept at the station for just such an emergency.

Fred got his cycle from the rack and began to make his way home to a flat in Victoria Road, not too far from the station. He had gone only a few yards when the dog's frantic barking gave way to the sound of wood splintering and the animal bounded out of the police station and down the centre of the main road in hot pursuit of Fred, dragging the kennel door behind him.

Tony Cook, another colleague, was a diminutive man whose shoulders were hardly wider than his helmet, but who in spite of his size was an excellent policeman. Tony was born and bred in Romford and his knowledge of the district was encyclopaedic. For example, one night when I was driving the Area Car and Tony was the observer we stopped to check a man walking along late at night alone. Having asked him his name and what he was doing etc, Tony asked for his address and he gave a road name.

"What number?" said Tony.

"Number forty-four" the man said.

To my utter amazement, Tony detained him on suspicion and put him in the police car. At the station he was questioned at some length, his identity established and a check was made at Criminal Record Office. It was found that the man was wanted in three counties for burglary, theft and assault. Later I asked Tony what had made him suspicious of the man.

"His address" he replied.

"What about his address?"

"The numbers in that street only go up to forty" said Tony.

There was Jock Semple, who I have already mentioned, Dennis Way a man with whom I became quite friendly and Jack Wadley, noted for always being able to get cheap pens, torch batteries and French letters! (the word condom was not used then). There were many others whose names have left my memory. I was proud to have served with all of them, but glad to be on my way.

# Harlow CID (1958–1961)

*"Singularity is almost invariably a clue. The more featureless and commonplace a crime is, the more difficult is it to bring it home."*
*- The Adventures of Sherlock Holmes (1892), Sir Arthur Conan Doyle - The Boscombe Valley Mystery*

Harlow New Town, as it was then called, boasted a new police station with every modern convenience and an adjoining Magistrates' Court building which was just as new and imposing. I had only been to Harlow once before, to do duty when the Queen visited the town, and was therefore a comparative stranger to its complex design. It was one of the first of the new towns to be built to house the overflow from east London, and the population consisted mostly of people from the Enfield and Edmonton areas. To qualify for a house in Harlow New Town it was merely necessary to get a job there, and work was not difficult to find in the early days.

Building work was plentiful, and there were jobs available in most of the many factories that had been completed or were soon to be finished.

Harlow CID had only a Detective Inspector in charge at the time, one Ted Bond, who spoke and behaved like an educated gentleman, quite unlike the previous DI I had known. I presented myself to him and was welcomed to the Division and introduced to the other officers of the department. There were three, Detective Sergeant Doug Heuer, who had his own office, and Detective Constables Ron Stark and Alan Wyatt. There was a desk for me in their office complete with empty in tray. Next door was a small filing office and yes, a typist! She was a married lady named Mrs Jackson whom everyone called "Slim" for obvious reasons. Slim was a good typist, a mine of information and one who could write a standard Crime Report for you given the barest of detail.

Later during my stay at Harlow another Detective Constable was posted there. One doesn't make many friends in the police force and even fewer lifelong friends. Cliff Stollery and I did become friends as well as colleagues, and we are still 'old mates' today. It was Cliff who introduced me to the pleasures of sailing, and for some years we owned a yacht on which we used to get away from it all at weekends.

Incidentally all CID offices in every station I have ever been to are on the first floor of the building if not higher, the ground floor always being reserved for operational police officers and offices.

The DI led me along the upper corridor to the Chief

Superintendent's office, which had a buzzer on the door. You had to buzz and wait until Fred Pettengel, the incumbent, deigned to press the little button on his desk to allow you in. The Chief's presence and his palatial office duly impressed me; Mr Pettengel was a large and rather portly man who was clearly conscious of his importance in the scheme of things. Even his Admin Chief Inspector in the office next door used to creep and hover about like Uriah Heep, obviously in awe of the man.

Once more I was welcomed and given a copy of Divisional Standing Orders to guide me through the days ahead. They were indeed a 'catalogue of other people's mistakes' and included one on how to put a pin in a sheaf of papers to hold them together: "The pin must go in the top left hand corner from above downwards and then back into the papers making sure that the point is concealed amongst the pages". When reading it I had a picture in my mind of poor Fred Pettengel angrily grabbing for his pen to compose a Standing Order with blood pouring from his thumb.

Fortunately only the Divisional Commander could issue a Standing Order; lesser mortals had to issue 'memos' and everyone, and I do mean everyone, had to initial them and 'obey'.

As far as CID officers' dress was concerned, a dark two-piece dark suit with shirt and tie was the order of the day except on Saturday mornings, when a sports jacket could be worn. Most CID officers also wore a trilby hat. In that however I was once again considered a rebel - I refused to buy one. Apart from the fact that I didn't like wearing a hat, the meagre allowance paid to detectives for their 'plain clothes' barely covered one suit a year. There was also a very small CID allowance that was supposed to cover out-of-pocket expenses and the overtime it was rightly assumed would be put in. I said that if the police insisted I should wear a hat then they would have to provide it. Mr Bond, as we all called him, 'Detective Inspector' and 'Sir' didn't quite seem to fit him, was not pleased. Shortly after my arrival at Harlow there was a visit by Her Majesty's Inspector of Constabulary. CID officers, as well as the Uniform Branch, all paraded wearing their trilby hats. I was given the day off!

However, that hurdle having been overcome, I got on very well with Mr Bond, and he was a capable detective, if rather formal in his approach, and as a beginner I was willing to learn all I could from anyone. Ted was a man of few words and very thorough. I once submitted a crime report, which contained a standard final phrase that I had learned at Romford: "Enquiries were made at all likely places without positive result". The report was returned to me from Ted and written in red ink on it were the words, "Well, make some enquiries at 'unlikely' places!"

Soon after I arrived at Harlow I was sent on a detective training course at Preston in Lancashire. It was a three-month course intended to teach prospective detectives some of the finer points of the practice of detecting crime. There was a good deal more law to learn and the finer points of case law and how to get round some of the restrictions imposed upon practical detective work. Detectives being rather more 'hard-nosed' than their uniformed colleagues tended to go out to pubs and clubs in the evenings, and there were definite signs there that some of those I met wouldn't go very far in the service unless they changed their drinking habits.

A detective had what was called a 'caseload', which was the actual number of investigations he was handling at any one time. Unlike the TV police programmes, where the detectives only ever seem to have one case to deal with, we always had up to a dozen or so ongoing investigations. Moreover, except when one expected to make an arrest, it was rare to carry out any enquiry except on your own. There are no 'partners' in the British CID system, and it was not until the inception of the Regional Crime Squad in 1964 that one began to see pairs and even 'gangs' of detectives working together. What is the collective noun for several detectives one wonders? Perhaps a 'gang' or a 'rabble', or even a 'confusion'!

How one managed to acquire a caseload worked like this. There was only one telephone in the CID General Office and if you were the one to answer it when a caller wished to report a crime, then generally that was 'yours' to deal with. When a uniformed officer received the report of a crime he first had to complete a Crime Complaint. In many cases he would write a recommendation that it be "passed to CID for further enquiries" on the bottom. This would then be passed to the Detective Sergeant, who, if he agreed with this course of action, would allocate it to one of his detectives. Occasionally someone would report in another police area a crime that had been committed in Harlow. The papers would then be forwarded and allocated to a detective to investigate.

In addition to your actual caseload there were 'other

enquiries' to be done. Officers from other stations would ring up and ask for people to be interviewed, warrants to be executed, arrests to be made and premises to be searched, to name but a few. Whenever a uniformed officer made an arrest a CID officer would be allocated to oversee the case. This always started by interviewing the prisoner, who might or might not have already admitted the offence for which he was arrested. It was essential to see if the accused had committed any other crimes before he was bailed or otherwise disposed of.

Before the questioning, or interrogation, of a suspect took place it was usual to search his house or premises. The law gave an officer the right to search the place where a person was actually arrested, so if he was arrested at home there was no problem. However, if he had been arrested in the street, or at work, then one could only search his home with his consent or with a search warrant. Usually the accused was easily persuaded that it would be to his advantage to give his consent, especially if he wanted to get home for supper!

The advantage of this routine search of a suspect's home could not be overstated. For example if he or she continued to deny the offence, evidence was often found at his house, or in the case of juveniles in their room at home. Many inexperienced officers used to spend hours talking to a suspect to no avail and then ask for CID assistance. The CID officer would first search the house, or 'tip his drum' as the expression went, perhaps to find the stolen goods, or evidence of some other crime or crimes. Hours of police time could often be saved by this procedure.

The 'tipping of drums' as a routine measure has now

stopped. The detection rate has fallen over the years from something like 45% to a little more than 20%. There are many reasons for this, but one of them is I believe due to the failure of officers to search premises in this routine way. There are many obstacles in the way of their doing this today, time available being only one of them, but the fact remains that hundreds of crimes were detected by this means which are no longer detected.

Having got an admission, it was routine to get out the Crime Complaint book and go through it with the accused, to try and get him to admit all the other crimes he had committed recently and wished to be taken into consideration when he went to court. It was not uncommon then for an accused to admit several other crimes, and even take the officers on a tour to point out houses or business premises he had broken into. Contrary to the general public conception of police these days, there was quite often an excellent relationship between police and prisoner. It is indeed a fact that when a prisoner had admitted his crimes, he became more relaxed and resigned to what the future might hold for him. That is of course if you were playing fair with him, which was not necessarily always the case.

My very first meeting with members of the Metropolitan Police 'Flying Squad' was when they came to Harlow to 'tip a few drums'. There had been a bank robbery in the Edmonton area of East London and the suspects all came from Harlow. I was detailed to go with the Squad to show them where the various addresses were for which they had search warrants.

At one house I went inside with the three officers from London and was asked if I would go upstairs and search a small bedroom for gold sovereigns, a number of which had been stolen in the raid and which were identifiable as having come from the bank in question. I did so, thoroughly, or so I thought. Afterwards the officer in charge of the Squad came upstairs as I was leaving the room and went in.

"There's nothing in here" I said.

"Fine" he replied, "I'll just have a check".

I was a little aggrieved and somewhat surprised, since I had already searched the room, and even more surprised when he came out with a handful of gold sovereigns he had found in a pair of shoes in the wardrobe. He winked at me and tapped the side of his nose with his finger. The suspect was arrested.

I later learned that all the suspects had been arrested and that gold sovereigns had been found at each of their premises. The men all had long criminal records for robbery and violence. I have no doubt that they were guilty of the bank robbery.

Another useful maxim that I learned early in the CID, and was able to pass on to many a less experienced officer, was that you should never try to get a confession from a suspect if you don't need one. It was always rather satisfying to round off an investigation with a 'statement under caution' as it was called, whereon the accused signs his confession. It was less satisfying when the case was lost because of some defect in the manner in which the statement was taken. A man might be caught at the scene of a crime loading the stolen goods into his car. Usually that was all the evidence to prove that he had stolen them. Why spend a lot of time persuading him to make a statement? After the man has been to see his solicitor all kinds of problems can arise with a statement under caution, including allegations that the statement has been completely forged, words put into the accused's mouth, or threats or other inducements made to persuade the accused to sign a confession. You name it, the defence will think of it. Juries and judges tend to lose sight of all the other evidence once the police or police conduct has been tarnished.

Having satisfied oneself as far as was possible that all the necessary evidence had been collected for the case, statements taken and so on, there were many forms to complete and antecedents to be compiled and verified. The uniformed officer was able to leave all this to the CID; not necessarily because he was incapable of doing this part of the job properly himself, but after all his place was out on the street, not in the station filling in forms.

So, when you had finished all the routine and other enquiries allotted to you, you were able to get on with investigating your own caseload, which usually began by visiting the scene of the crime and taking statements from victim and witnesses.

I was always, since my army days, an early riser, so it was usual for me to arrive at the station about 8.30am each day. Even when I realised that others took advantage of this trait, I couldn't break myself of the habit, although I confess that later I might go in at 8.30am but be 'out on enquiries' by

8.45. As with the uniform branch there was a duty register to sign in and out so that supervising officers would know where you were at all times. Alan Wyatt would usually make an appearance at 9am, but Ron Stark was never there much before five minutes past. You see at 9am sharp anyone who wanted the CID for any reason, especially to report a break in at their shop or factory, would ring up to report it. As I have said, whoever answered the phone had the pleasure of investigating the matter. I found at first that I was always first in the office and first to pick up the phone!

At Harlow there was only one CID car between three of us, four including Sergeant Heuer, although he was allowed to use his own car and claim a mileage allowance. Alan Wyatt didn't mind that very much as he was quite happy to plod around Harlow on his bicycle; he used to carry an old briefcase attached to the crossbar, containing all his forms and papers. His mode of dress for this usually included a cloth cap, and except for the local villains, who undoubtedly knew him, no one would ever guess he was a police officer.

Ron Stark was known by all as the 'armchair detective', and spent a good deal of his time in the office sitting at his desk sucking at his foul-smelling pipe. More often than not therefore I was able to avail myself of the CID car. I believe that the reason detectives have a plain or nondescript vehicle is so that they can call on members of the public without embarrassing them. It is not, as one might imagine, so that you can avoid being noticed by the ungodly. The local CID car is always well known to all those who have reason to want to avoid it.

All current investigations were put in a manila folder with a front sheet attached. The folders had to be displayed on top of your desk and as the case progressed the various forms and statements were placed inside the folder. The front sheet showed a list of matters that had to be dealt with as routine and the various boxes on the form were ticked as they were completed. The front sheet also showed the date when the Crime Report was due. In this way the Sergeant or Inspector could at any time, by looking through your case files, see from the front sheets how much work you had on and how you were getting on with it.

A report called a Crime Report had to be submitted within fourteen days of the receipt of a complaint of crime, giving details of the progress or otherwise of the investigation. These reports were then 'classified' and from them were produced the Crime Statistics everyone gets excited about from time to time. The reports had numerous boxes that had to be ticked or left blank so that the statistics could be calculated at Headquarters. The form had grown over the years because of the requirement for further information.

The reason why these Crime Reports were regarded as very important is largely because of statistics. From them the Division's crime rate and detection rate, the force detection rate and many other annual statistics were calculated. The number of burglaries in an area, and similar facts concerning all other crime, were regarded as vital to the future management and operation of the force. The Government also kept statistics on a national basis to amuse Members of Parliament when they asked questions about them and to publish for public consumption whenever it suited them or when for some reason they had to.

On one occasion a Member of Parliament asked the Prime Minister at Question Time if he was aware how many domestic pets were stolen in the course of a year. He was unable to give an answer on this occasion, but would never be caught out on that one again. A directive came down from the Home Office shortly afterwards and another 'box' was added to the form. Someone once suggested that the victim's and the culprit's ethnic group should be added to the form so those questions about percentages of crimes committed against and by these groups could be answered. It seems that this was too risky!

Ideally the crime would be detected and classified as one of say 'Burglary – Detected'. Such a crime was said to be 'cleared up.' If you had not been able to clear up the crime then the best alternative was to have it classified as 'No Crime.' To do this you had to satisfy your Sergeant and Inspector that for the reasons you explained in the report no crime had been committed. The reason might be that a person who had reported the theft of her purse might have later rung the station to say she had found it again. This was a genuine 'no crime', however it was often possible to manipulate the circumstances when writing a crime report to satisfy one's senior officers that no offence had been committed, which was known as 'writing off' an offence. Stones thrown up by passing cars were often used to explain how a shop window got broken, while other offences reported as fraud might well be 'written off' as a civil matter and therefore 'no crime.'

One had to be careful however, and there was one often-told story illustrating this of an officer who had received a report that some pigeons had been stolen from the local Squire's garden. Later in his report he suggested that they had probably flown away and therefore no crime was committed. Unfortunately for the officer the Squire was later at a social function with the Chief Constable and asked him how the investigation was going into the theft of his 'ornamental stone pigeons'. The following day the Chief rang the Superintendent, who sent for the report and later for the officer to explain how stone ornamental pigeons could fly away!

The more crimes one could write off, the higher would be the detection rate. It was a pretty good incentive to police officers generally, and detectives in particular to do their best to clear up crime on their 'patch'. If an officer was able to detect a crime at the time of its commission, that is to say before a crime complaint had been made, he got what was called a 'one and one'. It was far better for the crime figures than submitting a crime complaint in respect of an undetected crime. It also gave an officer, who also perhaps got a word of praise and encouragement from his senior officer, a greater incentive to keep his eyes open when he was out on the street. The theft of the smallest item from Woolworth's for example was a crime, for which a crime complaint had to be submitted. In my days at Harlow almost as many crime complaints were submitted by officers who had detected a crime on a 'one and one' basis as those which came by way of complaints from members of the public.

When I first became a detective the problem of drug

abuse, especially among young people, was in its infancy, certainly in provincial force areas such as Essex. As the problem became more widespread we did eventually have a 'Drug Squad' at headquarters consisting of one officer, Derek Wyatt, who used to visit schools with advice for the pupils, and give talks to anyone who was interested. In general these were women's clubs and other groups who might never see the problem at first hand, but did have a morbid interest. This officer, and he alone, kept himself up to date with the drugs available and in use on the street. Other officers might have a lecture on the subject next time they attended a course of some kind. Let us say the problem was not taken seriously, nor was it apparently envisaged that it would become serious.

The situation is now a national disgrace and successive governments have been unable or unwilling to deal effectively with a problem that kills many people each year. Not only are drugs responsible for death and misery for the individuals who take them, they are at the root of a large percentage of urban crime today. Like many other national problems, eventually the Government looks for someone to blame and one often hears that the police are not doing enough to deal with the problem!

For some reason that I can only think was political expediency, the Government did not make misuse of drugs generally a reportable crime, that is to say a crime for which a crime complaint had to be completed. Perhaps this was to avoid any statistics having to be published. If offences were not recorded then they were not counted either. In any case it was not the sort of crime that people came into the station to report.

It is in my view mainly because an officer would not get a 'score' or a 'one and one' for detecting such an offence that insufficient attention was paid to it in the early days. To have sat up and taken notice might have turned the tide, or at least held it back for a while. It is also true to say that no pressure was exerted from above encouraging officers to seek out and prosecute offenders who were contravening the Misuse of Drugs Act, although there was frequently pressure to make sure that there were no cars parked without lights in the vicinity of the Chief Superintendent's house.

On the contrary, while there was power to 'stop and search' anyone suspected of carrying a banned drug, it was almost taboo to do so, especially if the suspected person was from a local ethnic group or was 'known' for having been convicted before. To stop and search such a person was likely to result in a complaint for harassment or racial discrimination, and while this might have eventually been unsubstantiated, it would cause 'trouble' for the force and for the officer concerned.

It is true also that there was a perfectly good power of arrest for dealing with a person found to be in possession of cannabis or some other prohibited substance. However the procedure at the police station was long and tedious. The substance had to be sent to the laboratory for analysis before a charge could be brought, and not even a 'detected' crime to show for it! It needs little intelligence to work out the result of such a policy.

I said earlier in this chapter that often the relationship between offender and police officer was cordial. It is however an area of police work where there were strict discipline regulations. Not only could one not accept gifts from anyone, it was forbidden to associate with a known criminal. It did mean that detectives in particular had occasionally to tread a very precarious line between having a cordial relationship with a known villain and actually associating with him. Was having a drink in a pub with a villain you had put away and had recently been released from prison, 'associating with' him? Many a detective has fallen into the trap of stepping too far over this line. Not for his own gain necessarily, although this has no doubt happened, but for the benefit of obtaining information useful to him in his job.

Information is one of the most vital commodities used by policemen to detect crime and bring criminals to justice. This can be acquired in many different ways, but who better to know what is happening and being planned amongst criminals in a town than another criminal?

Getting a criminal to give information or 'grass' on his peers is not as difficult as it might seem. However the whole process is fraught with danger for the police officer who seeks to accomplish it. What some forget is that no one does 'owt for nowt' as the saying goes, and the reasons why a villain will willingly give information to the police are complex. Self-preservation is one good reason.

There is a great deal of psychology attached to being a detective and knowing when and how to 'do a deal' with a criminal. It's rather like buying a second-hand car, you listen to the salesman telling you all about the wonderful attributes the car has and perhaps, if you believe him, you find that it falls to pieces the moment you take it on the road.

When you have a prisoner in custody in the police station, he will often do practically anything to get out on bail, or even a 'refused charge'. He might promise you information about a forthcoming crime, or offer to give details of the activities of other criminals on your patch in whom you have an interest. While the chap is in custody you do to some extent have the upper hand, but as soon as he is released the boot is on the other foot, and you no longer have any control.

The bargain offered by the criminal is often, "Let me out and I will tell you what you want to know". On the other hand the police officer will say, "Tell me what I want to know and then I'll let you out".

Very often both know that the other will go back on his word. Less experienced police officers might take a chance, often putting their job at risk by letting a criminal off with a caution or on bail when he should not have done, merely on a promise by that criminal of some information. Usually such a risk is not worth taking, because the information either doesn't come or when it does it proves to be worthless. On the other hand the less experienced criminal might jeopardise his own position among his fellow ne'er-do-wells by telling the police officer about their activities, only to find that the officer goes back on his word and does not allow bail or freedom.

This conflict between potential informant and police officer in the police station went on all the time and rarely in my experience did either party benefit very much from any 'deal' made. Whenever any of my officers came to see me and said they had a prisoner who wanted to 'make a deal' my immediate reaction was, "Forget it!"

Another type of criminal informant is one who believes that he owes a particular officer a favour or is in some way beholden to him. It has been known that an officer will find stolen property or drugs in a person's possession and rather than arrest him, recruits him as an informant. The threat of arrest and a prison sentence in the future if the information is not forthcoming is used to squeeze information from the informant. Such information is likely to be of better quality since the informant knows, or thinks he knows, the penalty for failing to come across. What happens to the property is another question. It could be that if it was drugs for example, an officer could keep them in order to plant them on someone else. Strictly against the rules and common decency, you might say. There is not a lot of common decency required when dealing with drug addicts, but the rules should not be broken.

In fact the threat of arrest is an idle one, since an officer could not very well arrest the chap weeks, months or even years later for an offence for which he should have arrested him at the time. He could of course plant the drugs or other stolen property back on him, but that would be dishonest, wouldn't it? Of course it depends on one's conception of honesty. Is there any great difference between a villain getting dealt with for stealing, or being in possession of drugs, at the time or a few months later?

Perhaps a greater sin on the part of a police officer would be that he plants the 'evidence' on a person other than the one on whom he found it. This sort of allegation has been made many times against officers and comes under the heading of 'stitching up' or 'expediency'. I will have a little more to say about this aspect of positive policing later. However, as someone who has investigated many such complaints against police officers, I often think that if there is any truth at all in a complaint that drugs were planted, they almost certainly originated in the way described above. For this reason such a complaint is rarely likely to be substantiated, unless there is also proof that the officer obtained the drugs unlawfully.

Another type of informant is known as the 'professional informant' who gives information in order to receive reward money. He is usually a despicable and untrustworthy man who is an associate of serious criminals and is prepared to inform on his 'mates' for a reward. Insurance companies often offer 10% of the value of goods recovered, and this can be far more rewarding to a criminal and less risky than a night out 'screwing' on his own.

Such informants will usually only deal with one particular officer. Officers who regularly 'deal' with such informants are inclined towards devious behaviour themselves and are difficult to manage because of it. Their score of detected crime may well be far higher than those officers with a more conventional, some might say 'honest' and professional, approach to the job, but who deserves the most gratitude from the general public? I have always thought there was room for both types of officer in the service, provided their motives are the same - that is to say the desire to apprehend criminals. Modern policemen, especially those in high office, lawyers and politicians would not agree that occasionally the end justifies the means. However the criminals break the rules, why should the police not bend a few ever so slightly in order to put them away? (See Chapter Seven).

A tricky little informant is the 'runt' of the informing world and is usually a little chap who likes to feel important by talking to police officers and perhaps persuading them to buy him a drink or two in the hope that he might let drop a few words of wisdom. Generally he has nothing to offer and should be avoided at all costs. But first you have to find out the hard way, as I did.

One Friday morning there was a phone call and I picked up the receiver. "CID, DC Raven?" The voice was a rasping whisper.

"You don't know me, Mr Raven, but I have some information for you, can you meet me in the Painted Lady?"

I was naturally on my guard at once, but one can never turn down the possibility of some information, although only a very small percentage of such calls are genuine.

"OK," I said. "When?"

"I'll be in the saloon bar at eleven o'clock. I'll have a copy of the *Harlow Gazette* under my arm. I'll be at the bar, my name's Jock."

I told Ron Stark about the call. He looked his watch, smiled and nodded. I presumed he wasn't interested in coming with me.

All the public houses in Harlow were named after butterflies, probably because the architect was a collector: the Copper Kettle, White Admiral, etc. The Painted Lady was in the town centre a few minutes' walk from the police station.

I walked into the saloon bar a minute after eleven and at once spotted a little man in a cap standing at the bar with a paper under his arm peering furtively over his shoulder every second or so. He saw me approaching him.

"Mr Raven?" he asked.

"I presume you are Jock?"

He had an empty half-pint glass in front of him on the counter and I offered to buy him another drink. After all, that is what our CID expenses were supposed to be for.

"Thanks, I'll have a pint of Best" he said. Perhaps I should have realised then that I was being had, but it took another two pints before I wised up. Ron Stark had known!

Jock started to tell me details about recent crimes in Harlow, suggesting he knew the culprits, and although he was very long winded about it he seemed to be in possession of some information. He began to talk about rewards and how much it was worth etc, while drinking two more pints. It eventually became obvious, even to me, that he had no useful information and I let him buy the next drink for himself and left.

It was later explained to me that Jock used to buy the local paper early on Friday mornings and read up on the local reported crimes, burglaries in particular. Then he would ring up the police station, and if he was lucky enough to get some greenhorn such as me, he might get himself a couple of free pints by pretending to offer information.

Undoubtedly the best type of information came from a person who would only inform once. He or she had overheard something on a bus, in a pub etc, or had taken a car number at the scene of a crime, for example. On other, perhaps rarer, occasions a mother or father would contact the police wishing to inform on a son who they knew was committing crime.

More frequently the informant would be a disgruntled member of a gang who hadn't got his fair share, or frequently a jilted girlfriend who had a mine of information about her recent boyfriend.

Publicans were a good source of information, and at night it was common practice for detectives to go from pub to pub in the town stopping for a half-pint and a chat with the governor and then moving on. This was another way of 'keeping a finger on the pulse' of the town and often discovering who was 'flush' with money soon after a spate of burglaries.

In no case could an informant be assumed one hundred percent genuine. It was always necessary to check their information, and particularly their motives, before acting on it.

The question of associating with 'known criminals' is one I have touched on before. It generally included persons who were suspected of being of dubious character, although not convicted criminals. There are many such persons in any town; often they are the more wealthy types who could afford to have criminal associates and benefit from criminal activities, without themselves being directly implicated. I am thinking of people who receive stolen property as a matter of course.

Many people buy stolen property, or property otherwise unlawfully obtained, without question if it is cheap. Cheap tobacco, booze, cosmetics and clothing were regularly being sold to employees at factories and similar places of employment. It was rare that such a purchaser of stolen goods ended up in court, and on several occasions I received a phone call from one of them saying who was doing the selling and was able to get a 'one and one'.

For some reason receivers of stolen property, a good many of them in business for themselves such as builders, shopkeepers, publicans etc, rather like to associate with police officers. It gives them a sense of security and an ally in case of trouble. They hand out gifts of bottles of whisky at Christmas, and depending what business they are in they offer large discounts and cheap services to the police officers they are acquainted with. Harlow was full of such businessmen, and it was practically impossible to avoid contact with them. Of course to begin with you didn't know who was holding out their hand of friendship without an ulterior motive, but there were very few I would have invited home to tea.

One man I remember well was manager of a television shop. I had no reason to believe then that he was dishonest, nor do I now, but from time to time there were unsavoury characters in the shop when I called in to chat with him. On occasion he would ask me whether there had been any of a certain type of electrical goods stolen, as someone had offered him some and he was suspicious. This led me to think he was most probably honest, but was one of those local characters who liked to keep a foot in both camps.

One day he said he had had a van loaded with televisions stolen from the back of his shop. He didn't report it in the usual way but rang me to ask me to call and see him. I took all the details and circulated the details of the stolen vehicle, which was later found abandoned in Harlow. It was empty. Having had the van fingerprinted and examined by Scenes of Crime officers the vehicle was returned to the owner, who swore that he would get the 'bastards who did it'. He seemed to think he knew who it was and that they had in some way taken liberties with him. Later that day he called to tell me the name of the culprit and his address. He would only say that he had 'heard a whisper'.

I went to the address of the suspect with a search warrant and 'turned the place over', in the parlance. There were no stolen televisions in the garage where one might have expected to find them, and the occupier, a well-known CRO, was smug and confident. In the house I searched downstairs and upstairs thoroughly and on top of a wardrobe found a car key. The key, I later found, fitted the stolen van. I have no certain knowledge that the key was 'planted' for me to find, nor who might have planted it, but I have always suspected it was. In any event the thief in due course admitted his guilt and was convicted; the televisions were recovered from an associate's premises.

Many years later I was watching a programme on TV about self-made millionaires and was quite surprised to see my old acquaintance from the TV shop included. He had made his millions from buying and selling second-hand army surplus goods.

Informants and their reward money have got many officers into trouble over the years, and so have women. My advice to all young officers was always to avoid both at all costs. Few took it!

Today it is customary, in fact it's probably in Standing Orders, that a male officer should not go alone to interview a female person for any reason. I don't quarrel with that, although it is one more sad reflection on society that such precautions should be necessary. However it was not always possible to know in advance that you would be seeing a woman on her own. Frequently when calling to see a male suspect or witness, his wife would be in the house alone and in all innocence, or perhaps with ulterior motive, invite you in for a cup of tea.

There was a Jewish gentleman who owned a clothing factory in Harlow and one night it burned to the ground. There was a strong suspicion from the outset that all was not as it should be. The fire brigade was suspicious and so was I. The owner stated among other things that an order for several hundred dresses that had just been completed had been destroyed. There was of course debris in the area where the dresses had been, but no sign of the metal hangers that they were supposed to have been on. The owner and his wife, a rather large blonde woman, fussed around during the examination of the scene, making me even more suspicious that the fire had been set deliberately.

Enquiries led me to believe that the business was in financial trouble and I later interviewed several employees who asserted that there were no dresses made to fulfil this order. Later I rang the gentleman to tell him I would be along to see him later that evening. It was my intention to tell him of my suspicions and test his reaction and in all probability 'nick' him.

I arrived punctually at their rather large house on the outskirts of Harlow. The door was opened by the wife who, for a second, I failed to recognise. She was dressed to kill in a tight-fitting leopardskin playsuit made for someone much younger and much slimmer, and she smelled of exotic perfume. She ushered me into a huge and luxurious lounge and bade me sit on a large settee, in front of which stood a glass topped table with bottles of drink and glasses.

It was only then that she told me her husband was not at home and sat down on the settee. "What will you drink?" she said.

I must say that I have never felt really comfortable in the presence of women, especially women I didn't know, but on this occasion I was terrified. I could only guess at her motive for wanting me to sit beside her and drink. I had visions of her leaping on me just as the door opened to admit her husband, who would make all sorts of accusations and then want to do some sort of deal about his recent arson.

I hope I sounded suave and experienced when I said, "I'll just have to go to my car and tell them I'll be off the air for a while". She grabbed my hand and led me to the door.

"Don't be long," she whispered in my ear.

I got in the car and drove off, leaving a cloud of gravel dust in the air on the drive. Next day at the factory premises, in company with another officer I arrested the owner and he was duly convicted of attempted fraud on his insurance company. I dread to think what might have been the outcome of this enquiry if I had stayed for that drink!

This story reminds me fondly of another businessman I

knew in Harlow. Fred Rollinson, or 'Rolly' as he was known to one and all, was also a Jewish gentleman who ran a small draper's shop in Harlow town centre. I'm sure he or his descendants won't mind my mentioning his name, as I have nothing but good to say about him.

Fred was a sprightly, good-humoured man who liked nothing more than to have a laugh and joke with his customers, most of whom were women. I used to meet him from time to time in the Cock public house at Stock, just outside Harlow. He invariably had a new joke to tell, always about Jewish people and subjects. Some time after the case I have just described came to court, and was therefore in the papers, Fred had this one to tell:

Two Jews met in a pub and were having a drink together when one said to the other, "Izzy, I was so sorry to hear about the fire at your factory".

"Shhh! Shut Up!" said Izzy. "It's not until tomorrow!"

I have no doubt that Fred invented this story for my benefit, but it got laughs all round. I suppose that such jokes would be considered racist if told in a pub or anywhere else today. It raises the question though - would it be racist for a Jew to tell a Jewish joke?

Many of the enquiries undertaken by CID officers involve what is known as 'Obo' or observation. One learns to have a great deal of patience and to take disappointment in your stride. On many occasions 'information received' concerns an event that is to occur sometime in the future, and often the precise details of time are unknown. Watching and waiting is the only answer. Occasionally stolen property or vehicles would be discovered in circumstances that indicated the thief or thieves would be back for them. Once again, waiting and watching was the order of the day.

Harlow was a network of streets criss-crossed with pathways through wooded areas, havens of beauty in the daytime, but ideal places for weirdos and other unsavoury characters to hang about at night. Indecent assaults on women were particularly prevalent in these areas and for this reason, whenever manpower and time was available, these places were watched.

One often sees people interviewed on television asked to relate their most embarrassing moment. It always reminds me of the following story, which is mine.

One night, after a series of particularly nasty indecent assaults on a footpath in one of these wooded areas of Harlow, which was also a cycle track, Mr Bond decided to come out himself and do a bit of 'Obo'. I was chosen to accompany him. The big problem with all observation is concealment, and Ted's car was a bit of a wreck, an old Ford Anglia, and less likely to be spotted than the CID car, so he used that.

We found a secluded spot often used by 'courting couples' for the purpose of whiling away an hour or so, but within sight of a rather dark and lonely pathway. We sat and watched for half an hour before anyone walked past and as soon as they did Ted threw his arms around my neck and said, "Pretend we're a courting couple". My embarrassment was total and for once I was lost for words.

A few nights later an off-duty uniformed Sergeant whose

name was Pete Rison was riding his cycle along this same pathway on his way home. A young woman came running along crying. He asked her what was the matter and she told him that a man had just indecently exposed himself to her. The Sergeant dropped his bicycle and went off in the direction indicated. He found a middle-aged man with his trousers round his ankles busily masturbating just a few yards into the thicket.

Needless to say the man was arrested and brought to the station, where it was found that he had quite severe lacerations and scratches to his legs, penis and testicles. Sergeant Rison explained that the man had tried to resist arrest and had fallen into some bramble bushes, from which he had had to help him out. Justice was often a lot swifter in those days.

Men who expose themselves to women are not criminals, we are told, but rather sick people. However it is a crime and causes some women a good deal of distress - not always, however. Some years later when I was stationed at Chelmsford one of these sick individuals indecently exposed himself to a woman who was a market trader. It was early morning and she was setting out her stall in the market place not far from the old Chelmsford police station. She grabbed the man by his penis and dragged him yelling and screaming to the police station and would not let go until he had been duly handed over to the duty Sergeant.

The man arrested by Pete Rison was not the one responsible for the indecent assaults, who was caught a week or so later, but he did admit to a number of offences of indecently exposing himself. When his home was searched a good deal of ladies' underwear was found in his bedroom, which he later admitted stealing from washing lines. 'Knicker knocking', as this particular crime was called, was very prevalent in Harlow and there were frequent reports of ladies' underwear being stolen in this way. I never came across it anywhere else during my service, nor did I ever discover why.

Harlow New Town was quite different from Romford, an old-established town where all the local villains were well known to the police. In Harlow the vast majority of the inhabitants were from the East London area and a good many of them had criminal records. Many were later to be found to have convictions for murder, manslaughter, robbery with violence, grievous bodily harm, rape and many other serious crimes. None were known to the Harlow police when they arrived in town, and there was no information forthcoming from the police areas whence they came. Such passing on of information about a man's criminal record as a matter of routine just wasn't cricket.

In Romford there had been a 'safe blowing' one night; there were only about three local criminals capable of such a crime, and although they would all have watertight alibis no doubt, it was a place to start: often in Harlow there was no such starting point. Safe cracking with explosives and later with a thermic lance was prevalent in my Harlow days and a lot of hard work and hours of routine enquires had to be made before we began to build up the necessary local knowledge of the criminals on the patch to shortcut some of the footwork. So how does a detective investigate a crime such as burglary?

The work done at the scene of the crime is important, and much information can be obtained and evidence collected from the scene itself. Scene of crime officers dust everything for fingerprints, generally making one hell of a mess, and check for any possible evidence that might later connect a suspect to the scene. I say later, because all the physical evidence in the world is no good to you unless you have a suspect to compare them with.

I once found part of a broken knife blade at the scene of a break-in at a bookmaker's office in Old Harlow. I put it into a small envelope and slipped it into my pocket. I forgot about it for some days until I attended court at Hoddesdon in Hertfordshire, for some reason I can't remember now. There appearing before the Court was one of my local villains, who had been arrested the previous night in the locality and charged with carrying housebreaking implements by night. There on the table in front of the Court were the 'implements', which included a sheath knife with the tip broken off.

He was given a conditional discharge and was about to leave the court with a smug expression on his face when I stopped him and we had a little chat. He denied any knowledge of the offence at the bookmaker's office until I produced the broken blade and fitted it exactly to his sheath knife. He accompanied me back to Harlow and was in due course sent to prison for the burglary. If I recall correctly he had more than twenty other offences taken into consideration.

In my day there was no machine capable of comparing a suspect's fingerprints with marks found at the scene of a crime. This had to be done by hand and by eye by experts at headquarters. If there were marks at the scene that were attributed to a suspect they would be compared with the filed fingerprints of any CRO suspects you might like to pass up to them. The idea that they could or would search the several hundred thousands of fingerprints in the collection was not realistic. All persons who had legitimate access to the attacked premises would be fingerprinted and any marks found to correspond with them eliminated. Any that remained could be regarded as those of a 'suspect'.

Details of any particular modus operandi would be carefully noted. Many criminals leave their trade mark, even those that are wise enough to know they should wear gloves to avoid leaving fingerprints. It is worth knowing that 'glove marks' can sometimes be almost as valuable as a fingerprint, and that with modern science fingerprints have been taken from the inside of a suspect's gloves. Some offenders eat or drink from the refrigerator, others defecate on the premises, and one I knew left a half-eaten apple behind and was later identified by his teeth marks. It is not unknown for a villain to drop something out of his pocket while on the premises; one once left a newspaper with a pencilled number in the corner. Enquiries at local newspaper shops eventually identified the boy who delivered the paper and to whom. Nothing should be overlooked. I am reliably informed that the cursory examination of a crime scene today, if there is one, leaves a lot to be desired.

Witnesses are sought and interviewed, and the aggrieved person questioned at length to establish the times between which the crime took place and details of the stolen property for circulation to adjoining divisions, headquarters and New Scotland Yard, depending on the value and type of property and whether it was identifiable. House-to-house enquiries in the vicinity were always made where possible and details of any suspicious callers, persons or cars seen in the area noted.

Back at the station the paperwork begins, the crime complaint and circulations. The more people know about your crime, the more likely you are to receive a bit of useful information from another police officer or even a member of the public that might help you solve it. There were daily press briefings so that the local press could publish such details as you thought they should have. Obviously there were matters that only you and the burglar knew, and these you had to keep to yourself.

Details would be looked up of any similar crimes or MO and any suspects for those crimes looked into. Places and persons who were habitually offered stolen property, second-hand shops, pawnbrokers, jewellers etc were to be visited as soon as possible and the proprietors warned to be on the lookout. Many of these were not averse to accepting stolen property if they thought it wasn't too hot. By visiting them early they were more inclined to reject any later offered for sale and occasionally, but not often, they came up with some useful information.

After spending most of the day doing the routine enquiries associated with your current investigation, it was the evening when the more specialised job of detecting came into its own. Detectives used to work what were called 'discretionary' hours. This would usually be from 9am to 1pm, 2pm until 5pm and 7pm until 11pm, or on occasions much later. There was no 'overtime' paid for the extra hours worked and, apart from the meagre CID allowance, the only satisfaction you got from the sometimes long hours was a job well done and a prisoner or two at the end of an enquiry. This sort of existence was not conducive to a happy married life, as many CID officers have discovered. Happily that is one drawback to being a detective that has been removed with the modern idea that detectives should work a 35-hour week. On the other side of the coin very little real detective work gets done!

The evening was the time when you visited the local pubs and hostelries to find out what was going on in your manor. Informants, such as there were, might be promised vast rewards for information, and rivalries between local villains and associates exploited. Within a comparatively short time at Harlow I began to find that I had quite a few contacts who had information about the activities of local young thieves. The more serious criminals who lived in Harlow generally committed their crimes elsewhere on the basis that you don't foul your own doorstep.

Our local thieves at Harlow were usually between fifteen and twenty years of age, occasionally younger. Drugs were not a motive for committing crime then, as they are today, but rather cash and the sheer excitement of breaking and entering seemed to be what motivated them. There were still one or two older and more experienced 'burglars' and old lags still around and one got to be on nodding acquaintance terms with them.

When you did get a suspect it was usual to persuade him to come to the station, where you could interview him on your own ground with all the tricks of your trade at your disposal.

I frequently smile when I hear the expression, "Helping the police with their enquiries". They are words used by the press who for some reason are reluctant to say that a man has been detained on suspicion etc. Many of the people who are arrested on suspicion are released again and are quite innocent of any crime. Those suspects who are guilty of a crime are usually not helping the police at all, and on the contrary they are often making our lives very difficult.

'Interrogation of a suspect' is an art which some never acquire and others find a natural talent. There is a misconception amongst members of the public, and particularly politicians, that a guilty suspect will quite readily admit his crime and that no pressure is needed, or should be permitted, to induce a confession. It is also presumed it seems that to caution a man that he need not say anything will not be any obstacle to the policeman trying to detect the author of a crime. How then do they at the same time expect results?

In many instances of crime the police officer knows for certain who the perpetrator is, sometimes because of the MO, sometimes because of information he has received from an informant who was present when the crime was committed or for some other reason that cannot be disclosed or given in evidence. In such cases the only way to secure a conviction is to get a confession.

In training school you are taught all the rules about interrogating suspects, that the object of an interrogation is to 'obtain the truth' not to obtain a confession. In the real world you learn some tricks of the trade. It's fine when you have caught the guilty one red-handed or have real hard evidence to put to him, but I am referring now to the cases when a confession is the only way you are going to get your man to court.

The fact that you have the suspect in a police station is some help, because there you can begin to build up that 'mental ascendancy' which is necessary to begin your interrogation. You have to learn to talk to the suspect in his own language; it's not a bit of good calling a local market trader 'sir' or the bank manager 'mate'. Telling lies to a suspect is usually unwise; if he is the perpetrator he will know they are lies. He, of course, can tell you as many lies as he likes, and proving to him that he has lied might help, but is not evidence of his guilt. So how do you start with such constraints imposed upon you?

All questioning of suspects is governed by what are called the Judges' Rules. These were rules invented by certain judges years ago and were supposed to stop all the arguments about whether anything said by a suspect was admissible or not. Far from it, they only gave the legal profession more words whose meanings could be argued about. The first rule says that a police officer may question any person he thinks might be able to assist him when he is "trying to find the author of a crime". How nicely they put it. The next rule says you must tell him he needn't answer your questions. A bit silly really, don't you think?

Each case is quite a different challenge, and you have to

call upon all your experience and knowledge of the criminal mind to decide where to begin. The petty thief is a far cry from the hardened robber, rapist or murderer. For the most part you hope to trick him into an admission which you can then develop into a full-blown confession. Having put to the suspect some details of what it is he is accused of and getting the usual denial, the road ahead is like tramping through a minefield. Everything you say or do from now on is likely to be challenged as undue pressure.

"Come on, your mate has confessed, it will be better for you to do the same." A common ploy, often untrue, and not very likely to work. If it does it will surely be challenged as 'undue pressure' at court. If a defence solicitor knows that the only evidence against his client is a confession, you are in for a real pasting at court and chances are the case will get thrown out. No doubt that is why such interviews must now be recorded, videoed, witnessed and usually carried out in the presence of a solicitor for the accused. This innovation, while it might prevent confession being thrown out, does seriously reduce your chances of getting one in the first place.

As for beating a confession out of a prisoner, well what chance would you have of getting away with it? What good would it do in the furtherance of your case? And why do accused persons still make such allegations? All good questions.

One good thing about English law that hasn't yet been changed is that if physical evidence is obtained by unlawful means, it still remains 'evidence' and can be produced in court. So if under intense pressure the accused makes a confession in which he tells you where the stolen property is hidden, or gives other information which can corroborate his confession, then you are 'home and dry' as they say, or you have a 'result'. This is not so in America, where they have an expression "Probable Cause" so that if say a murder weapon is found during a search of a car, person or premises where there was no 'Probable Cause', this evidence would be excluded and the accused probably acquitted.

One trick that was surprisingly successful with petty thieves was to exaggerate the amount of money stolen, or in the case of an assault the seriousness of the injury.

"What have you done with the diamonds?" Might, with luck, receive the response, "There were no bloody diamonds!"

"The woman has serious head injuries and may die" might get a response like, "But I only pushed her, it was an accident". If you were lucky!

I have heard of various stories in my younger days of prisoners being taken before a mock court in the middle of the night and sentenced to imprisonment, of a doctor being called (a police officer in a white coat) to certify a suspect as insane. All in the name of 'interrogation of a suspect'. There was even one accused who said the Chief Inspector had played Russian Roulette with the gun pointed at his head, in order to get him to confess. How ridiculous!

The difference between arresting a man on suspicion and asking him to come to the station for an interview is largely an administrative matter. It can also involve the law, since to arrest on suspicion you generally have to have what our law calls 'reasonable suspicion'. Today, as the result of PACE, 'reasonable suspicion' means 'evidence'.

If you arrested a person on suspicion then he would have to be booked in by the duty Sergeant and duly processed. Getting him to come in voluntarily was a way of avoiding this procedure. The real test of whether a man is under arrest or not is whether you would allow him to get up and walk out of the police station. Generally the answer to that question is no, but fortunately I never had to put it to the test.

When you were questioning a person there might, and frequently did, come a point when you were pretty sure you had the right man. The question of the caution then arose, since if you later sought to give in evidence something the accused has said by way of confession it was likely to be ruled inadmissible unless it was said after caution.

Officially you only had to caution a suspect when you had evidence that he was guilty, so you could question him for hours without caution if he kept denying the offence, but had to caution him when he made an admission, if that was the only evidence you had.

On the other hand if you knew there were fingerprints or other evidence such as property found in his possession that linked him to the crime, you would have to caution him before asking any questions. This technicality often caused difficulties, which could usually be ironed out later when you made up your notes, but gave defence counsel in court hours of amusement.

There were no taped interviews or video recordings of interviews with suspects in my Harlow days and officers were trusted to make up their notebooks honestly and accurately. As time went by and more and more officers were accused of doctoring their notes, and technology improved which could sometimes prove this, there had to be a change. Many a guilty man would have got away with his crime had not officers manipulated their notes. Today many a guilty man is freed because they are no longer able to. The righteous would say that it is better that a hundred guilty men go free than an innocent one be wrongly convicted. Many, especially victims of serious crimes, would not agree. In 30 years I never heard of a truly innocent man being convicted. I did hear of a lot of guilty ones being found not guilty!

After you had charged your suspect, there were fingerprints to take descriptive forms to fill in, more circulations and then antecedents to prepare. You might think that was the end of the matter, but then there was the court hearing.

Many of the more minor offences, and juveniles generally, were tried by the Magistrates at the Magistrates' Court and one regularly attended there. In the case of a guilty plea, no evidence had to be given by witnesses, but the officer in the case, usually the detective, had to give antecedents to assist the court to come to its decision on sentence.

Antecedents were a potted history of the accused, including his jobs and his criminal record. Each of his last three or four employers had to be contacted and the antecedents contained details of why the convicted man had left. The antecedents usually finished with a summary of his financial situation, debts, income and weekly outgoings. As the law stands a jury, and in the case of the Magistrates' Court the Magistrates, are not supposed to know a man's previous convictions, or even if he has any or not, before a conviction. This whole subject is an absolute farce and at the end of a trial of several days, if a member of any jury doesn't 'know' or reasonably suspect that the man in the dock is a regular 'villain' then he must be a bit thick. As far as magistrates are concerned, with the same local villains coming before them on a regular basis, they too 'know'. If they don't then there are ways and means of having them find out in the magistrate's retiring room as I discovered at Harwich (see Chapter Nine).

It has always seemed strange to me that when a man is convicted in court the full details of his name, address and particulars of his crime can be, and usually are, published in a newspaper, yet only a short time afterwards such details are a closely guarded secret on a police computer. Why should an honest person who contemplates employing someone in a position of trust be prevented from finding out whether the prospective employee is trustworthy?

Once a month one would have to attend Quarter Sessions at Chelmsford and occasionally Assizes for the purpose either of giving evidence in a case or to give 'antecedents' in guilty pleas. Each detective would have a dark suit kept especially for Quarter Sessions, referred to as his 'sessions suit'. Many hours of police time were wasted in this routine administrative task, but the judge liked to see the officer there and be able to ask him questions. Now there is an officer permanently stationed at Crown Court to whom all antecedents are sent. It saves a lot of time, but it was always a great day out and lunch was on expenses.

'Not guilty' pleas were less common, but when a

defendant was facing a possible prison sentence it was often worth his while to elect trial, plead not guilty and try his luck with a jury who were considered to be less streetwise than the magistrates. A magistrate might have seen the face of a defendant many times before!

This advantage held by magistrates didn't apply to jury members, who I have occasionally heard gasp with surprise when, after deliberating for hours and hours about whether to convict, they hear a string of previous convictions for similar crimes read out by the detective in the case. A defence counsel had to be careful when defending a man with a bad record, because if he attacked the character of any prosecution witness, including the police officer, by suggesting he is not telling the truth, the judge might allow the previous convictions of his client to be put to the jury before they retired. You did not need to be a particularly good judge of character to see from a defendant's demeanour that he was 'an old lag.' Many had the letters l.o.v.e. and h.a.t.e. tattooed on their fingers; a sure sign they had been to Borstal.

During my time at Harlow I studied for my 'promotion exams'. There were two exams, one for Sergeant and one for Inspector. The exams were in two parts a 'Police Duties' exam and a general exam, which included subjects like English, Geography, Maths and General Knowledge. You were allowed to take the general exam for Inspector when you were still a constable, but not the Police Duties; it was only when you were a Sergeant that you could take that.

I passed the 'Police Duties' exams to Sergeant at the second attempt and the general subjects to Inspector first try.

It required more than a year's study, when not a lot of free time was available. Having passed the exams you would have to pass a 'Board' before you could hope to be promoted. The board consisted of the Chief Constable, your own Chief Superintendent and one from elsewhere. The Chief Constable usually asked you about your career so far and where you aimed to get. Your own Chief Superintendent might ask a few questions about general police duties and your views on certain matters, and the outside Superintendent was primed to ask a question about some obscure piece of recent legislation he was sure you wouldn't have a clue about.

I duly appeared before the Board at Harlow Divisional Headquarters. I was summoned and went in just as DC Ron Stark came out. He was a regular visitor to the board but had so far failed to impress them. When I entered and stood to attention before the Chief Constable, John Nightingale, he eventually looked up from his file: my file!

"We've just been talking to Detective Constable Stark" he said. "He complains that he has too much work to do. Are you going to tell me you have too much to do?"

"No sir," I said. "Of course I have enough to do and keep very busy but don't find it too much." Perhaps foolishly, I added, "I am hoping that one day all my efforts will be rewarded with promotion and then perhaps I won't be so busy".

The Chief let out a great guffaw, looked at Fred Pettengel and said, "He's after your job, Chief Superintendent".

At the time I was wearing a small lapel badge of the

Home Made Wine Makers' Guild to which I belonged at the time.

"What's that badge?" the Chief asked.

We spent the next ten minutes discussing homemade wine and I thought I was getting away very lightly, especially when the Chief looked at Fred Pettengel and said, "I don't suppose there's anything you want to ask him is there?"

Fred shook his head. The chief asked the same question to the other Superintendent, one Willis Vickers, whom I got to know better a year or so later.

"Just one" he said, "What's the maximum width of a caravan permitted under the new Construction and Use Regulations?"

"I haven't the foggiest idea," was my reply.

I was duly dismissed, feeling a little disappointed and thinking I had probably blown it. When I returned to the office Ron Stark told me to ring headquarters, as Jack Barkway the Detective Chief Superintendent wanted to speak to me. I lifted the phone with some trepidation, trying to think what I had done that warranted the Detective Chief Superintendent's personal attention.

He answered the phone, "Barkway!"

"DC Raven here sir."

"Oh yes" he said, "I just wanted to ask you what do you think of your posting up here to the Fraud Squad?"

"Sorry sir, but I don't know anything about it."

"Haven't you just been in with Mr Pettengel?"

"Yes sir, but he didn't mention it".

"I seem to have done it again," said Mr Barkway. "Well

you're promoted to Detective Sergeant and are coming up here to the Fraud Squad. Don't say anything to anyone until Mr Pettengel informs you officially."

"Thank you sir!"

When I eventually left Harlow I was called into the Magistrates' Court one morning before the Chairman of the Bench. He praised my work in the Division and said that the public of Harlow was sorry to see me go and wished me every success in the future. I felt my face redden with a mixture of pride and embarrassment and sheepishly thanked him and departed.

# Headquarters (Fraud Squad) 1961–1964

*It was beautiful and simple as all truly great swindles are - Gentle Grafter (1908) 'Octopus Marooned', O. Henry*

When I first joined the police force it was with no thought of promotion in mind. I wanted to be a detective, and was quite sure in my mind that I was capable of achieving such status. I was also determined that if I did not become a detective within four years, I would leave the force and seek my fortune elsewhere.

Elevation to the Fraud Squad was for me a very good step in the right direction. I was not aware of it at the time, but in hindsight I couldn't have had a better move.

The Fraud Squad was at the time a small section of men stationed at Police Headquarters Chelmsford, who while having the title Fraud Squad, also assisted in all major investigations, including murders, which were undertaken-in the county. Jack Barkway was the Detective Chief Superintendent, and his deputy was Detective Chief Inspector Harry Burden. They were both officers of long and great experience and in whom all of us had great confidence. The officers of the Fraud Squad were, it seems, his handpicked men upon whom he felt he could rely to perform the many sometimes long and often tricky, enquiries that were required to be carried out at Headquarters, rather than on Divisions.

Arriving at police headquarters was quite a different experience from arriving at a divisional station which represented the front line of policing. Headquarters was, one soon discovered, a hive of mainly senior officers and civilian staff, whose job it was to run the police force. The administration of the force was of course a major part of the function of headquarters, with departments controlling personnel, finance, records, training school, garages and so on. Overall policy on policing matters is the responsibility of the Chief Constable, aided by his heads of CID, Admin, Traffic etc.

An interesting little snippet comes to mind about the training school. They had a museum there containing many items of interest concerning the history of the force, one of them a revolver. One famous murder case from the archives of the Essex police history was the murder in 1927 of PC George Gutteridge. After shooting him dead, the murderer fired a bullet into each of his eyes, believing, it seemed, that the last image a person saw was recorded in the eye and could have perhaps identified him. Of course scientific advances had hardly reached that far then and probably never will. However the gun in the museum was labelled as the gun used in this killing. Some years later when I visited Scotland Yard's famous 'Black Museum', I saw an identical gun there labelled in the same manner. I never discovered which was the real gun. I am sure it is ours, but it was one more reason for me not to be too ready to believe what I was told by the Metropolitan Police.

At the time of my arrival on the Fraud Squad the Chief Constable, John Nightingale, a Trenchard Scheme man, would remain our boss for quite a few years more. He would later be knighted, as was the hope, vain in most cases, of all the subsequent Chief Constables we had during my service. There was also a Deputy Chief Constable as one might expect, and later several Assistants, but, as I later found out myself, deputies are pretty insignificant, so much so that I can't even remember the man's name. When I left the force I had lost count of the number of Assistant Chief Constables who had arrived on the scene and departed again. Empire building it seems was beginning, and each year Chief Constables would ask for more money and more senior ranks to control more or less the same number of constables and sergeants.

The force did grow, it is true, but the ratio between the number of chiefs and the number of Indians became bigger. I always found it odd that if the workload of a department became bigger the first priority was for another chief, not another Indian. Perhaps I was right, because for the last several years to my knowledge the trend has been the reverse. For a while all ranks preceded by the word 'Chief' all but disappeared and Divisional Commanders were all Superintendents. This didn't last too long however, and pressure from somewhere has reinstated Chief Superintendents as Divisional Commanders. I suppose it did seem a little dotty to have a Divisional Commander and his deputy both in the same rank.

Also at headquarters there were the more obvious 'police' rather than 'admin' departments such as the Fingerprint, Photographic and Scenes of Crime Departments under Chief Inspector Edwards, Criminal Records, with PC Patmore and the headquarters of the Traffic Division, which covered the whole of the county, and was not a territorial division in the same way as the other operational divisions. The Fraud Squad was a relatively new department, and in reality was just a small squad of detectives available for any task that the Detective Chief Superintendent required done under his immediate control.

Life at headquarters did not revolve around the day-to-day task of policing as I had been used to. With a large number of relatively senior personnel there were a lot more changes in personnel going on, with officers moving on to higher posts and others vying for their jobs. The day-to-day general conversation was not, as it had been on Division, "Who do you think committed such and such a crime?" but rather, "Who do you think is going to be the new Traffic Superintendent?"

Other moves and promotions of divisional personnel, such as my own, were discussed openly in canteens as well as behind the closed doors of the Chief Constable's office.

One officer in particular, Sergeant Roy Bloodworth, who headed the photographic section, always seemed to know in advance who was going to be promoted. We used to think that when his openly discussed forecasts of who was going to be promoted reached the Chief's ears it would somehow sow a seed in his mind and in some subliminal way he would recommend that person for promotion. Roy was quite proud of his reputation; it was quite uncanny!

I was aware after a very short time at headquarters that you had to 'watch your back'. Jealousy and pettiness abounded in the 'corridors of power' with many lesser mortals trying by fair means or foul to curry favour with the bosses. Some of the senior officers, I believe the Chief Constable himself was one of them, abhorred these 'arsehole crawlers' as they were known, but they were there nevertheless and some senior officers were impressed by them.

There was one officer I had known as a Sergeant who took seven attempts to pass his promotion exams and had very little to distinguish him from a thousand other policemen, yet he reached a very senior rank in the police service. It was not because he did anything especially good, but because of the way he always made those serving alongside him, and later beneath him, look foolish or inefficient. He was the head of the 'hindsight brigade' and made a speciality of telling his chief, whoever that might be at the time, what went wrong, whose fault it was and what he would have done if it had been left to him.

It behove one therefore to keep one's eye over your shoulder while walking these corridors of power, as there was usually someone there stalking in your footsteps hoping to get your job or to prevent you getting a promotion before them. I remember one such man, senior to me at the time, who took a report I had submitted, retyped the last page and signed it himself. I was surprised one morning to hear him being congratulated by the Chief Superintendent on a good DPP report. When I tackled him about it, he said that there had been some typing mistakes and that he had had it retyped. Then as I wasn't available and the report was required urgently, he signed it. It didn't wash with me and I never did trust that officer again.

A report that was going to the Director of Public Prosecutions (a DPP report) was always one with which you took particular care. Certain offences could, by law, only be prosecuted with the consent of the DPP, and such a report had to contain a summary of all the evidence and contain suggestions and recommendations. They were often lengthy and complicated, and all such reports submitted from divisional officers had to be vetted at headquarters. One wondered how many other good reports this man and perhaps others had taken the credit for.

However, being at headquarters had its good side too. You were at the hub of things and in a position to impress those in charge of you with your good work. You could just as easily of course tread on the wrong toes.

Once you had your foot on the bottom rung of your personal promotion ladder there were only two ways you could go, upwards and sideways. If you passed your exams and kept your nose clean, chances are you would make

Inspector in three or four years. If you offended in any way you could get a sideways move and someone would pass you on your ladder. A sideways move usually meant a move to another station or department with the same rank.

There was one other type of move that was known as a 'career move'. It was widely propagated that to reach high rank one should have experience in many departments. It was, I was frequently told as my career developed, necessary for CID officers to return to uniform for a spell in order to expect promotion to the hierarchy of the CID. While I did see some cases that tended to bear this out, I also saw many others that contradicted it. It is difficult to know whether this type of move was always genuine or whether a sideways move was sometimes disguised as a career move to soften the blow to the individual.

Detective Inspector Harry Batson headed the Fraud Squad. There were three detective sergeants, Chalky White, whom I knew at Romford and have mentioned earlier, Peter Joslin and Alfred Mitchell. I was to replace DS White, who remained only long enough to hand over to me his ongoing cases. Later there was another officer attached to us, Sergeant Colin Woodford.

Chalky White went on to become Detective Chief Superintendent in Essex and later a Divisional Commander. Peter Joslin became the Chief Constable of Warwickshire and Alf Mitchell an Assistant Chief Constable of Derbyshire. Colin Woodford studied law and left the force early to become a barrister and later a Recorder; he was killed in a road accident while still quite young. Me? Well that is what this book is about isn't it?

Peter Joslin, Alf Mitchell and I all studied for our promotion exams to Inspector together. We used to go back to the office at night, where there were reference books available, and quiz each other on matters we thought might come up in the exam. Colin Woodford was a loner and studied on his own. When we all passed we were all on a level footing as far as promotion was concerned. Having been promoted to Sergeant, one naturally began to think about the future and how far one might get. From then on a bit of luck and perhaps a bit of grovelling was all that was necessary to make it to the top. There were other matters that could limit how far one could climb up the ladder of success which I will be discussing in a future chapter.

Harry Julian Batson, his full name, was one of the most remarkable men I have ever met. He was at the time the youngest man ever to have been promoted to Inspector in the force and one would have thought destined for very high rank indeed. He was a brilliant detective and had the ability to concentrate on several subjects at once. He was relatively small in stature and must have stood on tiptoe to pass the minimum five foot ten inches height requirement for entry into the force. He was immaculate in his dress, and usually wore a British Warm Cashmere overcoat with a bowler hat. He carried a rolled umbrella and pig skin briefcase. He drove a brand new Ford Corsair, the very thing on those days – rented of course! He was efficiency personified.

Harry could be relied upon to get a job done and done well. He loved being in charge of his own department and was an officer we all looked up to from a work point of view, although none of us were persuaded to buy bowler hats. He did however persuade us to get contract hire cars, since we all had now a motor car allowance. The allowance just about paid the rental and we would then all appear a little cut above the rest when we appeared on Divisions in pursuance of our important work.

Harry was dedicated to the oath he had taken to carry out his duties without fear or favour. This and his desire to be in charge were probably the reasons he didn't make high rank. In theory a constable of whatever rank could decide to arrest any person he had reason to believe had committed a crime. Does that mean you can arrest half a dozen county councillors for fiddling their expenses? As I said before, 'Yes - in theory!'

Apart from the Lord Lieutenant, councillors and particularly County Councillors are probably some of the most influential members of society. The Police Committee, who appointed John Nightingale, comprises County Councillors, and the Chief Constable, while not answerable to them for police operational matters, is nevertheless quite naturally known personally to many of them professionally and socially. It is hardly surprising that when Harry arrested several of their number as they were walking down the steps of County Hall, it did not go down to well in the corridors of power and the Chief's telephone must have been red hot within minutes.

This was the first example I ever saw of a police officer's powers being subverted because of internal politics. In Harry's case it didn't actually succeed because he had acted first and told his senior officer second. I was to see many other examples of political expediency superseding the strict enforcement of the law, and to fall foul of it myself in due course. I learned a lot from Harry Batson, but unfortunately did not learn, as he too should have learned, that to be a successful senior officer, if not necessarily a good one, you should also be a politician, and be able to eat humble pie even when you know you are right.

Those that put Harry Batson in charge of the Fraud Squad failed to take into account his devotion to duty and the likelihood that he would not be amenable to internal politics. He was eventually given a sideways move to serve as Detective Inspector under the formidable Detective Chief Inspector 'Trunky' Sewell at Basildon. It was a cruel move. Perhaps the powers that be thought that 'Trunky' could tame him.

'Trunky' Sewell was famous in the force at that time for his dealings with a murder case known as the Pitsea Houseboat Murders. He was a detective of the old school and a law unto himself. It was said that his left hand never knew what his right hand was doing. Those who had served under him will vouch for that, and that he was a thief catcher par excellence. His methods would not always bear too much scrutiny however, and he and Harry Batson were like chalk and cheese. Anyone who knew either of these men must have known there would be problems between them. There were! Harry stood it for a while but resigned soon afterwards, a sad loss to the force. He became a successful private investigator in Peterborough.

So to the Fraud Squad. We were a pretty mixed bunch

but all got along well together. Each of us had his own cases to deal with and we would arrive at nine in the morning, discuss what we intended to do that day with Harry Batson, and then drive off in our new cars in various directions to various destinations in the county.

Fraud was considered to be too complicated or too long and drawn out for a divisional officer to undertake. This seemed reasonable, as divisional officers, with their busy caseloads, would have little time to take the many statements, sometimes hundreds of them, necessary in some fraud cases. At headquarters too we were only walking distance from the County Prosecuting Solicitor's office and many fraud cases required constant discussion with a solicitor on some of the more complicated points of law.

In addition to fraud our office dealt with stolen motor cars, which might, and often did, lead to a fraud investigation, and the misuse of drugs, although that was in its infancy then.

A fraud might be anything from a loan club treasurer running off at Christmas with all the funds (there was always one of those somewhere in the county at Christmas) to a building society going broke in suspicious circumstances. Any such crime that was reported at divisional level would be passed to the Fraud Squad by way of report, and Harry Batson would decide whether it was a proper case for us to investigate. Often however it would be reported direct to headquarters by a letter to the Chief Constable. In such a case we had no option but to deal with it.

I dealt with a fair number of fraud cases during my first spell on the Fraud Squad. I realised at an early stage that unlike the Metropolitan Fraud Squad, we did not have the benefit of trained accountants to assist us. Accounts frequently figured in such cases, so I resolved to remedy my ignorance of double-entry book keeping and did a correspondence course. Whenever a Fraud Squad Officer was ushered into a Managing Director's office to be appraised of the missing thousands, he was expected to understand the jargon and grasp the situation in an instant. At first I didn't know the difference between a balance sheet and an annual statement.

Fortunately Harry Batson, complete with briefcase, bowler hat and rolled umbrella, usually came to that first interview himself, to assess the seriousness of the case and to decide whether he should personally take it on. While I was sitting there desperately trying to follow him through the maze of words and figures Harry was nodding confidently and giving the appearance of understanding completely the complexity of the matter.

After that came the long process of taking statements from all those involved, except of course the alleged perpetrator. There is one important difference between fraud and other types of crime. When a crime is reported, generally you know exactly what it is that has been done: a burglary, robbery, assault etc. What you generally don't know is who did it. That will be the main thrust of your investigation. With fraud you almost always know immediately who is alleged to have committed the crime. What you often don't know is what crime has been committed, how it was committed or even if there has been a crime at all. The process of collecting evidence, mainly documentary, and witness statements is lengthy and can take several months or even years.

Taking a statement in a simple case is relatively easy; you know what crime is alleged and the points to prove, so you cover all those points in the statement. When you don't know what crime will finally be alleged or an accused charged with, you have to cover all possibilities. Otherwise you will be forever going back to get additional statements covering the points you overlooked the first time. Statements in fraud cases therefore can be long and detailed and sometimes take several hours to complete. Often a witness might refer to a large number of different documents and each has to be numbered and referenced in the statement.

When you have taken statements from everyone who you think can give any evidence or information, you have to sit down and decide where that evidence points. Often it is time to go to talk over the matter with your friendly County Prosecuting Solicitor (CPS). This should not be confused with today's CPS, which stands for Crown Prosecution Service, a whole different can of worms!

The CPS was based at Chelmsford and when I first arrived there it was a Mr Jones who had a staff of five or six solicitors. His clerk was one Peter Palmer, who probably knew more law than all the solicitors put together. He was a brilliant man and always ready at the end of the telephone to give help and advice. He would usually read your bulky file in record time and give an immediate decision.

The solicitors employed by the CPS were generally young men who had recently qualified. In the legal profession, unless you have a relative in the business, have qualified with exceptionally high marks or have lots of money, you generally have to take what work you can get. The CPS tended to get those who couldn't get a better job elsewhere. I don't say they were not good solicitors, but they certainly weren't the best, nor the most experienced, and they were often no match for the legal brains which even moderately successful criminals could afford.

There was the occasional exception, one of which was young Mr Bates. What he didn't have in stature and experience he made up for in guile. When defending a villain a solicitor would often quote some obscure piece of case law in favour of his client's defence. He had had weeks to look up such cases and prepare a defence. This would usually stump the CPS, who had probably seen the file of papers on the case for the prosecution only that same morning. Mr Bates, however, would jump to his feet immediately.

"There is a more recent case" he would say, "Smith v Jones" (for example). "Where in a case on all fours with this one it was ruled that…"This was usually enough to shoot down the defence in flames, and often we would get our conviction.

Afterwards I once asked him, "Where did you dig that case up? I've never heard of it".

"Oh that!" he said. "I just made it up." Living proof that there is something in the old adage that 'bullshit baffles brains'.

Together with Peter Palmer one would decide upon the charges which were made out by the evidence and plan the next stage of the enquiry accordingly, quite often an interview with the accused. The amount of evidence required was in the region of 95%. If it looked like there was a reasonable chance of a conviction we would proceed. It was always considered that the police had a duty to bring a suspect before the court if the evidence against him showed that there was a case to answer. It was a matter for the court to judge if the evidence proved the case beyond reasonable doubt. It was not the job of the police nor of the CPS to determine the case and decide on guilt or innocence. Nor was it policy to decide against a prosecution for reasons of political expediency, the likely cost to the taxpayer or any of the other reasons that are often today used by the Crown Prosecution Service to justify taking no action in a case the police have worked long and hard to prepare.

It was believed then that even if a chap did get away with at court, the experience of having been there probably did him a lot of good. In any case justice was supposed to be seen to be done!

It may be of interest that the Crown Prosecution Service is now a national rather than a local body. They still employ solicitors who lack experience and who have largely taken over that part of a police officer's role inherent in the definition of constable, "The prosecution of offenders against the peace". In my time I could take out a summons against a member of the public without reference to the CPS if I wished - not any more. The newspapers every day print details of cases that have resulted in acquittals or serious criticism of the police. Then there are others they have failed to prosecute, and one can only hazard a guess as to why.

Incidentally the criticism of the police is usually quite

unjustified, since the decision to prosecute is no longer theirs to take and should properly be directed at the Crown Prosecution Service, who are happy to skulk in the background. I don't know what amount of proof the CPS requires these days to take a case to court, but I do know that they will not prosecute a case if there is the slightest chance of an acquittal. They have taken on the role of judge as well as prosecuting solicitor, merely to save expense, for fear of criticism, or for any other reason you might think of. It seems that the first thing you have to do if you are ever unfortunate enough to get arrested is to make a complaint against the police. The chances are very high that you will not get prosecuted!

An interview with the accused was normally a lengthy business. Arrangements would be made with him or her to attend, and often he would turn up at the police station with his solicitor. Unlike the interviews I had had with accused persons up till now, these were well planned in advanced and the questions all typed out in the form of a questionnaire. Beside each question would be a list of the relevant documents he would be shown. His answers were carefully written down and afterwards he would be invited to sign each answer. This questionnaire would become a most important exhibit in the case and counsel would spend hours picking it to pieces and putting a spin on what was meant by a certain answer. A comma or full stop in the wrong place could be important.

A simple example of how words can sound rather than how they are written is usually given at training school. An officer giving evidence said, "I put it to him, your honour, cautioned him and he replied, 'I did it'". The accused version was that he had said in amazement, "I did it?"

During my time on the Fraud Squad I spent a lot of time in court. Most fraud cases were tried by jury at either Quarter Sessions or the Assize Court. These cases tended to last for weeks or even months and could be boring at times. The police in such cases were allowed to hire counsel and some of those employed by the CPS were excellent. Listening to learned counsel arguing a case in court has always fascinated me and I realised then that it was little more than a theatre. The judge and counsel for prosecution and defence had the leading roles and the defendant and witnesses were merely the rest of the cast. Each counsel would try to score points off the other as if playing a game, and neither really had any regard or genuine concern for the accused, the victim or the witnesses; the object was to win the game at all costs. There were often the odd chuckles at remarks that were made and even the occasional guffaw, usually known as the 'titter that ran round the court'.

There was a system of 'dock briefs' in those days. Any defendant who didn't have counsel could choose any barrister who was present in the court to represent him, provided that person was not engaged in another case that particular moment. Whenever a defendant was 'put up' for the purpose of choosing a dock brief there would be a quick exodus from the court of any counsel that didn't want the job.

On one occasion there was a young counsel, fresh from his bar exams and with a nice new clean wig, sitting in court and he was chosen by a defendant who was charged with burglary. He was an old lag and no doubt thought he could get away with the offence for which he was charged, as the main evidence was of identification. The young counsel went down to the cells for a brief interview with 'matey' and came back again to plead him 'not guilty'. The case commenced and the various witnesses were called to prove that the accused had entered the house in question and gone into a woman's bedroom and she had woken up, screamed and chased him off. Eventually the woman was called and gave her evidence; she identified the accused as the man she had seen and whom she had later picked out at an identification parade. The young barrister cross-examined.

"I put it to you madam that you couldn't possibly have seen my client's face as the bedroom light was out."

The judge intervened, "Are these your client's instructions?"

"Yes my lord" still the penny hadn't dropped.

The judge went on, "I think you had better go and have another word with him, I'm sure he might want to alter his plea". A titter ran round the Court!

The young barrister looked a little perplexed, until it dawned on him that his client couldn't possibly have known the light was out if he hadn't been there. There was a short adjournment before a plea of 'guilty' was entered and the case concluded very quickly.

Because of the amount of time spent on fraud enquiries, the time spent in court and in dealing with other matters, the Fraud Squad got a reputation of taking an eternity to conclude their investigations and get cases to court. This was true, but it was to be quite a few years before this situation was remedied with more fraud investigators. Because of this it was often decided to advise the aggrieved to seek civil remedy rather than to spend a great deal of time on the matter.

There was a time when, if you paid a bill with a cheque knowing you hadn't funds in the bank, you almost certainly would receive a visit from a detective and a fair chance you would end up in court. Now you will be told to seek civil remedy. It is still a crime, however!

When Chalky White handed over to me his outstanding cases, they were by and large complete; there was one however that was not. On a shelf in his office were a dozen or so box files full of statements and documents relating to what had become known as the Fisher Case. It was a case that was growing whiskers and for at least two years various officers had had a go at it. No one really knew how to finish it or write it off.

There was at the time a very complicated piece of law within the Larceny Act of 1916. It related to two crimes called False Pretences and Credit by Fraud. The subtle differences in these two crimes had been greatly amplified over the years by the dozens and dozens of cases that had been decided in the High Court. As fast as there was one decision that looked as if it had settled the matter, there was another that contradicted it. It was a fascinating subject and whole books have been written about it. The case of Raven v Fisher has been well documented, so I can safely mention the name of the defendant, who was in any case eventually cleared of all charges.

Maurice Fisher was a Jewish gentleman who travelled

around the Home Counties in a smart car visiting farms, usually owned by quite wealthy landowners and farmers. He would present himself as being from the 'farming world' and offer to produce a magnificent oil painting from their favourite snapshot or photograph. Many such prospective victims had a favourite horse or dog, but there were many other subjects to choose from. Fisher was well spoken and always well dressed. He had with him samples of his work and was a very plausible chap indeed.

There is a magazine called *Farming World*, although Fisher didn't actually say he was employed by the magazine and much later at court he always asserted that he meant he was from 'the farming world' as his father had been a farmer. He managed to persuade many people to part with sums up to £200 as a deposit and took away their snapshots. There were hundreds of statements from persons who had reported Fisher to the police. Many of them never saw him again. Some did get a painting but were most dissatisfied with it; none ever got their money back. There were the names and addresses of many others who had made similar reports, but who had been advised that it was a civil dispute and there was nothing the police could do about it.

As a newcomer to the Fraud Squad I was not too busy for the first few weeks, and spent a lot of time looking through the Fisher file. It was clear to me that the man had obtained a very large sum of money from a lot of people, and that he had done so dishonestly. Whether it was false pretences, credit by fraud or whatever I knew not, but I felt that something should be done about it. I took many more statements and eventually put together a file and produced a schedule of the offences, times, dates; places and the amounts obtained and went to have a chat with Peter Palmer. Meantime I had discovered that Fisher was an undischarged bankrupt, something that no one had known before.

It was decided that we should charge Fisher with thirty-two counts, sixteen relating to obtaining money by false pretences and sixteen alternative charges, but on the same facts, of obtaining credit while an undischarged bankrupt. Fisher was summoned to the Chelmsford Magistrates Court and committed for trial.

The case eventually came before the Essex Quarter Sessions. All charges before Quarter Sessions or Assizes are vetted by the Indictment Clerk, who decided in this case that there should be thirty-two separate counts on the indictment, and that the bankruptcy charges were not to be regarded as alternatives but as separate charges.

The trial lasted several months, the court was filled with large framed atrocious oil paintings that Fisher had hurriedly delivered when he knew the game was up, and a parade of important members of the community went in and out of the witness box. The local papers loved it, especially when at the end Fisher was convicted on all thirty-two counts. I was delighted too, as were the aggrieved persons; I even got a commendation from the Judge.

But Fisher appealed. At the Court of Appeal, no witnesses were called and the several days in court were spent listening to learned counsel arguing points of law. Fisher was eventually acquitted on sixteen of the charges, the false pretences, but the convictions on the other sixteen relating to the obtaining credit as a bankrupt were allowed to stand. It gives some idea of the complexity of the law involved that so many distinguished legal brains had different views about it.

At this time it was possible for the prosecution to appeal against the decision of the Court of Appeal, if there was considered to be an important point of law involved. The prosecution therefore appealed to the House of Lords against the decision of the Appeal court to allow Fisher's appeal in respect of sixteen counts. Fisher appealed in respect of the other sixteen counts on which he was convicted. I was completely bewildered by the hundreds of thousands of words that were spoken about the law in this case. It was inconceivable to me that such a relatively simple matter should be so complicated. In my view the man was a crook and wanted locking up! Nevertheless I was thrilled to bits at the prospect of going to the House of Lords.

The day duly arrived and all the words spoken at the appeal hearing were bound into a thick red volume bearing the title Raven v Fisher and Fisher v Raven, the first in relation to the prosecution's appeal and the second in respect of Fisher's. The wording bore my name as I was the 'informant' on the original summons. In cases of murder or other common law offences it would have had to be Regina v Fisher, etc.

The Lord Chancellor arrived wearing a lounge suit, somewhat to my disappointment, and sat on his woolsack while counsel for both sides duly argued their cases. Then everyone was sent home and the Lords went off to consider the matter. This took several weeks, but I was eventually informed that we had lost our appeal and Fisher had won his. It seems we were back to square one.

However the case was later to be of some importance and formed the basis of an argument for changing the law relating to false pretences generally. This is not a book on law and it would bore the average reader to pieces to read pages about why this was necessary. However the new law passed as part of the Theft Act 1968, contains a section on obtaining by deception (Section 15), which to a large extent has made life easier for the police in general, but sadder for the lawyers who must have earned a fortune arguing cases like Fisher v. Raven. (1963 All England Law Reports 389).

In addition to fraud cases reported in the county, there were many enquiries that the Director of Public Prosecutions would send to the Essex Police to be looked into. For example, whenever a judge comments that a witness has committed perjury, or that other misconduct by participants in a trial should be reported to the DPP, a report would arrive in due course for us to look into. Any suggestion of tampering with witnesses or jury members would also be dealt with by the Fraud Squad. In one instance a disgruntled candidate in a Southend by-election who had lost his deposit reported that the winning candidate had spent more money than was permitted in his election campaign. This developed into an interesting, if fruitless, enquiry. Who would expect the DPP to authorise a prosecution against the new local MP? However he did commit an offence contrary to the Representation of The People's Act and I was happy to tell him so and note his reply after caution, which was not as impolite as some I have had.

The Metropolitan Police on one occasion had cause to raid a house in London that was being used by a distributor of obscene pictures and other material such as films and tapes. They found hundreds of envelopes from all over the country containing money sent in response to an advertisement for these photographs, which had been published in one of those magazines you often find on the top shelf, or under the counter, at the newsagent's shop. All these people had committed a technical offence of attempting to obtain the passage of obscene material through the post, and enquiries were sent out to all the forces concerned to have the people seen and reported. It was proposed to prosecute in appropriate cases and for the maximum publicity to be given to warn others that such behaviour was not on.

Most of the men I visited readily admitted that they had sent for the pictures etc., and were appropriately embarrassed and ashamed. One on the list was a local vicar! He not only confessed to sending for the obscene material but also lifted a large crucifix on his desk, where prior to my arrival he had been writing his sermon for next Sunday, and handed me a pile of similar material. He duly appeared in court, without his dog collar on, and gave the excuse that he was actually doing some research on prostitution and needed the photos for his studies. It didn't wash with the bench and he was fined along with the rest. I don't think his parishioners thought too badly of him though - "There but for the grace of God".

Indeed I heard that his normally near empty church on Sundays was quite full for several weeks!

The Fraud Squad was also responsible for dealing with frauds involving motor vehicles, and they were quite considerable. DS Alf Mitchell generally dealt with motor vehicles and he had a Detective Constable, one Johnny Johnson, to help him. Whenever a motor car was written off in an accident a 'green form' was added to its file at the central registry of vehicles at Chelmsford (there was no DVLA or DVLC at Swansea in those days and every county kept its own records). A copy was sent to the police if ever that vehicle was re-registered and Johnny Johnson, who was somewhat of an expert in this field, examined it.

It was not unusual for thieves to buy a wrecked car, steal a car identical to the crashed one, put the original number plates on the stolen car and register it as a re-built wreck. If the police then examined such a vehicle it would generally reveal the true identity of the car through engine and chassis numbers, secret marks put on glass by manufacturers, dating features of the car etc. This was one of many frauds perpetrated by car thieves. It was known as 'ringing' and occupied a good deal of police time. Later this developed into 'cutting and shutting'. A part of a crashed car would be welded to a part of a stolen car, or several stolen cars would be cut up and the parts interchanged and welded together. Sounds difficult? It is, and the result can be a death trap, but it was done to try and confuse the police in their efforts to identify a stolen car. It didn't often work.

Dodgy garages would sell a car and obtain finance from

several finance companies. After they had done this several times, and the game was up, they would shut up shop and disappear. It was all good fun and interesting work for the motor vehicles section. In this same vein there has been more than one case of an estate agent who sold a house to a customer and obtained a mortgage from more than one lender. These types of fraudsters were always going to come unstuck in the end, and one wondered why such intelligent people didn't put their obvious talents to better and more honest use.

Divisional officers usually have a limited amount of law to enforce. The day-to-day infringements of the average member of the public usually involves the Theft Act, The Road Traffic Acts or the Offences Against The Person Act. This is why it is only these three Acts of Parliament that a police officer learned about at training school. Naturally there were occasionally other offences too, sexual offences, offences under the Children and Young Persons Act, licensing offences, the occasional arson and so on.

In the Fraud Squad one came across some of the more obscure Acts of Parliament, and this made life there a good deal more interesting. There were cases of perjury, election fraud, offences involving national security and of course murder.

There were several factories within Essex which had Government contracts for making items regarded as secret. One morning Jack Barkway sent for me and told me to go to Harlow, where it had been discovered that someone had been printing leaflets, regarded as subversive literature, on a duplicating machine at one of these factories. I was given the name of the person I was to contact there and warned not to mention anything about the enquiry to anyone; it was 'Top Secret'.

When I arrived there it was to find several members of the press waiting at the gate and they approached me hungrily demanding what was going on. When I contacted the man I was supposed to see, there was a real flap on and I was ordered back to headquarters immediately. Jack Barkway was furious and demanded to know whom I had told, blaming me for the leak that had resulted in the press being there. I protested my innocence, and I think I was eventually believed.

I never knew for certain who told the press on this occasion, but I had a pretty good idea. The subject of the relationship between certain senior police officers and the press is one about which I could write a lot more. Suffice it to say that there are those officers who succumb to the free meals and drinks provided by national newspaper reporters and in return leak information to them. Such men are dishonest and disloyal to their service. They would sell their souls for a mess of pottage! I do not suggest for a moment that the legitimate press representatives should be denied information to which the public is entitled, but it should be released by the Press Office and not by individual officers.

Murder in the county was a fairly rare occurrence, and although there were probably three or four a year, the majority of these were what the police call 'domestic murders' and were usually solved immediately. Husband kills wife, wife kills husband, husband kills wife's lover, wife kills husband's lover and so on. Police are called and find the culprit standing over the body with bloodstained knife or smoking gun. Such cases require a great deal of work from a police point of view, but the more difficult job of detecting the crime is already done.

Whenever there was a murder or other major incident in the county that required a prolonged investigation, the Fraud Squad became the Murder Squad. The 'team', as we were known, went to the division concerned and set up an 'incident office'. This might be in a police station or in the mobile police caravan that was made available when necessary. Often in such a case, and also in the case of a missing child for example, the police caravan at the scene was a great asset and a central point to which local people could come with information.

The Incident Office Manager, usually Harry Batson, would co-ordinate the enquiries under the direction of the Detective Chief Superintendent and we sergeants, together with officers from the division, would carry out the day-to-day enquiries. Initially the statements taken at the scene and from those immediately involved would be scrutinised. House-to-house enquiries would be made if thought appropriate, and a 'reconstruction' thought about. As a matter of interest the reconstruction is mainly to keep the media interested and rarely results in information being found that would not have been disclosed by routine enquiries. The longer the media keep the case on the front page and on the TV screens the better, from the investigators' point of view.

Every enquiry was initially made the subject of an Enquiry Log. These were numbered and handed to officers for the enquiry to be made. After completion the officer would write the result on the log and hand it into the Incident Office together with any statements he had taken. These were scrutinised once more by the Investigating Officer and Harry Batson, and further logs issued to clarify points thought to be ambiguous or to probe any new matters raised.

So the enquiry grew and the paper mounted. There were no computers to analyse the information or on which to store the indices of persons, vehicles, suspects etc that were generated. These were all on cards and filed in the old-fashioned way. It followed that at least one person had to see everything that came into the Incident Office, so that his memory alone could recall if someone or some vehicle had been referred to before. Now it is a simple matter of accessing your computer database.

Most murder enquiries I had anything to with were those of children killed by perverts, lovers killed by a partner fearful of being discovered by their lawful spouse, fights among youths, homosexual partners and old ladies or gentlemen killed for a few shillings. Later in my service I did deal with others, especially the domestic kind.

Of course there were many deaths that looked very much like murders to begin with but turned out not to be. One such was a woman who had tied a plastic bag around her head, and in order that she would not be able to rip it off when she began to become asphyxiated tied her hands to the side of the bed. At first it appeared she could not possibly have done this herself, but she had cleverly arranged it so that she could put her hands into a sort of noose on each side of the bed frame, pull it tight and then be unable to release herself. This was a suicide, as all the other facts surrounding the case confirmed.

On another occasion I went to a fire in a caravan which had been completely burned out. In the ashes was the body of a man who was completely cooked. His skull was split open and it seemed likely he had been hit over the head and his place set on fire. At the post mortem the pathologist said the apparent injury to the head had occurred after death and was caused by the heat popping the skull like a chestnut. It was wintertime and the caravan was being heated by a very primitive oil stove which had overturned. This, the coroner decided, was also an accident.

I recall a mock murder investigation at Detective Training School in Preston. It was like something out of an Agatha Christie novel and involved the local vicar being murdered in his study. It was supposed to be a realistic scene of crime, and from many points of view all murder scenes are the same to an investigator in respect of the immediate action that has to be taken and instigated. I suppose it was thought that up until about 1958 murders, other than those domestic murders I have described, tended to be of vicars or well-to-do squires in their studies, but not in my experience. However in crime fiction the local force generally called in Scotland Yard in such cases, and the local flatfeet took a back seat.

The impression this gave is that Scotland Yard has an inexhaustible supply of detective Superintendents, who with their Sergeant arrive at a remote place in some county they have never set foot in before and proceed to clear up the crime and arrest the murderer in a few days, if not hours. Nothing is further from the truth.

It is true that many smaller forces still called in Scotland Yard, for at least two good reasons. Firstly the Detective Superintendent from the yard could get things like forensic examinations carried out quickly and directly. He could send his Sergeant back to London to the laboratory with an article, spent bullet, bloodstained knife or whatever for a comparison to be made and have a result the next day. Provincial forces have to fill in a mountain of forms and wait two or three weeks for a result. Secondly, and perhaps more important, if the offence was not cleared up they could blame the 'Yard'!

Contrary to common belief the Superintendent that arrived from Scotland Yard may never have dealt with a murder in his life before. He was not an expert at all, but just someone who unfortunately happened to be walking past the Assistant Commissioner's door when the phone rang.

For some years Essex had been proud of the fact that they had an experienced detective at the head of their CID who took over the investigation of a tricky murder rather than call Scotland Yard. Before Jack Barkway it had been a man named Sid Totterdell for many years. There is a very good book written by him about the murders he investigated during his years as head of the Essex CID (*A Country Copper* by S. Totterdell).

Jack Barkway had almost a perfect 100% record of successful murder investigations during his reign, spoiled only by the murder of a girl whose body was frozen in a deep freeze for some time before it was found. I recall that eventually a man in Holland was strongly suspected of the crime and officers went over there to interview him. It still remains undetected along with several others since then but reported after Jack Barkway had retired.

One administrative peculiarity of murder enquiries is that the murder has to be recorded as having happened where the body is found. Of course we all know that many murders have been committed in one place and the body dumped elsewhere, but if that somewhere else is in another county then the question of jurisdiction as well as other complications occur.

One such case occurred during my early months at headquarters. The body of a young girl was discovered in a ditch in Suffolk, just across the border from Essex. It was, as it had to be, recorded in Suffolk, then a far smaller force than Essex. The young girl came from Earls Colne in Essex and it was obvious from the very beginning of the enquiry that she had been murdered in Essex and the body taken to Suffolk where it had been dumped.

Suffolk called in Scotland Yard, much to the annoyance of the Essex Police and Jack Barkway in particular, since all the enquiries relating to the murder would be taking place in his territory. The initial 'scenes of crime' work was done by Suffolk and then the enquiry turned to Essex. Our mobile police station was taken to Earls Colne, where it remained for several months during the enquiry. The Metropolitan Police Superintendent, whom I shall not name, arrived, and was duly ensconced in the little office in the caravan. Jack Barkway hovered around and was occasionally allowed into the office to discuss matters with him. As it was Suffolk's enquiry and they had called in this man, he was officially in charge, although junior in rank and certainly in experience to Jack Barkway, who was absolutely seething.

The man from the Yard proved to be a rude and arrogant man, full of his own importance and with little regard for the ability of any of the Essex and Suffolk officers who were dealing with the day-to-day enquiries. He sat in his little office most of the time drinking Scotch and would often disappear for a day or so without informing anyone when he was coming back. During his absences little could be done, as he insisted on nothing being done without his knowledge. Rumour had it that this was the first murder investigation he had handled. Needless to say the murder was, and remains, undetected. Jack Barkway was indeed grateful that it was a Suffolk murder, or his record would have been further tarnished.

As with many cases, murder or otherwise, the police knew who the culprit was from an early stage in the enquiry. In the Earls Colne case he was interviewed on several occasions, but there was never sufficient evidence to mount a prosecution. The family tried to get a private bill of indictment against the man later, but they were unsuccessful. It has always seemed to me to be a strange society we live in that would rather see a killer go unpunished and probably kill another child than erode what it sees as an individual's rights and freedoms. Are not the rights and freedoms of the majority important?

There are a good many routine matters that an investigator can be trained to do, but there are many other things that distinguish between a successful investigator and an unsuccessful one - tireless devotion to his task, flair, experience and so on. However so many avenues of investigation are now blocked by rules and regulations and laws passed in the name of 'freedom'. How many murderers have gone unpunished in our society? How many murders have been disguised as suicide or accident? How many police officers have misread the scene of crime and written off a death as an accident, which to others might have looked suspicious?

One morning the Divisional Detective Chief Inspector at Chelmsford, when making his morning report by telephone to Jack Barkway, told him that there had been shooting the previous evening. A farmer, it seemed, had taken his own life by putting a shotgun to his head and blowing his brains out. There were, no suspicious circumstances, he said, although there had been no suicide note found.

Jack sent for Roy Bloodworth and asked to see the photographs of the scene that had been taken the previous day. He spread them on his desk and studied them for a while before picking up the phone and sending for the Chief Inspector. He pointed to one photograph which showed the body on the floor, pieces of skull, hair blood and brains all over the place, the chair he had been sitting in on its side and the shotgun on the table.

"What do you mean no suspicious circumstances?" Jack said, "This is a bloody murder!"

The Chief Inspector looked puzzled. "What makes you think it's a murder? It looks like a perfectly straightforward suicide to me."

"I've never seen a chap blow his brains all over the room and then put the gun back on the table" Jack said.

Of course he was right and within a few days a farm labourer, whom the victim had sacked, was arrested and later convicted of the crime.

This was just one incident that taught me that it is not the guile, cunning and cleverness of a killer that makes for a 'perfect murder' but inept policemen and stupid rules that prevent the gathering of evidence. It was always emphasised at training school, and my own experience confirms, that a missed clue at the scene of the crime could be the reason why a crime was not detected. The meticulous examination of the scene, both visually and by specialist officers, is absolutely essential. Keeping the scene of crime free from contamination is paramount; everyone knows this. What no one seems to know is how to keep hordes of senior officers, from the Deputy Chief Constable downward, from trampling all over a scene of crime out of morbid if not professional interest before it has been examined. These same officers will no doubt be the ones to castigate the investigating officer if his investigation is not successful. In all these circumstances therefore, it is surprising that in the majority of murder investigations in which I was involved we did get a positive result.

It was recognised that if, after two weeks of intensive enquiries there were no suspects, the crime was either heading for the 'undetected' shelf, was destined to be a very long investigation or that something had been overlooked. It is the experience of most senior detectives that the murderer is usually someone known to or connected in some way with the victim, that connection revealing the motive. One exception to this is a political or contract killing, of which fortunately there are few in our country, although they are not unheard of.

After two weeks therefore, it was the practice of Jack Barkway to start at the beginning and re-scrutinise everything that had been done before. Once there was a night watchman at a factory in the Grays Division who had been murdered and his hut set on fire. His wage packet, received that day, and a bunch of keys were missing. At the end of a fortnight we still hadn't got a clue who was responsible and so all the statements and enquiry logs were re-examined. One of the statements was from the tea boy at the factory, who apparently had a watertight alibi for the night in question. He was with his girlfriend, so his statement read. The officer who had taken this statement had written on the bottom of the form, "Alibi checked". Jack Barkway wanted to see the girlfriend's statement, but none could be found. The officer was called in and admitted that he hadn't seen or taken a statement from the girl. He had intended to of course, but other enquiries had intervened and it had been overlooked. Needless to say the Sergeant concerned was severely dealt with.

The girl was brought in and stated she had not been with the tea boy that night. She knew him, but had not gone out with him. The boy, who was only sixteen years of age, was interviewed at length in the presence of his mother. The boy, a right 'tearaway', of course denied all knowledge but mother, unlike many in such circumstances, did not rush to his defence.

Bearing in mind his age, he could not be treated harshly. There was no other evidence and a confession was absolutely essential if this was indeed the murderer. After an hour or so of kid glove treatment the boy's mother suggested Jack leave the room and she would have a chat with her son alone. In ten minutes he went back in to find that the boy was in tears and had confessed. However this was a confession that might well have been thrown out in court because of the manner in which it was obtained. The boy agreed to show us where he had thrown away the keys on the way home to his house and after the search of a field beside the road, which took several days, the stolen keys were found. Jack Barkway had got his man once again.

One morning in April of 1964 I received a telephone call from Joyce Jones, who was then the Chief Constable's secretary. The Chief wanted to see me right away. I walked over to his office racking my brains to think why he could possibly want to see me, what had I done? You didn't get called into the Chief's office for any minor reason. I was all of a tremble when I arrived at Joyce Jones' door and office, through which one had to pass to get in to see the Chief Constable.

"What does he want to see me for?" I asked.

"I've no idea," she replied. "What have you been up to?"

Just then the Woman Chief Inspector came out of the Chief's Office looking glum, and walked out without saying a word to either of us. I was ushered in.

The Chief sat behind the same huge old-fashioned desk where his predecessor had once interviewed me, and in front of it there was a well-worn carpet. I stood at attention a respectful distance from the desk. I was literally on the mat. Was I in for a carpeting?

Nightingale carried on writing and looking down at the desk, no doubt to make me feel really uncomfortable before addressing me. It seemed like an eternity before he looked up. The irritability occasioned by his earlier interview with the Woman Chief Inspector clearly showing on his face.

"Are you pregnant?" He boomed.

"No sir" was all I could think of to say.

"Are you suffering from pre-menstrual tension?"

"No sir."

"Good, then is there any other reason why you can't go to the Police College next week?

"No sir." My relief was painful.

# Police College, Bramshill, 1964

*A university should be a place of light, of liberty, and of learning.- Speech, Hansard 11 March 1873, col. 1, Benjamin Disraeli*

The Police College is known as the policeman's university, and is indeed run on university lines. I have never been to a university, and so cannot judge for myself the difference, however there is no doubt that it is an establishment of academic excellence which does its best to impart wisdom to those fortunate enough to go there. It is undoubtedly considered to be the place where ambitious officers should go. However you cannot apply to go to the Police College; you have to be selected to be sent there by your Chief Constable if he considers you to be worthy, and a prospective senior officer.

Promotion in the police was generally thought to be on merit, but as I soon discovered, merit had very little to do with it. There were very few brilliant officers in the force, we were all pretty much the same, and there was nothing better than experience to make one more effective as an officer of the law. If there are several equals and only one can be promoted, those who have to make the decision have therefore to consider other factors. Ambition to reach higher rank never bothered many who were content to remain rank-and-file constables. It is perhaps fortunate that this is so, otherwise the competition amongst those who are ambitious would be fiercer than it is.

The 'Promotion Advisory Board' was designed to sort out the 'firsts among equals', but the board passed many more officers than there were vacancies, so there had of necessity to be further refinements to the method of choosing those to be promoted.

Much has been written and discussed about Freemasonry as a corrupt step towards promotion in the police force. I confess to being a Freemason and I am not ashamed of it. I joined later in my service when it could not in any case have affected my promotion and not for any reason of aggrandisement. The people I met and associated with at Lodges were all to the best of my knowledge and belief honourable men, and people of standing in the community. They were not, as many would have you believe, a bunch of corrupt individuals. So far as I am concerned Freemasonry is an international men's club, nothing more, which incidentally does give a considerable amount of money to charities and worthy causes each year. They do this without any publicity, unlike many stars of stage, screen and radio, whose interest in charity is far less sincere than their desire to achieve publicity for themselves. Am I being too cynical for you?

Freemasonry is not as some believe a 'secret' society; this term in itself implies shadiness, even dishonesty. On the contrary it is a perfectly legal organisation and membership is not a crime; there are books about it in any library. It does have its own confidential 'members only' aspects, as do many other clubs and organisations to set them apart from others. It is also true that members are often very shy about mentioning their membership, no doubt because of the plethora of misrepresentation that has been propagated about it by the media and others.

Listening to and reading about the ridiculous suggestion that it was a step towards promotion, I often wondered how one would know which members of your promotion board were or were not Freemasons, in order to make the necessary secret signs or whatever one is supposed to do to curry favour. After all you might come seriously unstuck if you were to make a wrong signal to one who was not of the craft but who knew, as many do, some of the so called 'secrets'. You would most certainly come unstuck if you made any signals to anyone who was a Freemason in these circumstances who would certainly regard you as someone who was abusing his membership and therefore less rather than more likely to be worthy of promotion.

I think membership of the force cricket team or the force choir or having an attractive wife who dances with the Chief Constable at the annual dinner and dance would be far more likely to have any influence on one's promotion prospects, all other things being equal.

Essex at one time had a Deputy Chief Constable called Charlie Waller. Until well past his prime he played cricket, and he personally selected the force team from his 'favourites'. Many of the force cricket team during Charlie's reign were promoted, some thought well beyond their capabilities. I rest my case!

It is possible, although I personally have no knowledge of it, that Freemasonry could be a corrupt influence on an officer performing his duty without fear or favour etc, but no more so than membership of the Rotary Club, the Bowls Club or a drinking school down at the local pub. A police officer had to rise above those influences if he was to command the respect of the public, and all those I knew did so.

If you passed a board you were said to have been given a 'Golden Ticket' to promotion. It didn't follow that you would get promoted, and some never did. Also on occasion, as in my case, the decision to promote someone was taken before they went before the promotion board and some officers were promoted without ever having been on a promotion board. Such decisions could and did cause ill feeling amongst holders of Golden Tickets. In my case the excuse was that I was best suited for the specialist job of Fraud Investigation. I don't know how this decision was arrived at or who made it.

In order to make the police service a more attractive career, and to attract a 'better class of recruit', there had to be a career structure. For some unknown reason the 'powers that be' thought that university graduates would make good policemen and that they might be attracted to the service if they had a direct entry scheme, as was the case in the Hendon or Trenchard schemes. These schemes failed either because insufficient university graduates thought the police force worthy to receive their talents or because the police force realised that university graduates did not necessarily make good police officers; perhaps a bit of both!

In spite of pressure from governments the police force has always resisted a new direct entry scheme, but has settled for an alternative way of recruiting those 'brighter' individuals it considers would make good officers. It involves sending suitable officers to university (not the Police College) for two years once they have joined the force. Nothing so far has removed the necessity for every new recruit to do his initial training and then two years' probation, on the beat. After that one or two officers each year, who are suitably qualified, are promoted to the rank of Sergeant and sent to university. In Essex it was usually Essex University at Colchester, which ran suitable degree courses. When they had their degree in sociology, criminology or whatever, they were promoted to Inspector and were on their way. There are very few Chief Officers around these days who are not products of this scheme.

Another facet of the promotion policy of the police service is that one should serve in several different departments, and also in different forces, to qualify for chief officer status. It followed that ambitious officers in general, and those who had a university degree in particular, were forever moving from department to department and from force to force. While this may have been good for their own personal careers it was not in my view good for the service as a whole. Nothing is worse than having a new broom move in over you every few months, especially someone with little or no experience in your field!

Senior officers had in the past always come from the ranks, and no one really found this a bad thing. However there was and still is a desire to create an officer class within the police force comprised of academic rather than practical men. Men of learning and breeding are considered more able to carry out the job of leading a service of men and officers, rather as it is in the army.

It might be helpful for me to first describe in some detail the rank structure of the police force. There are three levels of status so far as rank is concerned. First there are the Federated Ranks, Constable, Sergeant, Inspector and Chief Inspector. The next level is Senior Officer, which includes Superintendent and Chief Superintendent. The third and top level is that of Chief Officer and includes Chief Constables, Deputy Chief Constables and Assistant Chief Constables. In the Metropolitan Police the higher ranks are known as Commissioners and Deputy or Assistant Commissioners.

The Federated Ranks have a so-called 'union', the Police Federation. It is not a union really, but an organisation that liaises with Government (Official side) and Chief Officers (Staff side) on behalf of the Federated Ranks in respect of pay and conditions etc. It has no power to negotiate; it has no teeth and usually has to accept what is offered. It does however have a lot of members, as subscriptions are deducted from policeman's pay. Membership is not actually compulsory, but for all practical purposes it is.

After my appearance at court for careless driving, for which I was represented by counsel, appointed and paid for by the Police Federation, I was for a while totally disgusted with it. The counsel sent to represent me was just out of law school, hadn't got a clue, and I could have done a better job defending myself. I immediately resigned from the Police Federation and instructed the County Council Finance Department not to deduct the subscriptions. For several weeks I was subjected to intense pressure by the local Federation Representative, who was not able to persuade me to rejoin. However the rank and file members with whom I worked also put pressure on me, saying that as a constable I would derive the benefit from any successful negotiations regarding pay etc and that I should pay my share. For this reason I did eventually rejoin, but I have never really been a 'Federation man' and have yet to reap the benefit of any negotiations they made on my behalf that we wouldn't have got anyway. On the other hand each year our local representatives, together with representatives from all over the country and accompanied by their wives, spend a week at Blackpool attending the Annual Conference, housed in a good hotel and fed and watered in fine style. If anyone ever wondered what happened to their subscriptions, they need do so no longer.

Superintendents are represented by a quite different association, called, strangely enough, the Superintendent's Association. This august body does very little, since any negotiations for pay and conditions negotiated or awarded to the Federated Ranks also apply to Superintendents. They did organise an annual dinner every year, to which all the old and retired Superintendents were invited. It used to cost all the serving Superintendents about £5 a head to treat their old comrades. A few years ago they had a meeting and decided that if retired officers wanted to attend they should pay the full cost themselves. Very few of us took them up on the offer. Ex-police officers, from Essex at least, do not even receive a Christmas card from the force!

Chief Officers also have an association I believe, but one doesn't hear very much about it. They have a conference every now and again, but mainly to discuss operational matters and policy.

So, back to the Police College. There were in 1964 three courses being run for police officers, the 'A' Course, the 'B' or Superintendents' Course and the Senior Command Course. The 'A' Course was for six months and was for officers, usually of the rank of Sergeant, who their Chief Constable thought would probably become an Inspector in the near future and in his view had potential for further advancement. A force was allowed to send no more than one, two or three officers a year, depending on the size of the force. It is clear that with a force that has a fair number of inspectors, not all of them can be sent to the Police College. This did not mean that a Sergeant could not be promoted to Inspector, or that an Inspector might not achieve higher rank without having been to Police College. It did mean however that if you were selected to go there, and understood what it meant, then you could feel that you might well start being a little more ambitious, if you were not already.

I was later to learn that when you returned to your force the final paragraph of the report sent to your Chief Constable determined whether you would in fact go very far. It was supposed to be a well-kept secret, but like all well-kept secrets it was very soon a well-known fact amongst the Police College students. If your report said, "This officer will make a good Inspector". Then chances are that is all you would ever make. What your Chief Constable wanted to see was, "This officer is likely to achieve senior rank".

The 'A' course was in two parts. For three months you would study what were called 'liberal studies'. These included literature, history, abstract subjects such as 'conflict' and more important matters such as 'prejudice' and 'racism'. Yes, the police were studying racism as far back as the early sixties, but not because there was any suggestion that the police as an institution were racist. On the contrary they were looking at the subject objectively, as a fact that existed in society generally, the reasons for it and possible solutions to the problems it caused. From an academic point of view racism is an interesting topic. When it comes to the reaction of politicians it becomes an emotive subject, only discussed when it is thrust before them because of a problem or incident, and then they have to look for someone to blame, in many cases the police service as a whole. The enquiry and subsequent report on the Stephen Lawrence affair was a disgraceful slur on the police service as a whole and one for which the Government should be thoroughly ashamed. It will, I have no doubt whatever, live to regret it.

It has saddened me greatly to see the police force labelled

as 'institutionally racist' by people who should know better. The police are no more racist that any other section of society. The word 'racist' means a person who holds a belief that one race is better than another. Hitler was an extreme racist in his belief that the German race was superior to any other. There are many areas where the majority of the local population is coloured; it follows that as a matter of simple arithmetic that in such an area the police will arrest more coloured than white people. Are they racist?

The result of various reports and criticism of the police has been catastrophic as far as policing is concerned. The formation of no-go areas and 'soft' policing policies when it comes to dealing with ethnic groups distinguishes coloureds from whites in a way that discriminates against the white members of society. In turn this too creates ill feeling and conflict and has made itself all too apparent in certain areas of the country during the last few years.

For the second half of the course it would be 'police subjects', far more familiar to most of us. Generally the police subjects discussed were more general management matters, finer points of law, man management and suchlike.

When you drive into Bramshill for the first time, through the imposing gates and along the half mile of drive towards the 'big house', few could fail to be impressed. Bramshill House, just outside the village of Hook in Hampshire, was built in the fourteenth century and is a National Monument. It was originally owned by the Cope family, whoever they were, and like many great houses of their time has either been taken over by the Government, turned into a place of public interest or allowed to decay into ruins. The house itself is very large and a masterpiece of the architecture of the day, built by craftsmen who, no doubt, never expected that the beauty they created would one day be trampled over by hordes of what would then have been regarded as uncouth beings. There are now many other buildings in the vast grounds including a dining hall, lecture rooms and accommodation blocks.

The house itself has a very interesting and tragic history, about which books have been written, and it is said to be one of the most haunted houses in England. In the Great Hall at the bottom of a long and winding polished oak staircase is a huge wooden chest that was said to have contained the body of the bride of one of the family who died in tragic circumstances on the day of her wedding. The story of the Bride and the Mistletoe Bough Chest is one of the ghost stories you can read about in the great library. Others include *The Ghost of Peter Hawkins* (the gamekeeper) and *The Ghost of Henry Cope*, one of the ancestors.

In the house there are a number of bedrooms for the lucky ones and rooms used by the staff for their own student get-togethers and seminars. It also houses the library, probably the best law library in the country, and in one of the corridors is a museum of old police equipment, especially truncheons (batons), where several hundred adorn one wall.

The grounds include a vast lake and parkland, some of which has now been turned into sports pitches. The great lawn adjoining one side of the house is kept immaculate and is used on special occasions for cricket matches or summer garden parties.

On that first day the new intake of thirty officers would arrive from all over the UK and the Commonwealth; in the vestibule await your tutors. Each student will have two tutors, a senior police officer and an academic. The police officers are men who generally thought that a spell as a member of the Bramshill staff would be good for their promotion prospects to Chief Officer Rank. How many of them realised that they were probably getting a sideways move I'm not sure. The academics were middle-aged dons from various universities. Their fields of speciality were not generally advertised, but most were believed to have degrees in really useful subjects like literature, sociology and behavioural science.

Let me correct at once any impression I may give that I think Bramshill is not a great academic institute. Most places of this kind are what you yourself make of them; there was the opportunity here to learn if you wished. The staff were in my estimation not the very best available. Home Office wages were not, and are not, known to be the most generous and were the academics in particular of top quality, I have no doubt they could have demanded higher wages elsewhere.

The purpose of sending officers to this place was, as I have indicated, to assess your ability and suitability for higher rank. It was not really to teach you police work. You could gain a great deal from exchanging views and ideas with officers from other places and other countries, but it was regarded by most as a sabbatical, and no doubt it was thought that you would return to the everyday job of policing with renewed vigour.

After the introductions were made and accommodation

allocated, there was a parade and an address by the Commandant, usually a Chief Officer from some force or another whose place back home had already been taken by someone else. I often wondered what happened to ex-Bramshill Commandants when they had finished their two-year stints. Like the other police staff, it was considered by some a move in the right direction.

Every officer attending Bramshill had to wear uniform, so all detectives were issued with one before their arrival. It was the first time since my army days that I had worn a uniform with three stripes on the arm, and as I listened to the address by the Commandant I was feeling quite proud to be representing my force among such noble company from many forces around the world.

It became apparent at a very early stage that in order for your name to be glorified at the college you would have to do something special or different. There were, we were told, many ways this could be done. You could become captain of the cricket team, president of the Henry Fielding Society or director of the stage productions, to name just a few. The more ambitious rushed forward to put their names down to take part in the many activities that a college offers; quiz teams, indoor games, outdoor sports, debating society and so on.

Some of us hung back. The only sport I was ever good at was swimming and this was one of the few that did not figure, there being no swimming pool at Bramshill. There was no boxing team either, I'm happy to say; this sort of thing was for budding officers and gentlemen to watch, not to take part in. Special temporary membership of a nearby golf club could be arranged, but only after suitable vetting. I didn't play golf either, so that didn't bother me. I did later become quite good friends with a Metropolitan Police officer in my syndicate, Eddie Markham, and we used to slide off on Wednesday afternoons to play squash at a club some distance from Bramshill.

I had been an amateur photographer for some years, and when all the scrambling for every other activity had died down I found that the only club that had no names down was the Photographic Society. I quickly signed my name and became the Chairman, Secretary and sole member at a stroke. There was a room right at the very top of the main building which contained an old enlarger, developing tanks and all the basic equipment needed to process black and white films and prints.

At the time I had rather a nice Rolleiflex and one morning some weeks later when walking in the grounds, I took a picture of Bramshill House from across the lake. It was one of those shots that you dream about. The light was right, there was just enough cloud and the reflection of the house in the lake was perfect. When I left the college a framed copy of this photograph was hanging in the Commandant's office (perhaps it still is) and that year it was used on the front of the Police College Christmas Card. I said you needed a bit of luck in this job!

My luck didn't end there. Thursday night at Bramshill was 'dining in night'. Whatever you did on other nights, you had to attend dinner in full uniform or evening dress on

Thursdays. The mess hall was a grand new building and was able to accommodate the entire college plus their guests. Wives were allowed to attend on Thursday for dinner, or any other guest you might like to invite. These could include your senior officer or even your Chief Constable, if you really wanted to get on!

The display of finery from the overseas students, in their traditional dress uniforms, was a sight to behold, and I used to nip around the tables taking pictures of the students and their guests. During the following week I would print them and pin them up on a board, take orders and sell copies. After paying for the chemicals and paper there was still enough cash left to pay for all my social commitments.

The meal was always a little better than those provided the rest of the week, and of course you had to pay for your guests and for wine, which was for sale outside the dining hall beforehand. The top table consisted of the Mess President, one of the students nominated each week, Commandant, staff and official guests. There was an after-dinner ritual of the president banging his gavel and saying the words, "Gentlemen, The Queen". We all stood for the Loyal Toast, and then, "Gentlemen you may now smoke". Then came the ceremony of 'passing the port' which had to be done with precision and with the correct hand from right to left. The top table did not have to pay for their wine or port!

Thursday night was also the night when there would be 'official guests'. These would usually include one or two Chief Constables and some other important people, such as junior Ministers, trade union leaders, senior Home Office civil servants and so on. The students were expected to put on the 'after dinner entertainment' in the great hall. Following the meal everyone would stroll across to the hall to see the entertainment, or even to take part in it. Being able to play the piano, sing, dance or act, was a great asset and one more way to make a name for yourself at the college. I did at the time play the violin, but never admitted it. I couldn't face the inevitable jibes about a CID officer being 'on the fiddle'.

When serving at Chelmsford some time later, I was a member of the Chelmsford Symphony Orchestra for a while. A local press photographer spotted me one night at a concert and later in the local newspaper there appeared a photograph of me playing the violin and headed, "Rhapsody in Blue"!

It was quite amazing at times to see the array of talent possessed by some of the students at the college: singers, dancers, musicians, even conjurers and comedians. I used to think that had a talent spotter been amongst the audience, some of the performers might have been offered an alternative career to the police service.

The entertainment usually consisted of some kind of show organised by the students. It varied from some sort of play to a variety show, depending on the talents of the students available. Sometimes the entertainment would be what was called a 'balloon debate'. Those taking part would each speak for several minutes, and then the audience would vote on who should jump out of the balloon to allow it to stay aloft; the chap left in at the end was the winner. On other occasions it might be a quiz, which was run on the lines of University Challenge. Each course would submit a team and battle it out on stage.

The official guests would sit in the front row and hopefully enjoy the show and the social drinking in the bar afterwards. This was where students competed to get close to their own Chief Constable if he was there and buy him a drink, just so that he could get a glimpse of their face, and hopefully remember it.

When the entertainment was some sort of a show, it was usually a burlesque based upon some well-known musical, with words made up by the students to refer to events or people at the college. Often members of the staff, both professional and academic came in for some pretty heavy ridicule. The best show put on by the students while I was there was called Bramshilloma, the music being from Oklahoma and the words a cruel satire on some of the staff, who took it all in good part.

On another occasion there were three women police sergeants on the course. They were all fairly senior in service and were rather large and somewhat stern-looking women. One I remember was a Detective Sergeant in the Metropolitan Police who had a reputation for being a pretty hard-nosed lady. The three of them dressed up in short gymslips and tights and had their hair tied in bows. At one stage during the particular entertainment they came on and sang a version of *Three Little Maids From School Are We*, from Gilbert and Sullivan's *Mikado*. They got a great deal of applause.

The guest of honour that evening was a senior Home Office official; I have no recollection now of who it was, perhaps it's just as well. Later in the bar I overheard him talking to one of the other guests, a Deputy Chief Constable I believe. "I thought those three chaps who dressed up as women and did 'Three Little Maids' were rather good, don't you think?" he remarked. I'm not sure whether he was ever enlightened.

The thirty officers of the 'new intake' were divided into three syndicates or classes. One was to remain with the same syndicate for the entire course and most of the classes were conducted in those small groups. For some exercises we were divided into even smaller groups of three or four, and there were plenty of individual tasks to perform. For more general lectures the entire course – three syndicates – met in one of the larger lecture rooms. Then there were the occasions when visiting speakers would address the entire college. There was more than one 'A' course taking place at any one time, and together with the Superintendents and the senior command courses there were some three hundred or so student all told, which just about filled the great hall.

The first three months of the course, that is the 'Liberal Studies,' was said to contain subjects for a general broadening of the mind, academic rather than professional or technical. However it was apparent that most of the academics were more liberal in a political sense than policemen were generally. This made for some lively discussions.

Senior officers are often expected to speak to numbers of officers, or even at local government committee meetings, social events and other gatherings. It was apparent at the start of the course that one of the areas of expertise that was to be developed was the ability to speak in public - a task, incidentally, I would be called upon to do many times in the future, but never enjoyed.

One of the first things new students were required to do was to speak to the syndicate for twenty minutes or so. Each of us was given the name of a well-known character from history, the arts or politics. We then had a day or so to do research on the individual and then had to speak, or make a presentation, as it was known at the college, to the syndicate. Later there would be tasks allotted to groups and to the syndicate as a whole. This final task would be the subject of a presentation to the entire college in the Great Hall. It was good fun and generally enjoyed by all. With the group tasks, those who liked doing all the talking could do so, while others could take part in other ways, like preparing documents, slides and other 'aids' or props that might be required.

As for the academic subjects, these were intended to broaden one's outlook and to widen one's horizons. For those of us who had never read anything more broadening than Mike Hammer, Sexton Blake or even Hercule Poirot, the task of reading and writing a 'book review' on works about classical Roman history was daunting. The book I was supposed to review was *Count Belisarius* by Robert Graves. Whether it actually broadened my mind I'm not sure, it certainly bored the pants off me!

There was officially no political bias at the college and the subjects discussed and researched were not presented to us in a one-sided way. However if you ask anyone to write a paper about almost anything controversial, it generally tells a lot about the writer and his views. One wonders if this was taken into consideration when one's final report was assembled. Or am I being too sensitive? The trick was to be able to judge for oneself which political view was favoured. It was really not difficult to do this, given the views expressed by academics and the type of visiting speaker that came to talk to us. The difficult part was to decide whether to be a traitor to one's own views while at the college, or to express them freely and be thought of as a radical. Being a detective, and having therefore rather right-wing views about crime and the way to deal with criminals, I think I may have let my true colours show through from time to time, although I did stop short of propounding the death penalty for shoplifting.

The academic staff used to have cocktail evenings in their quarters when members of their syndicate were invited to partake of a sherry or two and have informal chats. They were pleasant enough, but I suspect all part of the detailed examination of all the students.

I mentioned earlier that some of the academic staff were behavioural scientists. It wasn't long before we realised that rather than students, we were looked upon by them as specimens for experimentation, and that for them Bramshill was a research laboratory for their benefit, rather than for ours!

On one occasion ten of us were shut in a room with a task. For example we had to decide whether there should be a village fete this year in our village and if so what events should take place etc. We thought it a bit weird, but set to the task with a will. A half-hour or so later the tutor came back in to see how we were getting on. We spent four hours on this task, but as we discovered later it mattered not one iota about the village fete. What the behavioural scientist was looking for was who had emerged as the leader or chairman, and who sat back and said nothing.

One of the more useful and, so far as I am concerned, previously unknown skills I learned at Bramshill was 'logical thinking.' So many decisions we make in our lives, both personal and at work or business, are made on the spur of the moment and therefore often turn out to be wrong. Logical thinking makes you sit back and carefully list all the pros and all the cons of the problem. The decision you arrive at is often not the one you would have made off the top of your head, and far more likely to be right. Next time you set out to buy a new car, try logical thinking and you will no doubt be surprised at the decision you make. Actually there are two decisions to make here: "Do I need a new car?" and then if the answer is yes, "Which car shall I buy?"

Many hours were spent in the magnificent library at Bramshill researching the various tasks allotted to us and writing our papers and presentations. There were no computers or world wide web in those days, and much of the research was slow and necessitated reading a good deal of small print. I started to get headaches each morning, and for a while thought it might have something to do with drinking in the bar in the evening. Eventually I realised it was not that and went to the doctor - there was a visiting doctor from Hook at the college every morning. He sent me to the optician and I have worn glasses ever since.

After three months of this liberalisation of the mind it was the turn of the police staff to examine what we were made of.

The reason why detective officers were issued with a uniform to attend the college was, I thought at first, just a simple device to ensure conformity, to remind us all that we were in a disciplined service and to ensure that parades - we did have parades - were not too ragged. They were bad enough with the various different uniforms of the many forces represented. I began to think afterwards however that there might have been a more subtle motive. There has always been a barrier between the CID and uniform branches. Detectives had a tendency to regard uniformed officers as 'woodentops', and they themselves were looked upon as superior, arrogant and often dishonest. Perhaps the uniform was a psychological ploy intended to humble this impudent bunch.

The CID generally was not very well thought of at the Police College. I believe I have already conveyed the impression that the majority of officers attending the college were rather more concerned about their career prospects than their police work. Most of them tended to regard detectives as rather uncouth types who talked a lot about crime and punishment rather than the social status in society of a Superintendent. Detectives were in a minority at Bramshill and during the many seminars I was to have with my tutors there was inevitably the question about why I was in the CID. This was followed by the advice that to get to the top in the police I should have to transfer back to the uniformed branch as soon as possible.

I knew of course that this was good advice, and that few of the Chief Constables, Deputy Chief Constables and Assistant Chief Constables around the country had ever spent more than a year or so in the CID to round off their overall experience. However I was undoubtedly already becoming uncomfortable in this atmosphere of egotistic talk of self-advancement. I had expected the Police College to be a place of learning rather than to be a specimen under a microscope for six months. I therefore usually could be relied upon in discussions to put forward a detective's point of view. I'm not sure on reflection how wise this was.

Police subjects were something most of us could understand a little more clearly and discussions upon which we could contribute more freely and knowledgeably. There were no lectures on specific laws, but rather about aspects of the law, its history and application; how such matters affect the community, the Government and different factions amongst the community.

There were lengthy discussions about such matters as the usefulness or otherwise of CS gas, whether there should be a national police force, a national CID, such as the FBI in America or a riot squad to deal with civil unrest. On one occasion we were invited to write a paper on a new law we would like to see legislation for. Then there were matters such as legislation to protect people from themselves; for example how far would the population be prepared to accept laws to make it a crime not to lock your car when you left it?

Most of the officers on the 'A' course received notification of their promotion to Inspector before they finished the course. Other Chief Constables were a little more prudent and waited until they had received the college report on their man.

As for the Superintendents' course, this too was a sort of short rest from active duty, but it was for officers who had already reached the rank of Superintendent. Since there was also a Senior Command course for Superintendents and Chief Superintendents who were destined for higher things, it can only be assumed that the Superintendents' course was indeed a sabbatical and intended to refresh the brain rather than to prepare you for higher rank.

I returned to Chelmsford after completing the 'A' Course in September 1964. I had received no information about the likelihood of my being promoted to Inspector within the near future; nor did the Chief Constable enlighten me when he interviewed me on my return from the course. As usual he said very little at such an interview and was as always a trifle sarcastic. He hoped that the course had done much to enlighten me and that I was prepared now to get down to some real police work.

A week or so later I was detailed to attend a meeting at Headquarters. There was a large wooden hall beside the main building, which was used mainly as a concert hall, theatre and to hold dances. It was known as "The Hut", and it was where such meetings were usually held. I had no idea what the meeting was to be about save that those attending were to be addressed by the Chief Constable in person.

CHAPTER SEVEN

# Regional Crime Squad (1964-1966)

*History is, indeed, little more than the register of the crimes, follies, and misfortunes of mankind - Edward Gibbon - The Decline and Fall of the Roman Empire (1776-88) chapter 3*

One of the serious drawbacks related to the enforcement of the law in the United Kingdom has been, and is still to a lesser extent, the differences between forces and the borders or barriers between them. Each Chief Constable has different priorities and policies, and while it is true that they each have different problems, these differences in policy do create difficulties, especially for example where one side of a street is in one police district and the opposite side of the road is in another.

There had long been a need to remedy the problem of these barriers between police forces, which have also led to them being rather parochial in their attitude to, and jealous of their differences from, neighbouring police forces. Officers in one force had no powers to act in another police district except in 'hot' or immediate pursuit of a suspect. If you wanted to carry out an inquiry in another police district, you either had to ask that force to do it for you, or go to the local police station in the area where you wanted the inquiry done and ask for a local man to accompany you. Lack of trust and lack of co-operation was not unusual and to expect another force to carry out an enquiry for you as thoroughly as you would do it yourself was, except in the most minor matters, too much to expect.

For example if you were investigating a burglary and had a suspect in custody who lived in an adjoining police district, you might well want to search his house. Asking the local force to do it for you had a number of flaws. First they would have no professional interest in the outcome of the case. Perhaps more important, they would not know all the fine details of the case and whether anything they found might or might not be pertinent to it. It was essential in such and in many other cases to do the job yourself. How much easier it would have been if you could have got on with it without having to call at the local police station for assistance.

Of course when the boot was on the other foot, you would be most upset to find that 'foreign' officers had been creeping about on your patch searching premises which might be of interest to you. Could you even trust members of your own force to do such an enquiry for you?

I once had a man in custody who was being most co-operative. In order to 'buy' himself bail, he was prepared to give information about a crime committed by an associate who lived in Basildon. I checked his information as best I could and there had indeed been a report of the theft of shirts from a local warehouse the previous day. My prisoner said that that very morning he had seen the stolen property in his associate's house and that he had arranged to go back that afternoon with some cash to buy them and a van to take them away in - I had arrested him before he could attend the appointment. The stolen goods were said to be piled in boxes in the front room of the house.

I telephoned Basildon police and asked them to go and recover the goods and arrest the suspect. About half an hour later I received a call that the enquiry had been done, no shirts had been found and the occupier of the house knew nothing of the matter. To this day I believe that if I had done the enquiry myself I would have recovered the shirts, got myself a prisoner and cleared up another crime. Afterwards my prisoner insisted that the goods had been there, but he also said the associate was a 'snout' (informant) for a senior detective. He didn't get bail! So, force boundaries and even divisional ones were a problem.

Crime and criminals on the other hand had no such constraints. For several years criminals had been widening their spheres of activity and spreading out from London to the provinces. There had been discussions and debates at Police College about the possibility of the formation of a National Police Force or a National CID. A study of the history of the British Police would give one some idea what a difficult task this would be. No doubt these debates were designed to test the temperature, as it were, of police feelings on the matter.

Government had by now reduced the number of police forces from over one hundred to forty-three, not including the Metropolitan Police, who have always been regarded as a special case. These amalgamations were said to be in the interests of efficiency, and there seems no doubt that there are many who favour a further reduction in the number of forces. To date the Government of the day has hesitated to take on this mammoth task, which is likely to be a very controversial undertaking.

Similarly there are many arguments in favour of a National CID. While this might solve some of the problems of stealth and secrecy when it comes to the sharing of intelligence and partisan behaviour of detectives generally, I doubt that any politician would have the courage to tackle the job, at least in my lifetime.

At the Police College there was one very good presentation called "The River of Time". It showed how the world has changed, how much more rapidly things progress today compared with just fifty years ago, science, technology, medicine and so on. The developments in all these and other fields has changed far more in the last fifty years than it did in the hundred years before that. It can only keep on changing faster and faster.

Unfortunately the British police force has not changed at the same pace, and while there have been vast changes, even since my retirement, there is still a long way to go, and a lot of old prejudice and stubbornness to overcome, before such changes as are clearly necessary can be implemented. Meantime modifications continue to take place slowly and piecemeal, rather than completely. The Regional Crime Squad was one of these changes, which may have been thought of as the first step to a national detective force. We were however told that it was just a temporary measure to combat certain types of crime. In my view it was ill thought out, and while it had its uses and did some good work initially, it was an expensive adventure.

If it was the first step to a national CID, then the experiment was clearly thought to be a failure, since there was never any talk of enlarging it. If it was a temporary measure, then why did it still exist, long after it had fulfilled its initial purpose? Perhaps no one had had the nerve to suggest that, like many government quangos, it was by then an expensive waste of time and of good police officers.

One of the most prevalent serious crimes committed by gangs of so-called 'professional criminals' in 1964 was the theft of lorries and their loads, crimes which invariably spanned more than one police district. It is worth remembering that the Regional Crime Squad was originally formed specifically to combat this type of crime, and for no other reason.

There were several other officers in plain clothes in attendance when I arrived at the Hut, some of whom I recognised, while others who were strangers to me; there were some fifteen of us, all seemingly just as bewildered as to why we were there. There were two detective inspectors whose faces I knew and one or two sergeants whom I knew by name. We sat and waited. Eventually the Chief Constable arrived with his entourage of several senior officers and began his address.

He announced the birth of the Regional Crime Squads, to take effect from 1st October 1964. Each squad would cover the same area or region, as did the various police districts. The 43 forces in England and Wales were grouped into six districts for administrative purposes and to share the costs of several 'common services' such as forensic science laboratories, driving school, training establishment etc. Essex was in No 5 Police District. The idea was that each of the police forces within the district would contribute a number of experienced detective officers who could now in theory, and without a change in the law, operate within the entire region. There would be small groups of one Inspector and four or five sergeants and constables stationed at various 'branch' offices within the region to form a network, which would be headed by a Co-ordinator with the rank of Detective Chief Superintendent.

In the case of Essex there would be three such branch offices: one at Basildon, one at Brentwood and one at Harlow. These would quickly become known as the Basildon Crime Squad, the Brentwood Crime Squad and the Harlow Crime Squad. There were to be other offices in different parts of the region, Bedford, Stevenage etc. The Co-ordinator, with a deputy, would be at Hatfield in Hertfordshire. Perhaps I should mention here that by this time the Essex Constabulary and the Southend on Sea Constabulary had been amalgamated.

After a great deal of protest and representations to Home Office, the deed had been done. Rather than offend anyone in Southend by saying they had been 'taken over' by Essex, the name of the new force was the Essex and Southend-on-Sea Constabulary. Some years later when the wounds had healed the name was changed once again to the Essex Police, which is what it is called to this day. Note the dropping of the word 'Constabulary,' a subtle change but a significant one.

The new squad had been formed, we were told, for the sole purpose of dealing with the rising tide of lorry thefts. This was to be our purpose in life, and each officer would be expected to serve on the squad for a maximum period of two years. The Chief Constable then announced the names of the officers who would be the founder members, as it were. There was every reason to believe, from what was said that the squad would be disbanded in two years. However, as I discovered many times in the police force, it was one thing to start something and quite another to stop it. "We will keep watch on so and so for a few days," is easy to say. At the end of a few days who has the courage to say, "Let's call it off?" Everyone knows that the day after you call off the observation the thieves strike!

So it turned out to be with the Regional Crime Squad. Many years later it still existed, without any clear task or directive. The National Crime Squad (NCS) was Formed in April 1998 and dealt with organised and major crimes and after the amalgamation of the six former Regional Crime Squads it merged on 1 April 2006 into the Serious Organised Crime Agency. The NCS reported directly to the Home

Office and had nationwide and international jurisdiction. It did not handle security matters, referring such matters to the appropriate security service. It primarily dealt with organised crime, major drug trafficking, murder for hire schemes, illegal arms dealing, human trafficking, computer and high tech crimes, money counterfeiting and laundering, extortion, kidnapping and murder relating to any of the above. Lastly, it augmented and supported regional forces throughout the United Kingdom. More recently (2013) we have seen the introduction of the National Crime Agency, which will also have many other functions. Going back to my early days of the RCS when our main concern was the theft of a few lorries and their valuable loads, I can only wonder at the speed with which times and crimes have changed.

Put someone in charge of anything in the police service and he becomes an 'empire builder', demanding more men and equipment and doing everything he can to make himself and his unit indispensable. I suspect that the various agencies and organizations that have been formed since the original RCS might be the creations of such people; or was it because each new organization was formed because its predecessor was not very effective?

I listened with some interest to the names the Chief Constable read out for the Brentwood and Southend squads; mine was not among them. I realised therefore that I was going back to Harlow for two years, and was feeling a little disappointed that it would be at least that length of time before I could expect to be promoted. But then the Chief Constable said, "The Harlow squad will be under Detective

Inspector Raven. He will have Detective Sergeant Clarke from Essex, Detective Sergeant O'Hara of the Metropolitan Police and Detective Sergeants Jones and Turner from Hertfordshire".

This was typical of John Nightingale, and while I was thrilled to bits at being promoted, I felt at the same time that the honour that was being bestowed upon me was a little tarnished by the manner in which the announcement was made. I tried to appear unmoved, as though I had known all along, as the rest of the proceedings continued. I even forgave the Chief Constable after thinking that probably someone else should have told me the news before the meeting.

I knew Detective Sergeant Clarke, who had a British Empire Medal. He was older and far senior to me in service. He had been a Detective Sergeant at Epping, within the Harlow Division, when I was a Detective Constable there. I wondered how I was going to get along with him now as his senior officer. As it happened I needn't have worried; we got along fine and indeed became quite good friends. The details of how he won his BEM were not widely known. The rumour was that one night when he was stationed at Basildon he had confronted an armed man, overpowered and arrested him. Nobby Clarke, as we all later knew him, rarely talked about the incident, but he did enlighten me one night after a social occasion when a good deal of alcohol was drunk. Nobby could hold his drink with the best of them, and I still don't know whether he was pulling my leg. However the story he told me was that he was patrolling in the middle of the night and checking the security of a small factory. As he turned a corner he came upon a burglar just exiting a window. Both he and the burglar were equally shocked at their sudden meeting. The burglar pulled a gun from his pocket and immediately lost his balance and fell out of the window, dropping the gun. Nobby pounced and the cuffs were on before you could say "Bill Sykes". Naturally the report when written up read somewhat differently and the recommendation for the award considerably enhanced the facts of the case.

Bill O'Hara was, like my other two sergeants from Hertfordshire, unknown to me. He didn't stay on the squad very long and went on to become a Detective Chief Superintendent in the Metropolitan Police. He was a quietly-spoken man with a vast amount of experience. Many years later, after I had retired from the police force, I met him again. I had applied for the job as a security manager with well-known national company. I was short-listed and went for interview at Enfield. There were three men on the interview board, the Managing Director, another executive and Bill O'Hara, who was now the Chief Security Officer for the company. I might have got the job but for the fact that they wanted me to move to and live in London and I didn't.

The two sergeants from Hertfordshire stayed with me for the full two years, and were useful members of the team. Jones was a big man who used to be slow to act but positive when he did. He smoked a Sherlock Holmes-type pipe and spent a lot of time lying on his back on the office floor doing sit-ups to reduce his midriff and strengthen his stomach muscles. Geoff Turner was something of a loner and used to disappear for days on end. He would ring in saying he was following a lead or chasing up some information given him by an informant, but when he returned to the fold he rarely had anything much to report. I don't know whatever happened to either of these members of my team.

The Chief Constable went on to explain how the administration of the squad was to be handled, and this is where I believe those who gave birth to this rather expensive and inefficient baby had not used a lot of the 'logical thinking' that was so praised at the Police College. The finance was to be provided by the forces that contributed the officers - Essex also provided the offices, motor cars and equipment - and day-to-day operational control was under the Co-ordinator. Wages and expenses would be paid to the officers by their own forces. It was clear that the cars and other equipment were to remain the property of the Essex Police and that I would be answerable for any damage or misuse of same to Essex.

These basic principles sounded fine, but there were many matters the creators of the Regional Crime Squad hadn't considered or even thought of. First, as the period of service on the squad was to be no longer than two years, there was no question of officers from other forces being moved to live near their offices. This meant a lot of travel to and from work, which was a new experience for many officers. Then the fact that each officer was a member of a different force caused administrative problems. Many of the other various defects in the scheme did not become apparent immediately, but as time went on they began to show. One of the early problems was that of having more than one governor. My boss was supposed to be the Co-ordinator at Hatfield, who was answerable only to the Commissioner of Police of the Metropolis, but I was still answerable to Jack Barkway and my own Chief Constable for anything that went on in Essex.

The Co-ordinator who was appointed to run the Regional Crime Squad was Gerald MacArthur, a senior Detective Chief Superintendent of the Metropolitan Police. 'Mac' as he became known to the members of the squad, was a formidable detective from the old school with a long record of successful arrests of major criminals. He had also dealt with a recent case of alleged corruption with the Metropolitan Police. The criminal fraternity and dodgy policemen alike feared him.

Mac was in the middle of a long investigation to crack the infamous Richardson gang when he was appointed to run the Regional Crime Squad. At first he was not pleased that he had received this apparent sideways move, but he did eventually see it as a boon. He now had a large squad of men under his total control and a free hand to pursue the Richardson gang pretty well as he pleased.

The Richardsons, like the Krays, were a gang of hardened London criminals. Their reign of terror in East London is legendary. It was Mac and his men who eventually put a stop to it. That is not to say that a few corners were not cut and a few rules broken. Mac was not known for his kid-gloved approach to dealing with the ungodly, and it became apparent that his methods were often in conflict with those of Jack Barkway, who clearly expected his own men to play according to the rules. I also believed in the 'rule book' and began to fall foul of Mac at an early stage.

The Harlow Branch Office was at Old Harlow, in the building that used to be the Police Station and Magistrates' Court. It was now being used by the Harlow Traffic Department, who somewhat resented our arrival to take over the upstairs offices. We were also provided with some suitable second-hand furniture and a secretary, who happened to be the wife of a police dog handler, PC Alan Loftin.

Alan Loftin was a very good and conscientious police officer stationed at Harlow (Dog Section). Bishops Stortford in Hertfordshire, which adjoined the Harlow Division, had no dogs at the time and occasionally called for assistance from Essex, which was readily given.

Soon after the formation of the Regional Crime Squad one of the biggest manhunts ever known was mounted for a man named Harry Roberts, who had shot dead three Metropolitan Police Officers who had attempted to arrest him. There was a large reward out for any information leading to his arrest and conviction.

Alan was called to Bishops Stortford one night, as a burglar had been disturbed at a factory there. He attended with his dog, a German Shepherd of course, and tracked the burglar from the factory to some nearby woods. He flushed out and arrested the burglar, who was from a 'travelling family' camped in the woods. The man had dropped several items stolen from the factory during his hurry to get away and after the arrest Alan spent an hour or so searching the woods for them. During the search he found a small one-man tent pitched deep in the woods. No one was in the tent, but it appeared to have been recently occupied and there was an empty whisky bottle there. This bottle was removed and found to have Harry Roberts' fingerprints on it.

A twenty-four hour watch was mounted and Harry Roberts was captured when he returned to the tent. He was later convicted and sentenced to life imprisonment for murder. As a police officer one cannot claim a reward in these circumstances, but it seems a criminal can. The convicted burglar who Alan had arrested earlier claimed the reward from a prison cell and it was given to him!

Alan was so disgusted that he sat down and typed out his resignation the very same day. He later ran a successful security business in Harlow called 'Rent a Dog.'

As well as our own private cars, for which we were paid a mileage allowance, we were to be provided with one new radio car by Essex. This of course had an Essex police radio, which was useless the moment we entered any other police district which used a different wavelength. Another small irritation that the boys in the back room hadn't thought of – the mobile phone as we know it today had not yet been invented. Today for the younger population the thought of life without a mobile phone must be terrible indeed. Since the amount of mileage each officer was allowed to do in his own vehicle was limited, and in view of the long distances now having to be travelled even to see the boss at Hatfield, the Essex police vehicle received a great deal of use.

The first day we all assembled in our new offices was a little strange. We had no specific instructions as to what we were to do and no current enquiries to carry out. We were all in due course summoned to Hatfield for an address by our new Co-ordinator, but meantime we discussed the things we thought it would be a good idea to do nearer home. Since our first priority was to be an offensive against the theft of lorries and their loads, we envisaged that the use of informants would be paramount and that we should concentrate for a time on contacting our current informants and trying to recruit new ones. We knew that most insurance companies were willing to pay 10% of the value of recovered stolen goods and there was therefore the prospect of some very good 'earners' for informants.

Next we foresaw that we would be working in groups rather than individually and in public places including pubs and clubs etc. It was decided to refer to each other by first names at all times so that no mistakes would be made when in the company of the ungodly by calling out, "What are you drinking, Inspector?"

The task ahead seemed quite daunting. First of all there were the gangs that actually stole the lorries to investigate. Then the places where the stolen vehicles were taken to unload and of course the receivers of the stolen goods which was to involve many different levels of society. There was very little the thieves would not steal, usually after they had already planned where and how to dispose of the goods. Alcoholic drinks, foodstuffs, electrical goods, furniture and practically anything that was hauled daily along our roads. Likewise there is no corner of our society that is immune from buying something cheap that has 'fallen off a lorry'. It has been said before that 'if there were no receivers there would be no thieves,' and so we began by looking for the receivers.

Most of the really good information came from Bill O'Hara, who had far better contacts that any of us provincial officers. It was interesting that he was soon able to tell us of various farms and places in Essex and Hertfordshire that apparently were known about in the MPD but not to us! We kept observation on these places as we found out about them, and on a number of occasions recovered stolen vehicles and goods and arrested lorry thieves and receivers.

Some periods of observation were easier than others, but I recall one night when we spent several hours watching a place in Grays in Essex. One of the squad was dressed as a scarecrow and stood in the middle of a field, the only spot from which the entrance to the farm could be seen. The rest of us were concealed in places where we could see him. Eventually he gave the signal and we pounced. Great fun!

It was easy once you had the intelligence. It is interesting to note that not once did we go armed, nor even think about it. On occasions one or more of the ungodly made a run for it, but rarely did they put up a fight. Today it would be unthinkable to carry out some of the operations we conducted without a squad of armed men.

Whenever the theft of a lorry and its load was reported to the police the information was passed to the nearest Regional Crime Squad branch office for investigation. It became apparent very early on that in almost all cases the lorry driver himself was involved. This meant that if a driver was found tied up on the side of the road, or managed to struggle free and phone for help, nothing he told the police could be relied upon. For example he might say he had been stopped by four men in a blue pickup truck on the M11, so the police would rush off to the spot and start making enquiries, never with any success. In fact he had probably handed over his lorry and keys to the gang in a roadside café somewhere quite some distance from the location he gave. After finishing his breakfast he would be duly tied up, given a mild beating and dumped on the roadside somewhere fairly near to habitation or a phone box.

You may wonder why drivers would do this. Most lorry drivers are from a class of our society which has to work hard for a living. Like everyone else they are not all entirely honest and quite a good target for thieves who promise them a very large slice of cash to co-operate. After all they have nothing to lose. The lorry and goods are not theirs to lose and anyway, "It's the insurance companies who pay, no one else", as we were often reminded by villains who had been apprehended.

The catch was that the money was promised to the drivers after the load had been successfully disposed of. There was usually no previous connection between the lorry driver and the gang, who had approached him at a workman's café or lorry drivers' stopping place. To my knowledge none of the drivers so approached were ever paid the money they were promised, and the gang had no fear that they would go to the police to implicate themselves. Because a driver was not proud of what he did he rarely discussed the failure to receive his cash with his mates, so it was a long time before the penny dropped.

We developed techniques for interrogating drivers who reported their lorries stolen. It soon became apparent if a driver was telling the truth about his terrible experience, and we soon became quite successful in getting to the truth. Unfortunately it didn't often help to catch the thieves because the driver couldn't identify them by name even if he wanted to. Members of the squad posed as lorry drivers and sat around in café with some success and even posed as prospective buyers of stolen goods. Nobby Clarke was very good at that and talked their language like a native. It was dangerous work however, and we had none of the modern equipment for eavesdropping on conversations between undercover policeman and villain.

On one occasion we dressed Nobby up like a real toff with his best suit and overcoat, a smart new Derby hat and a pigskin brief case. A local and most co-operative car hire firm loaned us a Daimler car and I dressed up as the liveried chauffeur. We arrived at the venue, which was a private club in Epping called Bruno's, and did the business. It worked a treat and a few days later when the villains came to deliver the goods and collect their money we nabbed them.

During our first six months our small squad recovered many thousands of pounds' worth of stolen property and arrested more than a dozen good-class thieves. When an arrest was made it was the practice to take the prisoner or prisoners to the police station nearest to the place where the crime had been committed. It was often a question of dumping the prisoners on the local police and dashing off again to make further enquiries. The local police often didn't know the full facts or what to do with the prisoners, and frequently resented the offhand and superior manner Regional Crime Squad officers seemed to use.

This type of work soon led to a distinct deterioration in the mode of dress and general appearance of detectives on the squad. For some reason they all began to dress like the villains they were after. I deplored this trend. While I could see some merit in dressing 'down' a bit for occasions when one did not want to be identified as a 'copper,' it did rankle with me somewhat. However it seems I was once more in the minority. In those days, if you saw four or five hefty yobs together, looking like the oldest swingers in town, you were probably looking at members of the local crime squad!

For many years the Metropolitan Police had been able to avail themselves of telephone taps. It was a closely-guarded privilege and required a Home Office warrant to listen in to private phone conversations. There was no reason I knew of why a provincial force could not avail itself of this mode of investigation, given the necessity outlined in the particular legislation that covered the procedure, yet no one to my knowledge had ever done so.

A few months into our new crime squad days, one of the team got hold of some reliable information that a certain farm out in the wilds of Saffron Walden in Essex was a centre for distributing stolen goods. We spent a lot of time watching the place both at night-time and during the day, but were getting nowhere. I approached Mac with a view to having a telephone tap put on the farm. At first he was reluctant to agree, but later he said he would see what he could do if I could put a report together which would satisfy the requirements for a 'tap'. Once more I was between the devil and the deep blue sea, with a duty to tell Jack Barkway what I was up to. Fortunately this time there were no repercussions, and Jack merely asked me to keep him informed.

My report was duly submitted and a Home Office warrant granted. I was then to be initiated in how the phone tapping system actually worked. The GPO would be asked to make the necessary connections and all calls to and from the phone number in question would be routed through a special office at Scotland Yard. There was no way the calls could be monitored anywhere else in the country except New Scotland Yard.

Bill O'Hara took me up to see the Chief Inspector who was then in charge of the special office at New Scotland Yard and introduced me to him. He took me into the large office, where there were some dozen or so recorders and operators. Messages were recorded on reels of fine wire and duly labelled and placed in trays ready to be transcribed by a group of civilian typists who had been suitably trained and sworn to secrecy. The officer in each of the cases being dealt with had to go to this office to read the transcripts; they were never allowed to pass outside.

It was pointed out to me by the Chief Inspector that his men had a boring job, missing all the excitement of the chase that might result from their work. It was suggested that if any rewards were paid out for property recovered as the result of a phone tap, the usual 10%, then he expected to receive some form of thanks - his 'lads' usually had a small party - and any money left could be split between me and my informant in whatever proportion I considered proper. I considered this for a moment before saying, rather naïvely I suppose, "What informant?"

It would never be appropriate; it seems, for any evidence to be given at a later stage to the effect that the information had been obtained from a phone interception. Rather the thieves and the loser would have to believe that the police had received information from an accomplice or just got lucky. If I didn't have an informant I would have to invent one. However, as I was prompted, someone must have given the information for the Home Office warrant to be obtained, so *he* could receive his share of the reward. This sounded to me like a pretty unsatisfactory arrangement, but fortunately my honour and honesty were never put to the test.

It was my job to go to New Scotland Yard every couple of days to read the transcripts, and this soon revealed to me a flaw in the system. I obviously wasn't the first person to see the transcripts and it soon became apparent that information gained was being passed to the Flying Squad who 'wiped our eye', as the expression goes, by beating us to the punch on every occasion. The end result was the same, but our squad didn't get the credit for it.

Another occasion when I had my eye cleanly wiped by the Met was as the result of searching some premises in the Loughton area. Our information was good, but rather than endanger the informant by searching only the farm where we thought the hidden stolen property was, we searched six neighbouring farms as well. For this we enlisted the help of the local CID at Loughton. We 'scored' that day and recovered quite a good haul, for which the insurance company was duly grateful. When I rang them up to discuss the matter it was to learn that Loughton CID had already claimed the reward for their informant!

The fact that the drivers who co-operated with the gangs didn't get paid, and the initial success of the Regional Crime Squad, were largely the reasons why lorry thefts soon died out and the thieves turned to something better like 'long firm fraud'. This was something the Krays were good at in those days. It was relatively easy for them to find a stooge from their many criminal associates and set him up in business with a warehouse and an office. He would then place orders for small amounts of goods on credit from a number of big suppliers and establish creditworthiness by paying for them within the specified thirty days, or whatever the credit terms were. Then they would place a massive order and fill the warehouse with goods they did not pay for. By the time the suppliers realised they were not going to get paid and commenced recovery proceedings, the warehouse was empty.

Occasionally, but not always, we were able to trace the stooge, but he would always plead that he was working for other people who we couldn't trace. A few such stooges were convicted and got a year or so inside while their families were 'bunged' or looked after by the real culprits.

The first serious clash I had with Mac was over the use of the Essex police car. Jeff Turner was in hospital in Hertfordshire for several weeks following an operation. I forget exactly why he had the operation, but his condition was never life threatening. Mac instructed that each of the Harlow Branch members take it in turn to pick up Mrs Turner from her home and take her to visit her husband in hospital, on a daily rota basis. The Essex police car was to be used, and petrol paid for at public expense. I spoke to Mac on the phone and told him of my reservations about such a procedure, suggesting that any officer who wished to use his own car, at his own expense, to do this task could be permitted to do so.

Mac was furious that his instructions should be questioned and ordered me to comply. I could see the sort of hot water I could be in if my own headquarters found out about this. What about insurance cover for the passengers? Suppose there was an accident in Hertfordshire with Mrs Turner in the car, how would I explain that?

I rang Jack Barkway with my dilemma and on hearing what I had to say he said, "Under no circumstances are you to use a police car for this purpose. I'll ring you back shortly when I have spoken to the Chief Constable". He did indeed ring back and say that the Chief Constable had personally spoken with Mr MacArthur on the telephone and that he would be in touch with me. Meantime his own instruction should stand and the car should not be used to take Mrs Turner to the hospital.

Mac was on the phone almost as soon as I hung up. To put it mildly he was not very happy and ordered me to attend his office immediately, if not sooner. I dropped what I was doing and drove to Hatfield for the biggest dressing down I have ever had.

I stood in front of Mac's desk and took it like a man for a while. I was accused of disloyalty, disobedience, and so on until he was red in the face and I could stand no more. I knew I was on firm ground as far as my own force was concerned and at that stage couldn't give a fig if I stayed on the Crime Squad or not, I exploded.

"Sir, I am an Essex Officer" I told him. "I have been trained to obey orders, but my first loyalty is to Essex and second to common sense. If you can't stomach that then the sooner you get me transferred back to my own force the better. That will suit me fine, and no doubt suit you too."

"Get out!" he shouted.

He never referred to the matter again and only once did he ask me to do anything that I considered 'shady'. On that occasion we had another shouting match, but my two years was soon to be up and I had already been told that I was to become the Detective Inspector at Harlow.

After the demise of the lorry theft gangs, there was a period of limbo for the Regional Crime Squad, who didn't really know if they were to be disbanded or not. They were seen as a two-edged sword by divisional officers. On the one hand they were this scruffy bunch of chaps who arrived at some ungodly hour at their station with prisoners that had eventually to be processed. On the other they were an additional force of experienced men who were not, it seemed, afraid to cut corners, and who could be called in to assist with any dirty job the division didn't fancy.

In the end the squad was not disbanded and was indeed used to augment divisional staff when there was a 'big' job or enquiry, and in the mean time for many years they used to target criminals and collect intelligence about them and their crimes. No one ever reported offences directly to the Regional Crime Squad, so there was no pressure to clear up any particular crime or case load to contend with.

There were occasions when their informants came up with a useful tip about a wages snatch or jeweller's shop robbery, but the real fun of pursuing the lorry thieves was over, and the era was fast approaching, especially after the Harry Roberts affair, when armed officers of the Firearms Unit would be called in to deal with such matters.

Harry Batson, during my Fraud Squad days, had thought of the idea of having an observation vehicle. We managed to acquire an old van and with the help of the headquarters garage got it fairly roadworthy. In the sides were some slits disguised by a painted tradesman's sign and there was a radio fitted. It was real Heath Robinson, but it did prove useful in catching thieves in car parks and so on. It was used mainly by divisional officers as and when they thought it would be useful.

The Regional Crime Squad thought this was a great idea and we used it, and the later model, with some success. However we were in London one day keeping observation on a house where one or more of a gang of thieves lived. Some London gangs were now using the thermic lance. A gas pipe was filled with welding rods and connected to a supply of oxygen and acetylene. The resultant powerful burning tool when the end was lit would cut through several inches of steel, and was being used successfully by a gang known at the time as the Charringtons.

We had been sitting in the van keeping watch on the dwelling in East London for an hour or so when a woman came out of the house with a tray of mugs of tea. She banged on the back door of our van and said, "Here you are lads, thought you would like a cup of tea, you've got a long wait ahead".

There was soon to be a Force Support Unit, which was the uniform branch equivalent of the Regional Crime Squad except they were not from mixed forces. They would be used to deal with matters of crowd control and public disorder within the county and were trained in the use of firearms. Over the years various Acts of Parliament in the form of Police Acts, Criminal Law Acts and Criminal Evidence Acts have done much to deal with some of the problems beset by the boundaries, but many still existed.

Probably the greatest fundamental difference between the work of the Regional Crime Squad and Criminal Investigation Department was that the latter investigated crimes that had already been committed and the former investigated criminals, and crimes that had not yet been perpetrated. This necessitated the use of informants, who were after all only other criminals, and planning with them the arrest of their associates and other criminals during the commission of a crime that was either planned or would be planned in the future.

Informants in these circumstances colluded with the police only for their own gain. It was only a short step from informing on a crime already planned to instigating one himself. If the result was a reward for him and prisoners and recovered property for the police, what did it matter?

I have known of lorryloads of stolen goods being driven into a receiver's premises while officers of the Regional Crime Squad were there waiting to pounce. The driver of the lorry, the informant, would be allowed to escape while the receiver and his associates were arrested. I have taken part in watching for robbers to arrive to make a wages snatch, knowing that at least two of them had to be allowed to escape as they had given information; one about this crime and one about some other yet to be hatched. Sitting there knowing also that we were going to allow the crime to be committed in order to get all the necessary evidence, in spite of the fact that some unsuspecting security guard might get injured, or even killed, gave me a very uncomfortable feeling.

I had sworn an oath when I became a constable and I was proud of being part of a great tradition and a fine service. The oath included the words, "prevention and detection of crime". It said nothing about instigating crime, or conspiring with criminals in the commission of crime, in order to arrest other criminals. That is what the Regional Crime Squad sometimes did. While I don't deny this was the only way to catch professional thieves, given the strictures placed around the police in making legitimate enquiries, I could see the need for a different force of men not associated with the British Police, and a different type of man from me to do this kind of work.

I used the words 'professional criminals' because that is a phrase generally accepted as meaning a hardened criminal, a perpetual criminal or recidivist. 'Professional' in my view gives the 'crook' a status he doesn't deserve.. He is a crook, a thug, criminal, gangster, hoodlum, miscreant, offender, thief, thug, robber, call him what you will, but please, not a 'professional'.

I was, not surprisingly, happy to hand over my Squad to another Essex officer, John Camp, who I believe enjoyed Crime Squad work more than I did.

# Return to Harlow CID
# 1966 - 1967

*The girl was beheaded, chopped into pieces and placed in a trunk, but was not interfered with (newspaper report).*

My departure from the Regional Crime Squad was not without a sigh of relief. I had realised for some time that I was beginning to sink into a quagmire of dishonesty and deceit that I found distasteful. It was as if we were becoming part of the very sub-culture of society we were there to oppose. I don't mean that we were becoming criminals, but we did dress like them, talk like them and in many ways behave like them. It would not have been so bad doing some of the discreditable things that needed to be done, and on occasions was suggested that I do, to catch villains, if I had had official backing. It was however rather like a spy being sent into Germany during the war and being told, "If you get caught we don't know you". There was tacit and even expressed approval for some of the dubious methods we used to catch thieves, but if anything went wrong it was 'down to you'.

Out there in the 'jungle' there are undoubtedly a good many very dangerous, disreputable and antisocial people. There is also no doubt that the public want them caught and put away. The dirty work of society! Dirty work usually means getting one's hands dirty, and yet the police are supposed to do this public duty while wearing kid gloves and with all the restraints placed upon them by the law and Government rules and regulations, while under the constant scrutiny of the media. In the heyday of the Flying Squad and to some extent the early days of the Regional Crime Squad many officers were prepared to take risks of physical injury and of breaking the rules, with all the possible unpleasant consequences of doing so. In the present day police force few are prepared to accept such risks, and who can blame them?

Now, happily, I was to go back to normal divisional CID duties that suited me better, and seemed to me more of a challenge to the 'little grey cells.'

In my few years away from Harlow Divisional Police Headquarters it hadn't changed very much. The population and size of the town had grown considerably and the CID now had a Chief Inspector in charge; I was to be his deputy. Detective Chief Inspector George Tame was known to me, but I hadn't served with him since the Romford days when he was a detective at Hornchurch. I knew him to be a forceful detective who would stand little nonsense.

I recall one night standing in the doorway of the Electricity Board showroom opposite Romford police station at midnight waiting to go in for a cup of tea, as was the custom. A scruffy youth, clearly the worse for drink, staggered up to me with blood on his face and a swollen eye.

"You got a detective in there, name of Tate?" he growled: I had seen George Tame go into the station a short time earlier.

"No," I said truthfully.

"Well some bastard just done me over, said he was a detective name of Tate."

"What did you do to upset him?" I said.

"Told 'im to fuck off didn't I?"

"Well what do you expect?" I said, "If you've got a complaint you'd better get across the road and make it."

"Lot of fucking good that'd do. I'd probably get another pasting." He wandered off down South Street, tail between his legs.

I thought at first that I would get on well with George, as we were both practical coppers and saw eye to eye about many things. He didn't much like the Crime Squad however, and I realised that I should not sing its praises too much. We shared an office unfortunately, which meant he was able to watch every move I made, and he occasionally disagreed with the way I was doing or proposed to do something.

I had a big advantage over him too, which I don't think he cared for. I had been a Detective Constable at Harlow and I knew the town well and had a lot of contacts there. He was comparatively new to the area and expected me to introduce him to all my acquaintances, which just wasn't on. It led to eventual conflict between us, although nothing that I considered serious. I suppose another factor was my independence. Many of my critics over the years have used that word in reports about me. I confess I am not a team player and like being in charge.

The department had grown too; there was now another Detective Sergeant, one Dick Ashby, and two more Detective Constables, Johnny Lambourne and Mick Patrick. Ron Stark was still there although Alan Wyatt and Cliff Stollery had moved on. The caseload had grown and everyone was constantly busy.

When I think of Dick Ashby I recall a very slim, quiet man with a lot of experience. He reminds me of much later in my career when I used to give lectures at the training school on a number of subjects including the interrogation of suspects. In my talk I used to give the following true example of the good guy, bad guy approach.

Harlow had been suffering for several weeks from a housebreaker who entered flats and houses during the daytime and broke open gas and electric meters. We called him our 'meter man' until he was eventually caught. We had a good description of him but for some time no idea of his identity. We analysed the offences that had been committed - we used to stick coloured pins in a map etc - no computer databases then. I calculated that he would strike again on a particular day between certain times and in a certain area. Officers were placed at various points in the area and sure enough we got lucky. The culprit was a ginger-haired youth about eighteen years of age who was spotted in the vicinity of a block of flats. We had taken out a 'descriptive arrest warrant' and his description was near enough to justify an arrest. A descriptive warrant, as its name implies, is an arrest warrant for a person whose description is known, but whose name is not.

The arresting officer interviewed him for an hour or so but got nowhere. I was asked to 'have a go at him' and did so, using all the skill I had, shouting, threatening, cajoling, promising leniency and so on, all to no avail.

Dick Ashby then suggested he had a chat with the lad, as he knew him vaguely. Dick sat down quietly with the suspect, tut-tutted and said, "Well well lad, what on earth is your mum going to say about all this?" The suspect, hitherto defiant and abusive, burst into tears and in a few minutes was making a full confession. He admitted over one hundred offences.

I must add that all the time spent on the interview by myself and other officers was not wasted. The softly-softly approach does not work by itself and has to be preceded by the tough guy bit. Even this simple psychology is today not permitted, despite what you see on television.

During the last war methods of interrogation were devised by both sides that would not be permitted in peacetime or when dealing with criminals. The methods were very effective, even the ones that did not include pulling out fingernails or attaching electrodes to their testicles. Of course they were fighting a war. Aren't we?

It wasn't long before I realised that as a supervising officer you didn't have much practical police work to do, and as a deputy, very little administration either. Of course there were always enough paperwork and reports crossing one's desk, but for me that wasn't enough and I soon began to look for some cases of my own. Crime was reported in various ways but rarely directly to a Detective Inspector. I was in the enviable position of being able to pick out any case I fancied and say, "I'll do that". There were also cases of a more serious nature that someone of the rank of Inspector was expected to take charge of, or at least have a hand in. These included suspicious deaths, armed robbery, safe blowing and rape. However for a while I did have some time to look around and pick up the threads of any outstanding cases that I thought I could look at.

I had moved house to a place called East Park, not far from the old Regional Crime Squad offices and quite near a junior school. Close to my house was a main road and opposite the school was a public convenience. I found that several complaints had been received from parents that there were improper things going on in the public conveniences and that on occasions men had approached and spoken to children. Nothing serious had occurred, but there was a lot of concern about the place. As I lived nearby I resolved to do something about it and keep an eye on it. The toilet itself was filthy and the walls covered in messages left by the various misfits that used the place. The wall facing the urinals was completely covered and one could hardly avoid reading some of the messages if you did stand there for a pee. Unlike many such public toilets where you saw messages such as, "Please don't put cigarette ends in the toilet – It makes them wet and soggy and hard to light," those on this wall were all too clear invitations to meet and perform acts of gross indecency, some of them with intimate details of what these acts would consist of. When I first examined the place I was amused at what one 'wag' had written, "A Merry Christmas to all our readers".

It was at first obvious that it was a place where people went to seek and invite acts of gross indecency, since the walls were a veritable notice board for such perverts. I contacted the local authority and arranged to have access to the roof space. I had a number of small holes drilled in the ceiling and had officers spend an hour or so up there watching, whenever they had some spare time. We kept a log of every incident that took place, but for a while nothing 'arrestable' happened. Incidentally the log, later produced at court in evidence, showed that a very small percentage of persons who went into the toilets used them for what they were intended.

I was having lunch one day when I was telephoned at home. The officer who had been watching had radioed in to the station to say that he had arrested two men. I dashed across to the public toilet to find my detective had arrested the police surgeon and a young trainee priest! He had watched them enter separate cubicles and pass notes to each other through a hole in the dividing wall. Then they both went into one cubicle and the doctor was participating in oral sex with the young cleric. 'Giving him a blow job' was the expression used by my officer.

There was a great deal of concern when we arrived at the station, scratching of heads, looking up the law on gross indecency and eventually consulting the County Prosecuting Solicitor before it was decided to grant them bail and to submit a file for further consideration. On many occasions the granting of bail was an admission by the police that they were not sure what to do. This was one such occasion.

The young would-be priest failed to answer his bail and it turned out that he had been sent off to Italy to work. The church authorities were not very helpful and after all it was not really a matter for extradition. The doctor was charged with procuring an act of gross indecency and public disorder and elected to go for trial.

The local papers had a field day after the committal proceedings and during the few weeks that it took for the case to come before the Quarter Sessions, I received quite a bit of criticism in the local press. I also received hate mail at the police station addressed to, 'Lavatory Inspector Raven', containing obscene and abusive words and material. Unfortunately none of this could be used as evidence against the accused, although the defence referred to it in their criticism of the police generally and me in particular.

In due course the police surgeon appeared at Chelmsford Quarter Sessions. Without the second man there were some matters of evidence that were difficult, but the County Prosecuting Solicitor decided it was worth pursuing. There was not a little criticism of the police methods in this case and at the end of a trial lasting several days the jury found him not guilty. However the *News of the World* went for him like a bulldog the following Sunday, so I had my day in court, and I have no doubt that it was a long time before he went into a public toilet again.

The council did then close the public convenience and

the parents of the schoolchildren applauded. The doctor was allowed to continue to practise, but not as a police surgeon! The matter was soon forgotten and my reputation restored.

Complaints of sexual offences were quite frequent in Harlow and on one occasion I arrested a schoolteacher after several complaints from parents that he had interfered with their children. He used to keep one or two back after school and teach them gymnastics, during which it is alleged he touched them unnecessarily and often indecently. He was the schoolteacher who produced the end of term play and always seemed to want the girls whose ages were between seven and eleven to wear vest and knickers when he photographed them, as he did quite often. One of the films he made, which was later used as evidence, showed a rather large girl of eleven bending over touching her toes wearing a pair of black knickers with the words, 'The End' pinned on them.

Statements were taken from every girl in his class and each had a similar tale to tell of him touching them between the legs, on the breasts and so on. The rules of evidence once again allowed him to get off scot free, as 'the evidence of a child of tender years cannot be corroborated by another child of tender years', even in this case thirty other children. There was just not enough corroboration, and with the help of an expensive counsel he got off. After the trial at Chelmsford we had to lock him up for his own safety. For a while thirty mothers and fathers went on the rampage and mounted a big protest at the court. They would no doubt have lynched him if they could have got to him.

It is interesting that men like this, and there are

unfortunately a lot of them about, would not appear on any register of sex offenders, yet they are just as potentially dangerous as those that are. He was allowed to continue teaching!

Complaints of rape were not so frequent, although there were far more complaints of rape than there were rapes. Some time later in my service, after I had investigated a good many rape allegations, I wrote an article on the subject which was published in the Police College Magazine, *The Criminologist* (1993) and an Essex University magazine called *Orbiter* produced by their Faculty of Law. It has, I am told, been read by many would-be criminologists and others. It does, you may feel, look at the subject objectively and realistically as opposed to the subjective and idealistic stance taken by many others who have pontificated on the subject. (See Appendix i).

It was during this period of my service that I attended my first post mortem on a child. Perhaps morticians and pathologists get used to post mortem examinations, but few police officers ever do. It is a necessary part of a detective's job and after a while one becomes a bit hardened to it; a body taken out of the sea, a villain who has been stabbed or shot and even the occasional wife who has been beaten to death. A child however is a different matter, and the tragedy of a child being murdered by a brutal parent or guardian is bad enough even for the investigating officer to bear, but to see the poor little mite on the mortuary slab being cut and sliced and the bits examined under a microscope is an ordeal I wouldn't wish on anyone.

In the early sixties the pathologist at the St Margaret's Hospital at Epping was a woman. She was a very senior member of the staff there and extremely good at her job. Not only was she a good pathologist but she was most co-operative with the police and an excellent 'expert' witness. The pathologist, whose name I just cannot now recall, was in her early fifties; she usually dressed in a tweed suit and flat brogues and spoke in deep clear tones. While preparing the manuscript for this book I asked an old colleague if he could remember her name, and he couldn't. "Oh, you mean the 'old battleaxe'!" he said.

She was, at first acquaintance, a formidable lady in whose presence one should have felt trembling and inferior. However she had a way of making you feel her equal and was warm-hearted and friendly. Often she would take you confidentially into her laboratory and show you slides through her microscope and explain the finer points of what she had discovered during the examination of your 'corpse'. A corpse actually belongs to the Coroner until any investigation and inquest is over, but as the coroner's representative, the investigating officer was always regarded as the owner of the body until such time as it was released for burial.

One morning I received a telephone call from the hospital. It was the pathologist, who told me a child's body had been brought in as a 'cot death'. She was not very happy about it and suggested I might like to go along to the autopsy.

The child was less than a year old, a little girl, whose body looked so tiny on the great stainless steel slab. It was pointed out to me that there was bruising on the arms and ankles, and I was shown x-rays which indicated to the pathologist, although I as a layman found it difficult to notice them, eleven healed fractures of the ribs and a hairline fracture of the skull.

After the first incisions were made and the rib cage removed, the pathologist started to make noises like, "Ah!" and "Mmm," and mumble words like, "Just as I thought," and, "Classical Battered Baby Syndrome". She pointed out to me the tiny lumps along the line of the ribs which were the healed fractures.

This pathologist had studied under Professor Keith Simpson, who was at one time the leading expert on Battered Baby Syndrome, and on many other things. She was not unnaturally very interested in the subject and most meticulous in her examination of the bodies of babies who had allegedly suffered 'cot deaths'.

Examination of the brain showed that there were contusions on one side of it that indicated that the brain had suffered a sudden and violent movement from one side of the head to the other. The pathologist suggested to me that the child had been picked up by its feet and swung against a wall or something hard causing injury to the head and brain and that this had caused the child's death.

Later at the parents' home I examined the cot, a wooden affair with plywood panels at head and foot. A careful examination of the headboard revealed a small split and the Scenes of Crime officer was able to find traces of the baby's head hair in the crack.

I arrested both parents, since neither would make any admission that the child had been ill-treated or assaulted in any way. They both in due course appeared at Lewes Assizes. It was not unusual for cases like this to be transferred to some remote court, if it looked like it might be a lengthy case and the Essex Assize list was pretty full. The case started on a Monday and was expected to last at least two weeks.

For me the timing was pretty inconvenient. I had booked and paid for a holiday with my family that was due to start on the following Saturday. It was one of the disturbances to family life that officers, and particularly their wives and families, had to suffer. Consideration might have been given and court dates altered to accommodate other witnesses, but not police officers. One of the better changes in police procedures that has taken place is that now you are required to submit your forecast leave dates with your file so that consideration might be given to them when fixing a court date. Of course it doesn't always work, because in our wonderfully speedy legal process it might be more than a year hence when your case comes up.

After the initial speeches and opening remarks by counsel the witness started to give their evidence. It seemed that the defence was going to be that any injuries on the child's body had been caused accidentally and in the normal course of the day-to-day handling of the infant. The second day started with the pathologist's evidence and she gave it in her usual concise and professional manner. The defence counsel stood up to cross-examine. After a few preliminary questions as to her qualifications, which were quite considerable, he said,

"Doctor, were the bruises on the arms and legs of the child consistent with normal handling of the baby?"

"Not unless one was particularly rough in the handling" the doctor said.

"But it is true is it not that some mothers, and even fathers are rather rough? They toss their children in the air and play with them, occasionally perhaps being a little rough and cause a slight bruise or two on a child's tender skin?"

"Yes".

Council for the defence smiled, thinking he was making a good start. "The injuries to the head. Are they not consistent with a fall?"

"Yes".

Counsel adjusted his robe and wig and made a significant glance towards the jury. "The sort of fall that might occur if a baby fell off the mother's or father's lap onto the floor?"

"No".

A frown crossed the counsel's face, "Well what sort of fall then?"

"If the baby fell out of an upstairs window onto a pavement below. That sort of fall." The pathologist looked directly at counsel and defied him to take the matter further.

"My lord," he said. "Might I have a few minutes' recess to consult with my clients?"

The recess was granted and after about ten minutes counsel came back and asked whether one of his clients, the father, could change his plea to guilty. The prosecution accepted this and offered no evidence against the mother, who was herself a battered wife, and the case was over. I went on my holiday as planned.

This was unfortunately not the last time I had to witness an autopsy on a child; they were all too frequent. Soon after this case there was another where the death was caused in a similar manner, except that the child was swung against the wall; this time it was the mother who confessed. On another occasion a young woman had a row with her husband and packed her case to walk out on him. When she got to the bottom of the stairs the husband came to the top and said, "You can take your fucking baby with you," and threw a three-month-old child at her. Neighbours heard the commotion and later at court described how the baby was then thrown from one to the other across a fence in the garden until one of them dropped it onto a concrete path.

Knowing how meticulous this pathologist was and how apparently less so were others I have seen, I wonder how many so called 'cot deaths' have actually been something far more sinister.

Fortunately not all post mortems resulted in police enquiries and subsequent prosecutions. Many proved to be accidental, suicide or natural causes. The body of a man was discovered one winter morning lying in a gutter, his face badly smashed in. The man was otherwise apparently healthy and uninjured and it looked initially as if he had either been attacked where found, or dumped from or even hit by a vehicle.

At the scene the man was found to have his hands in his overcoat pocket. Not surprising really, as he had no gloves and the morning was bitter cold with ice on the road. The post mortem showed that death was a direct result to a blow to the front of the head. The site and type of injury was consistent with a fall, and it was eventually concluded that he had slipped on the ice while walking to work, had been unable to get his hands out of his pocket quickly enough to break his fall, and had hit his head on the granite kerb stone. I always think of this case when I am walking along in the snow or on a frozen surface, and am always very careful not to keep my hands in my pockets.

On another occasion an old lady was found dead lying in the sideway between her house and a coalbunker. The cause of death was 'doubtful' and there was a post mortem. The oesophagus was blackened and it looked at first as though she had drunk a corrosive liquid. There was no smell of such however and the mouth was not burned, as one would have expected. It turned out that the old lady had choked on the acid contents of her stomach and had a heart attack, which was what had actually killed her. The blackened and burned lining of her oesophagus was caused by hydrochloric acid from the stomach.

As the Detective Inspector I was of course a senior officer to some, although still one of the federated ranks. I soon discovered for the first time that I was also a supervising officer. As a Detective Sergeant on the Fraud Squad I had no subordinates to oversee, and on the Regional Crime Squad we were all pretty much equals, being on first-name terms. There were no 'Progress' or 'Annual' reports for me to do and except when one of the bosses wanted to know something or to hand down a reprimand, I barely knew I was the 'Guv'.

As a supervising officer one is supposed to give 'on the job' training, guidance and advice as well as sort out many of the domestic and other problems of your men. I suppose that infidelity and alcoholism are no more prevalent in the police force than they are in most other jobs, but they certainly cause more headaches for the supervising officers. I don't know of any other job where a wife would come to a man's place of work to complain that her husband was being unfaithful to her and to suggest it was the fault of his supervising officers.

Drink and women have been the downfall of many men, and no doubt they will continue to be for many years to come; policemen are no exception. Sir Jonathan Peel took a very dim view of an officer who let down his wife. He considered that he had also let down the job and if he didn't sack him for misconduct he would certainly move him to a remote part of the county, as far away as possible from the cause of the complaint.

Unfortunately this policy of moving a chap every time he committed some infringement of the code of conduct expected of a police officer or other infraction of the rules was not an effective solution in many cases. It also punished other people, including the man's family, children who perhaps had to change schools, the innocent wife, who was perhaps chairman of her local ladies club etc, and not least another officer and his family, who might have to be moved to make way for the defaulter. However short of sacking an officer there was in many cases little else that could be done to punish such an offender and rectify the situation.

Sir John Nightingale (I believe he had received his summons to the Palace by this time) had a more liberal view of infidelity and of most discipline regulations. I had one married officer who was having an affair with an office typist at the police station. She became pregnant and the officer left his wife and was living with his paramour in a flat above some shops in the town. When the 'proverbial' hit the fan and we had all finished submitting large A57s, the Chief's decision was that the force would pay the officer's rent for the flat and allow the wife to continue to live in the police house for as long as necessary to resolve the marital situation. There was no 'move' and no other action taken. I scratched my head in disbelief, but there was little more I could do.

There was a police discipline regulation that no one could grow a beard without permission. One officer did so while on leave and when he returned to duty was ordered by the Chief Superintendent to shave it off. The officer refused and the Chief Superintendent sought to discipline him. Sir John overruled him and gave the chap permission to keep his beard.

Times and attitudes were of course changing, and even homosexuality was not treated as such a heinous crime in those days, although it was a little later when legislation made it legal between consenting adults. This decision by the Government certainly was a great shock and a blow to the police service, all members of which had been taught that a homosexual act was an offence against nature and a most serious crime. There is currently a great deal of concern about paedophiles in our country and one might laugh at a suggestion that paedophilia should ever be made legal.

That's what we all thought about homosexual behaviour. During my police career I met and had various dealings, professional of course, with men who were homosexual. I never knew one who wasn't also a paedophile. When searching their premises, amongst the other accessories kept by this type of individual we invariably found pornographic pictures of young children. Listening to their depraved conversation you always hear about their fantasies with 'little boys'.

Legalising homosexual behaviour, or decriminalising it, may have appeased a certain section of society who wish to behave in a manner contrary to nature, but it also gives a tacit nod and a wink to the paedophiles of our community. This is something our politicians don't know, won't admit or deliberately choose to ignore.

At the time when the law was changed there was a joke currently doing the rounds about a man who went to the Australian Embassy in London to apply for a visa to go to Australia.

"Why do you want to go to Australia?" He was asked.

"I want to get as far away from England as possible" he said.

"For what reason?" The official said.

His answer was. "When I was young, homosexuality was illegal. Now they have made it legal, and I want to get away from here before they make it compulsory!"

It was quickly apparent to me as a supervising officer who among the officers were earning their wages and who, if any, were not. There were two officers at Harlow at one time who lived next door to each other in police houses. The wives were friendly and one used to say to the other, "I can't understand why my husband is out at work every evening until late and yours is always home by 6pm".

The lady in question eventually came to see me to ask that I didn't work her husband so hard. Fortunately she didn't believe that he was doing anything other than work, and luckily she was right. This chap was as keen as mustard and was off like a ferret after any lead he turned up, day or night. No one complained if you worked overtime in those days, they didn't have to pay you for it! Of the two officers concerned, the hard-working one made Detective Chief Inspector and the other remained a constable. Hard work sometimes did have its reward!

I did not enjoy supervising, and while realising that it was an integral part of being a senior officer there seems to me to be something wrong with an organisation that pays an expert a lot of money to be an expert and then requires him to spend most of his time doing a job any clerk could do - make out duty rosters, ensure that cars are sent to the garage for service regularly, check on the mileage being used by the vehicles and officers' expense claims and so on. Much of the work I did at Harlow was not suitable work for a trained and now fairly experienced detective. I couldn't wait to get away from there.

I didn't have to wait long. I was called up to Headquarters one day and sent in to see the Chief Constable. On this occasion Sir John was not his usual sarcastic and abrupt self. He had me sit down, which was a rare treat.

I recalled the story of the little schoolboy who was asked

to write an essay about the police. When he had finished there were just four words on his paper: "All coppers are bastards". The teacher was appalled and decided something should be done. She contacted the local police station, who sent along an officer to talk to the class. Then he took them round the police station, showed them the cells and took them for a ride in the police car. Afterwards the teacher asked the boy in question to write his essay again. This time when he had finished there were five words on his paper: "All coppers are crafty bastards".

The Chief told me that he wanted me to go to Harwich as a uniformed Inspector. I was sure that news of my differences with George Tame had reached his ears and that I was going to get a 'sideways' move. I said as much, but he assured me that this was not so and that there had been a spot of trouble at Harwich and that he wanted me to go there as he knew I could 'sort things out and put matters to rights'.

"All coppers are crafty…" I thought again. The Chief went on to say that Harwich was going to be upgraded to a Chief Inspector station within two years and that if I made a good job of it there I would be the sitting tenant.

He could see that I was not at all keen to go back into uniform, and didn't insist. Instead he told me to go away and think about it, to have a word with my family and so on. When I left his office, his secretary told me that Jack Barkway wanted to see me in his office before I left to return to Harlow. That told me he knew I had been to see the Chief and no doubt knew the reason why.

In Jack's office I was also invited to sit down. He asked

me if I had decided whether or not to accept the post at Harwich. I told him of my misgivings and, like the Chief, Jack assured me that it was not a sideways move and that a spell in uniform was essential for me, whether I decided to pursue a career in the CID or not. He also filled me in on the 'spot of trouble' that they had had at Harwich. It seemed that one officer had been having woman trouble and another had been 'borrowing' money from the petty cash. He had been unfortunate in that there was an audit one day before he had had a chance to put it back. He was later to appear at court, and if I remember correctly was sacked.

I didn't think this was a really good enough excuse to warrant a Detective Inspector being sent to Harwich to 'sort it out'. It had already been sorted, and was no different from the problems at any station. Neither was it a sideways move for the Inspector at Harwich because, as I later learned, he was being promoted and going to Brentwood.

I could see that sideways move or not, I had to accept the job. To accept might mean a delay in any future promotion, and to refuse would have been foolish, as it would undoubtedly have alienated both Jack Barkway and Sir John. So reluctantly I accepted.

# Harwich
# 1967–1969

*And here the sea-fogs leap and cling*
*And here, each warning each,*
*The sheep-bells and the ship-bells ring*
*Along the hidden beach.*
*(Rudyard Kipling)*

On reflection I don't think accepting the job at Harwich was such a bad thing, and my two years there were probably among the most enjoyable of my service. Having gone there believing I had been moved sideways, I intended to do my job as best I could, but I was not trying to impress anyone to further my career, and as the months went by and I felt more comfortable in uniform, I began to realise that there were other things in life beside chasing villains.

Harwich was a sub-division of Clacton Division. The Chief Superintendent in charge was Bill Docker, a real gentleman. His deputy, another old soldier, was Reg Pearson, who sadly died of a heart attack several years before he was due to retire.

Reg's case was typical of a problem, still unresolved today, concerning police pensions, which were generally regarded as good. Police paid 11% of their wages into a fund for their retirement pension, and if they died before their wife their pension, or a large proportion of it, automatically passed to their widow. However the catch is that this only applies if you are still a serving officer when you get married, and a police widow loses her pension altogether if she remarries. Reg's widow lived comfortably on her husband's pension for some years after his death but then met and married Ken Alston, a retired Assistant Chief Constable who also had a good pension. As soon as Doris Pearson married Ken she lost her husband's pension, but that was fine because they had Ken's. However when Ken Alston died suddenly a year or so later Doris was left practically penniless, with nothing but a state widow's pension to live on.

Harwich was some twenty-two miles away from Divisional Headquarters across a large stretch of Essex countryside. It was therefore not every day one saw anyone from Clacton: most communication was done by telephone.

I was in charge again, and soon began to realise that being in charge of the police in a sizeable and important town like Harwich was a great deal more enjoyable than I had ever imagined it would be. I was virtually the Chief Constable of Harwich, and as I was soon to find out, ex officio, a member of the social hierarchy of the town. I also soon learned that I was not permitted to leave the sub-division for any reason without the express permission of the Chief Superintendent. I was for the first time in the position of having twenty-four hour responsibility, and someone else had to be designated as 'in charge' if I was not there. This is a little restrictive, but not at all as inconvenient as it might sound at first.

Harwich sub-division had several detached beats with constables at places as far afield as Manningtree, Oakley, Bradfield and Ardleigh, and a section station at Mistley with a Sergeant and two constables. At Harwich there were three uniformed sergeants and twenty-four constables and a CID department with a sergeant and two constables. There were two civilian staff a gardener/handyman and one typist.

The Mistley Section Sergeant was Dennis Murfitt, one of a dying breed. He was another pipe smoker and whenever I visited him, after the formalities of such a visit; signing of books etc, he would suggest we go across the road to his local for a pint. There his evil-smelling pipe would come out and we could discuss the various current matters concerning his section and personnel in a relaxed and friendly way.

It was at one such informal meeting that we were called back to the station. Some children playing in a copse about half a mile away had come across a body hanging from a tree. Sergeant Murfitt took the details and I went with him to the scene, where sure enough there was a man of about fifty hanging by a rope from a tree. It is always difficult to know in such circumstances whether to cut the body down and try resuscitation and perhaps destroy evidence, or to assume that the corpse is dead and send for the photographer, scenes of crime officers and the CID. In this case the decision was not so difficult since there were maggots crawling in and out of the eyes ears and mouth. There was little doubt that the body had been there for several days. There was an overturned stool beneath the man's feet and Sergeant Murfitt knew immediately who the man was. He had been reported missing by his wife a few days earlier and had apparently been suffering from depression because of money worries.

Suicide was infrequent in the rural areas of Essex, although not unheard of. However in the larger towns and urban areas it was all too common and many of the circumstances of such deaths were very sad indeed. I was to have dealings with several in the coming years.

Harwich was not by any means an unimportant town and was already known nationally for its passenger ferry to the Hook of Holland operated by British Rail. There was also another little-known British Rail ferry taking goods and trains across to Holland from a place called Gas House Creek. At Harwich itself there was another port, that of the Harwich Dock Company, was used for freight transport to Hamburg and Bremen. Later DFDS Ferries extended this to passenger services to Bremen and Hamburg.

There was a Warner's Holiday Camp, at Harwich too, which during the summer provided the sub-division with extra work, not to mention extra traffic through the town, and also free use of the swimming pool. In the winter the facilities of the camp were used for functions, including police dances, and for other shows and exhibitions arranged by local clubs and organisations. It is also where the TV series *Hi-De-*

*Hi* was made and there were usually a few celebrities around who appreciated the occasional sight of a uniformed constable.

On one occasion, after the filming had ended for the evening, there was a party going on in one of the bars. One of the stars realised he had locked his Mercedes and left the keys inside, so he rang the police. Realising that a Mercedes was supposed to be very up to date in the security department, and that it was not likely to succumb to the bunch of spare keys kept at most police stations for this kind of emergency, we rang a local locksmith, who attended forthwith. After a few minutes tampering in the car park he went into the bar and handed the star his car keys and a bill for £20, which was paid with alacrity.

"How did you manage it?" he said. "Those cars are supposed to have all the latest security measures".

"You left the sun roof open" said the locksmith without humour. "All I did was lean in and take the keys out of the ignition." We were surprised that the incident didn't feature in one of the shows.

At the station we had our own cell block, approved by the Home Office, although the cells were pretty basic and very cold in winter. In addition to our own prisoners, they were used frequently to house prisoners arrested by Immigration, Customs and Special Branch at Parkeston. On the wall of the cell block was a brass plate with an engraved horizontal line, which showed the level reached by the water during the great floods of 1953. On the bookshelf in my office was a book written about those floods, which I read in due course.

Stories in it included one about an officer who cycled down to the Harwich Quay to warn residents and was himself cut off and had to spend several hours in the Pier Hotel until he could be rescued. "A likely story" you might well say.

We also had an area car of our own, which was a fairly recent acquisition. Until then the Inspector was the only one who had a car authorised for police use, and he generally wasn't very happy to have to use his nice clean car for transporting prisoners, especially dirty or drunken ones. In 1953, when most of the east coast was flooded, the Harwich Inspector at the time was an Inspector Wood, known for some reason as Tokyo Joe. He had just bought a new car, which was in the garage at the rear of the police station the night the floods hit Harwich. It was totally immersed in water for several days, and a complete write off.

I moved into the Inspector's residence, which was a part of the Harwich police station in the summer of 1967. My house was connected to the part of the building used as the police station proper by a door on the ground floor giving access directly into the general office. There was also access through a door in my bedroom, which allowed me to walk down directly into the canteen and games room, where there was a snooker table.

I don't know how many of my predecessors had had their night's sleep interrupted by the click-click of snooker balls at three o'clock in the morning, but one of my first acts to 'sort things out and put matters to rights' as suggested by the Chief Constable was to ban the playing of snooker on night duty.

Many of us have a relative who has influenced us, given us good advice and become our idol. Often it was mother or father. In my case it was my Uncle Jim, who was a colonel in the Royal Indian Army Service Corps. As a small boy he used to come and visit us in his immaculate uniform and Sam Browne. I was so proud of him I could taste it and he always brought me a gift that I cherished like no other. It was a 'Smoker's Outfit' and contained sweet cigarettes, liquorice pipes and coconut tobacco. I would ask him how I could grow up to be an officer like him, and he'd say that he hoped I would.

"When you grow up to be an officer," he said, "Try to be a good officer, not a popular one. You cannot be both!"

I remembered this at Harwich when I made that first order. I was not going to be popular, of that I was sure, but as I began to assess my three sergeants and twenty-four constables I vowed that as their Inspector I was going to 'inspect' them like they had never been inspected before. There was an air of casualness about the station that I felt might be at the bottom of what the Chief Constable had said to me.

It was the practice for a constable to salute an Inspector or above when he was approached in the street by one. Indeed there was a Force Standing Order stating that this form or courtesy was to be paid. Within a few days of my arrival I approached one constable at a point who smiled and said, "All right sir?"

"Don't you salute your Inspector when he comes to visit you?" I said.

"No" said the officer, somewhat to my surprise.

"Why not?" I asked.

"No one does here" he said.

"You do from tonight Constable, and you can let your colleagues know that they do too." I examined his pocket book with a fine-tooth comb and found several errors and omissions in it. I pointed these out to him, as well as the dust on his helmet that hadn't seen a brush for some time. I reminded him that from now on it was I who would be writing his annual report, and that if he was in any way concerned that it should be favourable then he should buck his ideas up.

It rapidly got around that I was a new broom intending to sweep very clean. I examined books and registers and looked in cupboards that hadn't been opened for years. I went out in the middle of the night to the far reaches of the sub-division and made points with officers who I suspect had rarely seen an Inspector out after dark. Apart from appearing every morning at eight o'clock, I purposely avoided getting into any habits so far as my times of arrival and departure in the station were concerned, and the staff never knew when or where I would make an appearance.

Whether I would have chosen to exert my new-found authority in this way at Harwich had it not been for the hint of the Chief Constable that all was not well there, I am not sure, but while it lasted I enjoyed the power of wielding the new broom, and the station was soon buzzing with a new sense of efficiency.

There were few ways to communicate one's wishes and

instructions to a group of men who were never all together at the station, so the accepted way was by memo. A memo would be drafted and issued, and then circulated for everyone to initial. I confess to issuing several memos in the early days of my rule.

There was at Harwich a wealthy local businessman, also an eccentric, named Leonard Rose. 'Pummy' Rose, as he was known to all, was officially an estate agent, but I believe had other business interests. He was until his death some years ago a constant source of trouble to the police and to everyone else with whom he came into contact. In particular he had a long-running feud with the Harwich Golf Club in general, and their Chairman Mr Geoff Smith in particular, over a boundary between the golf course and his land. This dispute, which had become an obsession with Rose, was the main thrust of his constant demands that the police take action against the Golf Club and Geoff Smith for trespass, assault, theft, criminal damage and so on.

Geoff Smith and his wife Anne ran the Pier Hotel in Harwich and on one occasion Rose had been thrown out of the pub and barred. He took Smith to court, claiming that as it was an inn, as defined under some old obscure law, the landlord was obliged to serve any traveller who might call at his premises. The case was thrown out on the grounds that Rose lived in Harwich and was therefore not a 'traveller' as was also defined in the statute. This made him as mad as hell, and he frequently used to stand outside the Pier Hotel and shout abuse at Geoff and his wife.

Rose, although said to be wealthy, behaved badly, dressed

like a tramp and wore no shoes or socks. He went swimming in the sea most days throughout the year and was apparently as fit as the proverbial butcher's dog.

During my first week at Harwich my kitchen door burst open one morning as I was having my breakfast, and in stormed Rose, demanding that I take some action concerning his perceived problems. I was at first surprised, then shocked and then angry and ordered him out. I held his arm and he protested loudly and violently as I showed him through my hallway and out the front door. He threatened me with all kinds of evil, such as writing my name in his black book, getting me the sack and complaining about me to the Chief Constable.

Some years later I was actually to see the file on Rose at Headquarters and read some of the many letters he had written to the Chief Constable. They were all answered most courteously and carefully, but no action was ever taken about his complaints other than to write to him. When it became my job as Complaints Superintendent (acting unpaid) to draft the letters, I found it irritating that one had to give such a crackpot any of my time at all.

I asked the front office man how it was that Rose had been allowed to walk through the office and into my private quarters, and was told that this is what he usually did. A few moments later when I was in my office opening the mail Rose burst through the door, again demanding my attention. I was still a little angry at what had occurred in my house and this time I grabbed him in an arm lock and literally threw him out of the police station, telling him that if ever he came into my police station again he would make his complaint or whatever it was he wanted, known to the duty officer. He would conduct himself in a civilised manner. If he behaved like a wild animal he would be arrested and charged with causing a disturbance in a police station.

There was a flap in the front office counter which had until now always been left unlocked so that officers coming into the station through the front door, rather than the back, could lift the flap and walk through without calling for the office man, who also operated the switchboard, to open it. From now on it was to remain locked, although I never saw Rose in the police station after that incident, and he never bothered me again.

After a very short time at Harwich I applied to the Chief Constable for permission to buy my own house. Not that I particularly wanted to stay at Harwich for the rest of my service, but I did not like living in the police station and as other officers around the county were beginning to buy their own property I thought that the sooner I did the same the better, both as an investment and to have somewhere to live when I did retire. Until officers began to buy their own properties the best most could hope for on retirement was a council house.

My application was refused!

Harwich was one of those old towns that had a Mayor and one morning soon after I arrived at Harwich I received a call from the Mayor's office. I was invited, with my wife, to attend the launching of a new lifeboat the following afternoon at the quayside. I was tactfully reminded that ladies wore hats before 4 pm. I was introduced to the Mayor, who was ex officio also the Chairman of the Magistrates, the Harbour Master, Councillors, Elder Brethren of Trinity House and various other members of the upper echelons of Harwich society. In the months that followed there were several social functions I was expected to attend. I am not a social animal and don't play golf, so whenever I could I tactfully declined.

The Mayor's Ball of course was one that I couldn't avoid and was naturally one of the events of the year. Frequently too, so it seemed, there were cocktail parties thrown by Trinity House on board their flag ship, the *Patricia*. They were held in the afternoon and on the first occasion that I was invited to one I climbed the gangplank in uniform and mingled with the other guests on the aft deck, suitably screened from the hot sunshine by a canvass awning. I was soon holding a glass of a pink liquid and picking at the various canapés and things on sticks that were passed around by waiters in white jackets. The pink liquid was sweet and pleasant to the taste, but did not seem unduly alcoholic. The waiters filled up your glass as soon as it looked a little depleted, and after my third or fourth I began to notice a decidedly rubbery feeling in my legs. I thought at first that we had set sail and the sea was a bit rough!

While on the Regional Crime Squad I used to think I could hold my own in most drinking parties, so I stuck with it for a while before I excused myself and went to the heads (gents' cloakroom on a ship) and was violently sick. I was never able to acquire the recipe for this evil brew, not that I would have tried to make it myself, but I did learn that it included a large proportion of navy rum. I did attend future parties on the *Patricia*, but always held one full glass throughout and never drank any of it.

I was telephoned one morning by the headmaster of one of the local schools and invited to be the quizmaster at the annual inter-schools quiz, which was to be held at the local cinema the following Saturday. It was, so he said, a school tradition that the local police 'chief' carried out this task. I did agree on this occasion, but not long afterwards I was asked to be a judge at a school's sunflower competition. I declined this time, and later the Chief Superintendent telephoned me to ask me why I had declined and tried to persuade me to change my mind. It seems the school head, who had asked me, had spoken to him about it. I said that I had not joined the police force to judge sunflower competitions, but that of course I would go if ordered to, otherwise I would stick to police duty. Bill Docker tried to explain that in a place like Harwich the police chief was a respected member of the local community and was expected to take part in local events. I listened respectfully to what he said and in due course learned to identify more readily with the local people and events. I drew the line however at sunflower competitions and never did perform this civic duty, which I not only felt did not sufficiently identify with what the police stood for, but was beneath my dignity and position as Police Chief.

There were other social events too involving the police themselves, a tradition which I was expected to carry on, and indeed I saw no reason not to. At Harwich there were various other law enforcement agencies and services. There was a section of the Metropolitan Police Special Branch at Harwich Ferry Port (Parkeston Quay), the Immigration Service, the Customs and Excise and British Rail Police. Each month there would be a social at the police station, when one of the other services including the Fire Brigade and Ambulance Service would be invited to partake of beer and sandwiches and play snooker, darts and cribbage.

This was an excellent way to maintain a good relationship between all these services. Each had their own particular job to do, but often our paths crossed and area of operations overlapped. Good co-operation was essential and I am happy to say was always excellent. Neither before nor after my Harwich days did I ever know of such a social arrangement for promoting good liaison with other local services.

The officer in charge of Special Branch was a Sergeant Len Baker, who himself had an excellent working relationship with the port authorities and all the services that worked at Parkeston Quay. Often he would ring me up in the evening to invite me on board one of the cross-channel ferries to meet the purser or captain. Such meetings were always very good social occasions as well as another useful way of liaising with useful contacts.

Before my stay at Harwich ended, Bill Docker retired and the new Chief Superintendent was a man named Ray Long, who had quite different views as to how far police officers should integrate with the local community. He had quite different views about many things and was quite a different kind of leader from his predecessor. I had known Ray Long when he was a Fingerprint Officer. At the time I was a Detective Constable at Harlow and as there was no fingerprint department there an officer from Headquarters had to attend scenes of crime when requested by the 'Officer in the Case.'

The title, 'Officer in the Case' was important, because it meant that you and you alone decided what enquiries to make - that is unless and until you were given instructions by someone senior. I had asked for the Fingerprint Officer to attend a housebreaking and along came Ray Long. He dusted all the places he considered might have been touched or handled by an intruder and was about to pack up having told me he had found no 'marks'.

"Can you dust this post?" I asked him, indicating an upright post that I considered the perpetrator might have held on to as he jumped the fence and made his escape, evident by muddy marks on the fence and footmarks in the muddy ground below.

"No". He said, having packed his equipment away. "I don't think it would be of any use".

I reminded him that I was the 'Officer in the Case' and that I wanted the search done and that he was there to assist me, not to tell me what he thought. Further words were exchanged and Ray eventually dusted the post. Of course he didn't find any marks, and after the argument I really didn't expect that he would. However I had made my point and Ray and I always got on reasonably well at scenes of crime thereafter.

I wondered how, years later I would get along with him.

The answer is I didn't. No one ever 'got along' with Ray Long; he was a strange and I suspect lonely man who rarely socialised and was known for his gaffes. Ray saw himself as an autocratic leader who showed neither confidence nor trust in his subordinates. In return he was not revered by anyone.

One story about Ray I have told many times is when he and I (later, during my service) were both sitting on a Promotion Advisory Board with the Deputy Chief Constable, Ron Stone. Ray was the Divisional Commander and I was the outsider, in this case a Superintendent from Colchester. One of the interviewees was an officer who had joined late and had been a schoolteacher; he had been to university and had a degree in something or other. After Ron Stone had asked the usual questions about his service so far he turned to Ray Long, inviting him to ask a question or two.

"What are you doin' to improve your education?" he barked in his gruff voice. Ron Stone looked at me and smiled and I choked back what might have been a most inappropriate guffaw.

Coincidental with my arrival at Harwich was the introduction of the 'breathalyser' law in England and Wales. It was heralded by a lot of publicity and media hype and the local publicans were terrified that it was going to put them all out of business overnight. The Licensed Victuallers' Association invited me to their monthly meeting to talk to the members about the new law, how it was to be administered and police policy on the subject. I had never been to an LVA meeting before, nor had I met any of the local licensees personally. They wined me and dined me well and

I was introduced to Geoff Smith, whom I have previously mentioned, and several others who I got to know a little better as time went on. I had received from Headquarters several written orders and instructions about the new law with which to brief them, and I had also taken along a box of breathalyser tubes for them to blow into, just for the heck of it. However, in spite of the policy on which I was about to enlighten and hopefully calm their fears, I could see that there would be some problems that would require tactful handling. One licensee, I learned, drank a half a bottle of Scotch before breakfast every day and the rest after lunch. He drove around the town in a yellow Rolls Royce, normally completely inebriated. The wife of another was an alcoholic who had just bought a new sports car!

My talk went down very well, I think, and I was able to tell those present that the police did not intend to breathalyse everyone seen driving off their forecourts and that drivers could only be stopped and tested if they were committing a moving traffic offence or appeared to have been drinking. The offence was then 'driving or attempting to drive' a motor vehicle while your ability to drive was 'impaired', a subtle but important difference from 'being in charge of a vehicle while under the influence of drink or drugs.'

For a long time after the introduction of the new law there was a good deal of nervousness amongst the public and the licensing trade generally. Lawyers had a field day, as they usually do when a new law is passed and the police begin to try and enforce it. Loopholes were found in abundance and it was not until a myriad of cases and appeals that the law settled down to what it is today, a deterrent, but by no means a way of preventing drinking and driving. Look at any pub forecourt in the evening and you will see what I mean. From the police point of view the enthusiasm with which the law was heralded and enforced, when they believed it was going to stop the death and carnage on the roads, has dwindled. Now you are only likely to be breathalysed if you are involved in an accident or are doing something in a car to attract the attention of an officer.

In most police stations where I served, it was not unknown at Christmas time for traders, who were generally appreciative of the work of the local constabulary during the year, to drop in a bottle of drink or some cakes, sandwiches or whatever at Christmas, to enable the officers and staff to have a Christmas party. There were office parties in CID offices throughout the county. The one at Chelmsford, for example, was legendary, and it was open house throughout Christmas Eve. Senior officers from headquarters, magistrates, traders and others all popped in for a drink, a mince pie and to say Merry Christmas to the lads. All the booze and food was provided by the local traders and publicans.

At this LVA meeting I considered I had made a good impression on the local licensees and secretly thought that this might bode well for the Christmas boxes that traditionally came to the station at Christmas time. Until then it was so far as I knew a traditional part of local policing. Detached beat officers practically lived off produce provided by local farmers, and no one ever thought he was corruptly receiving gifts in the sense that police regulations were intended to guard against.

Christmas came and went and there was not a sign of any bottles or anything else being brought to the police station for the 'lads'. At midnight on Christmas Eve a box of spring rolls was sent in from a nearby Chinese Restaurant, but that was it. I thought it very odd and discussed the matter with my senior Sergeant, 'Trog' Parish. It seems my predecessor had discouraged local traders from sending gifts to the police station and in particular alcohol; he was himself teetotal.

Whenever property of any kind, 'lost and found', prisoners' property recovered from theft or from cars in road accidents etc, there is a specific procedure for dealing with it at the police station. First it has to be 'booked in' and labelled. Whenever it is handed over to anyone it has to be 'booked out' and signed for in what is called the 'Property Receipt Book.'

It seems that the first Christmas my predecessor was there, a bottle of spirit was sent in by one of the licensees. He insisted that it was first 'booked in' and then sent an officer to the pub to return the bottle and get a signature in the Property Receipt Book. It is little wonder that from then on there were no more Christmas gifts for the boys.

During the following year I did my best to renew cordial relations with the licensees and traders and we did fare a lot better for Christmas 1968, but already the breathalyser laws were doing much to curtail office parties generally and at police stations in particular. In future years local traders and business people began to stop this generous tradition of giving to the police. There were many reasons for this; economic, a feeling that the police were not as helpful as they once were, the police complaints procedure which was to appear soon and perhaps the feeling that policemen could afford to buy their own booze now as well as anyone else. It was an inevitable development in the march of time, but rather sad, since I don't believe any harm was done by this simple act of charity at Christmas.

Not too many years later, the Chief Constable issued an edict forbidding any office parties at Christmas, CID or otherwise. I was in charge of the Fraud Squad at the time and passed the order on to everyone, and we decided to have our Christmas Eve 'do' at a local pub instead. Imagine my surprise when a little later I was asked for a financial contribution towards the Detective Chief Superintendent's (Peter Crust's) office party to which I was invited. I refused to contribute or to attend!

My predecessor at Harwich was very keen on sea fishing and naturally knew all the local fishermen. They too used occasionally to call into the station on their way home in the evening, particularly if they had had a good catch, and hand over a bucket of whelks or a box of sardines. Fishing was not unnaturally a pastime of most of the policemen at Harwich. They had at one time clubbed together to buy a small boat, which was moored in a local creek. Six members of the staff owned the boat and when one moved on to another station, or retired, he had no difficulty selling his share to another officer who was just as keen to go out and catch some dinner.

The boat was a heavy old lifeboat from one of the Trinity House lightships. It had an old 4.5 horse power Seagull outboard engine which was powerful enough to propel the boat with the tide but not against it. It followed that you could go out fishing on an ebb tide, but had to wait for the flood tide before you could return. As the boss, I was privileged to go out in the boat, although not a shareholder, and did so on many occasions. There was cod in abundance just a mile or so outside the harbour, and if you went out about an hour before the flood and fished for a couple of hours you would always bring home enough fish for yourself and the other boat shareholders. Over the years the cod has almost left these waters, and one could fish all day now and be lucky to catch a couple of whiting.

There were frequent fishing competitions on the lightships, and those taking part would be ferried out to the nearest lightship in the Harbourmaster's launch and compete with the Trinity House men for several hours. It mattered not who won; in fact as far as I remember there were no winners or losers, just a lot of fish to take home.

Then there were the monthly sub-divisional jazz concerts at the Phoenix Hotel, organised by one of the officers, the sub-divisional annual ball and the Mistley section annual halloween ball, as well as other more spontaneous parties and 'dos'. There was a restaurant in the town called the Deva, where I recall we held some police dinners with some pretty risky after dinner entertainment.

All these functions were enjoyed by all the police at Harwich who were not on duty at the time, and I believe that these diversions for police officers, like any other group of hard working people, were essential therapy. It is sad that today a policeman hardly dare to be seen at a party of any kind, or even in a police bar drinking, without the eye of suspicion being cast upon him. Of course the Inspector received a good many more invitations; to attend the Mayor's investiture, his subsequent cocktail parties, the Harbourmaster's bash and so on, which of course it was politic to accept.

The election of the Mayor in Harwich was followed by a ceremony of throwing buns from the town hall balcony to the assembled 'peasants' below. The Mayor I remember most fondly who was elected during my period at Harwich was Peter Holbrook, a Trinity House Pilot, who like most of his peers was an illustrious member of the local upper crust. He was a popular Mayor and gave some very good parties. His wife Betty was a licensed slaughterer, and when it became popular to have a deep freeze I bought one, along with a side of beef and a pig at her suggestion. Betty came along to the police station with her tools and cut them up for me to put in the freezer in my cellar.

Humour plays a big part in police work, and if it were not so I have no doubt that the already large number of policemen who suffer from stress-related complaints would be far higher. Policemen are frequently the subject of jokes in the UK. Some comedians make their living making fun of policemen, and at police functions individuals are often picked out for derision. So far as I can recall, no one ever got too upset about it.

At one halloween dance I attended at Mistley Village Hall the place was decorated with the usual Halloween masks etc, with several coffins placed at various locations round the hall.

Each had an inscription or 'epitaph' written on it, about some member of the station personnel. For example, "Sergeant Parish. Died while waiting for a report from PC Green". Mine read, "Inspector Raven. Died while writing a memo".

One should not get the impression that life at Harwich was one long round of social activity. There was much police work to do and for the first and only time in my service, I was dealing with quite a different area of the law. Offences under the Oil on Navigable Waters Regulations, Importation of Cats and Dogs Orders and so on were daily fare for the Harwich Inspector. There were many bylaws at Harwich which did not apply to other areas of the county regulating the movement of waterborne traffic, including 'speeding' and other offences against the Merchant Shipping Acts.

Prisoners were regularly brought in to the station from Parkeston Quay, either by the British Rail Police, who had no holding cells of their own, the Special Branch, who might perhaps arrest a person who was on the 'wanted' list, or the Immigration Service, a person who had been refused permission to land, but had to stay anyway because of the rules! And then there were the smugglers arrested by Customs and Excise, who had to be booked in and usually bailed. Smuggling included anything from a few cigarettes over your allowance to a lorryload of contraband. Persons attempting the latter of course were less likely to get bail.

There are many amusing stories of people coming through Harwich with various items they shouldn't have had. Perhaps the funniest I can think of is when a man with a tin of black tablets was stopped by a Customs Officer. He suspected that the tablets might be some sort of drug and Special Branch were called. Sergeant Ron Stanley, a great character, attended and asked the man what the tablets were.

"They're carbon tablets for my indigestion" he said. Before the man could stop him Ron had taken two tablets and popped them into his mouth, saying, "I have a problem with indigestion, mind if I try them?"

Another officer then attended who had seen similar tablets before. The man and the tablets were detained and Ron spent several days in hospital getting over his 'trip'. The tablets contained a powerful concentrate of LSD, a popular hallucinatory drug at the time.

It was a local instruction that the Inspector must attend the scene of all fatal road accidents within the sub-division, an unpleasant duty, made more so by the fact that they always seemed to happen at night after I had gone to bed. It was one of the many instructions that seemed senseless to me, but at the time that they were written - when there was probably never a fatal accident unless a man fell badly when the wheel fell off his cart - perhaps it seemed prudent that the local police chief should take an interest. Nowadays the traffic division usually had the bodies removed and the road swept clean before the Inspector arrived to say "Everything all right?" and go back to bed again.

Many such instructions badly needed overhauling in the light of 'modern times', but no one seemed willing or able to do it. I am all for tradition, but I also agree with a gradual change coincidental with the changing times and conditions. In the last few years, after many years of stagnation with bobbies on the beat going about their work happily and things going pretty smoothly with little change, a big broom has appeared rather suddenly. Instead of changing with the times, conservative resistance to change had slowed it down, so that the police were in many areas well behind the times. Drastic changes were considered necessary.

A great many of the changes within the police service have been brought about by criticism of the service. Drastic new measures to restrict policemen's activities, police complaints procedures, laws and regulations about so-called racism, methods of interrogation of and taking statements from prisoners and so on have been a direct result of criticism of the police. Many of these changes would not have been necessary if the police had had the support of politicians, the public, the media and others and stuck to their guns instead of being forced onto the defensive to please their critics.

One example of how police investigation has been forced to change is in their dealing with reported cases of rape. These changes were largely forced upon the police by pressure from media, women's rights groups and the civil liberties lobby. All these experts purported to know far more about how to investigate a rape case than the police, whose many years of experience in this field suddenly had to be abandoned. The result of these changes is that many of the rape allegations that are made now either result in an innocent man being brought before the court, to be acquitted, or the 'crime' remains undetected because the police may not pursue certain avenues of enquiry, such as to examine the truthfulness of the supposed victim.

Other changes have come about through the advancement of technology, and many of these are indeed a great help in detecting crime, but there are still many areas where the restrictions imposed upon police in the use of technological tools are ridiculous. For example if a police officer needs to follow a suspect's car, there is now the means simply to attach a small device to it which can be tracked from a police vehicle or helicopter. The snag is that you have to get the vehicle owner's permission in writing and signed before you can put the device on his car. More often than not the owner of the car is also the suspect. Does that make sense to you?

At Harwich too we had our share of sudden deaths and bodies. There were enough bodies washed up on the shores to necessitate a mortuary on the sea front, where the corpses were deposited until they could be dealt with. Often such a body was too decomposed and odorous to be taken to the hospital mortuary at Colchester. There was a small cottage hospital at Harwich, but that did not have the facilities for post mortem examinations. Bodies dragged in by fishermen in their nets, amateur yachtsmen knocked overboard by their booms when jibing (or imbibing), suicides and even murder victims were not infrequent visitors to our little mortuary.

After the cause of death had been established, usually drowning, it was the job of the police to find out who the poor chap was. Sometimes this was not too difficult, while on other occasions it might end up as a photograph in Metropolitan Police Information. Such photographs were hardly suitable to show relatives, but often the description that went with it eventually matched up with a reported missing person.

Often it worked in reverse, in that we knew who had been drowned but hadn't yet found the body. Ferries from Harwich to Holland occasionally lost a passenger, and when he or she was not found it was assumed they had fallen overboard. In such cases the body might be washed up in England or Holland and liaison with the Dutch police and other continental forces was extremely good. In the snooker room in Harwich Police Station there was, and no doubt still is, a fine collection of police helmets donated by officers from the continent when they had visited us both on official business and socially.

Murders were still a pretty rare occurrence in the county, although they were on the increase. There was only one at Harwich during my reign, which became known as the 'Delilah Murder'. A young woman was found in her upstairs flat, having been stabbed to death with a carving knife. It was a pretty bloody scene and the investigation was conducted by the Detective Chief Inspector at Clacton who was then Trunky Sewell who I referred to previously when he was at Basildon.

The murderer was discovered pretty quickly; he was the young woman's lover. He had apparently discovered that she was seeing someone else between his visits and called to see her on the fateful night with a present. It was a record of the song *Delilah*, sung by Tom Jones. It is a song about a faithless woman, and the defence said later that he had played the record to his faithless girlfriend, hoping she was going to get the message, confess and they would make up, make love and all would be forgotten. However things didn't go according to plan and she didn't confess. When the song came to the words about how the singer took out a knife and plunged it into Delilah it all got too much for the poor chap and he grabbed a kitchen knife and stabbed his ex-lover, several times, to music!

It was in 1966 that police personal radios were first used in Essex, but not until 1967 that they first reached sub-divisions like Harwich. They were at first rather cumbersome things that had batteries rather larger than the radio itself, and these had to be recharged frequently. It was of course a great boon to be able to communicate with officers on the ground, or that was the theory. Often for various technical reasons one or more of the radios wouldn't work, and we used to say that they could send a man to the moon and be able to communicate with him fine, but that we couldn't even get to contact the chap at the railway station three hundred yards along the road. Still it was early days and things have improved a great deal since then. One development from the introduction of personal radios was that it was no longer necessary to make points at telephone boxes. The Sergeant could go out for a walk with his radio and call up the officer on the beat, say, "Where are you?" and make arrangements to meet him. Some officers soon learned the drawback with this system.

On one occasion the Sergeant was outside the post office at two o'clock in the morning and called up the beat chap and said, "Where are you?"

"Outside the post office" was the reply.

"I'll meet you there in five minutes" said the Sergeant with an evil grin on his face no doubt. About six minutes later the officer's boots could be heard running along the street and he arrived puffing and panting, his cape flying in the wind. Where he had been was never truly established, but it was apparent that the arrival of the police personal radio put a stop to some of the activities of officers on night duty.

Life was never dull at Harwich and every day something new would turn up that I hadn't experienced before. Occasionally something really unusual would happen, such as the morning I was called by my Chief Superintendent to say that one of my detached beat officers had been accused of rape by a local licensee's wife. Detective Chief Inspector Len White was on his way over and I was to meet him at the alleged rape scene.

It was usual, and so far as I know still is, for a Detective Chief Inspector to investigate any alleged crime by a police officer below that rank. In the light of the Police Complaints Procedure an officer of the rank of Superintendent would be the 'Investigating Officer', although the enquiries would be made in the case of a criminal allegation by the DCI.

Like many subsequent rape allegations I investigated, this turned out not to be a rape at all. The officer, although guilty of indiscretion, was not a criminal. The lady in question had, it transpired, been in the habit of entertaining the officer, and apparently other tradesmen, in the kitchen of the pub. Unfortunately it was the police officer who happened to be there the day the husband caught them at it. The word 'rape' was the first that came to the lady's mind when deciding how to explain her predicament to her spouse.

Harwich did have its own Magistrates' Court, which sat every Thursday in the town hall building. It was customary for the Inspector to attend court, both as a matter of courtesy, to offer no objections (usually) to applications by licensees for occasional licences at their premises, and to prosecute most of the minor matters that came before the Justices each week, such as traffic violations, and guilty pleas. When served with a summons a defendant was asked to respond, saying whether they intended to plead guilty or not guilty. It was essential to know this so that witnesses could be warned to attend if necessary.

Cases of more complexity, minor crime etc and the 'not guilty' pleas were dealt with by the County Prosecuting Solicitor, who would turn up as usual not having seen any of the briefs before that morning. The Inspector's presence was required also to enlighten the CPS on all matters that were not immediately clear to him.

The Magistrates' Clerk was also a local solicitor, who it was said liked to play golf on Thursday afternoon, and so it was assured that court would be concluded before lunch. Justice was often dispensed rather more quickly at Harwich for this reason than elsewhere in the county.

The way a 'guilty plea' was dealt with was that I would stand up, after the accused had been asked to plead, and give the facts of the case. This would be a brief summary concluding with the accused's reply to the reporting officer and previous convictions if any. Sentence would then be passed by the Chairman, inevitably the Mayor.

In the case of a 'not guilty' plea the CPS would call the witnesses for the prosecution and the defence would then be heard. The Bench would then 'retire' to consider the matter.

Not infrequently, I would get a message to go to the Mayor's retiring room and find him and one or two other JPs who might be sitting with him that day sipping tea or Scotch. I would be offered a drink, which I of course declined, and we would chat about things in general, fishing, Pummy Rose and so on. Then the Mayor would look at his watch and say, "I suppose we'd better be getting back". He would often turn to me and say, "What do you think we should do with this chap?" referring of course to the defendant. "It's a matter for you" I always replied.

Back in court the Mayor would put on his sternest look, stare at the defendant and wait for the Magistrates' Clerk to tell him to stand up.

"We have considered your case very carefully," he would say. "And find you guilty on all charges". Sentence would then be pronounced and justice was once again seen to be done.

When Sir Jonathan Peel was Chief Constable, he always boasted that he would visit every police station and detached-beat police-house at least once during each year. Sir John Nightingale also made regular visits to his divisions, although I doubt that he was able to live up to Sir Jonathan's boast. However he did try to attend functions at Divisions whenever he could and a great many personnel matters were dealt with at such functions. He was able to speak to officers of all ranks, ask them questions about their service and put suggestions to them about their future and note their reactions. He had a remarkable memory and knew many of the officers around the county by name.

In the autumn of 1969 the Annual Harwich Sub-Divisional dance was held, and as was the custom we sent an invitation to the Chief Constable. On this occasion he accepted and I naturally felt obliged to attend. It was the usual practice for the Chief to ask the local Inspector how things were going over a drink and I was no exception. I thought it a good opportunity to remind him of his promise to me two years earlier.

"I understood that Harwich was going to be a Chief Inspector station," I said. "I was expecting to hear something by now, it is almost two years since I arrived here."

"I'm afraid the Home Office have put this matter on the back burner for a while". he said, "I don't know when it will happen now."

I was disappointed, and it showed.

"Well," said the Chief. "Do you want to stay here or go back on CID?"

"I'd go back tomorrow if I was given the opportunity" I said.

A few days later I was notified that the Assistant Chief Constable, Charlie Waller, was going to visit Harwich Police Station. I duly made sure that all the books and papers were ready for him to examine and that the station was as clean and tidy as one could hope for. Charlie wasn't interested in any of these matters when he came in to see me. Uncharacteristically he was smiling. He offered me the job of Detective Chief Inspector in charge of the Chelmsford Divisional CID.

My successor at Harwich was Cyril Rand, affectionately known as 'Skid' for some unknown reason. The station was upgraded very shortly after that and he was made Chief Inspector, and later had a deputy! I sometimes think that had it not been for the Harwich Sub-Divisional Dance I might have stayed at that sub-division for a lot longer than two years. Cyril spent ten happy years at Harwich and was allowed to buy his own house there after a couple of years. He and I later became great friends and used to visit each other until he sadly passed away in 2012.

# Chelmsford Division
# 1969–1977

*Show me a congenital eavesdropper with the instincts of a peeping tom and I will show you a good detective (anon)*

It was a moment of great excitement and relief when I knew that I was moving back to the CID, and at the same time that my next step on the promotion ladder was at hand. Chelmsford was a big division, the County Town of Essex, and to be promoted to command the Criminal Investigation Department was, I had no doubt, a feather in my cap and an indication of the Chief's confidence in me.

My predecessor had been Len (Chalky) White, who was to be moved to Headquarters on promotion to Detective Superintendent. The Detective Chief Superintendent was now George Brown, the man who had preceded Len White in the chair I was now to occupy; all was boding very well for the future, I thought.

The Divisional Chief Superintendent was John Challis, another of the real gentlemen of my police acquaintance, and his deputy Long John Canham. One of the first familiar faces I saw was George Tame, whose deputy I had been at Harlow. However he was the Urban Sub-divisional Commander, and while having an administrative rank senior to mine, should have no say in the day-to-day running of my department. To be fair to him he rarely did, although with his CID background it must have been very difficult for him to see it all going on at a scene of crime on his 'manor' and not really have any say in the investigation. I know exactly how he must have felt, because some years later I was to be in the very same position. Chelmsford had only two sub-divisional stations, one at Maldon and another at Witham, each with a Chief Inspector in charge.

My deputy was Detective Inspector Mike King, who had transferred to Essex from Warwickshire. Mike was a beaver of a man who never seemed to run out of energy or ideas, a thoroughly competent detective and one upon whom I could rely with confidence. Having subordinates in the Criminal Investigation Department is unlike having them in other walks of life such as a factory. Detectives work very independently and it is often the end result of their work which the supervisor sees first. Whenever one of your officers lets you down, it is the Detective Chief Inspector who gets a blast down the phone from Headquarters and the department as a whole gets a black mark. 'Lack of supervision' is a phrase that has appeared on many an internal report into an incident or when something has gone seriously wrong.

There is a great deal of freedom in being a detective officer, freedom to work or freedom to play. Being able to rely on someone with every confidence is a great asset, especially in a deputy. There were about four detective sergeants and eight or nine detective constables, including one woman officer, Pam Arnold. Pam was a very experienced lady and her rather robust and occasionally stern appearance disguised a gentle and generous nature. She worked hard and could do the work of a Detective Constable as well as any of her male colleagues.

The CID Offices at Chelmsford in those days were in a separate building at the rear of the station, which was in New Street. The new Chelmsford Police Station was under construction and due to be completed soon. Ben Jenkinson, the Admin Chief Inspector, was fully occupied with this project and spent much of his day in the new building under construction 'supervising' the builders. He was probably the only one who knew his way around the huge new edifice when it eventually opened.

My office was as usual on the first floor, and compared to any I had occupied before it was quite palatial, with a reasonably new copy of *Stone's Justices Manual*, photos on the wall and a carpet on the floor. The position I now held was important, but not important enough to have a secretary - only the Chief Superintendent had one of those.

I had hardly been sitting in the comfortable chair long enough to make it warm when my first visitor was announced, without an appointment! It was the Chief Personnel Officer of the Marconi Company, one of the major industries in the town. He introduced himself and presented me with a list of some fifty names, with dates and places of birth and approximate heights. I guessed what he wanted, but affected innocence and asked him what I was supposed to do with this list. He explained that he had an arrangement with my predecessor that prospective employees of his company would be vetted by the police and we would tell him who had a bad record and therefore the ones he should not employ.

It was of course a serious disciplinary offence to divulge confidential information of this nature to a member of the public. Police officers are required to sign the Official Secrets Act, which is an additional deterrent. Of course the gentleman explained when I pointed this out to him that he understood this and that I need not divulge information, just put a pencil line through the names that were 'unsuitable'. I could see various other problems looming should I do this. Suppose a man was refused employment and discovered that it was because I had put a pencil line through his name. How would I stand legally? Perhaps the most important drawback was the one I told him about.

"My biggest problem in doing as you ask is that I couldn't trust you to keep it to yourself" I said.

"What do you mean?" he declared indignantly. "Of course you can trust me."

"But you have told me that you understand that in doing what you ask I will be committing a serious disciplinary offence if not a crime, and yet you come in here and tell me that my predecessor was doing that very thing. Could he trust you?"

I handed him back his piece of paper and said, "I'm sorry I can't help you. If you would like to take the matter up with my senior officers and they instruct me to do what you ask I will be delighted to assist you. However my predecessor is only up the road at Headquarters and no doubt he would be delighted to continue your arrangement."

The question of passing information about people's previous convictions is and has been the cause of much trouble, job losses and even prison sentences being handed out to officers who did it.

It was to be apparent at an early stage that being at Chelmsford Divisional Headquarters as opposed to Chelmsford Police Headquarters, some half a mile away, could at times have its drawbacks. It was extremely handy from a personnel point of view and any time Headquarters required extra manpower for a major investigation or incident, Chelmsford was the first to be 'hit'.

Chelmsford being the County Town and home of the Assizes and Quarter Sessions, there were always a lot of senior officers around, just 'popping in' as it were. I mentioned that there were now two Detective Superintendents. The second was a man named George Harris, the self-appointed deputy to George Brown, who was now the Detective Chief Superintendent. He and Chalky White, the other Detective Superintendent, used to float around the county generally supervising the CID. Either of them could appear at any time and want to know exactly what was happening, and one gradually began to resent their sudden appearance as if it was interference in some way.

I received a phone call at my home one evening about eight o'clock to say that there had been a robbery, and that my presence was required. It seemed that the manager of Budgens, the supermarket had been grabbed on his way home and hit across the head with an iron bar. The thieves had taken him back into the store and with his keys opened the safe and stolen the cash.

That evening there was a function of some kind going on in the County Hall, just across the road from the police station, and by the time I reached the station a detective superintendent who had been at the function and was in full evening dress, was in full command. Divisional stations now all had what was called an operations room as well as a front office. This is where the radio controls were and in the event of an incident such as this, where the officer in charge would generally be found during the initial stages.

The detective superintendent was in the operations room generally giving orders and apparently running the job. I walked in and expected him to hand over to me, as it was my division and my case. Instead he did no such thing and carried on as if I was not there. I tapped him on the shoulder and said, "If you want me I'll be at home" and left the station.

I didn't go home as it happened, but still being extremely hot under the collar, I went to my local for a pint and to cool down. When I did get home the phone was ringing. It was my Detective Inspector to tell me that the detective superintendent was tearing his hair out and had been trying to get hold of me for ages. He said also that he had got a lead on the robbery and did I want to go with him to pick up a suspect? I asked him if he had told the Detective Superintendent. He hadn't, so I told him to pick me up. Within half an hour we were back at the station with the robbers and the stolen money, not to mention the iron bar used to clobber the supermarket manager, who was alive and in hospital recovering well. Incidentally it was one of those occasions when some pressure could be put on one of a number of suspects who, not knowing the condition of their victim, might be persuaded that the charge could be one of murder! Invariably one would point the finger at the other and confessions would start rolling out.

I ignored the detective superintendent when we arrived and took our prisoners to the cells, interrogated them and duly booked them up and went home. The DS went back went back to the function and I fully expected a roasting next day at Headquarters. I never heard another word about it.

As head of a department I was expected to attend 'morning prayers' in the Chief Superintendent's office. This usually took place about 9.30am after one had had the chance to get up to date on what had occurred during the night. Those in attendance included the Admin Chief Inspector, the Divisional Superintendent, the Urban Sub-divisional Superintendent and myself. Chelmsford had the distinction of having the urban and rural sub-divisional headquarters in the same building as Divisional Headquarters. This meant that occasionally the Rural Sub-Divisional Chief Inspector also attended the 'morning prayers'.

These meetings were generally long and cumbersome, and I felt that they were often unnecessary and wasted a lot of valuable time. I might take no more than a few minutes to make my report and then have to listen to other people's often verbose dialogue relating to matters in which I had no interest whatsoever. My suggestions that perhaps it would be a good idea if I made my report earlier or later and so avoid these long-winded gatherings were always rejected. It was necessary therefore for me to occasionally resort to duplicitous means to avoid them.

Often I was able to telephone the Chief Superintendent prior to his meeting and say that I had been delayed and would be along as soon as possible. I would contrive to arrive just as the others were leaving. Occasionally the Detective Inspector would ring the Chief Superintendent just after the meeting had started and say I was urgently required for some matter. I couldn't get away with this on too regular a basis, but it worked fine on quite a few occasions.

The day started about 8.30am and mail was collected from the administration department, who opened and sorted all incoming mail. That included any that was marked 'Confidential' or 'Personal' and avoided any officer having his private mail sent to the police station.

Then, about 9am, there was always a call to or from the Detective Chief Superintendent, which might be short or quite lengthy, depending if anything important had happened during the night. There was in the police force a culture that presumed the senior officer in a department must know of everything that was happening in his sphere of responsibility. From the top downward information was passed only on a need to know basis; upward there was a duty to know and to report. If therefore the Chief Constable read in a morning newspaper at 7am that a body had been found in the river at Chelmsford, he would ring the Chief Superintendent and demand to know the details. If he hadn't been told he would ring the Divisional Detective Chief Inspector and demand to know the details, and pass on any irritation he had received from his hierarchy. It was of course impossible to know everything that was happening during the hours one was off duty and I was always one of those people who believed that if someone wanted me to know something, he or she would tell me.

I found that this was not the case in the police service at a senior level and that one had to demand to be told what was happening rather than expect that information would be passed upwards. This was a dangerous procedure, because there were always those who would take any instruction literally and ring you up at three in the morning to say there had been a flood warning or something equally inconsequential. It was necessary therefore between 8.30am and 9am to absorb as much information as one could from telephone messages, circulations and one's own staff in order to be in a position to 'know', if asked, about any incident that the Detective Chief Superintendent wanted details of.

There was little time between this call and 'morning prayers' to look at the mail and after the meeting it was already coffee time and half the morning gone. This used to irritate me no end, and although my deputy would deal with anything urgent in my absence I still felt my time was being wasted. I'd come out of 'morning prayers' often having had an argument with one or other of the sub-divisional commanders about why someone had parked the CID car in his space, or some other quite petty matter, and bark at everyone I came into contact with until I had had a couple of cups of strong coffee.

One of the greatest pressures upon any police chief, and in particular the CID Chief Inspector in charge of a division, is to get the crime figures down. Statistics are used to measure these figures and the efficiency of the department. If the percentage rate of detection drops there is a great debate as to why. Figures are also bandied about concerning the amount of reported crime, and each year Government figures are issued saying that there were more or fewer robberies, burglaries etc. Generally they tend to emphasise those figures that are down, such as burglaries, and minimise those that are up, such as sexual offences and violent crime.

I listen to debates regularly on television between politicians, newspaper people and other so-called experts. They pose questions such as "Why is violent crime rising in London?" and go on to talk some of the most implicit rubbish without having the slightest inkling of either the causes or the solutions.

There were at the time two simple reasons for the rising crime rate, drugs and the present legal system, which does no one justice. Drugs are the cause of most violent street crime and such crimes tend to get reported. Burglary on the other hand is down, because many more people now feel the need for a burglar alarm and reporting a burglary to the police is seen as a complete waste of time. Many crimes are reported only if an insurance company insists upon it, not with any hope of having your property recovered or the thieves apprehended. My own brother-in-law came home from holiday on a Sunday night a few years ago and found his house in Walthamstow had been completely stripped of every item of furniture, beds, clothing, rugs etc, even the kitchen fitted furniture and equipment was all gone. He phoned the police, who told him they would make an appointment for an officer to come along the following Wednesday to get a statement. You can imagine how he felt about reporting crime to the police after that.

Fortunately the people of Chelmsford could still in the 1970s expect better attention that that, and our success rate was in the region of 42%. Now the police response to any call from the public for assistance is 'graded' or prioritised. Burglary doesn't figure very high on the list of priorities. The most any government of recent years has done to try and stem the rising crime figures is to introduce more laws in some desperate hope that they will work. None have, since lack of laws is not the problem.

One such measure that was introduced during my latter service was the power of magistrates and courts in general to confiscate a thief's vehicle. It had to be his own vehicle and he had to have used it in the commission of a crime; driving it to the scene was sufficient proof of this. The risk of losing their car was, one can only imagine, intended to stop people committing crime. I have never known this law to be implemented. One or two courts did try to begin with, but were frustrated at every turn. Don't these lawmakers know that most thieves steal the car, and in almost all other cases it belongs to a finance company? Going out to do a 'job' in your own vehicle just isn't thought a very good idea by most thieves. In any case, what was supposed to happen to all these confiscated cars? Where were they to be stored and how were they to be disposed of?

More and more 'major incidents' taking more and more man hours away from normal duties kept the amount of time spent on day-to-day enquiries to a minimum. As in other services, the National Health Service, education and so on, more staff and money are always demanded and little by little the staff grows, but not by enough to make a difference, because the amount of crime to investigate and incidents to attend to increases just as rapidly.

Ten years earlier one or two murders in the county were all that were considered as major incidents. Such an enquiry might require twenty or thirty experienced detectives to be drawn away from normal duties for two or three weeks before, if still undetected, it would be scaled down to a mere dozen or so. Now in the seventies, missing children, rapes and serious robberies demanded similar attention and there was practically no period when one could expect to have a full staff.

It was probably by the late sixties that overtime payment for detective officers was beginning to be accepted as part of one's income, and it was usual for an officer to do enough overtime each month to increase his pay by more than fifty percent. The cost in the health and efficiency of the staff however began to tell, and for this, as well as for economic reasons, these payments were suddenly severely curtailed. It meant that detective officers had to go home in the middle of an enquiry or hand it over to someone else to do. Both of these situations were unsatisfactory and resulted in the job not being done at all or done badly.

It is understandable that the public would expect all the stops to be pulled out by the police when a child went missing. It was a first essential to ensure that the child is actually missing, as so many of them return in an hour or so. Children have been found asleep behind a sofa, under their bed or in a garden shed, or playing with a friend a few houses along the street. When these preliminary enquiries have been exhausted however, and time begins to pass, the omens are not good. Sadly, in spite of all our efforts and man-hours spent searching for children that were truly missing, the child was almost always found dead.

There was one happy exception to this rule that I recall, and that was a small girl who was reported missing from her home in Great Wigborough. The police mounted a search that evening and again next day. The police mobile caravan was taken to the scene, and as usual there were more than enough local volunteers to assist with the search, which was mostly conducted by the uniformed branch.

Because of the strong possibility that the child would be found to have been the victim of a violent or sexual crime, the CID were in attendance, as were several reporters from national newspapers, who were like vultures hovering around waiting for the body to turn up. Most of them behaved themselves pretty well and after the daily briefings they would go to the local hostelry and imbibe fairly heavily on the local brew. By the evening of the second day hopes were beginning to fade and the parents of the little girl, who stayed in the caravan most of the day, began to look more and more distraught. Incidentally the parading of parents before television cameras for the nine o'clock news is a relatively new phenomenon, which has been invented by the media. It has no bearing upon a police investigation except to throw public suspicion upon the parents by their demeanour on TV. The parents are usually quite innocent of murdering their child, though not always! Believe me, if there is any such suspicion, the police don't need the media to point it out to them, they will have already considered the matter and be taking whatever action they can to pursue this line of enquiry.

Eventually the reporters drifted off and only one remained. He was Charlie Leech, a photographer from the Daily Express, who had no particular place to go and had decided to wait until the police called off the search that the evening.

Suddenly in the fading light there was a shout and an officer appeared in the distance carrying a child. At first we didn't know if she was alive or dead, but Charlie quickly got out his camera and the parents rushed out to meet the officer. The child was theirs, and she was alive and reasonably well. The reunion between parents and daughter, the tears of joy and cries of relief made a most touching scene. Charlie took some remarkable pictures, which made the front pages of several newspapers the next day and no doubt a lot of money for Charlie Leech or his paper. Such happy endings were a rare occurrence in my experience, and I had the misfortune to be involved in many such searches which ended tragically.

There are few happy endings in police work generally, except when a long enquiry is successfully concluded. Happily for the police, that is, but not for the victim, who may never recover from the trauma of a severe beating, being raped, robbed or having their house broken into. Many have told me that the house subsequently feels tainted.

This must surely be the case when a member of the household commits suicide. Suicide was not uncommon at Chelmsford. All kinds of people from all walks of life and all ages took their own lives for a variety of reasons. One cannot really know how a person feels who contemplates taking their own life, except that it must be a feeling of utter desperation and hopelessness.

Probably the first suicide I went to at Chelmsford was that of a middle-aged man who lived at Witham. He had a very nice home, wife and family, a good job and was comfortably off. I happened to be making a visit to Witham police station when an officer who had been called to the house radioed in for assistance and to say that a man was hanging from the stairs and was apparently dead.

The report had been made by a neighbour, who had gone to the house for some reason and looked through the letterbox when he had received no answer to his knocking. He could see the man hanging in the hallway, suspended by his neck with a cord attached to the top of the banister.

It was necessary to break into the house, as no one else was apparently at home. We cut the chap down and administered artificial respiration, but to no avail. He left no suicide note and for a while there was some suspicion about the why's and wherefore's of the death. Unlike fiction, it is not unusual for a suicide not to leave a note, and it is usually the job of the Coroner, with the assistance of the police, to determine in all the circumstances whether the person has taken his or her own life or not.

These days the verdict is of suicide, as it was in this case. The words, 'while the balance of his mind was disturbed' are rarely used unless there is medical evidence of such mental derangement. It used to be thought that these words somehow softened the blow for the relatives, particularly if they were religious, and they were added as a matter of course in most suicide verdicts.

An even sadder case than this occurred one Christmas Eve, oddly enough also at Witham. A train driver was aware that he had hit something on the line and when he arrived at Witham stopped the train to report the incident. I went to the scene with other officers and we found a woman's body lying on the line. In fact the body was in two separate parts. The legs and pelvis had been completely severed from the head, arms and trunk, which had been carried some twenty yards further along the track. It was not far from some level crossing gates and we managed to get all trains stopped until the mess had been cleared up, necessary photographs and samples taken and the body parts removed.

It didn't take long to identify the body from the woman's handbag, which was found not far away. In this case there was a note in the handbag which contained words of love for her children and that she was sorry. There was no specific explanation of why she had decided on Christmas Eve to take her life.

I went to the house, where there were two quite pretty little girls of about eight and ten years. There was also their father, the woman's husband, who was a surly and unpleasant man. I broke the news to him and he appeared surprised and then somewhat angry that his wife had killed herself. I of course told him that until the coroner had had an inquest it could not be presumed that it was suicide, but that we would make all the necessary enquiries.

In the living room, which was sparsely furnished but had all the usual comforts of home, was a Christmas tree with a few presents underneath. The recollection of those two little girls sobbing and clutching each other in grief beside a Christmas tree, supposed to be an object of great joy and happiness, took a long time to fade in my memory.

The husband, as I had guessed, was a wife beater. The woman's doctor and neighbours all confirmed this, and it was evident that the poor woman had had all she could take. The coroner's jury, without hesitation, pronounced a verdict of suicide. Once again I was aware of the inadequacy of the law that allows a man to cause his wife's death in these circumstances yet is unable to punish him.

Bodies would regularly turn up in the River Chelmer, which flowed through the park in the centre of the town. Many were suicides, a few accidental deaths, when drunks on their way home had fallen in, and the odd misadventure, when someone tried to rescue a dog or cat. All were sad stories and tragedies for the nearest and dearest to suffer. For the police they were all in a day's work. Today I understand that an officer would probably need counselling after attending such an incident! This would have been laughable in the seventies and one can only wonder at the stature of constables today who find their work so hard to bear. I suspect that it may have something to do with empire building in the 'Counselling Department'.

Perhaps the strangest suicide I ever encountered was that of a young man who lived alone in a one-room flat above the shops in the centre of Chelmsford. He was discovered lying on his bed with a sheath knife sticking into his stomach. It was quite natural for the officer first on the scene to suspect foul play and the CID was called.

It was usual, when a death looked suspicious and likely to result in a murder investigation, to call upon the services of what were loosely called Home Office pathologists to do the autopsy in such cases. They were not actually Home Office pathologists, but a small number of specialist forensic pathologists who worked in a special department of the London Hospital, at that time under the leadership of a Doctor Cameron; before him it was Professor Camps and before that Professor Keith Simpson. They were approved by the Home Office to assist police forces anywhere in the country, and they had the accumulated experience of many hundreds of unusual as well as more common cases.

Having attended the scene myself I decided to make use of this service and contacted the London Hospital. Often the pathologist who attended would instruct that the body should not be moved until he had seen it and Dr Vanesis, who was the doctor on call, made this stipulation, having heard briefly of the circumstances.

The small room occupied by the deceased was at the top of a small flight of stairs, and I instructed a young uniformed officer to wait at the bottom of the stairs and let nobody up except Dr Vanesis when he arrived. At that time the scene was relatively unspoiled and the only people who had been in the room were the officer who found the body and the local police surgeon who had certified that life was extinct. After the body had been examined provisionally by the pathologist, photographed and removed, the scenes of crime people could do their work.

I returned to the scene some time later to meet the pathologist and went up to the room to wait. Unfortunately by this time news of the incident had reached Headquarters and the 'nosey brigade' had started to arrive. Detective Chief Superintendent (by this time it was Chalky White) ACC Crime, one Willy Petherick and Uncle Tom Cobley and all arrived a short time later and tried to pass my chap keeping guard at the bottom the stairs. I first realised this when I heard a commotion at the bottom of the stairs. The young officer was being castigated by Chalky White, both for not knowing who he was and for refusing to allow him up the stairs. I went to his rescue and explained the reason, but while Chalky was gracious enough to apologise to the officer he still insisted on the sightseeing tour by himself and the other senior officers, which I could hardly refuse. By the time they had finished trampling all over the scene and poking into cupboards and drawers there would not have been much hope of finding any forensic evidence if this had turned out to be a murder.

Dr Vanesis however saved the day by attending shortly afterwards and declaring almost at once that in his view it was a suicide. The post mortem confirmed this. There were the typical small incisions around the death wound where tentative attempts had been made before the fatal blow was struck. Stabbing oneself in the stomach is not such an unusual method of committing suicide as it might seem, and Dr Vanesis had attended several very similar cases; all had been homosexuals.

The police had a choice of calling the London Hospital for a pathologist or using one from the local hospital. This was no reflection on the ability of local pathologists, but they were not specialists in forensic medicine as were Doctor Cameron's men. A local pathologist would possibly have recognised this case as a suicide, perhaps not, but would have been far less positive in his assertion, and perhaps many days of police enquiries would have followed before sufficient evidence to convince the Coroner could have been found.

Unfortunately there are very few specialists available to the police to examine living people, only dead bodies. In my Romford days there was a Doctor Summers who was always called to examine victims of serious indecent assault, rape victims or victims of buggery. His expertise was often crucial at the outset of an investigation, since he had built up years of experience, studying and specialising in the subject of forensic medicine in relation to sexual offences.

For the most part the police have to rely nowadays on an examination by a local hospital doctor or their local police surgeon, some of whom do receive some training in forensic medicine, but many rely largely on the scenes of crime officer to tell them what is required.

Not all suspicious deaths however could be attributed to suicide or accident, and Chelmsford had its share of murders during my time there. Murder investigations, except where they were immediately detected and the murderer arrested, tended to be long and tedious affairs. The Detective Chief Inspector of the division in which the body was found was designated the 'officer in the case', and his involvement largely depended on his Detective Superintendent or Chief Superintendent, whose job it was to oversee the case. Some were content to do that, but others tended to take over or 'interfere', as some Chief Inspectors might have called it.

The body of a sixteen-year-old girl was discovered one morning on some land near Witham, an area quite frequently visited by courting couples. It was pretty obvious from the start that she had been murdered and an incident office was set up. The post mortem revealed that she had been strangled and there was a yellow duster rammed firmly down her throat. It was in a tight ball, which the pathologist wanted to remove without pulling it undone. To do so he had to dissect the jawbone, which while interesting to witness did not seem to be a problem at the time.

There was no identification on the body and no girl answering her description had been reported missing locally. During the preliminary examination of the body the pathologist had discovered sand between the toes and under the toenails and we therefore started to make enquiries at seaside towns, the nearest being Harwich and Clacton on

Sea. In fact a girl had been reported missing that morning, and she was soon identified as the daughter of a publican at Harwich.

Bringing a close relative into a mortuary to identify the body of a loved one is a harrowing experience for all concerned, not least the relative. Fortunately it was the father in this case and not the mother. The pathologist had done a good job of putting the face back together again, but had warned that it was pretty fragile and that no one who might come to identify the body should be allowed to touch it. Father was duly brought in and the white sheet removed. He identified the girl and then before anyone could stop him put his hand out and touched her face. We all shuddered as the girl's face fell apart and the jawbone came completely away from the rest of the face. Father was hustled out and consoled and explanations had to be made. A most embarrassing incident all round.

The girl had a younger sister, and when she was interviewed she told of a man in a black sports car that her dead sister had been seeing. The make of car was unknown but it was, we were told, definitely black and a two-seater. There were extensive enquiries to trace such a car and its driver, and several days went by before local records in all of Essex were perused to see if any such vehicle had been issued a ticket for a road traffic offence.

All such enquiries were negative, but one officer in Clacton on Sea did report stopping a car of similar description which had overshot a red light. He had issued a verbal warning, details of which, including the car's number, were recorded in the officer's pocket book. The vehicle was registered to a man in Northamptonshire, and the police there soon traced and arrested him on our behalf on suspicion of murder. Mike King was despatched with other officers to bring him and his car, back to Witham. He arrived late at night and our interrogation began. It was in the days before the introduction of tape recordings and video machines, and everything was prepared so that nothing could later be criticised.

During the interrogation the Detective Chief Superintendent arrived and wanted to sit in on the interrogation. I managed to persuade him against this, since it would mean he too would have to give evidence at the trial. I realised later that that was exactly why he wanted to sit in. The man confessed and made a written statement in the presence of his solicitor. He said that the girl was unhappy at home and that she had pleaded with him to kill her and he had obliged. There was plenty of forensic evidence in his car, and the case seemed pretty well tied up.

In the man's statement he had described in some detail where he had taken the girl on the evening he killed her. They had apparently visited five or six public houses in the district in his car. When the Chief Superintendent read the statement he decided to take the prisoner on a trip in the police car to show us the route he had taken. It was already past midnight and there seemed to me no earthly reason for such a trip, but I was overruled and we went. Right through the journey, which lasted over an hour and a half, the Chief Superintendent asked the prisoner questions and his questions and the answers were recorded on a portable dictating machine.

On arrival back at the station the prisoner was locked away for the night and I expected to be allowed to go home. However the Chief Superintendent insisted I stay there while he typed out a complete transcript of the tapes and his own statement of how and when they were made, which he insisted went into the file. This of course meant that he would be giving evidence.

At the trial, there was a good deal of legal argument about the admissibility of these tapes, which were eventually allowed in. Their contents were then subjected to a good deal more legal argument, which might have well resulted in a very confused jury and verdict of 'not guilty' had it not been for the judge's obvious irritation over them and his summing up. In it he told the jury to ignore them altogether and made scathing criticism of the Chief Superintendent for making them.

Another area of frequent criticism of the police is when they fail apparently to protect someone from some form of violence which has been predicted by a member of the public. It is a difficult area and one in which the police always come out with egg on their faces if the prediction comes true. It would be impossible for the police to provide personal protection for everyone who fears violence, and the standard response to any such request is that the person should dial 999 if and when the threat materialises.

One day, on my instructions, a woman was given that advice when she reported that her husband, from whom she was estranged, had threatened to kill her. I also instructed that the husband should be seen and warned as to his future behaviour. Before this could be achieved however, not that it would have done any good, the woman was found stabbed to death in the gutter outside her home in Maldon. Her husband was convicted of her murder, for which I also felt some responsibility.

Life at Chelmsford however was not all about death; there was a very varied and exciting diet of other crime a detective could get his teeth into. My experience of lorry thefts on the Regional Crime Squad came in handy on one occasion when two men came into Chelmsford police station to report that their lorry had been stolen and that they had been kidnapped and held captive in a house for several hours before being blindfolded, taken for a short ride and then released.

It seemed a 'likely story' but one that became more and more plausible as the enquiry progressed. It was most unusual for two drivers to be involved in a fake lorry hijacking, as I had experienced them in the past. Lorry hijacking was now a fairly rare occurrence, and kidnapping drivers and imprisoning them was unheard of.

The men, although blindfolded when they were taken to the house, could nevertheless see a little and described a builder's yard called Coward's which was opposite the house where they were taken. Officers went there and made enquiries, but the couple who apparently lived there denied any knowledge, and without a search warrant there was little more they could do. The men insisted however that this was the house and that they had been taken into a cellar and handcuffed with police type cuffs to hot water pipes in this basement. They were able to describe the basement in detail, as the blindfold had been taken off once they were there. They could give no descriptions of the men involved, who all wore masks, but they had heard a woman's voice.

I quickly obtained a search warrant and returned with officers to the house. This time the occupier became abusive and refused to open the door, which we kicked in 'Sweeney' fashion. Inside there was only the man and woman. There was no trace of any of the goods that had been on the lorry – wines and spirits – and no sign of a cellar!

Searching the wrong house is something to be avoided at all costs, but it does unfortunately happen. When it does there is usually a great cry of police harassment, abuse of authority, assault, damage to property and so on. Unfortunately it can and has happened and there is usually a perfectly good reason for the mistake. Failure to search because you think you might have the wrong house is equally a mistake, because until you do you'll never know. Searching the wrong house has happened to me on only two occasions, but in each case if I had to do the job again I couldn't have done it any other way.

In this case, after initial panic and realisation that we might have got the wrong house, I decided to lift the carpets. In a back room under a rug, there was a large hole covered with a board. The board was removed and this revealed a square hole with steps leading downwards to the cellar, where there were hot water pipes and a pair of handcuffs. Bingo! Sighs of relief all round.

The lorry was eventually found abandoned in the London area, but the stolen goods were never recovered.

Husband and wife were convicted of being involved in the crime and unlawful detention of the drivers. The other two men were not caught.

Armed robbery was a little less frequent in the seventies, and when it did happen it was usually a toy gun or finger poking through a raincoat pocket. One that was for real occurred at a sub post office in a back street of Chelmsford on a bright sunny afternoon. It was a street with terraced houses running alongside the railway with an embankment at the bottom their gardens. A man with a balaclava over his face went into the small shop, pointed a gun into the face of the middle-aged postmistress and demanded money. A gun pointed in one's face is usually a pretty good incentive to comply with such a request, and she handed over the cash in her moneybox with trembling hand and heart. The robber made off in a car, and no one, and there were several onlookers, bothered to take the number.

For the past week or more there had been a series of explosions heard by people in the neighbourhood and also several fires on the railway embankment, which the fire brigade had attended. It had become apparent that the loud explosions occurred just prior to a fire starting, and although no crime was apparent, or at least none had been reported, the police were concerned that something more serious might occur.

The description of the robber as given by the woman was a little vague, and of the gun even more so. Various witnesses described the man as between eighteen and sixty, between five foot six and six foot three tall, and the gun anything from a small automatic to one 'like the cowboys have on television'.

The car might have been a dark Ford, a light blue Vauxhall or a silver Toyota. Witnesses to such an incident are notoriously unreliable.

There was however a local flavour about the crime that suggested someone who had some local knowledge of this sub-post office, tucked away as it was in a little back street of Chelmsford, so our local suspects were looked at first. There was as it happened a chap who lived quite near the post office who was regarded as 'weird' by the locals and who may or may not have answered the description of the robber. We knocked on his door to 'ask him a few questions' and when he saw us he was off like a rocket out of his back door and along the railway embankment.

Thinking we had cleared up an armed robbery in record time, officers gave chase and soon brought him down. He wasn't as it happens the robber, but we did find a small bomb factory at the bottom of his garden. He had been making bombs with weedkiller and various other chemicals and trying them out on the railway embankment. He was not quite one hundred percent in the brains department. If he had been maybe he would have managed to blow up half the street.

The robber wasn't caught on this occasion, but like many similar criminals he carried on with his own personal crime wave until he was caught in a nearby town doing exactly the same thing. Unfortunately for him, there were more observant witnesses there.

During the summer a number of travelling families used to arrive in the farming areas around Chelmsford to do casual work and gather in the crops for the farmers. One other shooting incident I recall involved two travelling families who had an ongoing family feud and had the misfortune to be directed to park within a hundred yards or so of each other in a farmer's field. When each realised the other was there the feud began again in earnest and finished up with both families shooting at each other across the farmer's land with shotguns and air guns.

A number of charges were brought including the serious offence of Affray and the families finished up at the Assizes. I recall with some amusement the confusion, because one family was named Smith and the other Major. All the defendants were brothers and fathers, and the elder son in each family was named after the father. So we had John Smith, who was known throughout the trial as John Smith Major, and his son John Smith, who was John Smith Minor. That was bad enough, but then there was John Major Major and John Major Minor as well as the other Smiths and Majors to contend with. Each defendant had his own counsel paid for at public expense and the trial lasted several weeks. The result was heavy fines, all of which were paid in cash.

When searching the caravans of these travelling people it was astonishing to see the valuable glassware and other antiques they contained. Most had plastic bags full of money hidden in their 'vans', all of which they said they had earned doing casual farm work. Some also had building society pass books showing deposits of many thousands of pounds.

I have mentioned informants and my feelings about their use elsewhere in this book. I was only once ever given information by a newspaper reporter, although I know they have been useful to other officers. Of course I realise that as in the case of most other 'informants' they are hoping to gain for themselves in one way or another. This young man, who worked for the local paper at Chelmsford, told me that he knew of a restaurant at Chelmsford, which was also a place licensed under the liquor licensing laws, where they regularly held live sex shows. It appeared that tickets were sold to certain male customers of the restaurant who attended to watch young girls take part in sex acts with each other and with members of the audience. He was prepared to tell me the time and date of the next show, provided he could report on the outcome. He said that he had means of getting tickets and wanted to be there when the police raid commenced.

I could see no real objection to that; indeed if true an airing in the press about such a place could do nothing but good from the public's point of view. I had no reason to doubt the truth of the information and decided to mount a raid on the place. It was a real fun night, and I had twenty uniformed officers standing by to take the names and addresses of all the persons present. At the given moment when the 'sex' was being performed the reporter, who was also attending, unbolted the front door and we piled in.

There was a big scramble and our photographer got some good shots of the girls grabbing for their flimsy dresses and the men, who had agreed to participate from the audience, for their trousers. Various items of 'equipment' were strewn about the floor and it was pretty chaotic for a while. I went 'backstage' into the kitchen, where the girls were clutching their clothes to their ample bosoms and trembling, and arrested them. I wasn't quite sure what for, but it seemed a good idea at the time. The proprietor was also arrested and despatched to the local police station while the names and addresses were taken.

There were some thirty or so persons present, two of whom were recognised as members of the traffic division, and other well-known faces didn't altogether match up with the various John Smiths and William Browns whose names appeared on the forms used by the uniformed branch officers to record the names and addresses. Most of course were false, and I found no fault with that. We had ample evidence and the fact that the assembly gave false names and addresses added just a little weight to it. The two traffic officers were given the choice of giving evidence or facing discipline charges.

A day or two later I was having lunch at a local pub where they did a really good cheap bar lunch (the chef was the son of one of my sergeants) when I was approached by a reporter I knew. He was from one of the big daily newspapers and he wanted to know all the details of the raid. I told him what had already been published locally and said that I had no idea who was to be charged or with what. I also expressed my surprise and asked why such a big national paper might be interested.

"My editor was there" he whispered.

Later the proprietor of the establishment was charged with some offence about outraging public decency. The girls, one of whom was only sixteen, were let off with a caution. When being questioned the girls had said they were surprised that the police should be making such a fuss over this. "After all" one of them said, "we do this show at Southend for the Police and even the Chief Superintendent attends."

I spent seven years at Chelmsford town and they were among the most interesting, from a detecting point of view, of my police service. I enjoyed supervising a little more by now, especially as it didn't exclude me from getting involved in actual cases. However as I was so close to Headquarters it also meant that I would be one of the first to get called in to investigate allegations of crime made against police officers. It was not a job any police officer likes to have to undertake, and fortunately these cases were less frequent then than they are today. Happily only a very small percentage were, and are, substantiated.

I did have to arrest a serving police officer on one occasion at Chelmsford. He had been on night duty as area car patrol driver with a young constable as his observer. During the night he had stopped at a garage forecourt where a number of cars for sale were parked, and proceeded to prise off the headlight of one of the cars and steal a bulb. He did this in full view of his observer and told him that he needed it for his own car.

Probably one of the most difficult positions a police officer can find himself in is to witness a crime by a fellow officer, colleague or even a member of his own family, in a situation that if revealed, would make him appear as guilty as the actual offender. Loyalty is expected from all one's peers, and loyalty to the service as well as to yourself is considered essential by everyone else.

In this case the young officer tried to resolve the situation by confiding in his Sergeant. He failed to realise that this put the Sergeant in the same boat as he was in himself. The Sergeant quite correctly reported the matter and the young officer later had to give evidence at court against his fellow officer. The officer was dismissed and lost his job and his pension prospects. Quite a lot to lose for a two-shilling headlight bulb.

In my later dealings with complaints against police I came across this inner conflict on many occasions and in the vast majority of cases found that officers would rather risk losing their job and pension than inform on a colleague.

During the seven years I had spent at Chelmsford there had been quite a few changes within the force and there were now yet more chiefs and even fewer Indians. We had been through various so-called reforms, the Panda Car Scheme, the Noddy Bikes, Rural Beat schemes, Community Policing, Civilianisation and many other methods of trying to spread the existing force of men even more thinly over a wider area. We used to call it reinventing the wheel, because so many of the schemes dreamed up by those in high places had been tried before and a 'rose by any other name smells just as sweet'. Most of the schemes finished up as they began, nothing more than a good idea that didn't work. There seemed no substitute for competent policemen doing their job in the age-old way. This is just as true today.

More and more legislation was passed to learn and to try to 'enforce' and there was even a new department at Headquarters to distribute copies of all the new laws and 'bumf' that came from the Home Office to forces everywhere.

In addition I had lost my Detective Inspector, who had moved back to Warwickshire as a Detective Chief Inspector. It was a sad loss to the police service when later he was forced to resign after some bad publicity over a rape case he had handled in the old accepted way, but was now expected to deal with in the light of some modern thinking on the subject. There was now a new Detective Inspector, one Taffy Jones, who was a local man and a very good replacement. Sadly Taffy died tragically before he reached retirement age, following an accident when he fell from a ladder through a greenhouse roof. I attended his funeral, as I have those of quite a few other former colleagues in the past few years.

It was now 1977 and the Detective Chief Superintendent at this time was Alf Mitchell, who you will recall, if you have been paying attention, was a colleague of mine on the Fraud Squad way back in 1961. Chalky White was now a uniformed Chief Superintendent in charge of Chelmsford division. Alf telephoned me one day to ask me if I would be prepared to move back to Headquarters to take over the Fraud Squad.

I felt that seven years without a move was long enough, and after all it wasn't as if I had to move house. I had by now bought my own property at Springfield and at the time had no thoughts of moving from there. Alf, a colleague who I knew and got on well with, was in the chair. I saw that only good could come from such a move, so I accepted.

CHAPTER ELEVEN

# HQ Fraud Squad
# & Complaints (1978–79)

*Never apologise and never complain – it's a sign of weakness -*
*John Wayne, She Wore a Yellow Ribbon*

Detective Chief Inspector Barry Tarbun had been in charge
of the Fraud Squad for the past few years. This department
had now grown somewhat and had two inspectors and
several sergeants and constables. It was still called the Fraud
Squad, although that was to be change shortly to the CDU,
or Central Detective Unit.

Under my wing too was the Drugs Squad with an
Inspector Garrard, two sergeants and two constables. The
role of the Drugs Squad had changed somewhat and instead
of attending schools and ladies' clubs to talk about misuse of
drugs there was now an active move against such misuse. In
this respect the Drugs Squad had something in common with
the Regional Crime Squad, which I did know a little about.

No one actually reported crimes to the Drugs Squad, but they were now one of the specialist departments to whom others could turn for assistance. Drug abusers commit crimes against themselves, so they are hardly likely to report themselves to the police. People who supply them with drugs are the more serious offenders; they offend against society as a whole and not against individual victims, as with other crimes. It is rare therefore that a specific crime concerning the misuse of drugs is reported to the police.

One of the drawbacks of having a specialist department is that others tend to 'pass the buck' to them. If there was suspicion on a particular division that someone was supplying 'controlled' drugs, the Drugs Squad would be asked to deal with it rather than the division itself. The Drugs Squad personnel did have some up-to-date knowledge of the law on drug abuse and a copy of Mimms Compendium with which to identify the various pills and capsules they came across, but otherwise were no better qualified than any other officer to arrest suspects. It was generally thought however that they were the only ones who could deal with such matters.

Drugs, their misuse and its consequences were just beginning to dawn on the police and the 'authorities'. I really think that no one seriously believed it would ever be the problem it is today. The loss of life, the misery of people and families affected by drug abuse the thousands of crimes of violence against persons and against property that are perpetrated every day because of it are the direct result of ignoring the problem when it first appeared in the sixties. Now successive governments make a lot of noise about how the problem can and should be tackled, but nothing visible has changed on the streets of our big cities, and now in most of the smaller ones too, except that the problem gets progressively worse.

Like the Regional Crime Squad, the Drugs Squad relied quite a lot on information received in order to catch the suppliers of drugs. Misuse by individuals took up a great deal of their time too, because it was then considered a far more serious offence than it is today and the stopping and searching of individuals suspected of carrying cannabis was quite a frequent occurrence. Now of course we are led to believe that it is not so serious and that searching people on the streets, especially those from ethnic groups, is an infringement of their liberties.

Informants in the sub-culture of drug abusers are just as dangerous for a police officer to deal with as those I became acquainted with on the Regional Crime Squad. These creatures inform on others for three reasons: one is to obtain reward money to buy more drugs for themselves, another in order to avoid prosecution themselves and a third in order to repay a favour given to them by a police officer.

Although the Drugs Squad was under the direct control of an Inspector, it was my job to oversee the work of that unit and to ensure that it was done correctly. The three examples above of the use of informants did open up a minefield of problems that an officer, if allowed to, could create for himself and others.

First in relation to informants' money. There was, in the eyes of those in control of the purse strings, a suspicion that there might be 'fiddles'. Heaven forbid! And that officers might either invent informants or not hand all of a cash reward over to the individual in question. Over the years various cases had been reported in the press that might have given this impression. It was not unknown for some officers, believing they might be about to crack open a big case, to hand over some of their own cash to a so-called informant, but this was usually money wasted.

To ensure that informant money generally was paid out in a proper way and for good reasons, it was first decided that any money handed over should be signed for on a proper receipt by the informant. This proved to be something of a failure since either the informant refused to sign or he used the name 'Santa Claus' or something equally fictitious.

The next step in trying to control this perceived problem was an instruction from 'above' that an informant could only be paid reward money by or in the presence of a senior officer. This immediately reduced the number of payments to informants and to some extent proved the purse-holders right. At the same time in my view there did not seem to be any reduction in the numbers of arrests. However it did seem to me that there was a good deal more information coming in, which never did qualify for a reward but from which officers stood to gain financially. An officer might receive information that a 'deal was going down' (American jargon was now being used more frequently amongst drug squad officers) tomorrow, which happened to be a bank holiday. I fell for it a couple of times before I realised that having to work on a bank holiday the officers got paid double time and had a day off in lieu. The loophole here was that provided a reward was not requested, no senior officer was going to meet with the informant and it was hoped that he would give the authorisation to act on the 'information'. However when the result was constantly negative I began to suspect that the 'information' was manufactured by the officer. I could have been wrong!

From then on I insisted that I meet with the informant myself and confirm the information and the reason it was being given before I authorised any action. This, so far as I could see at the time, was the most effective way of ensuring that neither my officers nor I were being duped.

If an officer found a small quantity of a controlled drug on a suspect it was tempting to offer to let him go if he gave substantial information against another person, in particular the person who had supplied him the drug. It was a risk that officer might or might not be willing to take, and as I always reminded them, it was their risk alone. I did not condone this, nor did I encourage officers to do it. It was in the long run unproductive; it put the officer at risk of being dismissed the service and the informant of death at the hands of his 'pusher'. In spite of that it went on then, and goes on today.

The giving of information to an officer as a favour follows on from the above, in that having given information once, a drug addict might feel obliged to continue to do so. In fact the addict actually had more on the officer than the officer had on him, if he only realised it. The relationship that develops between a criminal and a police officer in these and similar circumstances is a most unhealthy one and will almost inevitably lead to the officer himself committing or participating in a criminal act. For drugs read money - large quantities of it - and many an honest man has been tempted from the straight and narrow by large sums of money.

Those in command of men engaged in and on the fringes of this kind of dangerous activity have a great deal of responsibility, and the risks of not doing the job effectively are equally hazardous. I was not in charge of the Drugs Squad for very long, but it did cause me more headaches than any of my other responsibilities. None of my officers were ever accused, I might add, of any kind of improper conduct or dishonest act; whether that was due to my supervision or their cleverness we shall never know.

Since my earlier period of service at Headquarters other new departments had been created, including one that kept up to date with and controlled the use of new equipment, surveillance items etc. We called it the 'department of funny toys' and no one had a lot of confidence in it, since as I pointed out earlier its use was very restricted indeed. One of the most effective and simple of the toys, which did work, was an electronic wallet. There were often reports around the county of a thief visiting changing rooms at golf clubs, schools and swimming pools etc and stealing cash and purses from clothing hanging there. The wallet used to be placed in a jacket and hung in a cloakroom and an officer stationed in a room nearby. As soon as the wallet was 'lifted' an alarm went off audible only to the officer, who walked in and nabbed the thief. It was questionable whether the use of this equipment did or did not offend against what is known as the law of 'agent provocateur', but no one ever questioned it and there were many guilty pleas as the result of its use.

The new Firearms Unit was ready to tackle armed raids and sieges and was responsible for the firearms training some officers were now receiving. For a good many years the police had seen the need for arming policemen on occasions. I myself had been issued with a weapon on one occasion during the search for Harry Roberts. Every Divisional Chief Superintendent had a number of handguns locked away in his safe and he alone had the power to issue them. There was a procedure for such an issue. After the necessary discussion to persuade him that there was an 'operational need', the Chief Superintendent would unlock his safe, take out the guns and ammunition and issue what he considered the necessary amount to deal with the situation. Then the rounds would be counted and, together with the guns, signed for. A warning concerning the use of the weapon had to be read to the officers being issued with a firearm, and a declaration signed by each officer taking a weapon acknowledging that the discharge of the weapon would be his sole responsibility and any consequences arising therefrom his alone to answer for. It was a long declaration in red and contained a good deal of legal jargon that had no doubt been formulated by a battery of legal brains to ensure the Chief Constable would be free of liability in the event that the officer needed to shoot someone. Had the officers had time to read the declaration properly, many would probably not have signed it.

One does not have to be a genius to see immediately that there was a problem with this system. It might be all very well for an occasion when armed robbers were expected to arrive at some place in the future and there was time to issue guns to officers to meet them. However no Superintendent was likely to be persuaded that a prospective gun battle at the OK Shopping Centre was an 'operational need'. Such an eventuality was not at the time an occasion for the issue of divisional firearms, perhaps an Armed Firearms Unit, now that there was one.

An 'operational need' might occur if an armed man entered a bank in the high street and threatened staff and customers. Fine, but then someone would have to explain all this to the Chief Superintendent and wait for him to unlock the safe, count out the rounds and read the warning. No doubt the armed robber would be happy to wait at the bank for all this to happen and for the officers to arrive and take him into custody.

The mind boggles at the imaginativeness of the people who dream up these procedures. You can visualise a dozen or more high-ranking officials sitting down together with politicians and Home Office officials, trying to arrive at a policy for the issue of firearms. It reminds one of the old quip that a camel is actually a horse designed by a committee.

It was obvious that there was going to be an occasional need for policemen to carry guns. Robbers and other criminals were using them more and more frequently, and if the police were to have any chance to combat the criminal use of firearms they would have to have them too. That was about the only thing anyone has ever agreed about. How to do it, when, what type of guns etc has been debated for years without any final policy being reached. The next stage was for police cars to have firearms locked in the boot of their cars so that they could respond more quickly to an 'operational need'. They still had to obtain the Chief Superintendent's authority to 'unlock' and hoped that he wouldn't be at lunch or playing golf when the 'need' arose.

Times and circumstances, terrorist activities, political murders and IRA activity have to some extent forced decisions upon governments and police forces, decisions which were not welcome and which have begun to turn police officers into soldiers. You just have to look at a typical airport policeman today to see what I mean. Where is the kindly chap who you can walk up to and ask the time?

At least somewhere at the top there was a realisation that if officers were going to have to handle guns, they would require some training. It was also felt necessary to have an American style 'SWAT' squad around to be sent in to situations too dangerous for the ordinary copper on the beat. They have been used on one or two occasions to good effect, and on hundreds of others the situations have been resolved without a shot being fired.

At Frinton one day a man walking his dog in a small wooded area found a bag containing the proceeds of an armed robbery. The Firearms Unit surrounded the place and when the robber came back for his loot he shot and killed one of them before being shot himself. At a pub at Ramsey one night a man with a gun threatened the publican and other customers. The Firearms Unit attended and shot and killed him. On each occasion the officer who actually did the killing was subjected to the most querulous enquiry and made to feel that the work he had been trained for was not only unnecessary but unlawful. The newspapers took up cudgels and the whole debate fired up once again for a few days.

Training for the ordinary officer, who one day will surely be carrying a sidearm as in the rest of Europe, consisted at first of an amusing fiasco in some woods near Colchester. There would be a pretence that an armed criminal was in the woods and teams of ten officers with 'loaded' guns would attempt to flush him out. The idea was to march in line through the woods with about twenty yards separating each officer. On the first and only occasion I was asked to participate in this farce, the instructor said, "Pretend that you have radio communication with the man next to you". This was the very last straw for me and I refused to attend any further sessions.

Firearms training was, and so far as I know still is, voluntary. Mostly the training now, except for the Firearms Unit, consists of firing a few rounds every few months on the military range at Colchester. After the training, officers were assessed as to their suitability for the handling of guns; some were said to be "temperamentally unsuitable". This indicated to me that at some time in the future this suitability test would have to be made before and not after a man was appointed as a constable.

The whole question of arming the police force will have to be seriously addressed sooner or later. There are serious problems in the half-hearted method of doing a simple job. It is like many situations in the world today - everyone knows what has to be done, but there is not the political will to do it.

Senior officers have been sent all over the world to study methods used by other police forces in order to improve our own. To my knowledge the subject of police use of firearms has not been included in these tours. It is obvious to me that all the misgivings held by people in the UK and the problems envisaged have all been experienced by other forces in other countries. Why should we not learn from them? An article by me on this subject was first published in *The Criminologist* (Appendix ii).

There was now also a fully-fledged Diving Section with a good deal of modern diving equipment and the means to search canals, rivers, and so forth. Sergeant Phil China was the officer in charge of this outfit; he had learned his skill in the Navy. He trained two or three other suitable persons and they proved to be very useful in recovering dead bodies from dangerous waters, searching weirs and water-filled quarries for missing children, sadly often finding them, and searching for stolen property, murder weapons etc.

About once a month as an exercise they used to go to Passingford Bridge in the Harlow division, where a river ran under the road. They used to search the river bed and almost always recovered something of interest. There were safes, guns, bicycles and once even a sack of stolen silverware. Why people used this spot to dump their unwanted or stolen goods I never knew, but it seemed a constant source of underwater treasure for the Diving Section.

The Crime Prevention Department was another of someone's bright ideas; no doubt with the rising crime rate it was thought of as yet another way to tackle the problem. A

Sergeant was the first Force Crime Prevention Officer and his job was to promote Crime Prevention within the County of Essex. He did this by driving a caravan full of exhibits to fetes, fairs, the county show and even town squares, anywhere in fact where it was thought people interested in crime prevention might want to visit and get his advice on matters such as burglar alarms, window locks and all manner of security devices that were available to the public. The manufacturers of course were very interested and supported this initiative with leaflets and free samples.

The constable's role in prevention of crime is well established from the definition of his office. I have always imagined, wrongly it seemed, that the constable's role in preventing crime was his very presence on the street. The sight of the burly constable plodding down the street in full view of the community was supposed to be the deterrent that prevented crime. The idea of a police officer being a super salesman for Chubb's locks and safes and for various other manufacturers of burglar alarms, security glass, locks and bars, was for me a hard pill to swallow. But who was I to argue with the Home Office, who regularly issued piles of 'bumf' on the subject for our CPO to digest and disseminate?

It is generally believed that fixing a burglar alarm to your premises is a way of preventing crime. My belief is that it prevents a victim, not a crime. The criminal is still out there and will commit his crime somewhere else. If there were no victims there could be no crimes, and the public might do well to think on this and do more to protect themselves in an age when the police and government can no longer protect them.

One spin-off from the Crime Prevention Officer, who incidentally soon became an Inspector with a CPO in every division, was the introduction of the Neighbourhood Watch. In many ways this was a good idea, but it depended rather heavily on the local CPO to generate interest and keep it going. I don't feel the need to go into any detail here about the scheme, and anyone who knows what a thankless task it is to get the British public motivated to do anything will know what an abject failure it was and is.

Various Home Secretaries have had some wonderful ideas about how this scheme could be developed, for example by having pensioners patrol the streets and encouraging people to inform on their neighbours. These ideas have done little more than to show that we really have some wonderfully imaginative politicians in charge of running the country. Every Home Secretary feels obliged to invent new schemes and ideas to improve the police, but they have all forgotten the wise old adage "If it ain't broke, don't try and fix it".

In addition to their other duties, which included teaching primary children how to cross the road and older ones how to ride bicycles, Divisional Crime Prevention Officers were supposed to advise householders and businessmen on the best means of protecting their premises. If any other constable were to be asked advice about such difficult and technical matters they had to refer the person asking to the Crime Prevention Officer, who would pay them a visit.

The Security Industry is now a major player in the big business stakes and experts on every kind of security you can think of are available at the end of the telephone. Television is a wonderful way of propagating information to elderly ladies that they should not open their door to strangers or let in the man from the Water Board without checking his credentials. Some may think that police officers, given the shortage of them, might be better employed doing police work and letting those that are good at it propagate crime prevention information and distribute leaflets for the security industry. An article by me on this subject was first published in *The Criminologist* (Appendix iii).

Perhaps the most significant department to have been formed at Headquarters since I was last there, and one that was to make so much difference to the efficiency, or lack of it, of the police service in the years to come, was the Complaints Department. The new legislation required that all complaints against police were to be investigated by an officer of the rank of Superintendent. In the case of Senior and Chief Officers the rank would have to be at least one higher than that of the accused officer.

It followed that a Superintendent was in charge of this new department and he oversaw all complaints. He was of course able to farm out the actual legwork to other lesser mortals, and as I said earlier any allegation of crime against an officer had to have the attention of a Detective Chief Inspector. An article by me on this subject was first published in *The Criminologist.* (Appendix iv).

Barry Tarbun had for the past two years or so been fully engaged in an operation called Operation Lager. No one really knew too much about what he was doing, but it involved drugs and lots of time spent in London. He also used some of the Fraud Squad personnel to help in the enquiries concerning this major operation and consequently most of them had spent less and less time on fraud enquiries.

Major incidents within the county had also interrupted ongoing fraud enquiries and in many cases, frauds that would otherwise have been passed to the Fraud Squad for investigation had been left with division, or just simply shelved until someone found time to deal with them. The whole Fraud Department had, insofar as fraud was concerned, come to a standstill.

Alf Mitchell had identified this problem soon after he took office and blamed Barry Tarbun for the situation, although to be fair it was not entirely his fault. Perhaps it was thought that he could have identified the problem earlier and suggested a remedy. However a sideways move seemed on the cards for Barry, and I took his place with a brief to get the matter straightened out.

I started this task as best I knew how and gave it a great deal of time and energy. Some short cuts were inevitable to get cases concluded and 'No Further Action' was occasionally stamped on the front cover of a fraud file that might otherwise have been 'worth a go,' as Peter Palmer used to say. I always did fancy myself as a good report writer, and a report can be slanted one way or another to fit your conclusions and recommendations. Mine were usually supported by Alf Mitchell and progress was made.

Almost as soon as I took my seat in the Fraud Squad Chief Inspector's office there was a report of a Building Society in Grays that was in difficulty. A senior member of the board, the Chairman in fact, had committed suicide and large deficiencies of cash were discovered. It was customary for the head of the Fraud Squad to attend to such a report initially and then to delegate if it seemed that his high office was not necessary to complete the enquiry. In this case I took along a Sergeant and we met the various members of the board of this quite small family-run business.

The chairman had been in his early seventies and although apparently happily married he had had, we discovered, a secret life. He had a flat in London where he kept a mistress and spent a good deal of time at the races and in the company of local bookmakers who were at first reluctant to divulge information to the police about him. Later we discovered that he would spend as much as a thousand pounds a day betting on the horses. When it all seemed about to be uncovered, as it must inevitably have done, he took the easy way out and shot himself in the head. He left no note!

This could have been a huge local scandal if it had become public knowledge and fortunately, as the perpetrator was dead, there was no prospect of a prosecution. Still the lid had to be kept on or savers would have rushed to withdraw their savings and all sorts of mayhem might have broken lose. Other larger building societies supported this small one in putting the finances right, and I had to trust to luck that no one would leak anything to the press.

Because of the circumstances, and particularly the pressure I was under at the time to bring dozens of other fraud investigations to a speedy conclusion, what at first looked like a job that might take a year or so to investigate was wrapped up in a matter of days.

Within a couple of months things were beginning to settle down, cases were prepared for sending to the County Prosecuting Solicitor or filed away forever, and we were once more open for business and ready to take on more new work. Alf Mitchell was delighted, and told me in confidence that he had put in a very good word for me with the Chief Constable, while no doubt taking a good deal of the credit, if credit there were, for himself.

Alf must have had great confidence in my ability with fraud investigations, because years later when I was myself a private investigator, and he too was retired and doing similar work, he used to recommend me to his clients when a job he thought was 'up my street' came his way. By now of course the police were turning away fraud and labelling it a civil matter. It is nothing of the kind, and the police are really neglecting their duty when they ignore the fact that a criminal offence may have been committed. Of course there are also cases where the aggrieved would not want the person they suspect prosecuted or they themselves ridiculed or embarrassed by having been duped. Such cases too were better left to a private rather than a public investigator.

I investigated a number of frauds as a private investigator, and very lucrative they were too. One local men's club at Clacton was making far less profit than it expected from the percentage profit they had calculated. They suspected theft, but had no idea whether it was money from the till, goods from the shelf or indeed how the losses were occurring. I spent many evenings at the bar drinking free beer before I discovered how the lack of profit was happening. The majority of members were working-class types who drank pints of 'light and bitter'. On every occasion when a drink was ordered the barman gave at least three-quarters of a pint of ale and a bottle of light. In this way some forty or fifty pints of beer was actually being given away every night! But I digress again.

The next incident to hit the efficiency of the Fraud Squad was a murder at Maldon. At least that is where the seat of the enquiry was. It meant that I and several of my officers were dragged off once more to deal with a major incident, to the detriment of our own work. The body of a woman of about thirty-five years had been found dead just over the Essex border in Hertfordshire. She had been murdered by strangulation and dumped, presumably from a vehicle. She was a married woman from Maldon and her own car was found locked and secure in a car park in Witham.

As the body was found in Hertfordshire it was their 'baby', and while it was clearly only an accident that the body had been dumped in Hertfordshire, nevertheless that force had to take responsibility for the investigation. A Detective Superintendent Jack Moulder came to Maldon to run the enquiries and I and others ran the incident office as if were our own enquiry. Jack Moulder I had known from my Crime Squad days; he was a competent and practical policeman. He is remembered by most who knew him for the expression, "Good thinking!" He used it every time anyone made a useful suggestion to him.

It seemed the woman was quite well known in Maldon and was a member of various ladies' organisations and clubs. There was little doubt that she had gone to the car park in Witham to meet a man, and had then gone off with him in his car. Her movements that evening were traced and both she and the man had called into at least one public house for a drink.

The enquiry dragged on for weeks, with nothing but suspects and plenty of worn shoe leather to show for it. I was eventually pleased to be allowed to return to my normal duties and in due course the enquiry was scaled down and active enquiries were concluded. Such files are never regarded as 'closed' and from time to time a new lead or enquiry would come up and reopened for a while. This murder remains undetected, but as it was not an Essex job that statistic did not concern us that much. As in many cases, after many weeks of intensive enquiries the police knew, or had a pretty good idea, who had committed the murder, but again like many cases, there was insufficient evidence to mount a prosecution. The suspect was interviewed on a number of occasions, but strong suspicion is no substitute for evidence and the police cannot voice their suspicions except to the suspect.

There was one positive result, however. One of the Hertfordshire officers on the enquiry met the wife of a local publican who later left her husband and married the officer. I hope they are both happy!

Although I was officially the head of the Fraud Squad, I soon became one of the investigators of complaints against police and spent more time doing that than anything else. The Complaints Superintendent was a man named Alex Ferguson, an officer who had transferred to Essex from a far distant force. He was a Scot, an alien so far as Essex men were concerned, and in view of his job as Complaints Superintendent not very popular.

I had known him before at Chelmsford, where he was the Rural Chief Inspector, but knew little about him except that he had been on the CID at some stage of his career for a short while. Any enquiry that was not a criminal allegation had to be carried out by a Superintendent, so all of the divisional and sub-divisional Superintendents had their caseloads to deal with of such matters as rudeness to a member of the public, smoking on duty, abuse of authority and so on. A Detective Chief Inspector usually handled only criminal allegations.

The first time Alex Ferguson asked me to do an investigation on his behalf he took me into his office and spoke to me as if I was a new recruit, explaining how I was to carry out the investigation, who I was to interview and in what order. I was by then one of the most senior detectives in the force and strongly objected to his patronising attitude. I told him if he wanted me to do the enquiry I would be happy to do so in my own way and without any advice from him. "After all" I said, "I am supposed to be the expert here. You don't employ a builder to build you a house and tell him how to lay the bricks."

The meeting was not as cordial as is should have been and a subsequent one was quite a battle of words. He rang me one day to ask if I had yet been to see a chap who was serving a prison sentence. I hadn't, but I told him that I had a letter of authority and was about to leave for Norwich prison to see the chap. He asked me to call and see him before I went to the prison, which I did. He said, "Who are you taking with you?"

I replied that I was going alone, which didn't suit him at all. I explained that I had been interviewing prisoners in prison for a number of years and that I had never felt the need to have anyone hold my hand or to corroborate my words. The interview would after all be in the presence of a prison warder. I resented the implied suggestion that my word would have to be corroborated to satisfy him and said that I would carry on as normal. I carried out my enquiries alone, much to Ferguson's vexation. As usual the complaint was unsubstantiated and the officer vindicated.

Most of the enquiries relating to complaints against police consisted of taking statements from witnesses. They were not necessarily persons who had witnessed anything significant but those who had some information or other which tended to prove or disprove the allegation against an officer. Because a witness in a complaint against police investigation was serving a prison sentence, he was still only a witness, and so far as I was aware there had never been any instruction issued that it was necessary to have two officers present for the taking of a witness statement. Nor was there any instruction that officers should go in pairs to a prison whenever a serving prisoner was to be seen about any matter.

For a while I gave the matter no more thought and

carried on with my work as normal. It did however crop up again a few weeks later, when one of my officers came to ask for a letter of authority to visit a serving prisoner. He told me that he and another officer would need to be named in the letter. I immediately asked why it was necessary for two officers to go and was told that that was now normal. I probed deeper and discovered that the practice had crept in without any official instructions and was generally approved of by most senior officers.

It was to me one of the first signs of a slide towards defensive policing. Since the introduction of the 'Complaints Against Police' system, officers were nervous about doing anything that might later attract criticism. I suppose some people thought that if two officers went to see someone the conversation later recorded in a notebook would be more likely to believed. That was short-sighted, because it was only a short step to both officers being accused of conspiring to produce a false record of an interview. It always struck me as strange too that even when an interview was recorded on tape there had to be at least two officers present. Not only was this in my view a waste of manpower, it was playing into the hands of those who would discredit the police. Why should we not hold up our heads and carry on interviewing and doing our job alone as we had done for many years, and face any criticism with firm assurances that were usually believed in the face of accusations by criminals?

My voice was a small one in this and many other crusades, and things only got worse. There were to be instructions (Standing Orders) issued about interviews in prisons and on many other matters which had previously been considered basic police work.

Like a number of other officers at the time, Alex Ferguson gave the impression that every complaint received was true and that the officer named in it was a liar, a cheat, a thief or worse. The Essex Police force, and indeed the whole of the police service, was at this time obsessed with complaints against the police. There were even leaflets printed in every possible language you can think of to distribute to the ethnic minorities, and others who don't speak English, instructing them how to make a complaint against the police! Trivial complaints that had been dealt with prior to the formation of the Police Complaints Board by way of a tactful chat between complainant and Police Inspector were now the subject of full-blown enquiries and reports to the Police Complaints Board in London.

The bulk of all complaints against police were trivial matters, never worthy of more than a quiet word in the officer's ear, but no longer could the Sergeant deal with things in this way and the Police Discipline Regulations and local Divisional Discipline Book became obsolete save for the most minor matters such as being late for duty or swearing at your Sergeant. There was even a debate as to whether a complaint by one officer against another was an official complaint. Yes, it was! Or so the powers that be ruled, to be on the safe side.

The Deputy Chief Constable (at the time it was John Duke) was, according to custom and the new Police Act, responsible overall for discipline with the force and it was to him therefore that Alex Ferguson had to report. There was a daily meeting in John Duke's office in the morning when progress on enquiries into complaints, together with details of any new ones, were discussed. There was another each evening when reports that were ready were signed by John Duke before being forwarded with his recommendations to the Police Complaints Board in London. If disciplinary proceedings followed they were held by the Chief Constable personally. The Complaints Superintendent presented facts and the officer could either defend himself or have a 'friend' do it for him. 'Friend' was the word used in the regulations, and was not necessarily a friend in the usual sense of the word. The 'friend' could be anyone of his choosing but it had to be another police officer and one who agreed to act for him. At the time an officer accused of a disciplinary offence could not have a solicitor to represent him. There were at Headquarters a Police Federation Office and a full-time force representative. The representative was often considered to be a 'friend' to lower ranks and they often used to ask him for advice and to represent them before the Chief Constable.

If it were a question of criminal proceedings, then these would be heard at a Magistrates' Court or a higher court in the same way as any other criminal proceedings. John Duke would also sign suspension notices for service on any officer accused of, or who had admitted, a criminal offence.

I had had little experience of the complaints procedure until then, although I had at one time while in Chelmsford been interviewed by an officious officer from the Metropolitan Police who demanded that I make a statement detrimental to one of my detectives who, it seemed, had been accused of some trivial matter by a London villain while in the MPD carrying out enquiries. The Met officer introduced himself to me as a Chief Superintendent, but I had been forewarned that he was in fact a Chief Inspector, the same rank as myself, and had been given this acting rank for the business of the enquiry in hand only, an enquiry which went far beyond the alleged misconduct of my own officer. His manner was so rude that I walked out of the room and slammed the door, refusing to answer his questions or to make a statement.

The Metropolitan Police had had a department or branch called A10 for some time which was on a par with the Internal Affairs Division of the police in the USA. There had been some pretty bad cases of police abuse and dishonesty in the Met in recent years and this branch had a reputation of being pretty ruthless in dealing with allegations against policemen. Besides being my first contact with anyone from A10 I do believe it was also the first occasion that he had had to come out to a provincial force to pursue his enquiries. No doubt we both learned something from it.

Later, after an interesting conversation with John Duke, I wrote out a statement as to what I knew about the matter and forwarded it to the Chief Inspector. I heard no more about the matter.

Now I was to learn much more about the procedure, because one morning John Duke called me into his office to tell me that I was being made an Acting Superintendent and was taking over the complaints department temporarily, as

Alex Ferguson was going to the Police College for three months on the Superintendent's Course. The handover was a less than good-natured affair, but we managed it without rancour and I wished him good luck on his course. The next three months were something of a rest for me, because apart from a lot of paperwork, on which I thrived, and the morning and evening meetings in John Duke's office, there was little to do except farm out enquiries to other people. There were so many complaints to deal with on a day-to-day basis that I couldn't possibly spare the time to do any myself.

As time went by more and more complaints began to roll into the department and I found it increasingly difficult to get divisional Superintendents to accept them. It became necessary in the end for John Duke to send them out with his written instructions. The days of ringing up and politely asking if a Superintendent would mind taking on another case were over.

Most of the work done by the Complaints Superintendent was carried out in plain clothes. Divisional officers too were encouraged to visit complainants and take their statements in civilian dress. As I knew from experience, the vast majority of complaints were from criminals and their families, who would hardly welcome a police officer in uniform knocking on their door. The idea was to try and get the complaint withdrawn, and to rub such complainants up the wrong way by any form of officiousness was not the way to do it.

As I didn't have a uniform that was fine, but there was one important task for which a uniform was necessary, and that was the presentation of cases to the Chief Constable at a disciplinary hearing. In the police, certainly in the Essex Police, when an officer was acting in the next rank up he did not generally wear the badges of rank of the officer he was acting up for. Nor, incidentally, did he receive an increment in his wages. However in my case I was issued with a Superintendent's uniform and all the badges of rank that went with it. I thought this might well be a good omen.

There were not too many cases that went before the Chief Constable, but when they did it was a very formal affair and the Chief appeared in his full uniform, a sight not often seen except on very formal occasions. After the verdict and sentence was handed out there were usually a number of forms and papers to serve on the officer concerned. Such hearings were often circumvented by the resignation of the officer concerned, and then I would have to formally take possession of his appointments and Warrant Card.

In the case of an officer having been convicted in a criminal court of any crime, he would appear before the Chief Constable immediately afterwards, who would formally dismiss him. In such a case similar procedures would be adopted, but in addition a dismissal notice would be served, which among other things told the officer he could whistle for his pension.

Having nearly reached the end of my three months I was beginning to wonder what was to become of me. Construction was well on the way with the new Police Headquarters building, which was to be very large and with palatial offices for many, with new furniture, modern equipment, a canteen, bar and gymnasium. I wondered whether I would be lucky enough to occupy one of these new offices when they were completed. Since another officer had already taken my place on the Fraud Squad and Alex Ferguson was due back from the Police College I had a horrible fear that he was going to move on and I would be required to stay in Complaints.

I was enlightened by John Duke one morning when he casually told me at one of our morning meetings that there was shortly to be a vacancy at Grays for a Divisional Superintendent and that the job was mine if I wanted it. Although the offer was made as though I had a choice, I wondered whether I could refuse, as to do so would be seen as a refusal to accept a promotion.

CHAPTER TWELVE

# Grays
# 1980

*The Common Law of England has been laboriously built about a*
*mythical figure; the figure of The Reasonable Man. – A P Herbert,*
*Uncommon Law (1935), The Reasonable Man*

The initial notion that I would be going to Grays was
something of a shock. I had given Sir John Nightingale a very
positive indication that I wanted to remain on the CID in
spite of the disadvantage this might hold for further
promotion. Of course I couldn't refuse; after all it was a
promotion, and elevation to Senior Officer level was a big
step forward in monetary terms as well as the feeling of
achievement that went with it.

I discussed the move with John Duke and we talked about
my having to move house - I was in my own property - or
alternatively the travelling. Grays was more than forty miles
from my home at Chelmsford and I thought it most unlikely

that I would be allowed to travel, not that I really wanted to. John Duke said we could do a deal and that if I agreed to travel at my own expense I wouldn't be required to move house.

I pointed out to him that it would be a great disadvantage being so far away from my division and that the opportunity to call into the station for supervisory visits at off times would be lost. John Duke agreed, but said he was sure everything would work out fine. I agreed to think about it and let him know my decision later that day. I left his office wondering why such an unusual arrangement seemed to be agreeable to him.

I went along immediately afterwards to see Alf Mitchell and told him the news. He was already aware of it and said it had been discussed in the Chief's Office. Alf was most encouraging and said that the move was not going to be for long and that he was sure that as things were I could expect a chance at getting his job some time in the future. It was, he said, a pre-requisite for the job to have a period as uniform Superintendent; all those who had held the job of Detective Chief Superintendent in the past had done so.

Of course it was not within Alf Mitchell's power to make any promises, and he did not do so, but he had Sir John Nightingale's ear, and I felt that with his support, the prospect of one day becoming the Detective Chief Superintendent was a real one, and one that I could not afford to jeopardise by turning down this promotion offer.

I informed John Duke at our evening meeting that day that I would accept the promotion and the move to Grays, but that I really wasn't at all happy about the travelling arrangements and didn't want to move house to Grays under any circumstances. I may have also said that I didn't think that the arrangement was likely to be any great advantage for me or for the police service, since my heart was not in it and my ambition was not to be a Divisional Chief Superintendent.

I was fifty years old now and had completed twenty-six years' service. A Superintendent could serve until the age of sixty, but I had no intention of remaining in uniform for another ten years. After twenty-five years' service one could retire with a reasonable pension and still be young enough to get a job in the security business. I resolved to go to Grays for a while and see what transpired in a year or so, then if it looked like this move was another sideways movement I would leave the service as I had done my twenty-five years.

Grays was like a foreign country to me. I knew nothing about the area, had rarely visited the division, and apart from the Detective Chief Inspector, a man named Eric Smith, I knew few of the personnel. The Divisional Commander was Chief Superintendent Joe Bird, who had been a Southend Officer before the amalgamation. He was one of those who had found himself promoted far beyond his wildest dreams because of it.

Southend, although a Borough force, had been quite a large one, and at the time of the amalgamation there was an agreement that none of its officers should be downgraded or in any way penalised because of the amalgamation. It was apparent from one or two subsequent promotions that rather than appear to be treating ex-Southend officers as second class members of the new Essex Police, several of them were promoted more rapidly than they otherwise might have expected.

There were two Detective Superintendents at Chelmsford Police Headquarters; one of them, Bill Brown, had been a Detective Chief Inspector in the Southend Force. He was a very senior member of that force in age and length of service, and one who would in my view never have made the rank of Detective Superintendent in Essex, had it not been for the amalgamation. After all, that force had only one Detective Superintendent and many more better qualified men competing for the post, as well as many more from other forces.

I knew very little about Joe Bird and had never met him before. He was a lean individual and some six feet six inches tall. I discovered that he was a religious man and a teetotaller. Joe was cordial and apparently most willing to accept me, though he may have viewed me from my background as a rather coarse and outspoken individual who could cause him problems. I for my part was beginning to acquire a little more discretion and vowed that I would try my best to make my stay at Grays as free of conflict with Joe, or anyone else, as I possibly could.

Grays police station was one of the older police buildings. It had served its purpose well for many years, but was far too small for a modern Divisional Headquarters. Plans had already been drawn up for a new police station and work on this was due to start soon.

As always with these stations there had originally been no need for an office or parking space for a Divisional Superintendent, as there hadn't been one. It was therefore a surprise and a great relief to find that I did have an office of my own and a parking space in the very small yard.

Joe Bird lived in Southend, and since neither he nor I was able to travel home for meals, and there was no canteen at Grays, we both took sandwiches and a flask of tea or coffee, which we ate and drank alone in our respective offices. After a few days Joe came into my office after he had eaten his lunch and suggested we might both go for a walk. It was a bright sunny day and there seemed no better way of spending a half hour or so. I readily agreed to his suggestion, and noting that he had a civilian jacket on over his police shirt and tie, I did the same

There had naturally been many changes in the police service since I joined in 1953. Most of them should have been advancements, but in the field of discipline I regret that the direction was backwards. Wearing a civilian jacket or 'mixed dress' as it would have been known in the Army and in the Police a few years ago was a serious breach of discipline. However we all tend to copy those who are there to set us an example and I did likewise. Had I not made a promise to myself to keep my mouth shut on all controversial matters I would have undoubtedly brought the matter up, but as it was I did not.

In many things, especially as I was a new boy and the Deputy, I took my directions from the leader. I did not always agree with him, but true to my promise I kept quiet even when it hurt to do so. Such matters as scruffy uniforms and appearance, calling sergeants by their Christian names, smoking and failing to wear their hats when driving police cars, things I would never have permitted at Harwich, were the rule rather than the exception here. I did gently and slowly influence such matters, but not with memos or a big new broom. A quiet word here and there seemed to be all that was necessary to improve standards. Reminding officers that a senior officer had actually noticed the infraction worked wonders.

The first walk I did with Joe Bird was quite a surprise and looking back, very enjoyable. He walked at a pace that made me recall some of the marching I had done many years before in the Kings Royal Rifle Corps. The Rifle Brigade and the Kings Royal Rifles were two of the few Regiments in the Army who marched at a very fast pace; it was some sort of tradition no doubt, and on Saturday mornings when we paraded on the Square at Winchester Barracks we marched round and round to the music of the Regimental March at ninety paces to the minute.

So it was with Joe Bird, and in the three quarters of an hour or so we marched around Grays we covered at least four or five miles. There were many parts of Grays I had never seen, even a beach! How many people know that there is a beach at Grays? I certainly didn't. Our conversation covered many subjects, few of them police matters. Joe, it seemed, apart from being connected with many activities of his local church, was a very high official in the St John's Ambulance Brigade and had many tales to tell about that service. I was unaware that the Elder Brethren, with a very ancient and honourable history, governed the St John's Ambulance Brigade. Joe was one of their leaders and had his impressive uniform in a cupboard in his office. Occasionally when he was off to some meeting of the brethren or other such function he would appear in all his glory and bid me look after the shop while he was away.

These walks became a daily ritual and except when the weather was really inclement we did our walk come what may. Joe naturally had his day off, as I did, and then I walked alone and at a much more leisurely pace.

Anyone who has ever served as a deputy to someone will know that it is really a 'nothing' job. A deputy is really quite unnecessary as a deputy has no function at all when his boss is actually present. The Chief's days off, annual leave and other absences give a little relief for the deputy who, for a short while, becomes the boss.

The second in command of all divisions now held the rank of Superintendent and for a long time the name 'deputy' stuck to them. In fact it was eventually discovered that they were not deputies in the true sense of the word and could be given specific responsibilities and duties. It is nowadays more correct to call them Divisional Superintendents, and in most cases this is the title they hold and prefer.

In general Divisional Superintendents are responsible for operational matters, leaving the Chief Superintendent free to concentrate on the overall administration of the division, personnel matters, the use of resources and policy. There is of course very little policy that has not travelled down from Headquarters, although there are some local matters over which the Divisional Commander does have some say. He also has the final word when proposals are put to him for approval in operational matters and CID operations.

'Operational matters' covers practically every aspect of day-to-day policing. While I did not make day-to-day decisions about the work of the various departments, I was frequently consulted about specific matters when, for example, the plans of one department might overlap or stray into the work of another. CID operations were most likely to do this. Frequently the CID Chief Inspector would require extra men, and for the most part I was able to mediate between the CID Chief and the Sub-divisional Chief Inspector, who naturally would resist any such request as strongly as possible.

Joe Bird had his morning prayers, as did the other Divisional Commanders I had worked with, and any small matters such as I have mentioned concerning personnel that hadn't been sorted out amicably were put to Joe for his final decision. He was usually diplomatic, and the road he preferred to travel was in the centre of any such dispute.

I was interested to note that Eric Smith was frequently absent from 'morning prayers' and the excuses we heard were not dissimilar to the ones I had used at Chelmsford. He too obviously thought they were a waste of time, and did his best to avoid them. I did once tentatively touch on the subject with Joe Bird, but could see at once that he was unlikely to agree. I began to see his point too, and there were some advantages in the Detective Chief Inspector attending the meetings. There had always been a rift between the CID and the uniformed branch; a rift which many uniformed personnel felt was compounded by the superior attitude of some CID officers. Such a rift would not be healed or improved if that branch, although an important one, were made to feel 'special' in this way. It was also more important that busy Detective Chief Inspectors realised that they should be aware of what was going on, on a day to basis, in the rest of the division. I started to feel as though I was a poacher turning gamekeeper.

The plans for the new Grays police station were well advanced and were discussed most mornings at 'prayers'. The Administration Chief Inspector was the station expert on matters concerning the new station, and everyone was putting in their bids for office space and equipment. The site for the new station was directly behind the old one. As in Romford the Grays Magistrates' Court was adjacent to the police station, and access to it was through the same double gates through which police vehicles and personnel came and went.

It was obvious that when heavy building equipment, lorries and materials were using this entrance too, there would be many problems of security, access, safety and not least parking spaces for the Chief Superintendent and myself. Attempts were made to forecast all these problems and prepare contingency plans for them. It made for lively and interesting morning meetings, perhaps a lot more so than the ones I had been used to in Chelmsford. Fortunately I had already left Grays by the time the first sod of earth was lifted for the foundations of this new building, so I did not have to suffer the inconvenience and mess the construction work caused for many months.

What was apparent however was that the County Architect, who was the designer of this wonderful modern edifice, had not had a lot of help or advice from the police side. His idea of a police station was no doubt very good from a design point of view, and it was obviously going to look very nice and cost a fortune. However there were some very basic defects in the placement of and access to the cell block, general security and so on. Various suggestions and amendments were mooted as the result of our meetings and in due course a building was designed that incorporated some, but not all, of the requirements of a police station.

I recall that later, when the building was completed, it was found that by going onto the roof and bending back four lead-retaining clips a large semi-circular glass dome could be lifted off and access given into the police canteen and so into the rest of the building. In this age of increased awareness of the vulnerability of police stations and other public buildings this had to be changed very quickly.

It was about this time that I learned of the departure of John Duke as the Deputy Chief Constable. Duke had arrived in Essex from another force, I don't remember which, but so far as I recall it was in the North East of England. This was apparent when he got angry and his loud cultured voice began to become coarse and take on a distinct Newcastle Upon Tyne accent. He had at first alienated a lot of people by his brusque nature and tendency to appear at crime and murder scenes when his presence did little more than slow down proceedings. However he had made a name for himself as a practical copper who didn't mind getting his hands dirty, as he had done at the Weely Pop Festival a few years earlier, and by 1980 he was well thought of and respected.

As I had served him as the Complaints Superintendent I was also known to him personally, and his departure meant a new Deputy would soon be in place who had probably never heard of me, and perhaps never would. I began to realise that having friends in high places was all very well until they moved on. It was common practice now for all senior posts to be advertised in the *Police Review*, and the idea that local officers were local men was a concept of the past, a sentimental thought for the older members of the Force, the remnants of the Essex constabulary.

When not actually deputising, although Joe Bird was away from the Division quite a bit, and not specifically engaged in 'operational matters,' I had quite a bit of time on my hands and spent some of it visiting the Magistrates' Court as kind of a figurehead, and travelling round the Division to visit sub-divisions and section stations.

There was a sub-division at Tilbury and another at Pitsea. Visiting any station as a new Superintendent presented a challenge, in that there was bound to be a scrutiny going on by the Sub-Divisional Commander of his new Superintendent and by the new Superintendent of the Chief Inspector. Tilbury was one of the oldest police stations in the county, in the heart of what might have been called a deprived area, and the work of the police there involved a lot of petty theft and many assaults. There were fights between drunken sailors from the many foreign ships that docked there and disputes between the fishermen, sailors and other workers who lived in the rows and rows of old terraced houses, and their wives. There were a number of pubs, seamen's homes and working men's clubs, all of which were potential flash points of violence late in the evening.

It surprised me that a small sub-division with no more than a handful of men managed to keep the lid on this potential high explosive cauldron so well. They still managed to carry out their duties in the old-fashioned way of commanding rather than demanding respect. The sight of a local officer in uniform still calmed down the natives and brought peace and quiet in the streets once again. Perhaps that is why one felt reluctant to alter this fine balance by moving an officer and replacing him with a new one. A strange face might have made all the difference to the status quo.

It was however known to be the 'punishment station' of the force, and anyone committing a heinous crime such as sleeping with another officer's wife could well end up here for quite a long stint.

Pitsea was a rather newer police station and also had a Chief Inspector in charge. The first time I went to visit him I was shown into his large and well-furnished office, far better than mine, and offered tea and biscuits. It has often been said that most policemen are a bit odd, or they wouldn't have chosen the police force as a career, but this chap for me was odder than most. He closed his office door with a surreptitious look out into the corridor to see if there was anyone there, then locked it!

On one wall was a large framed print of a fishing boat in dire trouble on a wild sea, and he carefully removed this to reveal a large sheet of graph paper pinned to the wall. He explained that the graph represented crime figures, road traffic accidents, numbers of prisoners and prosecutions for all manner of offences within his sub-division. The figures, when one began to fathom the myriad of little lines and dots, showed comparisons on a month-to-month basis and from year to year.

I was invited to study this work of art and to deduce from it no doubt what a first-class chap we had running the Pitsea sub-division. I was not wildly critical. After all he probably had plenty of spare time to spend on his chart, and if this was his idea of how to make use of the mass of statistics we all had to read and submit, then good luck to him. It didn't impress me, however, and I realised on my drive back to Grays that as a senior officer I had some influence, if not great power, over this officer's future. One's immediate senior officer submitted reports each year; I was his, and I began to wonder what I would write about a chap who kept such a highly secret document in his office!

Back at base I did a little homework and discovered that this officer had been removed from the list of people permitted to be issued with a firearm; he was, so it was said, 'temperamentally unsuited to carry and use firearms'. I was relieved of the duty of having to write a report on this chap, and it's just as well. I was suitably surprised to see that in future years he was to become a Divisional Commander with the rank of Chief Superintendent. Perhaps I should have been more impressed with his chart!

I seem to remember that about this time I was required to attend a full day of lectures on Man Management. It was a subject that someone had obviously found a book about, perhaps a copy of Mr Bunyard's book on Police Administration, and thought it a good idea to have all the officers in the force indoctrinated. It was, and I suspect still is, the system in the police force when any new idea or subject is to be propagated to send someone, as junior a rank as absolutely necessary, on a course on the subject. Usually two or three days is sufficient to turn them into the force expert on the topic when he returns.

In the case of man management the chap selected was a Sergeant from Brentwood who, after the three days, returned to Essex with the brief to lecture everyone with the rank of Sergeant or above to make them experts too. I am not sure I was any better a manager when I had received my lecture, but did feel that there were a lot of wrinkles I could have added to this very academic look at the subject.

I felt when I was first promoted to Sergeant in the army and again in the police force that far too little time was spent in teaching NCOs and police sergeants and above, anything at all about management. It certainly appeared to me that it was leaving it a bit late to try and teach the subject to Superintendents with only a few years left to serve (perhaps less). I found that practical man management was something you acquire by experience and that theory doesn't always work in practice.

When I first took over as Detective Chief Inspector at Chelmsford, a Detective Constable of considerable experience one day tapped on my door and asked if he could speak to me. He laid out for my consideration the facts of a robbery he was investigating and then suggested how he thought he might go about investigating a certain aspect of it. I could see immediately the avenue he should pursue and felt that with his experience he should have seen it too. It was however apparent that he was not keen on the extra work that this would entail.

"Have you discussed this with your Sergeant?" I asked

"Yes," he was forced to admit.

"Well, what was his suggestion?"

The officer told me that the Sergeant had told him exactly what I would have done had I been his Sergeant. I dismissed the chap with a curt reminder that matters of this sort should be taken up with his Sergeant and that if he thought he could get the Sergeant overruled by sneaking in to see me, then he was wrong. However I also added that my door was always open if he had any problems the Sergeant couldn't deal with

In many CID offices there is usually one Sergeant to three constables and their desks are in close proximity or they share a small office so that the Sergeant can easily supervise the constables. At one time I had a new Sergeant who had no doubt been promoted on merit and was a conscientious and able man. I noticed for a few weeks after he arrived in my department that every time the phone went and a new job came in he answered the phone, made a few notes, picked up his hat and was off. At the same time two or even three of his constables were sitting around in the office.

I called him to one side one day and asked him why he dashed off out to answer every call, and reminded him that he was now the Sergeant and should send one of his subordinates out to do the donkey work unless it was something worthy of his senior rank. It was something that just hadn't occurred to him, and no one had ever told him.

While at Grays I do confess to a feeling of being wasted. I was, so I thought, a capable investigator, and here I was driving around the division visiting officers at sections and sub-divisions, drinking more cups of tea than I really needed and wondering why the force didn't want to make use of my skills. There was of course the not infrequent 'complaint against police' to investigate.

Unlike Harwich there was little social life, although I did sneak the occasional half-hour in a local pub for a chat with Eric Smith. All the invitations to functions, grand balls and so on were directed to Joe Bird of course, and he used to graciously offer one to me if he didn't want to go to it himself. Mostly I refused, both on the grounds of pique that I was considered only second best, and secondly because it was a hell of a long way to come for a social function, and with the drinking and driving laws now beginning to have an effect I couldn't well set the wrong example, nor did I want to sit all evening at a dinner and dance with only a glass of mineral water!

There were occasions when Joe Bird was invited to attend a function where it was considered a 'must' for the police chief to make an appearance. Joe, like me, did not like judging sunflower competitions, and by virtue of his office and because he had a deputy, he would avoid responding positively to invitations to which he could not take his wife.

One such was to the annual speech day of the largest

elementary school in the district. I was duly instructed to attend in his place and he encouraged me by saying that it was only for an hour or so and I wouldn't be expected to make a speech or anything. On arrival at the school I was more than surprised to see the dirty state of it. There was graffiti on the walls of the outside of the buildings and on the corridors inside. The grounds were untidy and looked neglected and in general I got the sort of impression a foreign visitor gets when arriving at Kings Cross underground station. I knew that schools were, as they have always been, a bit short of cash, but for this kind of wilful damage to have been permitted surprised and disappointed me.

I was to meet all the school governors, one of whom it turned out was Taffy Llewellyn, an ex-Chief Inspector whom I knew and liked. After the formal business of handing out the prizes Taffy and I had a good chat about old times, and after the cup of coffee and a few canapés we adjourned to the nearest pub for a proper drink and finished our chat over a half of ale.

On another occasion I wasn't so lucky. Joe had told me to attend on his behalf at the annual prizegiving of the GPO 'Safe Driving Awards'. I listened with muted interest to the laudatory remarks passed on the winners and clapped when it seemed to be appropriate. Just when I thought it was all over the Chairman said, "Ladies and gentlemen, we are honoured to have here tonight Superintendent George Raven of the Essex police, our local Divisional Superintendent, and I will ask him now to step forward and address you".

I was to say the very least stunned. I stood up in a haze

of panic and desperation as I tried to think of something appropriate to say, and anger at Joe Bird for placing me in this position.    I have no recollection of what I did say, only of the relief when I was in my car afterwards driving home and preparing my words of reproach to Joe the next morning. As it turned out we both managed to have a good laugh over it, but I was never without an emergency speech and a few 'police jokes' after that.

My stay at Grays turned out to be a short one and within six months I received notification of my return to police headquarters as a Detective Superintendent.

# Headquarters CID, 1980–1981

*How long soever it hath continued, if it be against reason, it is of no force in law - Sir Edward Coke, The First Part of the Institutes of the Laws of England (1628) bk. 1, chapter 10, sect. 80, p. 62 recto*

There had been enormous changes at Headquarters in the few months I had been away. The new building was open and the establishment had apparently grown, along with the size of our new premises. There were now three Assistant Chief Constables as well as a Deputy, and there were to be three Detective Superintendents in addition to the Detective Chief Superintendent, who was still Alf Mitchell.

John Duke had been replaced by Ron Stone, who was an 'import' from another far distant county. One of our new Assistant Chief Constables was also an import and two others were from Essex. One of these was William 'Willy' Petherick, who was probably the oldest serving officer in the force. He was already past the usual retiring age but was being granted year-by-year extensions on the grounds of his vast experience. At least that was the excuse given for his continued service in this exalted position. It was of course, as I explained earlier, a necessary qualification for the post of ACC to have served in three different forces. The rules were apparently wide enough, or elastic enough in Willy's case, to allow Essex constabulary, Essex and Southend on Sea Joint constabulary and Essex Police to be three different forces. Common sense dictates otherwise, but what does common sense have to do with expediency? Willy Petherick was a beloved old soldier even if he was a 'duffer', and no one really minded. He never did anyone any harm and on the contrary did one or two people a great deal of good.

The three ACCs were given responsibility for crime, administration and operations. Willy Petherick had crime, Peter Simpson, the other Essex man, administration, and the new guy, whose name I cannot remember and who in any case changed two or three times in the next couple of years, was operations.

George Harris was still a Detective Superintendent, Bill Brown, who I have mentioned, ex-Southend, was there too and then there was myself to make up three. The new Police Headquarters now housed what was known as the Central Detective Unit (CDU) which incorporated the Fraud Squad, Drugs Squad, Stolen Motor Vehicles Branch and Special Equipment Section (funny toys). The CDU was now greatly enlarged and had several more officers than before. There was also a fully-fledged Firearms unit, with a firing range for training in the basement, and Force Support Unit, which were under the control of the ACC Operations.

It had been decided that George Harris was to be the Detective Superintendent in overall charge of the CDU and that the other two would each supervise the work of the CID in half the county. This would apparently alternate every six months, although I never could see the logic of that. Perhaps it was to give us a change of scenery. I was, at least for the first six months, to supervise Chelmsford, Harlow, Colchester, Clacton and Saffron Walden Divisions. Bill Brown had Grays, Southend, Basildon and Brentwood. We had specific instructions that we were to attend every case of suspicious death and serious crime occurring within our areas of responsibility. I was to share an office with Bill Brown, an idea I didn't relish very much, but as it was we didn't spend a lot of time there.

In many of the divisions by now there were senior detectives I knew well, some of whom I had supervised previously. I did not envisage any problems with them but there was one, Barry Tarbun, now the DCI at Chelmsford, who I did feel might well resent my presence as a supervising officer. He was not pleased at having been moved sideways, which he blamed on my apparently friendly relationship with Alf Mitchell.

On the first occasion when a suspicious death required my attendance at Chelmsford, Barry made it quite plain that he neither needed nor wanted any help from me. We had to have a behind closed doors session to sort matters out and from then on we got along in a state of armed neutrality.

Barry was indeed a proficient officer who didn't need my help, but nevertheless he was a member of the same force that I was and not a law unto himself.

Barry's big case Operation Lager eventually concluded with the arrest and conviction of a number of people for supplying drugs. It was considered to be a successful operation and a detective learns that in the eyes of his leaders he is only as good as his last case, or as bad! Barry made the most of the success of Lager and was soon on his way upward. He eventually finished as Detective Chief Superintendent of the City of London Police.

The Detective Chief Inspector at Colchester was Derek Wyatt, known throughout the force as 'short fat', due presumably to his resemblance to Ernie Wise, although I couldn't see it myself. I had known Derek when he was the sole member of the Drugs Squad, and although my presence might have irritated him he never showed resentment and we got along fine.

On one occasion I had attended a post mortem examination with Derek Wyatt on a man whose body had been discovered in suspicious circumstances in his division. Dr Vanesis had attended and was able to state categorically that the death was from natural causes. I had never seen the inside of a man's heart before and we were shown the white patches of the inner wall, which we were told was evidence of several previous heart attacks; it was where the blood vessels were dead and no longer carried blood. In addition Dr Vanesis had gone through the procedure of taking samples of liver, lungs and all the usual bits and pieces for further laboratory examination.

Relieved that we were not going to have to mount a murder investigation, Derek offered to buy Dr Vanesis and myself lunch. There was rather a good restaurant at the Colchester Catering College where the cooking and serving was done by the students. It was necessary to book a table and Derek rang and did so. When we sat down it was rather late and the restaurant would be closing shortly. A very nice young lady came to serve us and apologised that the only thing left on the menu was grilled kidneys!

The first time I went over to Harlow was after a report of an armed robbery at a supermarket. I arrived amid a hubbub of activity as witnesses were being interviewed and sought. It turned out to be a rather amateur crime; a youth had pointed what appeared to be a gun at the cashier at the checkout and grabbed a handful of notes.

Harlow was my old stamping ground and I knew the area well and many of the likely lads who lived around there. We decided to pay some of them a visit. Most petty thieves don't like anyone committing a serious crime on their territory because it always creates a lot of police activity and stirs up the mud in the pond. After a few calls we had the name of the robber.

Strictly speaking we should have then called in the Firearms unit. As it was I knew the youth and had arrested him on several occasions in the past. I was sure that even if he had a gun he was unlikely to produce it in answer to his front door, especially when at that stage he could still protest his innocence. We were in luck; he was at home. He came quietly and the cash and gun (a child's toy) were recovered.

Harlow did then cover Stansted Airport, but there was no CID stationed there and the policing of the airport was done by a small section of men with their own police station within the airport complex. This unit has grown considerably over the years and now has armed officers patrolling throughout the day and night.

Saffron Walden was another of the old police buildings in the county and there was relatively little serious crime there. I used to visit occasionally for a cup of tea and a chat, but little more.

In addition to supervising, the two 'outside' Detective Superintendents, as they were known, were a pretty good target for the Complaints Department to offload some of their investigations. Bill Brown and I were constantly being called into the Deputy's office and briefed on some dastardly and serious crime that some constable was alleged to have committed. Bill Brown always started every investigation with gusto and an enthusiasm that I found impossible to match. It was almost as though he enjoyed the prospect of investigating a fellow police officer.

I did these tasks because they were required of me, and so far as I am concerned, dealt with police officers in just the same fair and firm manner afforded to members of the public. I never did enjoy the job however, and often one commenced a complaint investigation, knowing that the complaint was trivial and the complainant a hardened criminal. Often it was a question of making sure that an officer's name was cleared rather than gathering evidence enthusiastically to try and convict him.

I investigated complaints big and small, many and varied from misappropriating informants' money to abuse of authority and from stealing another officers pay cheque to sexual harassment of the office girls.

One interesting point cropped up in an investigation into a complaint by a man who had been questioned by an officer following a report of a child having been approached by a man and asked to get into his car. She had run off and told mum, who had called the police, and an officer went to the scene, which was by a children's playground. Nearby there was a man sitting in a car and doing nothing else in particular. He was questioned by the officer, who took his details, but he was unable to take the matter any further. The man said he often stopped there to eat his lunch. It appeared from further enquiries that he had been seen there on several occasions in the past but there was no evidence he had actually committed a crime and he had no previous convictions. He was clearly a suspect and the police quite rightly in my view regarded him as such.

By 1980 only a few police records were being kept on a computer database, although the Police National Computer was in use as well as the National Motor Vehicle and Licensing Records at Swansea. While factual information could be kept on a computer, provided it was correct, intelligence about what was suspected by the police could not. The Data Protection Act later put several annoying restrictions on what could and could not be kept, even on police computers. It was therefore the practice in each division to have a Collator. His job was to record all intelligence, piece it together and occasionally, it was hoped, he would come up with some useful conclusions. In the case of information such as a suspected child molester the details would be put on a card and filed with a blue tag or a red tag, whichever applied to that class of information.

The complainant in this case insisted that he should not have been questioned and that if the police had made any record about him it should be destroyed. In my report on the matter in due course I concluded that the man must have had something to hide for him to want any record destroyed and that his apparent deduction that a record would be made was further indication of his devious behaviour. The officer, I recommended, should receive nothing but praise for his conduct and the records should be retained.

On the first point my recommendation was agreed to, but it was ordered that the record card be destroyed. The only reason it was destroyed, I believe, was so that the complainant could be pacified. A letter to him signed by the Deputy Chief Constable and giving him the result of the investigation into his complaint stated that the record had been destroyed. It couldn't in truth say that there had been no record made and to say that it had not been destroyed might give rise to a further complaint or even civil action. On the other hand important intelligence that might have assisted in a future child murder was lost forever.

The question of police intelligence is a very sensitive one and it is not surprising therefore that by and large police are very loath to pass it on to any other organisation or person, even if the objectives of the two organisations are the same.

Since 1980 the subject of sexual abuse of children has raised its ugly head far more frequently than in earlier years. Society has woken up at last to the fact that there are paedophiles out there and that they are a danger to our children. They expect the police to put their finger on these people, and there is even a Register of Sexual Offenders that has a very restricted circulation.

Persons whose names are not in the Sexual Offenders Register and who either have never offended before or have never been convicted before, will commit most of the future offences against children. Intelligence about all these people should be available to all the services that are responsible for law and order. How you reconcile this with the rights of the individual to privacy I can't tell you.

I hadn't been in my new post many weeks before I was notified that I was to attend the Police College again, this time for three months on the Superintendents' course. Neither Bill Brown nor George Harris had been to the college and both were senior to me, that is to say they had been Superintendents for longer. In the circumstances I felt that it was good news, and I resolved to enjoy the course and do well if I could.

I discovered that for the most part the Superintendents on the course were quite senior in service and were not as I might have imagined keen younger men and budding Chief Constables. It did begin to look as if this course was in fact some sort of reward for long service and good conduct, not really a promise of promotion to come. For that reason we were generally a more relaxed lot, with less emphasis on where we were going, and after a while I began to forget about the two Bath Stars that go with a Superintendent's Crown to make him a Chief Superintendent and decided to enjoy myself.

We did have rather more senior subjects to discuss than those on the 'A' Course, like the management of major incidents and liaison with other services, and spent days on several exercises that were interesting and informative. We were privileged to visit Sandhurst Military College and be given talks by Generals on what might happen if government was ever to collapse. It was refreshing to know that there are plans for such an eventuality, but a chilling thought when you see it happening regularly in other countries.

We had a three-day exercise in Sunningdale where an aeroplane had supposedly crashed on a railway bridge hitting a passing train and causing the maximum possible damage and casualties. Afterwards we spent several more days poring over a large scale sand-model of the town and surrounding area discussing what we had done right and what we had done wrong or failed to do. I found such exercises useful, as they showed how the initial chaos at such incidents can, given the right training, be brought into order in a short space of time.

One mistake everyone made was to allow all the emergency vehicles to arrive at the scene together and cause an almighty traffic jam. It is a mistake, but there seems no way of avoiding it, and at the major incidents I have read about and attended since then there is always this problem to begin with.

We also had lectures and talks from all sorts of interesting and important people such as Lord Hunt (Henry Cecil John Hunt, first Baron of Llanvair Waterdine) which I didn't find so useful. Lord Hunt was at that time Chairman of the Parole Board. It was he and his colleagues who decided which criminals to let out before their sentence was fulfilled, and under what conditions. He had been an Army officer and a mountaineer; how that qualified him for the job I don't know.

When it came to question time I asked him if he had any knowledge of a case I had dealt with in Chelmsford a year or so earlier. A man in his sixties attacked his housekeeper with an axe, and but for the fact that a police car was in the next street when the neighbours dialled 999, he would have killed her. As it was she had terrible head wounds which left her a nervous wreck. I arrested the man, who was sent to prison for ten years for attempted murder. One day his victim was standing a queue at the local post office to get her pension she was aware of someone standing close behind her and turned to see it was the same man who had attacked her. This shock sent her over the edge and into a mental institution.

I asked Sir John why this man had been released so soon, and why he had been permitted to return to live in the same street as his former victim. Sir John waffled as I expected him to, saying he had no personal knowledge of the case but would look into it. I don't suppose he ever did, and even if he did it was far too late to do anything about it. Some of the other students had some pretty good questions for him too. I reckon he was glad to get out of Bramshill with his hide intact.

The little gathering in the bar on Thursday night after the student entertainment was, as I have already indicated in an earlier chapter about Bramshill, an opportunity for students to speak to their Chief Officers. It was not only good for the ego to be able to chat informally with the people who could influence your future for good or bad, but you could sometimes receive a tip or suggestion from them. The Chief incidentally actually expected to see his men when he visited the college and appeared to have a genuine interest in how they were doing.

The Superintendents were generally more mature men and many of them would have had a good deal of contact with their Chief Constables during the day-to-day business of running their divisions, sub-divisions or departments. It was not unusual for Chief Officers to drop hints to their senior officers at Bramshill as to jobs that had been recently advertised, or that might well be advertised soon, and which they might wish to consider making application for.

Police regulations required that all senior posts in the police service had to be advertised nationally. Officers who were suitably qualified could make application in writing, which had to be endorsed by their own Chief Constable. Such advertisements appeared in the *Police Review*, which is a weekly publication anyone can buy.

On one occasion John Duke, the former Deputy Chief Constable of Essex, who was by then Chief Constable of Hampshire, was a guest at the college. He drew me to one side and said that there would shortly be a vacancy for the Detective Chief Superintendent's job at Hampshire. He suggested that it might be a good idea if I applied for the job. A nod being as good as a wink to a blind horse, as they say, I fully intended to do so when the advert appeared.

It never did. The Detective Chief Superintendent of Hampshire was a man named Holdaway. He was known as 'Tanky' Holdaway and had a reputation for being a formidable man as well as an experienced and good detective.

When John Duke was in Essex, it often used to irritate senior investigating officers to find him at the scene of a crime at a very early stage. I later discovered that on one occasion, just before I had the above conversation with John Duke, there had been a shooting incident in Hampshire. Tanky Holdaway arrived at the scene to find Mr Duke already there and busy prising a bullet out of a wall with a penknife. There was an almighty row and Tanky threatened to resign. Unfortunately for me he never did.

When I returned to Chelmsford after my three months away at college it was to find that a number of changes had been made. First of all Alf Mitchell had departed and a new Detective Chief Superintendent was installed. It was neither of the incumbent Detective Superintendents, both of whom might have expected to be considered for the job, but an outsider. The chap who got the job, and his name has gone from my memory, was only there a few months before stepping off to become Chief Constable of another force - I believe it was the British Rail Police or even an airports authority somewhere. It matters not, because the next Detective Chief Superintendent was Peter Crust, the ex-Metropolitan Police officer who had been a Detective Sergeant on the Regional Crime Squad. I'm not quite sure of his entire antecedents, but he had at one time been the Detective Chief Inspector at Colchester and then uniformed Superintendent, but where I'm not sure, probably Southend.

I was never to feel comfortable with Crust as one of my leaders. This was in no way due to any feeling of jealously that he had been promoted so rapidly, but because it was my personal view that he brought with him some of the ways and means no doubt learned in the Metropolitan Police. My experience of the Met, especially on the Regional Crime Squad, the Chief Superintendent called in by Suffolk to deal with the Earls Colne murder, the Flying Squad and various other members of the Met CID I had met, made me very wary of him and some of his methods, effective though they might be.

He took office and it looked probable that he might inhabit that position for some time to come. In view of that I decided to start making application for jobs outside Essex. It was a decision that had to be taken with the consent of one's family. Fortunately none of mine wanted to stay in Chelmsford when I retired.

It was considered to be something of a drawback to getting a job in another force if you were living in your own house, since that force would then have to fork out the expenses involved in selling up your house and moving. House prices had risen considerably since I had bought my house and it was a good time to sell. There was a very suitable police house available not far from Police Headquarters and Sir John Nightingale was agreeable to my suggestion that I move into it while I sold my own house, which I did without difficulty. I was now in a position to move at short notice if I was lucky enough to secure a position in another force.

I sent off several applications for the post of Detective

Chief Superintendent, and no doubt with the good word of recommendation appended on them by Sir John I was short-listed for two.

The first was in Hertfordshire, and I appeared before the selection committee of the Chief Constable of Hertfordshire and two others. The other two on the short-list were Jack Moulder, whom I knew and who was already acting in the rank, and another chap from the City of London. As expected, Jack Moulder got the job.

The next time I was short-listed was for the job of Detective Chief Superintendent in Warwickshire. Unfortunately Peter Joslin, my old colleague from the early Fraud Squad days, who was to be their Chief Constable for quite a few years, hadn't arrived by then and again the local man was appointed. One of the questions I was asked concerned what I thought about the role of policewomen in the police service. My answer on reflection might have been one of the reasons I wasn't selected!

It had become the rule that senior posts like these had to be advertised and were open to any qualified officer in England and Wales. However there was no rule that said an outsider had to be appointed, so it was not really a surprise that in many instances it was the local man who won. So for a time I went back to investigating complaints and supervising, and eventually gave up the idea of moving out of the county.

Perhaps the most exciting and amusing complaint against police I was ever involved in investigating was the 'Wibbly Wobbly' affair. It was called the 'Wibbly Wobbly' affair because it involved a policewoman who had rather large breasts which she frequently flaunted in a provocative manner. She also had large 'come to bed' eyes which she flashed invitingly at most of the men she looked at. It is at first thought surprising that anyone at Headquarters should have ever accepted her as a police officer, but on second thoughts all these decisions were made by men!

Miss Wibbly Wobbly was stationed at Clacton on Sea, then a Division, but subsequently a sub-division of Colchester. A Detective Sergeant had been promoted and was due to leave the division in a few days. A party had been arranged for him, to be held after normal licensing hours at a private club at St Osyth. The policewoman was at the time a CID aide, although what she was aiding them to do makes the mind boggle!

About three in the morning Miss Wibbly Wobbly staggered into Clacton Police Station in a most dishevelled and drunken state, claiming that she had been raped by the Detective Chief Inspector. There was a young constable at the front desk who as one can imagine was very glad his Sergeant hadn't decided to go out for a walk at that point. Sergeant Jacobs was an older and much more experienced man, and while he knew who the woman was and that the chances of her being raped were about as high as his ERNIE Bond coming up with one million pounds, he did the right thing and informed the Chief Superintendent. This resulted in the Detective Chief Superintendent, Peter Crust, and myself being despatched forthwith to Clacton to investigate.

When we interviewed the policewoman concerned,

whose real name I won't mention for obvious reasons, she withdrew her complaint of rape, but did reveal details of what must have been a most lascivious and drunken evening. There were tales of activity upon a billiard table that did not conform with the rules of any of the ball games usually played there, as well as lewd and unruly behaviour which was quite unbecoming, one might have thought, of police officers.

It was, so it seemed to Peter Crust, incumbent upon us to investigate all the circumstances surrounding the affair, and this all took several weeks. The motive behind the policewoman's complaint was her own anger at the less than gallant treatment she had received at the hands of the officers, none of whom, after her most co-operative performance, would take her home. She therefore contrived to make things as hot for the officers as she could and made allegations that they had misused the CID car on this and other occasions, fiddled their expenses and a number of other serious accusations relating thereto, such as falsifying documents.

In the long run, although there were a few sideways moves as the result of the investigation, most of the allegations were resolved as rather minor, and cautions and severe warnings as to future conduct were the order of the day.

The whole episode seriously backfired on the policewoman, who was revealed as a promiscuous lady whose ambition, it seemed, was to sleep with every eligible (and some not so eligible) males in the station. The local and Sunday papers even made some nebulous connection between her and her landlord, a wealthy local businessman and Councillor.

I was left to tidy up the paperwork after the dust settled and was called in to see Mr Stone one day, who said that the woman had to resign. There was no question of her having a hearing in front of the Chief Constable and dragging all sorts of names in the mud in her vindictive state of mind.

I subsequently had a long interview with the lady in question, accompanied; I hasten to add, by another woman police officer. She was at first adamant that she would not resign, but was eventually made to see sense and go and think it over, having been convinced, I hope, that dismissal was the alternative. I reported back to Mr Stone, who was equally adamant that he wanted her Warrant Card at all costs and when I next saw her in the presence of her father, a very nice and respectable gentleman I might add, it was he who persuaded her to hand it over; she threw it at me with abuse worthy of a fishwife, as my mother used to say. Apologies to all fishwives!

I was sorry to learn about now that Sir John Nightingale was to retire and the new Chief Constable was to be Robert Bunyard. I was sorry to see Sir John leave in spite of his Liberal views, and wondered how I would fair under the new leader.

Mr Bunyard had previously been in the Metropolitan Police, and we in Essex saw him as a career policeman without the slightest interest in Essex except as a way ahead. I was introduced to him a short time after he arrived, and there were several people in the company at the bar in Chelmsford Police Station. During the small talk he made some remark about having his photograph taken. I can't recall what I said, but it was a light-hearted remark about our very proficient photographic department and their very strong cameras. The remark didn't go down at all well, and I saw in the glance that Mr Bunyard gave me all the credit marks I had stored up with Sir John Nightingale gurgling quietly down the drain.

Something else comes to mind when I think of Robert Bunyard and photographs. When he came to the county of Essex he naturally didn't know any of his senior officers, or his junior ones come to that. He had an album made containing the photographs and a few details from the personal records of all officers of the rank of Inspector and above. Rumour has it that whenever there was a promotion in the offing Mr Bunyard used to look through his album to find a suitable face to promote. It seems that if your face didn't fit you didn't get on. No doubt this gem of Police Administration came straight out of the pages of his book!

With the new chief, an expert on Police Administration, came several sweeps of the new broom, as one might expect. One of these was a determination to stop the improper use of police telephones. Bearing in mind that there were several hundred people at headquarters, most of them with access to legitimate use of telephones, it was not surprising that many calls of a private nature were made.

In due course the GPO installed a high powered monitoring system and for a month or so, unknown to all the staff (although it leaked out after a while), all calls were monitored. A printed list was produced of every telephone and extension in the building and a random selection were checked daily. No one was ever disciplined, and after a while the machine went away and the whole thing died a natural death. Rumour had it that Willy Petherick's phone ran up a bill larger by far than anyone else's and that there were calls to Australia and many more to numbers that were said to be 'private calls'. Perhaps that is why we heard no about this scheme.

Another job the Chief's new broom did was to sweep away one of the three Detective Superintendents, something I would have done myself if I had been in his shoes. Last in first out was the rule, so it was me who was soon packing my bags and preparing to move to my new post as Divisional Superintendent at Colchester – sideways!

Robert Bunyard stayed with the force for a few years and was the first of several Chief Constables in quick succession. He left before his fame had reached the ears of the Birthday Honours list committee, or his book on Police Administration had hit the best-seller list. He was off to be Commandant of the Police College. A 'sideways' move? Perhaps not - I hear he is now a "Sir".

CHAPTER FOURTEEN

# Colchester Division, 1981–1983

*If you've got a nice fresh corpse, fetch him out! - Mark Twain, The Innocents Abroad (1869) chapter 27*

Soon after Mr Bunyard arrived in the county I gave up the idea of transferring to another force and applied to buy a property in Walton on Naze, where I hoped to live on retirement. I told the Chief that I would not expect to live in the property while working and would therefore not have to travel or to receive rent allowance. Permission was granted, and I bought a bungalow which required some renovation. I have always been a handy DIY enthusiast, and I spent many weekends and days off making repairs and decorating.

When I was offered the job at Colchester, perhaps to soften the blow, I had been told that I could now live in my bungalow in Walton and receive a rent allowance. This suited me very well, and for the next two years I was able to exploit a rather silly police regulation. One of the conditions of a policeman's service was that he should have free housing. When it became common practice for policemen to buy their own properties a rent allowance was paid to them which was based on a set sum worked out by some official somewhere. For Superintendents the allowance was higher, even if he lived next door to an Inspector and in a similar property. The allowance was also fixed so that no matter how much your mortgage was, in my case £163, the allowance remained the same, in my case about £400. I never could see the sense in this, but didn't complain. It took a long while for the penny to drop, but no such rent or housing allowance is paid today.

I now had only two years left to serve until I had thirty years' service. I would then be fifty-three years old and still able to serve another seven years if I wanted to. I could not see myself remaining a deputy for that length of time and thought my chances of returning to CID were remote. I thought also that as a Divisional Commander I might like to stay on, but made a conscious decision that if that hadn't happened by July 1983, when my thirty years was up, I would leave the force. The police force is really a young man's job and there is a strong incentive to make you leave after thirty years' service - your annual pension decreases for every year you serve after thirty.

Colchester Police Station was then in Queen Street. Previously, like many other old police stations, it had been a school building. Now there is a large new station in Butt Road, Colchester, but like Grays this was not completed until after my departure in 1983. I did however have a small but comfortable office and a most agreeable boss. Derek Dighton was one of the last real old-type policemen and probably the nicest man I ever served under. Almost all the new breed of Divisional Commanders are university graduates and career policemen, who while perfectly adequate commanders do talk a different language from us old 'uns. Clacton was now a sub-division, but it did later regain divisional status, and there was another sub-division at Braintree.

Derek Wyatt was the Detective Chief Inspector and looked like remaining so until he retired. Apart from his police activities, he was known for his ability to make after-dinner speeches. It was something he liked to do, and he was in great demand. He could hold forth on many subjects and make the audience laugh. Derek liked social life and there was plenty of that in Colchester if one wanted it.

One of the many bright ideas reaching ground level from the Home Office was known as the Victim Support Scheme, and Derek was given the job of getting it off the ground in Colchester. As it involved talking to groups of people it was something he did well and enjoyed. The fact that it had nothing to do with police work didn't seem to bother him.

It seemed that as the police couldn't catch criminals the next best thing was to console the victims, and volunteers from the 'do good' brigade were recruited to learn how to do this from Derek. Whenever there was a serious crime against the person or property the police would inform one of these volunteers and they would go round to see the victim and let them cry on his or her shoulder. I know I am cynical, but I also believe I am practical, and I firmly believe that this did nothing to aid the prevention or detection of crime and little to aid the victims. Indeed if this work was necessary then it was the work of some charitable organisation or even the Probation Service, but not the police.

For me it was really back to the medicine as before. I did find however that Colchester was a much more lively and interesting division to work in than Grays. Supervision, the occasional Operational Order to write and the usual batch of complaints to investigate were the order of the day.

Supervision as always did nothing to excite me and when coming to work in the morning I used to read the messages, circulations and crime complaint book with interest to see what had been going on during the night. When I got to my office I would find that perhaps first on the daily agenda was a complaint by an area car driver that he had found fish and chip papers in the car when he took over. Perhaps another memo was required, or even a Divisional Standing Order, to remind officers that they should not leave fish and chip papers in the area cars, even an enquiry into who was the culprit. What a job for a Superintendent!

It was around this time that instructions were received that women police officers were to be allowed maternity leave and the stream of other concessions that soon followed, which the men considered discriminated against them, caused much inconvenience as well as heartache. When approving duties for the division one had to consider those officers on leave, those off sick, those injured, those on courses and now those who were pregnant! With shifts of eight or nine officers this usually didn't leave many. It was interesting to find that prior to 1953, when Colchester was a Borough Force, there were twelve men to a shift, and now there were nine – on paper! By the time you had manned the area cars and the office and catered for those wanting to do reports, is it any wonder that the public didn't often see a bobby patrolling the High Street?

Each time there was a police operation for an event that could be forecast in advance there had to be an Operational Order. One had learned how to do these at Police College, if you had been there, and it was based upon a mnemonic:

I   Information
I   Intention
M  Method
A  Administration
C  Communications

Whenever you saw a police Operational Order there were always these five headings, with as many sub-headings as were required for the occasion. Many of the Orders related to events that had occurred before, so it was just a question of getting out the old one and re-hashing it to suit.

There were regular Point to Point Race meetings at Marks Tey and occasional visits by important people like politicians. I did have a new one to do for the Queen who once came to visit the local Grammar School. It was a very important occasion, although fortunately security was not quite so intense as it is today. She duly landed in the school grounds in her bright red helicopter and I was there to salute.

It was one of the very few occasions, except at Police College when I actually wore the white gloves I had been issued with. There were no snags, no one threw eggs or tomatoes and I went home that night, a very relieved and happy man, to see myself on TV.

I often used to wonder if, when politicians decided to visit a town, school or factory, they ever gave a thought to the amount of work and inconvenience his or her visit caused to the police. Few ever said "Thanks". You didn't really expect a thank you from the Queen of course, after all she was our boss, but she always said it!

There were weekly football matches at Layer Road, where Colchester United were based. They were then in the Third Division of the Football League and the ground was quite small and with a pretty basic pitch. One week during the football season the first team would play at home and the following week they would be away. The weeks they were away saw the second team at home, so there was a match of sorts every week.

The local Sub-Divisional Commander had things pretty well sewn up and took care of the manpower required by asking for volunteers. The football club was required to pay for eight police officers each week according to some formula I never understood. It always struck me as odd that a football club, a private concern, could put on an event each week that required twenty or more policemen who were after all public servants, and only be required to pay for eight of them. It seems that better men than I had decided that what went on inside the ground was the club's responsibility and what went on in the street was that of the police. So if we needed a hundred men outside the ground to control traffic the public had to pay for them. This contradicted the law on the subject, which says that a person is responsible for any problems he causes such as crowds or traffic outside his premises.

However, who was I to argue? The club was poor in those days and couldn't even afford to pay for the eight officers. Before I left the division it was a regular monthly debate as to whether we should sue the club again for some of the money that they owed us.

Probably the biggest Operational Order we produced between us in Colchester was when we learned that Colchester United had drawn Ipswich Town at home in the League Cup. Ipswich was a First Division side and was well known to have a pretty rough crowd of travelling supporters. United's small ground could probably pack in four thousand at a pinch and they had promised to limit ticket sales to that number.

Four hundred policemen were on duty that day and there were many arrests and unruly incidents in the town. The police did their best to escort the supporters from the railway station to the ground, but many were lost en route and managed to get themselves full of beer before arriving at the ground.

It was my first experience of football hooliganism close up, and believe me it's ugly. When the media recall the rioting at other grounds both in UK and abroad and the resultant death and destruction, I thank my lucky stars that nothing more serious than a few cuts and bruises and broken shop windows occurred at Layer Road that day. Of course whatever goes wrong at this type of event or at any other, the police get the blame. It is true that our job is to protect life and property and there is no doubt we do a good job. Sometimes things turn out badly, but those who actually cause the death and destruction are usually only mentioned in passing.

I earlier mentioned that some officers were off with injuries. Some of these were caused in the heat of battle with the ungodly on the streets, but a few by their fellow officers. In the 1970s there was a big increase in the number of riots, strikes and civil disobedience in cities all over the UK and the police, as usual, were expected to control and quell such outbreaks. It became necessary for them to train for this unwelcome task and regular 'riot training' was undergone by all officers who were fit enough and under a certain age, I believe it was forty. They would be bussed to an old and now disused military establishment at Shoeburyness, where they would put on their riot gear, plastic shields and helmets and run the gauntlet. The 'gauntlet' was often a street between buildings on top of which would be members of the Support Unit who would hurl bricks down at them. There would be shouts of delight when an officer failed to deflect the brick and caught it in the face or other part of his body.

Then they would be asked to confront the same Support Unit officers on the ground and beat their shields with their sticks to terrify them, and push and shove and battle them until all were totally exhausted.

This rather futile and expensive use of manpower and equipment was supposed to make them ready to meet the real thing on the streets of Britain. I don't know whether the powers that be really didn't believe that it would ever be necessary or were just stubborn in the face of the need for a proper riot squad. In the light of the continued liberal approach of our society towards wrongdoers I am surprised they didn't issue the lads with wet lettuces with which to beat off the rioters! On almost all trips to Shoeburyness for riot training one or more officers was injured and it became an accepted loss of manpower, which always infuriated me.

Before Mrs Thatcher came to power in 1979, and even for a while afterwards, society was battling with the problem of striking workers in nearly all fields of endeavour. At Colchester we had our share and they included firemen's strikes, ambulance strikes, postal strikes and a printers' strike. In the case of the first three the police had a lot to do, since they were expected to act as guides and assist the Green Goddesses provided by the Army to do the job of the strikers. Operational Orders were needed! A police car had to accompany every 999 call to a fire or for an ambulance.

A postal strike was usually a bit of a damp squib and resulted in a good deal of frustration for the public but little trouble for the police. The printers' strike looked like being more serious and followed a long-running strike of print workers in London that had been ongoing for months and which had severe consequences for relations between police and the public.

In Colchester there was a fairly large printing works where, among other things, all the newspapers for the Essex area were printed. Nightly there would be a hundred or more workers outside the premises, blocking traffic and causing mayhem. They were breaking the law and should of course have been arrested and charged with rioting, causing obstruction of the highway, lighting fires on the street, assault on police and many other criminal offences, not to mention unlawful picketing. As it was, with only a handful of police there was little, in fact nothing, we could do, and the public had to put up with the disruption and inconvenience until common sense (and Mrs Thatcher) overcame the problem of strikes. There was no criticism of the police for this apparent lack of action on their part, strangely enough, since it was Home Office policy!

Essex University was only a mile or so from the centre of Colchester. It was known for its speciality of courses for social rather than practical sciences. As such it attracted the most radical of students, who in addition to their studies, if they ever did any, caused as much trouble as they could for the police and their own security staff.

Their Rag Day in the town, which required yet another Operational Order, did usually go without too much trouble, and no doubt provided a reasonable sum for charity. I often used to wonder how much of the cash collected in their grubby little tins ever ended up as a charitable donation. Whether it was worth the closing down of the entire centre of Colchester from 6pm to 10pm I'm not sure. However the public loves a carnival and it seems they are still prepared to put up with inconvenience to enable them to have one. It goes without saying that there was always a string of complaints from motorists who happened to get caught in the road-blocks around the town and had to stay there for some hours. Still that was the price they had to pay if they missed the advance publicity and the signs that were put up offering them alternative routes.

The students' protests and occupation of university buildings was a regular source of annoyance to the authorities there and to the police, who were notified as soon as one began. As these 'sit-ins', as the students called them, occurred totally on private premises it was largely out of our hands except for possible criminal offences that might be committed. So it was to the County Sheriff's department we had to turn, and still nothing could be done before a Court Order was obtained to evict the students from the canteen, lecture hall or wherever else they had decided to 'occupy.' At that stage the police would accompany the Sheriff and his officers and break down the door and the students would all march out meek and mild. This process usually took about a week and meantime the students had painted graffiti on the walls, urinated all over the place and generally turned it into a pig sty, which is where most of them should have been made to live permanently. It was a feature of all students' protests that a certain element, not all of them students, would appear for the occasion and disappear just as quickly afterwards. They were referred to as 'rent a mob' and could be relied upon to show up whenever there was a student demonstration within the university or in the town.

Apart from the difficulty of proving who did what, and the general reluctance of the university to support proceedings being taken against any student, no doubt for fear of further protests, there was rarely any criminal prosecution following such protest.

Within the university grounds were the students' accommodation blocks and their own bars where dances were held regularly. Some local youngsters were allowed to attend, and what went on afterwards in the accommodation blocks was often hard to believe. Apart from the promiscuous behaviour, fire extinguishers were always discharged and thrown out of windows, fighting took place and a general air of student merriment, acceptable only in the highest of academic establishments, ensued.

At the time of General Elections there was a special polling booth within the university especially for the students - who are actually allowed to vote. This caused conflict between various factions and the Students' Union and there were fun and games for the police to 'supervise', since the law requires an officer to supervise all polling stations. The Student Union used to try and ban the presence of police officers on campus, but on these occasions they were overruled. However the officer attending was always made to feel most unwelcome.

Not all the students at Essex University were drunken, uncouth and arrogant or behaved like animals, and I felt sorry for the many genuine students who were trying to get on with their studies. One can only compare our liberal establishments with those once-famous universities abroad such as Leipzig and Prague which turned out many of the world's great men and women in a much more disciplined atmosphere.

One of the more unusual events that occurred at the university was the kidnapping of the son of a wealthy Middle Eastern gentleman. Kidnapping is an unusual event in the UK, so there are not many experts on the subject. The force did have such an expert, but he was not available at the time, having been sent away on a course. The father was notified and flew to England the next day about the time the ransom note was delivered. Derek Wyatt handled the matter properly and when the ransom was obtained by the father he made all the necessary arrangements for the money (I forget the actual amount but it was not excessive) to be delivered to the specified place.

Discussions with the father about his son and the relatively small amount of money that was demanded began to create a few doubts in our minds about the genuineness of this crime, but we nevertheless went ahead with the 'drop', which was to be into a litter bin on the campus. The litter-bin was 'staked out' and I believe it was Derek Wyatt who delivered the satchel with the money and left the area in his car. Shortly afterwards a student arrived to collect the money and was duly arrested. He quickly shopped his friend, who, as we had begun to believe, was the missing son. It seemed he had thought up the entire scheme to get money from his father, who was otherwise reluctant to give him enough for his extravagant tastes.

This was a kidnapping contrived by a couple of youths without any great imagination or thought. In a genuine case this crime requires very careful and expert investigation, with the co-operation of the media and others in order for them to be brought to a satisfactory conclusion. Officers are now trained in the techniques required for this type of investigation, and I wonder in this age of multi-millionaires at every street corner if it will not become a more popular crime in the future.

Colchester had its share of crime, as well as the many activities that were not classed as crime that made up the day's work. Both local and visiting thieves and criminals regularly performed most of the activities proscribed by law. The use of firearms in their commission was not a frequent occurrence and incidents involving them were far less frequent than they are today.

I was having supper at home one evening when I was called back to the station as there was a reported 'armed siege' taking place. It seemed that a man had had a row with his wife and disturbed the neighbours, who had called the police. The neighbours said that they believed the man had a shotgun and was now inside the house with wife and children, refusing to come out and shouting abuse at anyone who went near.

There was so far as I could see no evidence that the man had a gun, other than an assertion by the neighbour that he thought he had one. He certainly hadn't a licence, but then what criminal does? Nevertheless by the time I arrived the Firearms Unit were in attendance and the place was surrounded by officers with rifles protruding from behind hedges and vans, waiting presumably for a target to appear.

Preliminary enquiries showed that the man in question was in his early fifties. There was a history of domestic disputes at the house and, as luck would have it, an officer present at the scene, not a member of the Firearms Unit, had dealt with several disputes and felt he knew the chap well enough to go and talk to him. I gave authority for him to do so and the incident ended a few moments later when he came out and agreed to come to the station for a chat. The wife and children were apparently fine and although a diligent search was made of the house, no firearms were found. This sort of 'incident' was, years ago, an everyday occurrence for the bobby on the beat.

One of the special tasks of the Divisional Superintendent was to sit as an ex-officio member of the Colchester Borough Traffic Committee, whose monthly meetings took place at the Town Hall once a month at seven in the evening. It was a gathering of councillors representing all the different areas of Colchester with different traffic problems. There were usually discussions about the need for pedestrian crossings at certain places, traffic lights, No Parking areas and so on. The meeting was usually pretty uneventful.

There was a good deal of reconstruction and building work both under way and planned for the centre of Colchester, one of which would eventually be a shopping precinct and occupy a space now used as a car park. The car park was where the Colchester market was sited twice a week including Saturdays. The discussion inevitably came up about where the market should be sited when the car park was closed for the work to commence.

One councillor decided it would be a good idea to have the Saturday market in the High Street and close it to traffic.

There was a great deal of discussion as to the pros and cons of such an idea, and the thought of closing this busy street to traffic on a Saturday, or any day come to that, was just out of the question. However, it was eventually proposed that the Saturday market should be in the High Street, but that traffic should be allowed through; it was at least a one way street, as usual.

They all looked at me for the police view on the matter. I had fortunately been briefed as to what it was. The head of Traffic Division, my own Chief Superintendent and presumably the Chief Constable were strongly opposed to the idea of a Saturday street market in Colchester and I set out the problems of danger and inconvenience to the public, disruption to traffic and so on as I had been briefed.

My words were not very welcome, and those present could see that if the police remained opposed to the idea, there was very little chance of it becoming a reality. I was soon to learn a bit about politics!

Immediately after this meeting the local newspapers took up the cry and I became something of a local hero. My photograph loomed large in the newspaper with headlines, "Police Oppose Street Market". So far as the council was concerned it was I rather than the police who was the villain of the piece. Naturally when interviewed by the press about the matter I continued to spell out what I had every reason to believe was the Force policy on the matter, opposition. The very idea of market stalls on both sides of a narrow and very busy street with buses and other traffic passing between them and the hordes of shoppers seemed a recipe for disaster.

Shortly after this the Council scored a good point when one of them discovered an ancient Royal Charter in which some king or other had once visited Colchester and granted them the right to have a street market. Despite the passing of hundreds of years and the invention of the motor car this charter, it seemed, was still valid.

Before the next meeting of the Colchester Traffic Committee I received a telephone call from the Chief Constable rebuking me for taking the stand I had taken on the matter of the Colchester Street Market and ordering me to back off and go to the meeting and give the scheme our blessing. Eating 'humble pie' isn't very pleasant, especially when it isn't home made, but I managed it with as much grace as I could. I wondered whether this was another nail in my coffin so far as Robert Bunyard was concerned. If it was, it wasn't quite the last!

It was not all routine however, and there was the occasional relief from day-to-day police work. On one occasion I went to Cranborne for a week's Civil Defence Course. Most of the other officers present were Chief Constables or Assistant Chief Constables, It somewhat confirmed my view of Mr Bunyard as an arrogant man that he would send a mere Superintendent to represent him at such a distinguished gathering. The subjects for discussion were interesting, the company illustrious and the food absolutely wonderful.

On another occasion I had occasion to attend a week's course at Stansted on co-operation between the services likely to be required in the event of a plane crash. One of the most illuminating lectures was from a representative of Kenyons, the company whose personnel attend plane crashes all over the world to assist in the recovery and identification of bodies. Such a gruesome task requires experts and it is a little known fact that in general local law enforcement officers are not required to do this grisly work.

For the duration of the course, those attending were housed in a very smart hotel in Bishops Stortford and wined and dined very well at the county's expense, one of the few perks I ever received in the police force. It was all too soon at an end and it was back to work again.

One morning a Detective Sergeant came to see me in my office and said that he had a problem with a policewoman who was at the time a CID Aide. She was apparently a useful and conscientious police officer who was sorely troubled. It seemed that there had been a complaint made against her by a magistrate concerning neglect of duty. The matter had been investigated and she had been charged with a disciplinary offence. The case was due to be heard before the Chief Constable on the morrow and on the advice of the Police Federation representative she had notified the Deputy that she intended to plead guilty to the charge.

This morning however, she had gone to her Sergeant in tears and said that she didn't see why she should have to plead guilty to something she hadn't done. It was, it seems, well known by now that I knew a lot about the complaints procedure, and this was why my advice was being sought.

I told the Sergeant that my advice would be that if she wanted to plead not-guilty she should notify the Complaints office at headquarters at once, but to expect that she might be criticised for leaving it so late. If she did intend to plead not-guilty then she should consider getting a 'friend' to act for her and then the Chief would probably allow some time for her to prepare her defence.

A little later the Sergeant returned with the policewoman concerned and she then asked me if I would act as her 'friend' in the matter. It is a request that is not usually refused in the police force, but even I was a little uncertain whether an officer's own Superintendent could act in such a role.

I telephoned the Deputy and told him of the situation. He was, not surprisingly, a little annoyed that the hearing should have to be cancelled, and said that so far as he knew there was no reason why I shouldn't act for her. I promised to get the matter sorted out as soon as possible and to let him know when the new hearing date could be fixed. Mr Stone pointed out to me that this matter had already been sent to the Complaints Board with the details of the charge and that they would be awaiting the result.

Then I listened to the girl's story. She had been on duty in the front office at Colchester Police Station along with a male officer who was not, like her, a probationer, on a Saturday morning. Two giggling young girls had come in and said that a man had indecently exposed himself to them in the High Street. The policewoman had taken a brief description of the man and the location and told the girls she would go and get someone to attend the scene immediately. She had left the front office and asked the officer in charge of the control room to get a message out to the nearest officers. She had returned to the front office to find the girls had gone.

She had asked the male officer where they had gone, as she wanted to get their statements. He apparently said that he thought she had finished with them and had told them they could leave. At this point the policewoman hadn't even got their names and addresses.

It transpired that one of the two girls was the daughter of a magistrate, a lady of some standing in the community and one who was at a cocktail party some days later attended by Derek Wyatt. The magistrate during the course of the evening asked Derek what was being done about her daughter's complaint and he confessed to knowing nothing about it. He personally later took statements from the girls involved and this formed the basis of the subsequent complaint against the officer.

It was apparent to me when I read the file containing the evidence against her that very few of the facts had been covered and that her interview with the investigating officer later was full of loaded questions. I had no doubt that the disciplinary proceedings were a showpiece for the benefit of the magistrate. Many of the important facts had been omitted from the report, which was a travesty.

I submitted a report to the Deputy pointing out in great detail all the defects in the investigating officer's report and recommending that the charge be withdrawn. Alternatively I would be happy to defend the policewoman on the basis of a 'not guilty' plea, when it would be necessary to call as witness the Magistrate and Derek Wyatt as well as several other people who were directly involved.

Within twenty-four hours Mr Stone was on the phone in very angry mood. I was he said being disloyal to him and would force him to write to the Complaints Board and explain that he had been wrong in recommending proceedings. This he was loath to do and thought it best that I rewrite my report. I stuck to my guns. The result was that the Deputy had to write his letter and I successfully hammered the final nail into my own coffin. As it was, he made matters less embarrassing for himself by deciding to issue a caution to the officer, and she later had to attend his office to receive this verbal admonition. It is well known in police circles that a caution can only be given when a person admits his or her guilt and is willing to accept it.

Later the policewoman came to thank me for my efforts on her behalf and said that the Deputy had been very nice and apologised for the trouble that had been caused her and that it would not in any way affect her career. It was the strangest caution I have ever heard!

It was customary for a senior officer to receive a visit from an ACC each year to discuss their Annual Report. Peter Simpson came to see me a few weeks after this affair and I discussed my future prospects with him. He shook his head and said that I had recently upset the Deputy and that it might be quite a while before my name would come up as a prospective Divisional Commander.

Derek Dighton had already retired and had been replaced by Bert Dawson, a younger man than me and one who was clearly far better placed in the league table. In mid-1983 I could see that the writing was on the wall and that it was decision time. It was not a difficult decision to make; there were opportunities out in the big wide world for officers with my experience and my pension would be sufficient to live on even if I decided to go sailing and to hell with working ever again.

I drew my trusty old typewriter towards me and typed out my resignation effective from 1st July 1983. One of the last things I had to do was hand in my uniform and appointments, and I duly did this to the Admin Chief Inspector, who asked for my glasses. I thought he was joking, but he was not. He said that if I wanted to keep them there would be a charge of fifty pence.

Police officers who wore glasses were provided with them free of charge, but they had to conform to a special pattern with unbreakable glass etc. Of course they were made by your own optician and were to your prescription and as such were not the slightest use to anyone else.

It wasn't his fault of course, but I placed the glasses on the desk and said I hoped that they would prove useful to some poor soul. Then I feigned blindness and stumbled towards the door with arms outstretched.

My last journey home from Colchester police station was not without sadness and reflection.

# Reflections on a career

*Look with favour*
*Upon the chapters in your hand*
*The mind's reflections coldly noted,*
*The bitter insights of the heart.*
Alexander Pushkin, Eugene Onegin (1833)

It is impossible to condense everything that happened during thirty years of an interesting and sometimes exciting career in the pages of one small book. I have merely scratched the surface, but in recalling some of the episodes I hope I will have interested and amused anyone who reads these pages as much as I have enjoyed my trip down memory lane. Perhaps it will also serve to stimulate the mind to think about some of the issues I have covered in a new light.

One of the few certain things in this life is that you will get old, if you don't die first. In getting old there is less to look forward to and much to reflect upon; past good fortune, happy times and the mistakes one has made. Young people have everything to look forward to and little to reflect upon, so it is natural for them to scorn the elderly and their supposed wisdom. They too will get old, they too will reflect and they too will make mistakes. It is sad perhaps that in general we cannot learn from the mistakes of others, nor can people of strong temperament heed advice. One of the things one should avoid doing when you reach a mature age is to regret and say, "If only!" It's already far too late for that.

I have survived to enjoy thirty years of retirement, and all I can look forward to are a few more years soaking up sun and Spanish wine and reflecting on the past as I watch the TV and read the daily press about the activities of the present-day warrior in the war against crime.

I look back on my career with a great deal of pleasure, recalling the days on the beat, the days spent as a detective and all the other jobs I did and the places I served. They were for the most part happy years, and I can truthfully say I enjoyed my service in the police. There is a little sorrow too, sorrow that it is all over, sorrow that things have changed so fast and sorrow that the police force today seems to be a force of disgruntled and unhappy men, unlike the ones I knew.

I would dearly love to be able to say that society is a little better for my efforts and that crime was under control, but sadly that is not possible. Some ten years ago I read in the newspaper that street robbery in London was getting out of hand and that 400 officers of the traffic division were being formed into a special unit to combat this type of violent crime. Won't they ever learn that the problem cannot be solved merely by more officers on the street? They might catch a few more, but even if with luck they convict them they will back out on the street committing more robberies tomorrow.

There is a distinct difference between Law Enforcement and Crime Detection, and perhaps the future lies in separating these two things. If the law is not enforced it will be broken, and only then do the two areas of police work coincide. The better the enforcement the less detection is necessary. There is a third subject connected with Law & Order which is often completely forgotten or ignored, and that is punishment. Punishment has nothing to do with the police and everything to do with society. It is only society who can demand that criminals are punished rather than given holidays abroad and every chance and opportunities denied to honest folk. People who believe that this is the best way of dealing with criminals are misguided. They have never been raped, indecently assaulted, robbed or mugged or had their valuables stolen and their houses violated. They are a minority of the public now! It is, I believe, time for a change in attitudes.

Reflecting upon our society leaves one with the overwhelming sensation that today 'looking after yourself' is what life is all about. In Spain they are well aware of this and have an expression for it, "¡Vivo Yo!" which means in English "I'm all right Jack". We have become a selfish society where kind people are the exception rather than the rule and are often regarded as 'do gooders'. It is not a new phenomenon. In the 1950s my grandmother, then in her seventies, fell outside the railway station in Bromley, Kent. Commuters coming home from work on the train stepped over her! It was only later when the Ticket Collector helped her and called an ambulance that it was discovered her purse had been stolen. What good are mere policemen in a society like this?

I have not mentioned the Probation Service in this epistle, although as a police officer I came into contact with it a good deal. It seemed to me that our tasks in life were miles apart, he trying to reform the sinner and me trying to lock him up. Today there is little to choose between the police service and the probation service, as their areas of responsibility have come far closer together. It is often said to me by members of the public who once respected and were proud of their police that we have become just another branch of Social Services. This of course is not true, but from some perspective that is how we appear. When the police are dealing with armed gangs of criminals and terrorists they are more efficient, it seems to me, than in helping the old ladies of our society to retain their purses as they walk along the high street, and the totally inadequate punishments imposed by our pathetic legal system hardly help in this regard.

Whenever firearms are used in committing a high profile crime the debate about arming the police force is opened again, and closed just as quickly when politicians rapidly sweep the subject under the carpet once more. It is not a popular subject with politicians, who know that the public prefer to see the British bobby as a portly figure on a bicycle riding round the country lanes and along the village high street.

Indeed if you ask the average member of the public about the subject he or she will usually express the view that the police should not be armed because they would probably shoot some innocent bystander. Of course they don't realise that the police force is being steadily armed by stealth, a government's favourite way of doing things unpopular with the population. All the officers at airports, channel ports and on protection duty are armed. Officers of special patrol units, force support units and other such squads are armed, and in many of the police patrol cars you see on the streets there are firearms locked in the boot.

Sooner or later the subject will have to be approached realistically and in earnest. We are the only country in Europe that doesn't have an armed police force. Whether Britain decides to remain a full member of the European Union or not seems to me to matter little. The European criminal knows no boundaries and has no allegiance to Queen or country. The idea of police at one end of a short tunnel bristling with guns to tackle the many criminals that use it and bobbies on bicycles with little sticks at the other end expecting them to respond to "'Ere 'ere 'ere, wot's all this?" is ludicrous in the extreme.

Police on the continent don't go around shooting people; in fact many go through their entire service without firing the gun except on the range. The gun is there as a symbol of their authority, to protect them from harm and to give them the necessary confidence to do their job in this age of lawlessness and violence.

The need is now apparent for more and more co-operation between the police forces of the UK and Europe, and the future will be interesting to see for as long as I can manage to survive the ravages of this Spanish sun.

I have looked back, so now what of the future?

In the next ten to fifteen years I see a fully armed National Police Force with the traffic wardens becoming a local police department, taking on a new role to include the enforcement of local bylaws and traffic control. In addition there will be a Third Force, a semi-military body of men fully trained and equipped to deal with national emergencies, riots and civil unrest, and there will be a lot of that in the next fifty years.

And then?

OK, so they have got their Single European Currency, and the next thing to tackle will be the Single European Language. When they have got that sorted, how about a European Federal Bureau of Investigation?

Remember you read it here first!

# Rape?

Rape, as understood by the average member of the public, is the act of a man forcing a woman to have sexual intercourse with him against her will. In the minds of the public, rape is associated with violence, fear and intimidation, since any report of this crime, whether it has just occurred or is currently being tried, is almost always made more sensational by the media. In fact many of the more mundane cases reported to the police are dealt with without ever reaching the eyes and ears of the community.

The crime of rape is one of the most loathsome offences in the whole gamut of criminal behaviour and one that causes almost as much public of horror, disgust and anger as offences against children. Even hardened criminals have no time for their fellow men who have been convicted, or who are merely suspected, of such offences.

In most societies in the world rape is considered a serious crime, although not always for the same reason. Talmudic law makes little discrimination between seduction and rape, emphasising the violation of a woman's virginity. In many African tribes rape is heavily fined because it is considered a violation of property rights, the woman belonging to either her father or her husband.

In the past, and today in some societies, situations of permissible rape exist. A number of ancient peoples customarily ravished their conquered women. Among some American Indian tribes forcible rape by twenty or more men is the prescribed punishment organised by an aggrieved husband against an adulterous wife.

As society has advanced through its various stages of development, attitudes towards women have changed considerably. During the 20th century there were many important changes, including the Representation of the People Act 1928, wherein women were given equal voting rights with men, legislation regarding equal pay and opportunities for woman and sexual discrimination. There have more recently been a number of cases of sexual harassment unheard of twenty years ago.

Likewise the law appertaining to the crime of rape has changed somewhat. as has the attitude of the police to such investigations and their treatment of victims of this and every other crime.

Originally a felony at common law, rape was reduced to a misdemeanour in 1275, but in 1285 was again declared a felony, no doubt following some notorious case. It remained a felony for many years and the penalty was increased to life imprisonment in 1575. In 1861 on the passing of the

Offences Against The Persons Act, rape became a capital offence, but with the abolition of hanging the maximum penalty is now once again life imprisonment.

For nearly one hundred years thereafter rape was dealt with under this Act of Parliament and policemen throughout the country were trained to investigate the offence according to established practice and procedures found to have been successful over all these years.

In 1956 we had the Sexual Offences Act and later in 1976 the Sexual Offences (Amendment) Act wherein changes were made to the law appertaining to this and other related offences. The offence of Rape is currently covered by the Sexual Offences Act 2003, wherein even the definition of the crime has been changed.

The policeman's attitude to rape and indeed to all other crimes is not surprisingly dissimilar from that of the general public, who almost always see any crime from different points of view. They may have sympathy for the victim because they are a friend or relative; they are themselves a potential victim, they have been prejudiced by newspaper reports, or they may be supportive of the accused for similar reasons.

The great lawyer Blackstone once said that there are three sides to every story: the prosecution, the defence and the truth. He was never more profound.

It is the duty of the police to discover the truth in an investigation. They can be, and often are, misled at the outset by being given false information by the witnesses. The reasons for this are too many and too complex to discuss at length in this short article, but there are generally three reasons. These are prejudice, malice and genuine mistake. Most honest citizens are reluctant to assert what they are not sure of and so the last of these, mistake, is not often a problem.

Just a brief word about prejudice. A person who hates women drivers may witness an accident between a coloured man on a bicycle and a car being driven by a young woman. When asked to give his version of the accident this witness, entirely without malice, may well describe events as though the woman driver were at fault. The same incident witnessed by a person with a prejudice against coloured people will undoubtedly give quite a different picture. This is one of the many problems facing an investigator.

Malice or self-interest is by far the most important reason why people mislead the police when making reports and statements to them.

As a police officer I was constantly reminded "It's not your job to decide who's telling the truth and who is not. It is the job of the courts". In theory this is true, but in practice it is a very different matter. If the police were to prosecute every person accused of any crime – particularly rape – just to enable the court to decide, then the whole justice system would grind to a halt. More than half the cases would be thrown out and the police would come under some very heavy criticism. So when a woman reports that she has been raped, they will quite naturally want to know a great many details, and the female, whoever she is, will have to undergo a pretty thorough questioning and later medical examination, both of which may be unpleasant.

The first job of the police when investigating is to establish that a crime has been committed. If they are satisfied that it has, then their next job is to try to establish who committed the offence and to prove it with evidence acceptable to the courts. It would for example be unacceptable for the police to dismiss every complaint of rape as probably untrue and go ahead with their enquiries on this assumption. It would, I believe, be equally wrong to assume from the outset that everything the complainant has said was reliable and rush off to lock up a man who might later to be shown to be innocent.

How then does one proceed? There are a number of factors to aid the investigating officer, not the least of which is experience. If you have ever seen the victim of a genuine rape then it is unlikely you will have any doubt about her truthfulness.

In the early 1980s, following a television series made with the co-operation of the Thames Valley Police, there was much public debate about the somewhat insensitive treatment of rape complainants by some officers. Since that time police forces throughout the country have introduced special training for officers dealing with rape complaints and in all major police stations there are now what are called 'Rape Suites' wherein victims can expect to be treated sympathetically by experienced and specially-trained women police officers.

It is a fact that many of the offences reported are eventually recorded as "No Crime" or a lesser offence, and many complainants withdraw their complaint after the enquiry has got under way.

However, just because a woman is not bruised, bleeding and terribly distressed, it does not mean that she has not been raped. The law says "in proving a charge of rape it is not necessary to prove that what might otherwise appear to have been consent was in reality merely a submission induced by force, the fear of force or fraud, but merely that the victim did not consent" (R v. Olugboja (1982)). There does not have to be violence, merely lack of consent or a recklessness on the part of the rapist as to whether the woman is consenting or not.

The law is wonderfully ambiguous about consent. For example, in the case of R v. Thomas (1982), the Court of Appeal said, "A man is reckless if either he was indifferent and gave no thought to the possibility that the woman might not be consenting, in circumstances where if any thought had been given to the matter, it would have been obvious that there was a risk she was not, or, he was aware of the possibility that she might not be consenting but nevertheless persisted regardless of whether she consented or not".

On the other hand a mistaken belief that the woman was consenting, however unreasonable it may appear to have been, is a complete answer to a charge and the prosecution must eliminate the possibility of such a mistake if it is to succeed.

I trust anyone who is reading this who is not a police officer will begin to see some of the problems which beset an investigating officer faced with an irate rather than distressed woman who alleges that a named man whom she has been with at a party all evening has raped her in his flat where they were having a drink and he was 'showing her his etchings'.

Why do women report that they have been raped when they have not? It is a fact that they do, and the reasons are many and varied. Lack of knowledge of the law may be the answer in a few cases, but not many. Here are a few true examples from my own experience. I am sure many other officers, and former officers, could give you any number of similar examples.

A sixteen-year-old girl reported that she had been raped. She described the man responsible and gave a detailed description of the events that had taken place in a local churchyard. The medical evidence was not conclusive but scientific evidence showed that she had lain on the ground in the place where she had claimed the events had taken place. She was not however injured in any way. A number of local men were interviewed and some twenty officers worked for over a week on the enquiry. One of the girls' parents then brought to the police an exercise book found in their daughter's bedroom which contained a detailed description of the events she had reported but in the form of a story. It was dated a month before the alleged attack. Faced with this, the girl later retracted her story of rape and the matter was recorded as 'No Crime'. Her motive was fantasy.

A twelve-year-old girl was reported missing one Christmas Day and a search was under way when she walked naked out of some woods near her home claiming a man had taken all her clothes off and "done things" to her. She had a number of scratches on her legs and appeared very distressed. The medical evidence showed that she had been penetrated, but by a piece of wood rather than a man. After a long day and a spoiled Christmas we discovered the truth. The girl had been adopted by the family, who had two children of their own, and both of these had had lots of present and loving attention for Christmas. The alleged victim had none, and was treated quite differently by the mother and father. The girl had gone out for a walk with the intention of frightening them into paying her more attention.

A local publican had complained that a police officer had raped his wife. She persisted with the story for a while and the officer was suspended and interviewed. He confessed that he had been having an affair with the lady in question and that the husband had come home unexpectedly. He had escaped through the back door, but she was caught by her husband in a state of undress in the kitchen where the act had been taking place and cried "Rape!" The fleeing uniform was unmistakable and detection inevitable. Not rape however.

There have been other cases of women reporting that they have been raped because they thought they might be pregnant, to excuse being late home, to explain venereal disease and as revenge for being jilted. In all such cases the truth can only be arrived at by some pretty hard questioning. Often police officers are criticised for asking embarrassing questions and apparently treating victims unsympathetically. If such criticism affects the way police do their duty it will inevitably lead to more and more charges being preferred and either more acquittals or more wrongful convictions if juries are as sympathetic as some would like the police to be.

It has been argued that a victim's harsh treatment in the police station prevents genuine cases from being reported. I do not believe this to be the case. The last thing a woman who has been raped thinks about is how she is going to be treated in the police station, and often the matter is reported by a friend or relative to whom she has gone in her distressed state. Such a victim has always, in my experience, been treated with the utmost consideration and sympathy.

In England and Wales some 3,400 rape offences were recorded in 1990, an increase of 3% from 1989 and just under three times the number recorded in 1980. Much of this increase is thought to be attributable to changes in police practice, resulting in an increasing proportion being recorded as offences when the police have serious doubts that the crime was committed but are prevented from pursuing this line of enquiry.

It is clear that the police have a duty to thoroughly investigate allegations of rape and if the thought that one might undergo a careful medical examination as well as detailed questioning at the police station prevents some mischievous or malicious allegations, then I for one am quite happy.

# Law And Disorder - the Judicial Use of Firearms

## INTRODUCTION

In 1829, Sir Robert Peel, Secretary of State for the Home Office, carried through the Police Bill of that year, creating the first disciplined police force for the Greater London area. Many events have occurred since that momentous year to change and develop the Metropolitan Police, some of which might well have caused that gentleman to turn in his grave. The thought of constables patrolling the streets of London carrying firearms, however, would undoubtedly make him spin round in his tomb like a top.

When the Metropolitan Police, and subsequently the County Police Forces (County Police Act 1839), were created, constables were recruited on the basis of their physical strength and appearance. A plethora of brains was not required to carry out the tasks envisaged by their political creators. Indeed it was important that unlike Cassius, they did not 'think too much', and that officers remained servile to the landed gentry and politicians, who often regarded themselves as above the law. Constables were expected to deal only with the criminal classes, in a firm, positive manner, and at the same time touch their forelocks to the magistrates and gentry as they passed by on foot or in their grand carriages. White-collar crime was virtually unknown at that time, and Fraud Squads, Serious Crime Squads and the like, would have been stifled at birth.

## THE CONSTABLE

The office of constable is very old, and dates back to the Roman and Byzantine Empires. It was the name usually given to the head of stables (*comes stabuli*). During the reign of Henry I, the principal duty of the constable and the marshal was to command the army. Sometimes the appointment was coupled with that of conservator (later justice) of the peace, who assisted the sheriff in enforcing the law. This gave rise to constables exercising civil jurisdiction, and under the Statute of Winchester (1285) the civil and military organisations were linked.

It is perhaps ironic that the chief (or high) constable in every area (hundred or franchise), was responsible for suppressing riots and violent crimes, and for arming the militia to enable him to do so.

Today a constable is defined as: "A citizen, locally appointed, with authority under the crown, for the protection of life and property, the maintenance of order, the prevention and detection of crime and the prosecution of offenders against the peace". Now of course, the responsibility for the prosecution of offenders has been removed from the police and given to the Crown Prosecution Service, although many police officers believe that this change has benefited only the wrongdoer. The removal of power from the police and the denial of new power is undoubtedly a throwback to the early days, when constables were there merely to serve the rich and powerful. There is also heavy apprehension among many that the police should ever become an instrument of the Government. Arming the police would be to give them far more power than they already have, and from a political viewpoint such a move has dangerous implications.

## RESOURCES

The need for adequate manpower, weapons and equipment to achieve the prime objectives of the modern police service has never been greater. The refusal of the Government to consider a 'third force' or military style riot squad - perhaps by way of a 12-month National Service - has meant that more and more police time and resources are now spent on the first two objectives, and less and less on the third, the prevention and detection of crime. Public order, or disorder, brought about by industrial and other disputes, demonstrations, protests, civil disobedience and racial problems, has become the single most pressing duty for the police to deal with. The struggle to maintain order, and thereby to protect life and property, has been responsible for a huge drain on police manpower and funds.

There is no doubt that the respect for the office of constable which should exist in a well-ordered society has gone. It has been replaced by a fearless disregard for the law in general and the police in particular. This process has been encouraged by the trumpeting of insidious minority groups, a media hostile to everything but its own freedom, the vast traffic in drugs and their distribution amongst the young people of the land, an economy and legal system which are seen by many to favour those who flaunt the law, and mistrust of the police fostered by minority ethnic groups and in some cases, by the well-publicised misconduct of the police themselves.

This lack of respect for the law, its officers and all they stand for is in my own opinion the largest single reason for the disorder now occupying so much police time, effort and expenditure. Society is accelerating down a slippery slope. Would the issuing of personal sidearms to all constables on the streets of England and Wales help to reverse the situation?

## THE ARGUMENTS

The arguments for and against the carrying of firearms by the British police have been debated for many years. Whenever yet another police officer is murdered in a senseless and unnecessary manner, the matter is raised, the subject aired, and - like the death penalty – it is put once more on the `back burner' to await another tragedy so that it can be ventilated yet again. When I was researching this book the latest name to appear on the ever-growing roll of honour, of those who died in the line of duty, was that of Constable Ian Dibell of the Essex Police, who was shot dead on 9th July 2012.

Politicians usually react to the idea of arming the police as if it were some sinister fascist move, fearful that the public might see it as the first step towards a National Police Force and a Police State. It might therefore be a long time before any serious proposal that the police should carry arms is debated in Parliament.

The arguments against arming the police, which I have heard repeatedly, are: tradition; that it would encourage criminals to carry firearms rather than deter them; some innocent person might get shot; the high cost; many officers are not emotionally suited to the use of firearms; and, in particular, that the police themselves don't want to carry guns.

Let us examine each of these arguments to see whether they are valid, if they have been stated with knowledge, facts and authority, or merely emotionally or with self-interest in mind.

## TRADITION

It is said that to arm the British police would go against all the traditions of our policing methods. Unlike many of our allies in Europe and elsewhere, the British police force is founded on a system of policing by consent. The traditional `bobby' was portly, genial and patrolled the village, or his beat, on a bicycle. He was not a servant of the state, but of the community where he lived. The sight of his blue uniform sent shivers down the spines of mischievous children and caused second thoughts to enter the minds of potential criminals lurking in the shadows. Little old ladies could not resist asking him the time, or asking him to lead them safely across the road. He was a well-respected member of the community, often a regular churchgoer and friend of one and all.

Tradition, to put it simply, is the handing down from generation to generation of customs, beliefs or institutions. Tradition, however, has to be earned, and is not just an apathetic repetition of what has been done before.

Compare our traditional 'bobby' with the sight of today's officer in fireproof riot gear, body armour, helmet and shield. He has already been dubbed 'Robocop'. One could hardly say he was traditional. For the purpose of trying to keep order in serious cases of large-scale or politically-motivated strikes, police from several districts have to combine to tackle the problems. They can hardly be regarded any more as 'local' officers, nor be seen by the public as anything other than 'Government forces'.

The need for this new police image has been brought about by change. One can discuss at great length what has caused the present state of law and disorder in our cities, but the fact that this change has taken place cannot be continually ignored. The rioters; so-called 'professional criminals'; drug abusers, dealers and armed gangs; juvenile criminals; muggers; terrorists and other murderers of police officers, are all out there. They have to be faced and dealt with by courageous policemen and women, not by those, be they politicians or other 'experts' on law and order, who, in the comfort of their offices, contemplate how best the job should be done. Can traditional methods of policing in Britain really still be thought of as relevant in today's war against crime?

## CRIMINAL USE OF FIREARMS

It is averred that to arm the police would encourage greater numbers of criminals to take up arms. Criminals have used firearms against the police in this country for many years. One of the earliest murders of a police officer by shooting was that of PC Gutteridge in Essex in September 1927, referred to earlier. The sad fact is that if one were to draw a graph showing the number of police murders and unlawful killings through the years, the line would start fairly level and then, more recently, would shoot right off the page.

There can of course be no reliable evidence that arming the police of this country would either reduce or increase the use of firearms by criminals - It hasn't happened yet! No doubt the hindsight brigade would carefully watch the statistics, should it ever happen, so that they could deafen us with their silence if the figures showed a downward trend, and smile smugly and say 'we told you so' if the opposite were the case.

Police officers over the years gain a great deal of experience of the criminal mind. They probably have more knowledge of how the petty crook and the sophisticated lawbreaker think and behave than any psychologist does. This on-the-job training does, I admit, make the police officer somewhat cynical of his fellow man, but it also makes him an expert on criminal behaviour.

I have no doubt, from my own dealings with offenders who have been apprehended, that they are indeed motivated by fear of the consequences of their actions, are as afraid of physical assault and violence as any other citizen, and are undoubtedly more cowardly than most when on a 'level playing field' as the politicians say. This does not include persons who were under the influence of drugs at the time of their offence, nor of course persons who have not yet been caught, and who may also feel that they are invincible.

If the police carried guns, the more hardened and violent types, who already carry firearms, would no doubt continue to do so. I feel strongly that many lesser offenders would be more reluctant to embark upon an armed raid, or to carry any weapon, that might provoke an equal or greater force to be used against him by a police officer. What is important of course - and often overlooked - is that armed, the police officer at least has a fighting chance against those who do choose to break the law with a clear intent to resist, by force, any attempt to apprehend them.

This country has probably the most rigorous control of firearms, legitimate firearms that is, in the civilised world. In spite of that, experienced and determined criminals have little difficulty in buying them, or even hiring them for a specific criminal enterprise. The petty thief does not have this easy access to guns, or the relatively large sums of money needed to get them. I do not believe therefore that your average thief or burglar would be able to obtain weapons, even if the prophets of doom were right in saying that arming the police would be an invitation to them to do so. It is one thing to pick up a gun, but quite another to have the will or intent to use it. The knowledge that the law would always make the presumption that those unlawfully in possession of guns do intend to kill people with them is also a strong discouragement to those who might carry them to frighten or intimidate.

Much useful information on this aspect of arming the police is readily available from the many forces throughout the world whose police do carry weapons and have done so for many years without any of the problems we seem to fear in this country. It seems to me from my own travels in Europe that determined criminals, terrorists and the like will always carry firearms. Arming the police will not stop them. It may stop some of the others, it may not, but it will level the playing field and certainly prevent many murders of police officers in the line of duty.

On the continent you most certainly do not see officers being punched, kicked, spat upon, abused and otherwise rendered unfit for duty in the way that is now all too common in the UK. It may be that the attitude to the police there is due to fear rather than respect, but in my experience the Continental police are feared only by the criminals, not the general public. Is that such a bad thing? I walk around the local Sunday market here in Spain and see the local Guardia patrolling with their sidearms clearly visible on their belts. It gives me and the rest of the local people a sense of security that is missing in society at home in the UK.

## PROTECTION OF THE PUBLIC

If the police carried guns, say the 'anti' lobby, members of the public or innocent bystanders would get shot in the crossfire. One wonders what is worse, getting shot by a criminal, or by a police officer trying to do his duty. I have every confidence that police firearms training is as good as it can be at present. The criminals don't have any training at all, and the chances of an armed robber hitting an innocent bystander while shooting at a police car or police officer are far higher than those of a trained police officer missing his mark. It is true that there is a risk that some day, somewhere an innocent person might get injured or even killed by a police officer. In all other countries where the police have guns, it seems that it is considered to be a risk worth taking, in order to have some chance of winning the battle against those who continually flaunt society's laws and fill the lives of so many ordinary honest citizens with constant apprehension, terror and grief.

## ECONOMICS

The cost of arming the police would be too high, say those opposing the motion. It may surprise some of them to know that the police in England and Wales are already armed to a considerable extent. Individual officers do not yet carry a sidearm on normal patrol. However most forces have weapons concealed in patrol cars and most police stations have a number of handguns locked away for an emergency.

All forces now have highly trained Firearms Support Units; officers on protection duty carry guns; at airports guns are openly carried, and there are many other exceptions to the general rule that the police go unarmed.

Most officers, in most forces, undergo firearms training on a regular basis, and others such as the FSU officers receive special and intensive training. This all costs a considerable sum of money each year.

The additional cost of equipping patrolling officers with their own personal weapon would I believe be a comparatively small additional expenditure, and a one off. One wonders too whether in time, as respect for law and order and of its officers was restored, far less expenditure would be necessary in trying to maintain public order.

## EMOTIONAL STABILITY

I have only just recently heard it said, by a serving police officer, that some officers are emotionally unsuited to carry, and be expected to use, firearms in the line of duty. That is perhaps not an argument one might expect to hear about officers who nightly have to go out on the streets to tackle armed criminals, with nothing but their bare hands and a small stick of wood. It makes one wonder whether these same officers are emotionally suited to do that! I accept that there are officers who do not like guns, nasty, noisy, dangerous things that they are. This problem was not unknown in the army, when national servicemen lined up on the range for the first time. Proper training served then to solve the problem.

There seems to me to be absolutely no reason to worry that an unsuitable officer would parade for duty, if firearms training commenced at Initial Training School. Any officer who was genuinely unsuited would be 'weeded out' at an early stage, and perhaps persuaded that he, or she, might do better in some other field of public service.

One cannot expect that the arming of a police force for the first time could be done overnight, nor that it could be achieved without teething problems. There would be a good deal of preparation, and I expect the introduction of guns being carried by officers on normal patrol on the street would be achieved gradually. Indeed the process has in my view already started.

## THE WISHES OF THE POLICE

It is believed by some that the police themselves do not want to carry guns on patrol. So far as I know there are no reliable statistics to prove this point one way or the other. There was a 'referendum' in Essex a few years ago and a small majority was against the proposition. I don't know how many other forces have had a similar exercise nor, if so, what the question was on the voting paper.

If you ask, for example, 'Would you like to see the British police force carry guns?' you might get one answer. However if the question were put, 'How would you prefer to go out on patrol at night, armed with a gun or a stick?' then the response might be quite different. It is well known among pollsters that it is important to ask the right question, and that you can almost always get the result you want by careful wording of the inquiry.

I have found when talking to police officers that the older they are in service the less inclined they are to opt for police carrying guns, although they think that this is now inevitable. The younger ones also accept that it is inevitable and for the most part, the ones I have spoken to welcome it.

It is strange that anyone should, for once, care what the police themselves think of a development, or to believe that what they think might have any effect at all on the outcome. It would indeed be a unique happening if a government were to abandon a future scheme that they considered to be in the nation's interest because the police were not in favour of it.

One other reason why many police officers would be reluctant to carry weapons is the current official attitude to their actual use, and the unfair publicity that seems inevitably to follow any positive piece of police action. An officer is trained that when he fires his gun at someone he must presume that he will kill him. That he could be taught to shoot to wound is an idea that might appeal to John Wayne fans, but not to anyone who has any experience at all of firing a handgun. Many officers presume, I believe quite rightly, that until this entire question of culpability is thoroughly gone into, they would not be treated fairly. Experience has shown that after any fatal shooting incident, the officer responsible has been tried and convicted by the media the following day, and serious attempts to prejudice the outcome of any proper enquiry into the facts are made by screaming minority groups and the gossiping of the uninformed. Pressure has been exerted on senior officers to suspend officers before anyone has found them guilty of anything. Officers expect to be accountable for their actions. They expect also to be treated fairly and with total impartiality.

Rather than ask the police, who after all are the servant, not the master, would it not be more important to discover what the public - who are the masters - thought of arming the police? If letters to the editors of newspapers are any indication of public opinion, it seems that many are in favour of the idea. Among such letters I have read was one from the wife of an officer who was a colleague of the late Sergeant Derek Robertson (stabbed to death in 1994). She wrote of her hope that 'this tragedy will be a spur to giving our police the protective equipment they deserve'. Another was from the wife of an officer who had also been stabbed, although not fatally, and who had been told he could wear a stab proof jacket if he wanted to pay £100 to buy one. Emotional stuff it might be, but they are real people with real feelings. Policemen have wives, children and mothers who all suffer stress each day when their loved ones go on duty. They know that the chances of a senior officer appearing at their door with bad news are increasing rapidly day by day.

## FINAL THOUGHTS

Whether one is for or against a political union in Europe, there is inevitability about the direction we are going. No one has yet said we should arm our policemen and women to bring us into line with Europe, although I expect someone will before long. The Channel Tunnel is a fairly recent development, bringing us all closer together. Already there is a close economic bond between us and our European neighbours. We often hear politicians discussing the future of Europe and making comparisons, suggesting that we should do this or that, because it is done in Europe.

When the tunnel opened for business it was an interesting paradox that the police on one side of the channel tunnel were armed, and those on the other side were not.

Although I believe it is inevitable, it may be that the time when we shall see the British police officer patrolling with his personal sidearm is yet still some way off. Sadly it will take many more dead policemen to convince those who make the laws that you have got to have someone 'out there' who is capable of enforcing them.

# A Different View of Crime Prevention

## RESPONSIBILITY

The prevention and detection of crime are two of the duties imposed upon every police officer which, with the authority of the Crown, he swears upon his oath to fulfil. So far as I can discover the police are the only body, apart of course from the Government, who have such a legal responsibility.

However a constable in England, Scotland or Wales is no more than an ordinary citizen, with some extra powers given by the Crown. It is the sworn duty of a constable to prevent crime, but it is, I believe, the moral duty of all citizens, young and old, to deter wrongdoing. Today any interference by a member of the public with the activities of another is almost immediately followed by court action or serious injury. It is therefore unreasonable to expect the public to actively engage themselves in the prevention of crime. This task, as it is perceived today, is left almost exclusively to the police.

Crime is disobedience of the law, a simple definition of a very complex subject. Crime in general is rising year by year, no matter how politicians try to spin the statistics to try and prove otherwise. All kinds of reasons - one might say excuses - are submitted to explain, if not to justify them. Could it be that there is something wrong with the effectiveness of Crime Prevention? Let us have a more serious, in-depth look, at what 'crime prevention' means and how it could be tackled to reverse the crime trend. Is it indeed possible to actually prevent crime, rather than to merely push it into the next street?

Perhaps we should first decide exactly what crime prevention is. Ask your average 'reasonable man' in the street what he understands by the expression 'crime prevention'. I have no doubt he will say it relates to locks, bars and burglar alarms. I regret that many police officers also regard crime prevention as advice given to members of the public on how best to protect themselves from burglars and thieves.

It used to be said that the best crime prevention officer was the uniformed constable, patrolling up and down his beat. There can be little doubt that in the days of the detached beat officer, crime prevention was an extremely effective part of his daily life. As a supervising officer, part of my job was to visit detached beats and, among other things, to examine the crime complaint book. There would often be no entry in it from one visit to the next, a fact that the officer concerned would be very proud of.

Today, the police force operates exactly like a fire brigade, responding to calls from the public. There is little time for leisurely patrols when the uniform can be displayed, door handles tried and would-be thieves deterred. It is also true that the sight of a police uniform does not deter in the same way it once did. When the definition of constable was first formulated, I suspect that those responsible for it used the words 'prevention and detection of crime' with the vision of the bobby on the street in mind. We have come a long way since then.

Nowadays Chief Constables attempt to fulfil their duty to prevent crime by means of Crime Prevention Officers and Crime Prevention Departments, dedicated to this subject. Unfortunately this does have the effect of relieving other police officers from this responsibility, although of course it should not. When it becomes necessary to explain to Her Majesty's Inspector of Constabulary what is being done in this field, the Chief Constable usually calls upon his Chief Crime Prevention Officer to speak.

Of course there are no facts or statistics to prove or disprove how effective the department has been during any particular period. On the contrary, if crime figures showed an increase on the previous year one might say that the Crime Prevention Department had failed miserably. No doubt the HMI will consider whether the amount of money spent in this department is a reasonable part of the whole budget. He will also listen with interest to details of the Crime Prevention Campaigns held, the number of Crime Prevention Surveys carried out and talks given to members of the public. Many old-time cynics such as myself, however, frown and wonder whether the vast sums of money and man hours spent on this type of crime prevention are anything more than an exercise in public relations.

What are the ways in which crime prevention, as a significant subject, can be approached? Education, self-help schemes, security systems, deterrents, legislation and intelligence are some. Perhaps this list is not exhaustive, but it will do to show that there is more to this subject than merely locking out the criminal.

## EDUCATION

Let us begin with the Crime Prevention Officer, for it is he who is the backbone of crime prevention in this country. It is he who does his best to educate the public in how to protect themselves from becoming victims of crime. This is how he perceives his prime function, and he attempts to carry out this role in several ways.

The work of the crime prevention officer in the field of crime prevention is almost exclusively directed to crimes against property. There are many other crimes in the 'book' which society has chosen to legislate against, and I sometimes asked why no attention was given to them. "Ah!" cried the CPO in protest. "We give talks to groups of women about being attacked. We tell them how to protect themselves, how to ward off would be attackers. That's not a crime against property!"

True, but neither is it crime prevention. Crime prevention in this area would be to prevent the attack in the first place. A woman who can protect herself against physical attack by a man is at an advantage over one who is not, but the crime is not prevented. Likewise if a burglar sneaks up to your house at night but cannot get in because of the expensive locks, bolts and bars you have purchased, he will undoubtedly move on to the next house. You have not prevented a crime. Indeed the attempt to commit most crimes is a crime at common law, and usually the penalty is not limited by Act of Parliament. In theory the maximum punishment for attempting to commit a crime is often greater than for actually committing it.

The Crime Prevention Department of a police force offers a service to the public, for those who ask for it. It will attend premises, private or business, and carry out a survey to advise what, if any, security precautions need to be taken to prevent theft and burglary. The CPO can advise on the best and most suitable equipment available, since he is naturally in touch with all the manufacturers. They in their turn see the CPO as a most desirable ally in selling their particular equipment.

This service is also available from civilian, and of course commercial, security organisations or manufacturers. The CPO will argue that he is unbiased in respect of one lock maker or another. Naturally he would not, as has been alleged against at least one company I can think of, recommend equipment that was not really necessary. This of course is true, but your own insurance company will gladly tell you the minimum requirements needed for your security. Their advice, though not always unbiased, is equally competent.

This activity cannot be passed by without a comment that the time and energy spent on it is designed to protect individuals who can afford it. It really does nothing to prevent the incidence of theft and burglary, and if anything it moves crime nearer to those less well off, who rely on the police and society to protect them from crime.

No security device can be relied on to prevent a determined criminal from achieving his aim. Alarms and devices will usually protect one from the casual or even full-time burglar or thief, but if there is something specific of value in certain premises that a highly-skilled thief must have, then in due course he will get through the locks, bolts and bars to get it.

Besides surveys, CPOs seek to educate the public by giving talks to schools, clubs and other groups, and by means of Crime Prevention Campaigns. These talks are illustrated with videos and films, which can also be hired, all of which teach people how to protect themselves from becoming victims of crime. The campaigns too are intended to be educational, but no matter how many times you tell elderly ladies not to open their doors to strangers, the bogus gasman and other officials still succeed in getting in.

Ignorance of the law, we are often told, is no excuse for committing crime. Neither should there be any excuse for failing to educate our children at school how they should behave in society. The once-a-year talk by the local bobby is not, I suggest, the right way to do this.

The whole thrust of crime prevention departments is towards putting the lid on a known and accepted problem, rather than trying to eliminate it. It is just a matter of moving the crime on to someone else's property, rather than preventing the criminal from having the desire, the need or the opportunity to commit the offence. Perhaps it would be better to call this subject 'crime protection' rather than crime prevention. The fact that we need to spend so much time and money on protecting ourselves from crime is evidence of the failure of the forces of law and order, the courts and the lawmakers.

The CPO in each Police Division spends a great deal of time preparing charts and diagrams in glorious colours. He or she can instantly tell an enquirer how many burglaries there were this month compared with last, what percentage of them were detected, the value and type of property stolen etc. This in my own view is not really the realm of the CPO. However it used to be the theory that the CPO would analyse current crime and so be able to advise the CID Chief of the trends, stick pins in maps etc, and so forecast where the ungodly would strike next. Then by strategic use of his resources the CID Chief could prevent or check a particular series of crimes.

Sadly this theory seldom comes through into practice. Most CID Chiefs in my experience, struggling with their rising crime, and pressure from 'above' to do something about it, are less than enthusiastic about the help they get from the Crime Prevention Department. In my own experience, whenever I called for the CPO I found he was educating the public at the local fete with his 'circus', otherwise known as a Crime Prevention Exhibition. I hasten to apologise to any CPO who reads this; they are invariably fine officers doing their job as prescribed, in a conscientious and adequate way. I am not critical of them personally.

## SELF-HELP

In most police forces various self-help schemes have been launched under the general heading of crime prevention. I think it is fair to say that for the most part these ideas have been more in the nature of crime protection, and sometimes more useful in the detection field.

One such scheme was called the Vehicle Observer Corps and was designed to try to make use of the vast network of CD (Citizen Band) radios in use daily on our roads. It did however call for lorry drivers to help the police in tracing stolen motor cars and reporting suspicious events. Truck drivers are not always the best allies of the police, particularly traffic police. While they may be keen to help them in a hunt for a child killer or a rapist, their enthusiasm for helping catch minor offenders could not be relied upon. In addition there are just as many dishonest users of CB radio as honest ones, so if the police did use the network, they could never be sure who was listening. Such schemes as this are now for the most part in disuse, if not abandoned altogether.

Another scheme, quite popular in most areas, is the Crime Prevention Panel. This consists of several businessmen, shop managers, hoteliers etc who meet once a month, with the CPO to discuss crime trends, and how best they can protect themselves and their fellow traders from the machinations of the wicked.

Many schemes have been tried in the past, some still in being, which band together groups of people with similar problems. Shopkeepers, for example, would join a scheme to form an early warning network of information about shoplifters. Several in the group would be willing to notify other members, and so pass information along quickly. If a shoplifter were detected in one shop but not detained, the shopkeeper would call the police, who would notify the description of the suspect to all the other key members, who would in turn pass the information on.

Such schemes as this and the previous one, all administered by the CPO, are really not cost-effective in terms of the good they do for society in the field of crime prevention. The notifying of say 100 shops that there was a shoplifter in town, and expecting them to notify all their staff to keep a special watch, is really living in cloud cuckoo land. On the other hand the public seem to approve, and think a great deal is being done for their benefit.

Perhaps the most popular of all self-help schemes, and the one that is perhaps closest to crime prevention, is Neighbourhood Watch, which has taken root all over the country. Insurance companies seem to like the scheme, but there is no evidence that I can find that crime is prevented in areas that endorse the scheme. Its value is more in the nature of bringing the community together to help and 'watch' each other, especially the aged who live alone and people who go away on holiday and leave their properties unattended. Some groups organise coach outings, coffee mornings and other social events. Great, but is it really a job for the police to manage? Could not the local authority look after it?

In my experience most Neighbourhood Watch Co-ordinators are elderly and retired, and they have little to do but try and whip up enthusiasm among the neighbours. I myself tried, and eventually gave up in disgust at the apathy I encountered. They have monthly meetings at the police station and complain about boys cycling on footpaths and noisy motor cycles.

The Home Secretary, the Rt Hon Michael Howard MP, at a national meeting of co-ordinators once suggested that members of the Neighbourhood Watch should carry out patrols of the streets at night, as a further development of the scheme. I wrote to my own MP at the time, Iain Sproat, to ask whether the Home Secretary was actually serious about this, or having just watched an episode of Dad's Army, he was having a little joke. I was told that he was indeed serious, although I have heard no more about it since.

I repeat that all these schemes do not prevent crime. What they do is help those involved in the scheme to be more aware of the dreadful state of criminality in the country, to guard themselves against the inevitable attack, and to make such an attack less likely to be successful. 'Don't burgle my house - go next door' should be their motto.

## SECURITY SYSTEMS

Because of the escalating crime rate, a new industry has evolved over the past thirty years or so. Starting with Securicor, there are now dozens of uniformed carriers, guards and patrols on our streets doing jobs that the police, for various reasons, cannot do. The Yellow Pages is full of security organisations and detective agencies, each offering to do tasks for us that most feel should not be necessary in a civilised society, but which are becoming essential. Each year there is a national security exhibition at Olympia where the hundreds of companies manufacturing every conceivable type of security device and equipment to protect homes, business premises and persons, from attack by criminals display their wares.

This is the society in which we now live. Crime has not been 'prevented', perhaps because no one really knows, or is willing to confront, the cause. Is it because successive governments have not had the courage to deal with it, the police have not had the power and the public has not had the zeal?

## INTELLIGENCE

In many everyday cases it is possible to prevent crime by either removing the object of the crime or eliminating the means by which it is committed. Often simple common sense is the answer to a very vexing problem

A licensee I knew was troubled during the summer months by his beer glasses being stolen or smashed. He had a pleasant beer garden at a seaside resort, frequented by the type of drinker who found it amusing to steal or smash the glasses. He was advised to allow only tins of beer or minerals and paper cups to be taken from the premises. His problem was solved.

In another case a village was troubled by hooligans who left a local youth club at 10pm each evening. While waiting for the last bus home to town at 10.30pm, they caused a nuisance by urinating in people's front gardens, shouting and generally being an irritation to the locals. The bus company was approached, and agreed to alter the timetable. After that the last bus went at 10.05pm and there was no more trouble.

Shops with attractive open displays can easily put them behind glass, or raise them out of the reach of would-be thieves. There are many ways crime can be prevented by using intelligence when planning or operating a particular enterprise, or when designing buildings and housing estates.

Criminal intelligence is of course used to forestall serious crimes, often with great success. The use of informants however is fraught with hazards and has been mentioned in earlier chapters.

## DETERRENTS

Surely the most effective way of preventing crime is to deter people from committing it. Why do people not want to swim in shark-infested waters or put their hands into a fire? The answer is simple, they know the consequences would be unpleasant.

Judges and magistrates in our fair country have a duty to see that defendants are tried properly and fairly according to law and to mete out appropriate punishment. They do not have a direct responsibility for crime prevention. It is surprising therefore that many judges, and particularly magistrates, are misguidedly asked by probation officers, psychiatrists and others speaking for villains not to impose a custodial sentence, because he or she believes 'chummy' will not commit a further offence. In such cases they are being asked to consider crime prevention rather than punishment, and are being side-tracked from their prime function, which is to punish the offender appropriately.

Some years ago there was a punishment known as 'preventive detention' where a persistent offender could be sentenced to 14 years 'PD' as it was known. It was, and is, sometimes forgotten that all custodial sentences are preventive detention, and that besides punishing the offender, they prevent him from committing crime for the duration of his sentence. However it is neither logical nor appropriate, in my view, to argue that because an offender is not likely to commit a further offence he should not be punished.

Perhaps it would be a good idea to impose upon the judiciary an obligation to prevent crime as well as to punish offenders. It is not essential to send a person to prison to prevent him from committing crime. Suspended sentences were a good idea, but unfortunately persons who re-offend now know that it is unlikely they will be sent to prison in spite of it.

Confiscation of property, redeemable only after a period of good behaviour, might be considered. There are already many sanctions such as penalties that can be imposed on the parents of criminal children, confiscation of cars used by criminals and compensation orders etc, which are sadly ignored by most courts.

Perhaps it is time for fixed penalties for crimes other than minor parking or speeding offences. Why should murder be the only serious crime in the book for which there is a fixed penalty? If people knew that if they committed theft they would go to prison for a year, no matter what their age or excuse, would this have an effect on preventing crime? Three convictions and you got the grand prize of 10 years. Wow! That would make them think.

## LEGISLATION

Each time the Government makes a new law it makes new criminals. Laws are often made without consideration of the problems of enforcing them. No one complains that an act or omission that interferes with the peace of others should be outlawed by a law. What does seem a little odd is that the Government should impose laws upon us to save us from ourselves.

One such law is the wearing of seat belts. No one can doubt that they make driving safer. Why is it necessary to make the failure to wear one a crime? Surely anyone with common sense would want to wear a seat belt.

Smoking cigarettes, on the other hand, is known to seriously damage your health, even the health of others around you. This is not considered a matter for legal sanctions, while the wearing of crash helmets is insisted upon by law, no doubt gladdening the hearts of the manufacturers.

Some time ago there was a serious debate about whether it should be made a crime to leave a car unattended without locking it. So far the Government has not been persuaded that this should be illegal. Could it be that there is nothing in it for them by way of tax, or for a manufacturer by way of sales? Or am I too cynical?

It might be a good way to prevent some crime if all the old laws, now completely unnecessary, or all those that ban acts or omissions not offensive or detrimental to others were repealed.

Crime prevention is, I acknowledge, difficult to legislate for. It is not however, impossible. Perhaps the law should give people - after all it is the people who are the victims - more power to deal with criminals and some protection from civil action when acting with reasonable cause. Police officers can arrest someone on reasonable suspicion of having committed a crime, or being about to do so (crime prevention). An ordinary citizen cannot; he/she can only do so only after actually witnessing the crime.

Politicians should bear in mind that the more laws we have, the more criminals we create. The law-abiding public are unanimous in their view that the law is heavily weighted in favour of the criminal, rather than the potential victim. Laws relating to granting of bail, rules of evidence and edicts that prevent a jury from knowing that the man they are trying is a habitual criminal are all crime creation laws, not crime prevention!

## SUMMARY

In a perfect world there would be no crime, because no one would have the motive to commit offences against their society or fellow men. In our imperfect state, criminality gets steadily worse. Who is debating how far and how much more serious the situation will have to get before something is seen to be done about it? We all know that the only logical ways of preventing crime are strong deterrents, education of the young and where necessary preventive detention. Who will have the courage to vault over the backs of those motivated by self-interest, political opponents, pressure groups and the lethargic, to tackle the problem head on?

# Complaints and efficiency - the modern police force

I remember being told by a lecturer at the Police College many years ago that the difference between psychology and psychiatry was that the first is the study of the normal mind, and the second the study and treatment of the abnormal or sick mind. Although somewhat simplistic, this distinction is basically correct. If one accepts that criminology is the psychology of crime, then we come to my first contention: that crime is committed by normal human beings. The madman who goes berserk with a gun or a knife is not in control of himself, and therefore not responsible for his actions. He has not the *mens rea*, the 'guilty knowledge', required for a crime to have been committed.

Criminologists study, as a science, the causation, correction and prevention of crime, including penology, as well as in some countries - particularly America – so-called criminalistics, the science and practice of criminal investigation. The advice given to governments by these experts on the causes of crime often results in changes in legislation, procedures and even attitudes to the criminal. In most cases these changes, over the years, have been towards a more liberal treatment of offenders; community policing, more lenient sentencing etc etc. So far these changes have had little overall effect upon the crime rate, which continues to rise.

Far better brains than mine have wrestled with the problem of why crime figures rise faster than they should, given the population increase. No one has been able to pinpoint the reason. Perhaps this is because there is no one reason but several. This brings me to my second contention: that the efficiency of a police force has a direct bearing upon the causation of crime, as well as detection.

How then does one measure the efficiency of a police force? It is obviously not a straightforward matter. An efficient business can be rated by the profits it makes - the more profits, the more efficient. A police service does not make and sell goods, nor is there a balance sheet at the end of the year showing 'income from sales'. How can a police force be made more 'cost effective'? I have a few ideas about that which I will mention later, but can you really reconcile efficiency with cost effectiveness? Of course certain tasks can be done more efficiently with modern technology, but this always costs more rather than less.

The Sheehy report (1993) into police responsibilities and

rewards made 272 recommendations. It sought, so we are told, to deal with both these questions. It brought a great gnashing of teeth from the police service nationally, who saw it as nothing more than an exercise to cut costs, to the great detriment of efficiency, as well as to the wellbeing of the service generally. Most police officers, and I'm happy to say some politicians, agree with this view. No doubt the police forces of this country could be run at less cost, but at what price?

Crime figures are published annually which tell us how many crimes have been reported, how many detected, and percentage detection rates. Everyone knows however, that statistics are like bathing costumes - what they reveal is interesting, but what they conceal is vital. Such figures as are published do not truly reflect the efficiency of a force, neither does a poll of how popular they are, nor what percentage of the cases taken to court are thrown out because of a defect in the evidence. I have yet to find any reliable indicator of efficiency. After all, what is the good of sending a car in response to a 999 call in two minutes if the person who dialled 999 is left dissatisfied with the action taken by the officers when they do arrive?

An efficient police service, in my own estimation, is a well-motivated body of dedicated and conscientious men who carry out their tasks well and, as they are sworn to do, without fear or favour, malice or ill will. This is not, from my own observations, and knowledge, the situation today.

Let us look for a moment at what motivates us normal human beings to commit crime. Oh yes, we have all done it, we are all criminals. Whether it was a few paper clips from the office, the fiver picked up in the street and pocketed, parking on double yellow lines or something more serious, we have all broken the law. Why?

The main reason is because we thought we would not get caught. If we did think there was a slight chance of detection, well so what, the punishment would be negligible, or we could well afford it.

When a burglar decides to go out at night to break into houses and steal, the same thoughts surely go through his mind. What are my chances of getting caught? A quick look at the local crime figures will tell him that his chances are 30% or less. Recently quoted statistics show that out of every 50 crimes committed there are only two convictions in court. Not bad odds, one might think. So what if I do get caught? Glance at the 'burglar's charter'. If I'm under 14, no problem, under 21, can't go to prison for a first offence - first offence? Ha! Ha! first time caught, they mean. Bail? Certainly! Wife pregnant, no job. They'll probably give me a 'sub'. Off he goes merrily with his striped jersey and bag marked 'swag'.

What if that same burglar knew the chances of getting caught were 85% or greater? That if he were caught he would surely go to prison or be suitably punished? I suggest that in a large number of cases he would put his feet up and watch his colour telly - provided by the 'social' of course.

Sir Robert Mark was probably the father of the present police complaints procedure. When he took over as Metropolitan Police Commissioner in 1972 he vowed to clean up the force. There had at that time been some publicity about serious wrongdoing by officers in that force, and no doubt it was long overdue for some 'cleaning up'.

It is a difficult task to wheedle out bad police officers and convict them in court, but Sir Robert persevered and succeeded in clearing out the worst of the corruption that had been going on for many years. The success of the operation and the establishment in the Metropolitan Police of A10 (Police Complaints Department) had, I believe, a knock-on detrimental effect on the remainder of the police forces in the country.

The Government of the day was persuaded that all police forces were tarred with the same brush, that they needed some sort of inducement to purge their own officers, and to regulate how and when officers should be investigated for misconduct, as well as to open them up to official complaints from members of the public. The fact that there was already a well-established and exacting discipline code and procedure in all forces was not enough to satisfy the minority groups, who were pressing for more accountability and openness among police forces.

The Police Act of 1976 (referred to by Sir Robert as an 'unacceptable act' in his autobiography, and the reason for his premature resignation) was born. Offices of the Police Complaints Board were set up in London, with a staff of civil servants, appointed by political patronage under Lord Plowden, to oversee the investigation of police officers by police officers - a matter highly disapproved of in many circles. Every force opened its own complaints department with a Superintendent in charge, and a number of lower ranks and civilians to staff it. One of the objects, we were told, was to give the public confidence and satisfy them that their complaints would be investigated fairly and properly. It miserably failed to achieve this objective. No complainant is ever satisfied unless he gets his own way.

The law relating to complaints against police was revised in the Police & Criminal Evidence Act 1984. The 'Board' was now the Police Complaints Authority. In October 1993, the Home Secretary announced a further package of proposals to deal with police misconduct, intended to be part of a new Police Bill. The proposals once again were fiercely opposed by the police, and the Police Federation has said "It's not justice, it's oppression". In 2002 a new Police Reform Bill was passed, Part II of which introduced the Police Complaints Commission, a bigger and better stick to beat the police with. How's that for empire building?

Following the introduction of the Police Complaints Board in 1976, much publicity was given to how members of the public could go about making a complaint against the police - indeed in the press they were virtually encouraged to do so. A leaflet was printed in many different languages to be given to anyone who wanted to know how to go about it. Ironically these leaflets were available at all police stations. A complaint could be about anything at all, from the manner the officer spoke to a member of the public to giving false evidence in court. The public could - and often do - complain about a police officer's conduct while off duty. Initially these are all given credence by the 'Investigating Officer' who has to be a Superintendent, and much paperwork results.

The officer being investigated is first served with a notice telling him of the substance of the complaint. In more serious cases or where the allegation is of a criminal offence, he might well be suspended from duty for a long period while the matter is dealt with.

A situation now exists where a constable can investigate a serious crime and arrest the culprit, be he lord or peasant, but if a complaint is made that a police officer was drinking a cup of tea at the back of a shop while on duty, the investigating officer has to have the rank of Superintendent. The rank and file believe that they do not have the same rights as a member of the public who is 'innocent until proven guilty' they are quite clearly 'guilty until proven innocent' - why else would they be suspended? The police are the only public body - or private one for that matter - who have this statutory framework of complaints imposed upon them, constantly plaguing, and interfering with, their daily work. They resent this distinction quite strongly.

Complaining against the police soon became almost routine for the 'criminal classes' - if I dare use such words - who, caught red-handed committing some crime or other would complain that the officer assaulted them, or put words into their mouths at an interview. Solicitors too saw it as a 'ploy' in the defence game, which could often be used to the advantage of a client. Although such complaints are usually put aside until after the court case, they are not forgotten, and following a conviction, if the complainant did not withdraw it, the officer, who had been 'served' his notice and been under threat since the complaint was made, is investigated. One might well ask why, when the matter had been fully aired at court.

Making a false complaint against a police officer is a criminal offence, because it wastes police time to investigate. The police thought initially that this fact would deter false complaints, but there is no evidence that it does. The great majority of complaints against the police are unsubstantiated. Many of them are false and made out of malice, or to try and mitigate the complainant's own wrong doing. Seldom, if ever, is a prosecution brought against the complainant. Perhaps it is thought that such action by the police would seem rancorous, or might deter a genuine complainant, one wonders.

In a very short time the number of complaints grew to great proportions. Complaints departments expanded in size and stature, and soon every Superintendent in a force found that in addition to his proper supervisory duties he had a caseload of matters to investigate, delegated by the Deputy Chief Constable, who is the person in a provincial police force responsible for 'Complaints and Discipline'.

The annual report of the Complaints Authority, as one might expect, serves mainly to justify its own existence. Statistics show that in the County of Essex, where I served, there were 540 complaints in 1991, of which only two disciplinary charges resulted (Chief Constable's Annual Report 1991). You can easily multiply these figures by the 43 forces in England & Wales, plus of course the Met, to see what a colossal amount of time and public money is expended on this exercise.

If only one were able to work out the precise cost in money, and loss of police time for other duties! The price the public are paying to satisfy a few minority groups with questionable motives that their police forces are 'squeaky clean' would interest, perhaps even alarm them. At one time investigating officers had to log time and mileage spent on investigations. I often wonder what happened to these figures.

Governments are very good at setting up departments to deal with certain problems. The trouble is that when the problem has gone, the department stays. No one could now say that we have a corrupt or dishonest police service, and yet here we have a great machine churning away at great public expense to investigate complaints, the majority of which are trivial in the extreme, totally false, or made by persons whose own criminal conduct was responsible for their initial contact with the officer concerned.

In 1964 Regional Crime Squads were formed throughout the country for the purpose of combating the theft of lorries and their loads, prevalent at that time. Lorries and their valuable loads were being stolen by the hundreds nationwide. Within two years this offence had been practically eliminated, due to the work of the RCS, but we still had the Crime Squads for years afterwards, generally undisciplined and autonomous squads of men drifting around the counties trying to find something to do. They could have been far better utilised back in their Home Counties and divisions. No one had the courage to disband them, although since that time, at huge cost, they have done work of questionable value and were certainly not 'cost effective.' The RCS has now been superseded by the National Crime Squad and more recently the National Crime Agency. More empire building?

Remember the 'quangos' (quasi-autonomous non-governmental organisations) set up during the last war? It took years to get rid of these, long after they ceased to serve any useful purpose.

Officers have generally adapted to living under the new complaints system, as they have adapted to new laws and procedures since the time Sir Robert Peel first introduced them on the streets of London in 1829. They do not like it, however. Constantly under threat of investigation, the once-conscientious officer is now 'going by the book', the less conscientious believing that 'if in doubt, do nothing' is the best policy.

For many years the police of this country, who by tradition police by consent of the public, invented little tricks of the trade, rules of thumb and other unofficial ways of dealing with situations. How often have you heard someone say of the police, "In my day they would have given Johnny a clip round the ear, then taken him home where he'd have got another one from his Pa"? Today that same officer knows that he would be prosecuted for assault and lose his job if he dealt with Johnny in this way.

I was once asked to investigate a complaint against two officers who had been on patrol one night and driven past three youths who had shouted as they passed, "Fuck off coppers". The car stopped and the officers got out to speak to the youths to warn them of their conduct. They were treated to a tirade of the most obscene and abusive language. The officers arrested the three, and at the station they were charged with behaving in a manner likely to cause a breach of the peace. Subsequently the Crown Prosecution Service decided not to prosecute. They argued that a breach of the peace was not likely, as the officers were there to prevent it. Despite police protests and the quoting of case law on the subject, the CPS would not relent. The parents of the youths then complained that their sons had been harassed and arrested needlessly.

As the investigating officer I had to go and see these louts and their parents, and then interview the officers. I was expected to soothe the parents and let them believe I thought their complaint was reasonable, or else they would have complained against me! Subsequently, although the complaint was unsubstantiated, the officers were warned as to their future conduct. In answer to a question as to what he should do again in a similar situation he said, "Drive on and ignore them".

When I served as a young constable, the local youths knew that if they assaulted a police officer they would, the very next morning, go to prison for six months. There was nothing more certain than that in Romford. Magistrates in those days were very supportive of their constables. The three youths in the foregoing example would undoubtedly have been charged with assault on police in days gone by and probably had a thick ear to boot. I was assaulted only once in two years at Romford. Today officers are assaulted daily, and more often than not, the defendant will allege that he too was assaulted by the officer, who will be duly served with a notice of complaint and investigated, perhaps suspended.

Today the old-fashioned methods once used by police

that most of the public appreciated, and I believe would still appreciate, have disappeared. Officers operate strictly to rule, although I doubt anyone would wish to describe it as such. The rule book, Police Standing Orders, gets ever larger, and officers dare not bend or manipulate them by using their own initiative, lest they fall foul of the complaints system.

Even prospects of promotion are affected by the 'brown envelope' attached to an officer's record, which contains 'For Eyes Only' particulars of former complaints - even those that have been unsubstantiated - against an individual.

Almost daily I hear or read about comments from members of the public who have called the police for some reason and are dissatisfied with the action taken. The police officer has tried to explain that he has done everything he officially can, but the public want more. They will only get more if they support the police officer when he acts in a positive and forthright manner. It has been said that the public get the police force they deserve, and I heartily support this view. If the public want a police force that can win the fight against crime, somehow it will have to raise its voice against the minority whose cry is always louder, more persuasive and motivated by self-interest. You cannot put a canary in with a fighting cock and expect it to win.

In an earlier paragraph I referred to the Sheehy report as an exercise in cost effectiveness, and said this meant trying to get the same results for less money. I have discussed Sheehy with former colleagues as well as my local Member of Parliament, but there is no mention in that report of saving money by disbanding the Police Complaints Authority (Now the Police Complaints Commission), which would, I suggest, save many millions of pounds each year, and give the police back thousands of man hours to use more effectively in the battle against crime.

What is even more important is that police forces would then, in time, get back to policing without the constant fear of criticism, which will almost certainly be dealt with as a 'complaint'. My third and last contention, if you haven't already guessed, is that the present complaints system is an unnecessary and expensive institution which seriously affects the efficiency of the police service.

A senior civil servant, speaking a while ago on television in opposition to the Home Secretary's declared determination to 'get tough' with the criminal, said inter alia that the police would be 'confused' if they now had to change from their present community policing role and start 'feeling collars and arresting villains'. I think he is out of touch with the current mood of the police, who would, for the most part be delighted to get back to 'feeling collars and arresting villains' and to give up their present duties, which seem to many to be those of just another branch of the social services.

How many Home Secretaries have talked about being 'tough on crime'? Talked is the operative word; you can never get tough on crime without a police force unhampered by the fear of petty complaints and by punishing offenders for their misdeeds rather than blaming others for them.

# Rioting in the Community

In the criminal law of most countries, riot is an offence committed against public order involving three or more persons and the use of violence, however slight. Like an unlawful assembly, a riot involves the gathering together of persons for an unlawful purpose. Unlike an unlawful assembly however, a riot includes violence. The concept is obviously a broad one involving a wide range of group conduct, from a bloody clash between pickets and strike-breakers to the behaviour of a street corner gang.

In Anglo-American legal systems, the offence lies mainly in the breach of the peace that riot causes. Under the Continental European codes, the offence requires the interference with, or resistance to, public authority. Our own laws relating to Unlawful Assembly, Rout, Riot, Affray and Breach of the Peace were all common law crimes, varied by statute from time to time, until 1986. A new Public Order

Act of that year repealed all previous legislation, updated old offences and created new ones. It was considered by some and hoped by many that this would cure the evils of our society, which by that date had festered and then, for a variety of reasons, erupted into commonplace public disorder, violence and outrage.

Two of the most important duties of the civil police are the maintenance of order and the protection of life and property. In recent months it has been apparent to many law-abiding citizens, the vast majority of our society, that the police have been finding it more difficult to carry out these duties effectively. There is a vast difference between sitting in a comfortable office in Whitehall passing laws that give the police a power of arrest and being one of a relatively small number of officers confronted by hundreds of raging demonstrators. In such a case, the arrest of one or more of the number would be likely to enrage the others still further. Another problem for the police is that for every arrest, their numbers at the scene are depleted by at least one, and often with violent and disruptive persons, by considerably more than one.

Does this mean that law and order has effectively broken down, or that the more aggressive in our society may now commit offences and breaches of the peace without fear of arrest, punishment or any other sanctions at all?

## PUBLIC DEMONSTRATIONS

We have seen public demonstrations in support of many

causes in the past few years, but perhaps the one that has caused the greatest strain on police resources and public funds during the early part of 1995 was the campaign against the export of live animals. It was the main objective of the anarchists who organised and took part in this campaign to bankrupt police services, and force them to divert their resources away from day-to-day policing. All members of society are entitled to hold views on this subject. All persons, that is, except police officers who are expected to do their duty whatever their personal feelings. Many otherwise quite normal people are, it seems, enraged by the thought of live animals being exported for slaughter. Many citizens who have never before been in conflict with the police, old age pensioners and children, suddenly became involved in serious confrontations with authority. Some police officers may sympathise with them, although this should not interfere with their zeal in enforcing the law. Does it in fact do so?

What is it that turns ordinary law-abiding citizens into a lawless rabble, cursing and spitting at police, sending them obscene mail and telephone calls, blocking roads, threatening violence against anyone who does not agree with their point of view and even urging their very young children to join in this process?

Just as every member of the community is entitled to hold and express a view about this activity, so surely are others in society entitled to what was once known as the Queen's Peace. That is to say the right to expect that they can go about their daily lives and lawful business without let or hindrance and especially without interference from minority groups, who inevitably will use any demonstration, march or protest to further their anarchistic ambitions, anti-government views or other political motives, and are always prepared to use violent means to prevent others from exercising their own more peaceful rights. I have heard it said by a senior police officer that "the police service is being used to come between those who are trying to ply their lawful trade and those who have a lawful right to peacefully protest in order to prevent violence". Is this really the case? The very fact that police have had to wear 'riot gear' in which to perform this task is a clear indication of how they see this job. After all you don't wear riot gear to police a peaceful protest.

These words also imply that there is some legislation that gives people the right to protest peacefully. There is not. In an unprecedented letter to every household in Brightlingsea, where most of this protest took place, the Assistant Chief Constable wrote, "Be noisy, make your protest in accordance with your legal right to do so, but please stay within the law". People in this country can of course do whatever they like if they do not break the criminal law or interfere with the civil rights of others. Many would argue therefore that because people are assembled merely to peacefully protest - encouraged it seems by the police, to exercise this questionable right - any subsequent violence that results because of confrontation, can be excused and blamed upon police provocation, or the actions of those against whom the protest is directed. This is not however the legal position. Protest is a public, often organised, manifestation of dissent.

When it is directed towards other members of the community who are behaving lawfully, how can such a protest be, or remain for long, either peaceful or lawful?

What then is the legal position? What laws do the police have to enforce? What do the public expect of the police in these situations? And what other factors influence the way in which various police forces deal with such matters in practice? The law is there to be enforced, no one can seriously argue otherwise. It is not the prerogative of any police officer to decide which laws to administer, which to ignore. Yet on occasions it does seem to the citizen that those, whom the law should protect, are the ones who suffer most when riots take place. Let us then look in more detail at the law, passed in 1986 to protect us from rioters and the like. (Public Order Act 1986).

## OFFENCES

The most serious crime created by this legislation is that of Riot. The offence is committed when twelve or more persons who are present together use or threaten unlawful violence for a common purpose, and the conduct of these persons is such as would cause a person of reasonable firmness, present at the scene, to fear for his personal safety. One might ask, "What is unlawful violence?" I cannot think of any sensible answer to why the word 'unlawful' was included here. It seems to imply that there could be cases of riot excused because the violence was lawful, a suggestion too absurd for further argument.

It is the law that such conduct may be committed in private as well as public places, that it matters not whether all twelve or more people threaten violence simultaneously, nor whether a person of reasonable firmness is actually present at the scene, merely that if one were, then he or she might fear for their safety. It is also written into the act that the common purpose may be inferred from the general conduct of those present. The maximum penalty for this arrestable offence is ten years' imprisonment or a substantial fine or both. It must be tried on indictment, and is clearly regarded by those who make the laws as a very serious crime indeed.

Well now, what has been happening on our streets since the Act was passed, particularly at ports around the country and at one airport, Coventry? On a daily basis several hundred persons attended at these locations together, and in the streets nearby. They chanted, waved offensive placards and hurled bricks and other missiles at police and lorries loaded with calves or sheep bound for the Continent. This export trade is a perfectly lawful activity. Protesters have crowded round the lorries and aircraft, sometimes chaining themselves to the axles and to one another, or engaging in other dangerous and unlawful acts. Attempts by the police to remove these people were met with resistance. The drivers of the lorries would all tell you that they feared for their own safety. The fact that a woman was killed under the wheels of a lorry at Coventry is evidence that safety is in jeopardy at these events.

Incidentally, eye witnesses have told me that these so-called animal lovers who were hurling bricks at the lorries, were quite happy for their missiles to hit the poor creatures, by this time in a state of panic, and far less happy than had they been left alone. Do not the circumstances of these events constitute a riot? I suggest that they surely do.

The next most serious crime defined by the Public Order Act is that of Violent Disorder. This offence is exactly similar to riot, except that there need be only three or more persons present together for a common purpose and who use or threaten unlawful violence etc. This offence carries a maximum penalty of five years' imprisonment. It can however be tried summarily at a magistrates' court, where the maximum penalty is six months' imprisonment or a fine (or both).

The only difference between the offences of Violent Disorder and Riot is the number of persons involved. If parliament thought that twelve persons present together and threatening violence was a serious crime, what of several hundred?

The next crime in order of seriousness is Affray. In years past, this was the most serious common law offence involving public disorder. Now a person is guilty of affray if he uses, or threatens, unlawful violence towards another, and his conduct is such as would cause a person of reasonable firmness to fear for his safety. Here there need be no common purpose, and the threat has to be more than just the use of words. The offence carries a punishment of three years' imprisonment on indictment, or six months and a fine if dealt with summarily.

Because the maximum sentence is less than five years

(which would make it an arrestable offence), the Act gives police officers a specific power of arrest for this crime.

The next section of the Act defines the offence of Fear or Provocation of Violence, formerly known as Breach of the Peace. This section of the Act defines the offence: A person is guilty of this offence if he uses towards another person any threatening, abusive or insulting words or behaviour, or distributes or displays to another person any writing, sign or other visible representation which is threatening or abusive. In this offence there has to be an intention on the part of the offender to cause the other person to believe that unlawful violence will be used. The behaviour or display of writing, signs etc, has to be within sight of a person who is likely to be caused harassment, alarm or distress by it. The police have power to arrest such an offender only if he continues the behaviour, display etc after a warning to stop. The maximum penalty is a fine of £1000.

It would be reasonable I suggest to deduce that the Government of the day, fearful that this new law would be unpopular, since it was obviously created to prevent the public from demonstrating (other than peacefully), wrote into it a statutory defence under the heading 'Mental Element'. This means that it is necessary for the prosecutor to prove not only that the behaviour complained of was violent, threatening, abusive etc but that the offender actually intended that it should be so. The old presumption that a person is responsible for the natural consequences of his actions seems, in this Act, to have been specifically written out of the law. Does not the question 'Why?' come again immediately to mind? A reasonable man might wonder how a person shouting abuse and throwing bricks at police officers could possibly argue that he did not intend his behaviour to be violent, threatening or abusive. It would surely make more sense to put the onus upon the defendant that he had no such intention.

## PREVENTION OF DAMAGE

An interesting aspect of the present law, seldom applied except in Northern Ireland, allows the police to give directions to persons organising or taking part in a public assembly. If, having regard to the circumstances, the Chief Officer of Police considers that such an assembly may result in serious public disorder, damage to property etc or that the purpose of the assembly is the intimidation of others, with a view to compelling them not to do an act they have a right to do, then this part of the Public Order Act (Section 14) may be applied. It allows the Chief Officer of Police to direct when and where such an assembly might take place, the number of persons involved and its duration.

If after such direction has been given, either verbally (if the assembly has already occurred) or in writing (in the case of a future event), the person organising the assembly, or any person taking part, who fails to comply may be arrested. The penalty is three months' imprisonment or a £2500 fine. A 'public assembly' consists of 20 or more persons in a public place or in the open air.

The police still have a liability to pay for damage caused by a riot (Riot Damages Act 1886) so one would think it was in their interests, and also that of the public, to implement this particular part of the Public Order Act where appropriate. One can hardly think of a more appropriate case than that of several hundred persons under the collective name of BALE (Brightlingsea Against Live Exports) who daily threatened to turn back lorries laden with sheep for export at the local docks and disrupt the life of the town.

It seems common sense to some, particularly to those who, while sympathising with the genuine protesters, do not turn out to protests at these daily assemblies, that if the sheep are exported on Mondays, Wednesdays and Fridays, the protests should be allowed by the police only on Tuesdays, Thursdays and Saturdays and limited to a manageable crowd.

## PROOF

It is surprising to many that having amended the law relating to public disorder as recently as 1986 (Public Order Act 1986), following a number of serious outbreaks of disorder - including the one that resulted in the death of Police Constable Blakelock the new law seems just as ineffective as the old. Is this because the law is hard to enforce and the offences difficult to prove?

Take the Brightlingsea case in particular (Operation Gunfleet it was called), as it was on my own doorstep. It was ongoing for ten weeks, over one and a half million pounds of extra expenditure was incurred for the huge police presence required daily, and only a small number of persons were arrested (280 up to 29 March 1995). Of these 76 were charged, mostly with offences of obstruction, either of the police or the highway. Many have been released without charge, or 'De-Arrested' as allowed by PACE.

One lady boasted that after five hours in police cells she was released without charge, but refused to quit the police station until, as is her right, she had been supplied with a meal. This was duly provided and she sat in the cell with the door open and took her time to eat it before walking free.

Case law, however, does provide some help in proving offences under the Public Order Act. For example, in the absence of identification to show that a defendant was part of a group of people arrested, a magistrate may take judicial notice of the due process of arrest, charge and bail, and where a defendant appears in court and pleads to the charge in his name, he has a case to answer (Allen v. Ireland (1984) WLR 903, 148JP545).

Insulting behaviour does not lose its insulting character because the persons who have witnessed it have not been insulted (Parkin v. Norman (1983) 2 All ER 583), and behaviour may be insulting even though it is not deliberately aimed at a particular person or persons, if in fact it could be insulting to any member of the public who might see it (Masterson v. Holden 1986 3 All ER 39).

In determining whether violence is likely to result from threatening, abusive or insulting behaviour, it is proper to take account of the reaction of others who might have observed the behaviour, apart from the persons to whom the behaviour was addressed (Parkin v. Norman (1983) 2 All ER 583).

# ENFORCEMENT

Why then, one asks, does the law passed to prevent public disorder apparently not apply to incidents such as the current wave of animal rights protests, anti-hunt demonstrations or even the 'poll tax' uproar? If such events are not riots, then why do the police attend in numbers dressed in riot gear? If, on the contrary they are riots, why is the law not enforced? Do not youths wearing balaclava helmets, waving wooden sticks and banners, throwing bricks, spitting and cursing at the police and others who are pursuing their lawful trade constitute an offence under the Public Order Act? Do not all those who associate themselves with these rioters place themselves in the same category? Is the Act really unenforceable?

Many police officers think it is. How can they, they ask, arrest a crowd of several hundred persons? How can they prove specific offences by individuals?

The Chief of Police, not, as many think, the Government, has the right to request the assistance of the Army to maintain peace and public order. What Chief of Police however, is likely to admit that he is unable to fulfil this, his own particular responsibility, without help? The means are available to deal with a large crowd of persons committing public disorder, and yet we constantly see that they are not employed.

Similar protests in Europe usually last for one day only. There they have a 'third force' to deal with rioters, and do not depend upon the civil police. After being doused with water cannons, belted with heavy truncheons and/or heavily fined in court, the so-called peaceful protesters invariably decide to carry on their protest, if at all, by writing to their MP, or better yet to take up some other less painful and frustrating occupation.

The attitude of the Essex Police, concerning Operation Gunfleet, has been from the outset, "To defend the right to demonstrate lawfully, but equally to keep the highway open for legal trade". What seems to have been missed is that the actions of the people who attend daily at Brightlingsea to obstruct the roads by force and obstruct the police in their duty to keep them open are not lawful. What would occur if the police did not turn up to 'police' this event each day? Surely we know, and the police know, hence their presence, that mayhem would ensue.

## THE SOFT OPTION

Here it is, one feels, that politics creeps in to the enforcement process. 'Let us not antagonise the public, albeit it a tiny minority, by bringing the full weight of the law to bear upon them.' You can almost hear a politician uttering these words. How is this political influence, if it exists, communicated to the Chief Officers of Police around the country? It is not difficult for senior police officers to receive signals as to how the Home Office feels about matters such as this, even without written directives.

Today the decision whether to prosecute any offender is made by the Crown Prosecution Service, not the police. This is a very debatable subject, but it does mean that once the CPS has made a decision not to prosecute someone who was arrested by a police officer, there is a knock-on effect. The officer concerned and his colleagues, when the news percolates through, are not likely to make a similar arrest in the future, although it was, in the first case, perfectly justified. If officers know that arrests for certain matters are not welcome few will 'buck the system' or 'rock the boat', as is said in the trade.

It is well known in police circles that the CPS will always take the soft option when considering whether to prosecute following a police arrest. They consider, inter alia, the likely cost, the chances of obtaining a conviction, and, one presumes, the political climate. Former senior colleagues tell me that they have no confidence at all in the justice system, so why go to the bother of taking people to court?

What is the result of this policy? In the ten weeks of the Brightlingsea riots, for that is exactly what they were, what was achieved? By the protesters, absolutely nothing so far as their aims were concerned. They did of course achieve huge publicity and received much financial support thereby. The police have incurred a great deal of additional expenditure, a rift in police public relations that will probably never be repaired, depletion in the workforce for normal duties and great pressure on those who do remain on patrol and in offices. The public have experienced a loss of police services generally, considerable loss of trade in the area of the protests, and great disillusionment of the life and times in which we live. It is, of course, the public who will pick up the bill eventually by way of increased Council Tax or other taxes. The police from other areas are committed to selfish 'nimbies' and anarchists at Brightlingsea instead of chasing burglars, perverts and car thieves on their own patches.

What would have been achieved, I wonder, if on the first occasion that protesters arrived at Brightlingsea, they had been arrested for 'Threatening Violence' and dealt with by way of heavy fines? Some say worse riots would have followed, some that it would have ended the protests.

# Racism

In July 1995 Sir John Condon, the Metropolitan Police Commissioner, published some statistics showing that 80% of street robberies in the London area were committed by coloured men. One does not know the real purpose behind the publication of these figures, although the Commissioner stated that it was done after consultation with the local leaders of the black community. It was certain to be a controversial utterance, and I personally doubt whether it was made without prior consultation with the Home Office. The real purpose of making such pronouncements in public may or may not have some political objective. The results of making them are matters we can discuss and witness for ourselves.

As one might expect, the pronouncement brought immediate and loud cries of "Racist!" and for several days the press had a field day, dragging up once more the suggestion that the police are motivated by racial prejudice, and that they deal with coloured offenders differently from whites by discriminating against them. Indeed the argument is put in a way that suggests the police treat coloureds unjustly, that is to say they fabricate evidence and tell lies when it comes to dealing with coloured people. These are arguments I cannot accept, for reasons I will go into later.

It follows that the figures published by the Commissioner were not accepted by community leaders such as Bernie Grant and Paul Boateng, who presumably think the victims of street crimes are also racially prejudiced - the figures are of course based upon the descriptions of the offenders given by ordinary members of the public.

I personally believe that many of those who use the words 'racist' and 'prejudice' in relation to policemen and the coloured community have not recently looked up the words in a dictionary. It might be as well therefore to remind ourselves of the true meaning of these so frequently misused words.

Racism is the theory or idea that there is a link between inherited physical traits and certain traits of personality, intellect or culture and combined with it the notion that some races are inherently superior to others. It is the word 'superior' in this definition that causes those who support this theory to practise discrimination, and to be prejudiced against other ethnic, religious, linguistic or cultural groups.

People who believe these groups are different from ourselves, but not inferior, do not suffer from 'racism' as if it is some kind of disease. They have no problem accepting other groups within our society and making allowances for the differences in everyday life.

Racial discrimination denotes all forms of deferential behaviour based on race. The notable form of such discrimination is physical segregation, but there are many others. The term 'racial discrimination' always refers to behaviour, and indeed to social behaviour. The term 'wog' used to describe a black man is no more or less discriminatory than the term 'white honkey' used to describe a Caucasian. It was once quite common to use nouns such as this to distinguish between races; a 'Wop' for example meant an Italian and 'Frog' a Frenchman. There is nothing racial in the use of these words but they are usually insulting in the manner in which they are used. The Italians and the French no doubt have similar expressions for Englishmen. Today society has become so obsessed with the subject of racism in its throes of racial integration, that it has outlawed many such previously used words as racist rather than merely insulting.

A second aspect of racism is racial prejudice. Prejudice is a psychological phenomenon. It is defined as an attitude, usually emotional, acquired without, or prior to, adequate evidence or experience. An opinion held by someone, or by a group of persons based upon evidence and experience cannot, by this definition, be prejudice.

It is important to distinguish between the psychological and social aspects of racism, that is to say between prejudice and discrimination, although the two are closely linked. If society has set groups of persons apart and subjected some of them to discrimination, then it is likely that prejudice will develop within that society to justify its behaviour towards them. Conversely it is hard to envisage a society in which discrimination against groups within it is practised unless prejudice was present to begin with. In this case prejudice is the reason for the discrimination.

Charges of racism have frequently been made against the police in general and occasionally against certain officers in particular. Those who make these allegations are naturally from groups who feel they are discriminated against and who feel, or are persuaded by their leaders, that the reason for this discrimination is racial prejudice.

Some time ago I wrote an article about complaints against police in which I quoted statistics which showed that the vast majority of complaints are found, after investigation, to be unsubstantiated. It is also true that many complaints are made by persons who have had 'dealings' with the police, and whose complaint is made to try to mitigate their own misconduct. While there are likely to be bigots within the police service as well as in any other profession, or group with society, I have no doubt that such charges of racism are for the most part made with malice, and if investigated would be found unsubstantiated for the same reasons.

It is quite another matter to suggest that the police dislike, even hate, criminals. This is not prejudice, since to regard criminals as their enemy is their very reason to exist. As an officer progresses through his service, he sees the misery and injury caused by the criminal to our society. He sees also how society deals with them when caught. Perhaps he even sees himself as discriminated against.

# What a caution!
# The right of silence

The publication of the Criminal Justice and Public Order Act 1994 caused much debate among politicians, analysis by lawyers and tearing of hair by police officers. Perhaps the aspect that has caused the greatest despair among those sworn to keep the peace and enforce the law is the apparent desire to restrict even further the way police officers question suspects. It underlines the ever-widening and dangerous gap between the lawyers who anatomise evidence, long after an event, and those who have to deal with crime and criminals, and obtain that evidence, in conditions far removed from the courtroom.

Some provisions of a proposed new law (Police & Criminal Evidence Bill in 1984) were defeated in the House of Lords. The arguments for and against the proposals were widely publicised, sometimes with humorous comment by the media. The alleged 'removal of an accused's right of silence' has been most fiercely opposed. That was not, of course, the intention of the proposed new law.

None of the proposals in the Bill provoked such passionate condemnation of the Home Secretary, the Rt Hon Michael Howard QC, as the publication in August 1994 of 'his' proposed new Caution. This evoked almost as much humour as his earlier suggestion that Neighbourhood Watch should patrol the streets to help the police. The press (*Daily Mail* 22nd August 1994), usually a reflection of public feeling, described it as "Just the latest in a series of ministerial cock-ups, all of them foreseeable".

In America when a person is arrested they 'read the prisoner his rights' (the Miranda Warning). In this country the prisoner is 'cautioned'. The difference is buried deep in our legal histories, and that of our respective law enforcement methods. It is worth considering our own case somewhat more seriously than the media have done.

## JUDGES' RULES

It was as recently as 1984 when the Government, by means of the Police & Criminal Evidence Act, sought to cure the problems there had been in a few well-publicised cases with the way police dealt with suspects and prisoners. Many of the original proposals in the Bill were modified after pressure from the Association of Chief Police and Officers and others. It was another example of the real experts on law and order not being consulted until a very late stage in the process of law making.

For many years prior to PACE police officers had been guided by the Judges' Rules when questioning suspects, or indeed anyone. Most people recognise, quite fairly, that a person in police custody can be misled, tricked or even beaten to make him confess. The Rules, drafted many years ago by the most senior High Court Judges, were for the guidance of police. They were not the law, but woe betide anyone who did not obey them.

The rules were made for a number of stated reasons: first to standardise the procedure for questioning people in the many different police forces in the land; second to ensure that there should be no misconduct by police officers when questioning suspects; and most important of all, to ensure that anything said by a suspect which the police wanted to give in evidence should be admissible.

The first rule, the most important one in my view, was that "When a police officer is seeking to discover the author of a crime he may question any person whom he thinks may be able to help him in his enquiries". The rules went on to say that when the police officer had evidence that the person he was questioning was the author of a crime he should caution him in the following terms: "You are not obliged to say anything unless you wish to do so, but whatever you say will be taken down in writing and may be given in evidence".

It was not essential to use these actual words, as long as the person concerned understood the nature of the caution. Police officers were taught that they could question someone as long as they wanted to without caution, provided they did not later seek to give what the suspect or prisoner said before being cautioned in evidence. This is why a police officer's evidence often read, "I had a long conversation with the accused, and he then said, 'All right guv. It was me wot done it.' I cautioned him and he replied....."

The reason police cautioned people therefore, until PACE, was not to let them know their rights, but to ensure that the case against them in court, if it relied upon the accused's confession, would stick. For many years these rules worked well, until lawyers began to realise that all they had to do to get an accused off was to assert that any incriminating words or written statements attributed to their client were obtained under duress, or by other improper means. Alternatively, and better still, that their client did not make the statement, or utter the words at all.

We have all heard the word 'verballing' to describe the process of putting words into an accused's mouth. One has to admit this has occurred, but I venture to suggest on far fewer occasions than it has been alleged.

More and more cases were thrown out of court after such allegations, which were as unsubstantiated in many cases as they were ridiculous. For example accused persons have been acquitted after swearing on oath that they were intimidated by being in the police station, and confessed merely to get out. The defence had only to sow the seed of doubt, often elegantly expressed by expensive counsel. It seemed to the police that they could do nothing to prevent such calamities. Then came PACE.

## PACE

Whatever the rights and wrongs of PACE from a police officer's point of view, it is now the law. With it came several codes of practice for the police to digest and follow. I will deal here only with questioning of members of the public. The police guidance for the questioning of suspects etc is contained in the Code of Practice for the Detention, Treatment and Questioning of Persons by Police Officers. The code is not law, but has the effect of law.

Since the arrival of PACE it has seemed to many that the courts seek to punish police officers who do not comply with the Code of Practice to the letter, by letting their prisoners off scot free. This is a mistaken view, since it is not the police who suffer, except from frustration, it is the public.

It is interesting that although the Code of Practice purports to cover the questioning of all persons by the police, the Act itself only deals with suspects and persons in custody. Nowhere in the Code, apart from the title, can one find any reference to questioning members of the public who are not 'detained' or 'in custody at police stations.' Part V of PACE itself tells us that the Act codifies police powers and responsibilities for the questioning and treatment of detained persons.

There were now some subtle, but important, differences in the way police officers could question suspects. One of these is that the new code says, inter alia, "A person whom there are grounds to suspect of an offence must be cautioned..." The difference is that a police officer has only to have 'grounds to suspect'. Prior to PACE he had to have actual 'evidence'. A huge difference! In the past, for example, you could question a suspect because the modus operandi used in a crime was the same as the one used previously by your suspect. It was not evidence, and you could still question him without caution. Under PACE you could not. The caution too was changed; it was now somewhat shorter: "You do not have to say anything unless you wish to do so, but what you say may be given in evidence".

The need to write down what the accused has said was omitted. Perhaps someone realised that when you are arresting a violent man in a torrential storm, it is not always easy to get out your pocket book and write down his reply, even if you could understand his vernacular. No, the alteration was undoubtedly made with tape-recorders in mind.

The code also insists that a person must be cautioned once there are grounds to suspect, before any further questions are put to him for the purpose of obtaining evidence... etc. It follows, in theory at least, that an arrest might be unlawful if the caution was not administered at the appropriate point, even if the prisoner said nothing further and sat upon his right to remain silent. It does suggest also that if your grounds for suspicion are the suspect's verbal confession, you need not caution unless you wish to ask further questions. The code of practice was in this respect, so far as the police were concerned, a very badly worded piece of advice indeed.

Since the 1984 Act things have not improved. The problems the Police and Criminal Evidence Act sought to solve are, it seems, still with us, and Criminal Justice Acts since then have attempted what PACE had failed to achieve.

The procedure for interviewing suspects at a police station is dealt with in the code of practice in minute detail. Records, recording, documentation etc are all provided with rules that the police have to obey. Reading through the code of practice one might think there could never be any excuse for a suspect, or prisoner, to complain that a statement, or confession, was made under pressure of any kind.

Is it merely because the court is told the prisoner was cautioned that any verbal statement made by him/her afterwards is viewed with such suspicion? Is it the natural assumption of an upright honest citizen, lawyer, juror or even judge that having been 'cautioned' no one in their right mind would say anything to incriminate themselves, and that ipso facto the police officer must be lying? Is this the cross the police, and the public, have to bear for the misdeeds of a few police officers in the past?

Perhaps it is. Perhaps this is why it is so easy for an accused person at the time of his trial to allege all kinds of intimidation, threats or even just that he didn't feel well, in order to escape the consequences of his criminal conduct and big mouth. Perhaps it is not the right of silence that some would seek to remove, but the right to confess!

In practice, there are very few prisoners who will not talk to you. Most seek to justify their actions, or to deny at great length what has been alleged. Many readily confess when confronted with the evidence. As long ago as 1953, when I joined the then Essex Constabulary, young recruits were told, "If you've got the evidence, don't worry about a confession. If that gets thrown out, your case will be lost, no matter what other evidence you have". In later years I have often repeated this to young officers, but many of them, in spite of that, have written down a statement under caution only to have it torn to shreds by lawyers when he got to court. Sometimes you just can't shut prisoners up. In those cases it used to be the practice to give the accused a pencil and paper and tell him to write his own confession. A procedure more difficult, today as prisoners are not always literate in English.

It is ironic that evidence discovered by the police as a direct result of something the accused said while not under caution is still admissible evidence. The fact that it was found as the result of what the prisoner said is not (Edwards' Creameries Ltd v. Smith (1922) 86JP155). Even as far back as 1922 it is evident that the caution was aimed, not at repressing the recovery of the stolen property or the murder weapon but at restricting the evidence of police officers. In practice it has become a rebuttable presumption of law that, in respect of verbal confessions, a police officer is lying and that his memory is fallible.

## THE NEW CAUTION

Let us then look at what all the fuss has been about. The wording of the new caution was to begin with: "You do not have to say anything, but if you do not mention now something which you later use in your defence, the court may decide that your failure to mention it now strengthens the case against you. A record will be made of anything you say and it may be given if you are brought to trial".

Not surprisingly criticisms were made of this caution, 'It is too long for officers to remember', 'Prisoners would not understand it or its implications' and 'Lawyers in court would have a field day picking holes in it'. I can think of others.

Let us first look at the reason for the new caution. It seems that, unlike the Judges' Rule caution, this one is not merely to ensure that evidence is obtained properly, but also to inform a prisoner of a change in the law. In this land it has always been said that ignorance of the law is no excuse. Surely few criminals in the future will be ignorant of the fact that their right of silence has been modified. It has not been taken away, as many newspaper articles have asserted. The innocent will still have nothing to dread from remaining silent, and the guilty, one hopes, everything to fear from cooking up lies and excuses at a later date which might now be exposed more easily.

Why then should it be necessary to remind a prisoner (or suspect) of this change in the law before he is questioned? It would make just as much sense to explain to him the law relating to the offence under investigation, that theft means the unlawful appropriation of the property of another with the intention of permanently depriving him of it, etc.

One suspects the notion that a prisoner's right of silence can, if exercised, be used as evidence against him is such a revolutionary idea that the Home Secretary, or those who advise him, have had some serious misgivings. Is this caution perhaps a way of salving their own consciences, or in anticipation of whimpering of minority groups?

After much deliberation and realisation of the

implications the 'new' caution was revised yet again and is now: "You do not have to say anything. But it may harm your defence if you do not mention when questioned something which you later rely on in Court. Anything you do say may be given in evidence".

The Code of Practice goes on to say: "I am going to ask you some questions. You do not have to answer any of them unless you want to. But if you go to court and say something there which you have not told me about, and they think you could have told me, it may harm your case. Anything you do say may be repeated in court".

Is it really anything so very new? The right of silence has already been removed in respect of alibis (s.11 C.J. Act 1967). A prisoner's right of silence has always been a two-edged sword. Take the example of an officer giving evidence, "I pointed to the stolen jewels on his kitchen table and said, 'would you care to give me an explanation for your possession of these stolen jewels?' I cautioned him and he made no reply".

What would a jury make of that? Suppose the defendant later gave evidence that some unknown chap had asked him to look after them for him. Would not the accused's earlier silence weigh heavily against him? Of course it would. It is an insult to our jury system to treat 'good men and true' as if they were incompetent. Surely they would not be on a jury if they were!

The fact that the caution is full of legal jargon is obviously a serious handicap to it being ever used properly, except in a police station where it can be read out to the prisoner from a suitable card. The more words it contains, the more mistakes the police officer can make and the more loopholes a lawyer might find. In any case the wording is quite inappropriate for the day-to-day questioning of people by police officers, some of whom will be suspects, but who will never be arrested or charged with any offence. Blinded by a misplaced sympathy for criminals, has someone forgotten the purpose of cautioning a suspect? Have they forgotten also that it is out on the street, sometimes in very 'exciting' circumstances, where questioning takes place, and the caution is administered, not in a cosy police station?

## PRACTICAL DIFFICULTIES

The new caution uses the words "your defence" and "court". The older caution merely informed the suspect that what was said "may be used in evidence", quite possibly in someone else's trial. However the Code of Practice says that a person must be cautioned if an officer has grounds to suspect him/her of an offence. There are many occasions when an officer will have such grounds, whether because of hearsay, a previous record for similar offences, or just the circumstances. It would be absurd to first caution such a person in terms that refer to his defence, the case against him and his trial.

It might be possible to define more specifically what 'grounds for suspicion' means, but that sort of fine-tuning is for lawyers, not for police officers trying to do the job in practice.

One can presume that a police officer's common law right

to question people other than suspects and persons in custody, in pursuance of their enquiries into crime, and reinforced by the Judges Rules, has not been 'codified' by PACE. It follows that officers will often be questioning a person when there are no grounds for suspicion, but during such interview a confession is made. There are several precedents for this, and such confessions have usually been accepted, provided the caution is administered as soon as possible afterwards. It is still however a matter for argument in court.

If police officers are to be hampered even further by such legal red tape, surely some of them are going to try to 'get round it' for, as they see it, the best possible motives, ie the conviction of the criminal.

Except for interviews conducted in police stations under the antiseptic conditions of PACE, the only opportunity for an officer to manipulate what is said by a prisoner is at the time of the arrest. No one but the officer(s) and the prisoner will know exactly when and how the caution was given, and this will continue to be a source of controversy in the witness box. The only way to subvert this, if Police Officers are all to be considered liars, is to haul the prisoner off immediately to a local court, and to admit in evidence at a later trial only what he has said to a magistrate.

Another real difficulty to be considered is the position of undercover police officers, who cannot reveal their identities to criminals. The work of such officers, working as they do under great pressure and in dangerous situations, often includes obtaining incriminating evidence from the mouths of criminals. Are they not to be allowed to give this evidence against them? If the answer to this is 'yes' then one must ask why. Are these officers any more truthful than their conventional colleagues are? If the answer is 'no' then surely undercover work will be a thing of the past. Officers seeing all their efforts frustrated at court would not volunteer for such hazardous work.

## OTHER FORESEEABLE PROBLEMS

Many persons who are interviewed by the police are nervous and guilt-ridden, whether or not they committed the offence under enquiry. Some offences are more complex than others, and an explanation, if given, might be long and involved. Many prisoners, in my own experience, will wish to say nothing at the time of their arrest. It is, as has been said, their right, and in their confusion the best and most truthful answer to a question might not be apparent to them. A person might, for example, have a perfect alibi in the shape of another sexual partner, but being married would not want to reveal this. There could be a thousand and one reasons why a person being interviewed might not want to answer questions at the time of his arrest. It would be unreasonable to hold this against him/her, and indeed it seems to me that this is not the intention, since the caution says that the court may decide that failure to mention it before strengthens the case, etc. This leaves the whole question about whether the 'silence' was or was not reasonable to the court's discretion. It will lead to long and expensive trials within trials, making proceedings at court even lengthier than at present. Usually such a trial within a trial is to decide whether some damning piece of evidence should go to the jury. Here they would be discussing something the jury already knows, or is bound to know in due course. Only the effect of the 'silence' on the minds of the jury is in question. You cannot really expect members of the jury to disregard an incriminating piece of evidence once they have seen (or not heard) it, even if you tell them to.

Perhaps even more relevant is the fact that any admission made after the caution has been administered could be said to have been obtained under duress. I confidently forecast that the first time this matter is tested, the accused will say he only made an admission because he was told that if he did not, this fact would be held against him at court. What a dreadful rod we are making for our own backs!

The rules introduced by PACE only apply to police officers. Today on the streets there are almost as many security officers as there are constables. There are private citizens, and perhaps we will even have 'Dad's Constabulary' - the Neighbourhood Watch. All of these have powers of arrest under the law.

The difference between the power of arrest for an arrestable offence, given to a constable and that possessed by a private citizen is that the latter must actually witness the crime (grounds to suspect, one would think!) Such crimes as theft and criminal damage are arrestable offences, as well as those some people might regard as more serious. It would be unreasonable for any court to refuse to admit a confession or incriminating statement made to a private citizen because he/she wasn't cautioned. This seems to suggest that in the eyes of the court a private citizen's evidence is more reliable than a police officer's.

## CONCLUSIONS

Whatever happened to common sense? Magistrates at lower courts know the score; they generally know who is telling the truth and who is lying. Surely the common sense of magistrates, jurors and High Court judges should be sufficient to decide whether a person's silence should be held against him or not.

Often in the summing up at a trial, the judge warns the jury that they should not hold against a defendant the fact that they did not give evidence. The judge, however, often comments on that very fact in his summing up, something he, and he alone, is entitled to do. This clearly leads the jury to the same conclusion reached by the judge.

There seem to me to be two separate matters here. First the question of admissibility of a statement made by an accused, and secondly a person's right of silence. The two are quite distinct and should not be linked in this way. There is already enough controversy about when and how a person is cautioned, in respect of the admissibility or otherwise of verbal admissions. Would it not be a very foolish and retrograde step to risk increasing the number of guilty offenders who are acquitted although patently guilty? Logically, a person who has made an entirely free and voluntary confession could argue for an acquittal if he wasn't reminded that if he had remained silent, this too could be held against him.

Whenever a prisoner or suspect is taken into the police station, there on the wall of the charge room is a very large notice headed, 'Prisoners' Rights'. It covers everything a prisoner could wish to know about his rights and entitlements, not forgetting how to make a complaint against the police. How simple it would be to make this notice a little bit bigger, to include the Caution.

ND - #0050 - 270225 - C0 - 203/127/30 - PB - 9781861511782 - Matt Lamination